D1528257

Codex Bezae is one of the most important primary sources in New Testament scholarship. Since its rediscovery in the sixteenth century it has continued to fascinate scholars, who have remained intrigued by the riddles of its general appearance and textual characteristics. David Parker here makes the first comprehensive investigation of the manuscript for over a century, and sets out to uncover the story behind this most enigmatic of manuscripts. By studying the characteristics of Codex Bezae, both physical and textual, and by comparing its Greek and Latin texts, the author aims to show how a bilingual tradition developed, and thus to discover as much as possible about its earliest stages. This leads to an important new theory about its origins. In a final section, the general character of the text is assessed with a view to what this can tell us of the earliest traditions about Jesus.

Codex Bezae

Codex Bezae

An early Christian manuscript and its text

D. C. PARKER

Tutor in the New Testament, The Queen's College, Birmingham

CAMBRIDGE UNIVERSITY PRESS

Cambridge New York Port Chester Melbourne Sydney

Published by the Press Syndicate of the University of Cambridge
The Pitt Building, Trumpington Street, Cambridge CB2 1RP
40 West 20th Street, New York, NY 10011-4211, USA
10 Stamford Road, Oakleigh, Victoria 3166, Australia

First published 1992

Printed in Great Britain at the University Press, Cambridge

British Library cataloguing in publication data
Parker, D. C. (David C.)
Codex Bezae: an early Christian manuscript.
1. Bible. N. T. Luke. Codex Bezae. Critical studies
I. Title
226.4048

Library of Congress cataloguing in publication data
Parker, D. C. (David C.)
Codex Bezae: an early Christian manuscript and its text/D. C. Parker.
p. cm.
Includes bibliographical references and indexes.
ISBN 0 521 40037 6
1. Codex Bezae. 2. Bible. N.T. Gospels – Criticism, Textual. 3. Bible. N.T. Acts – Criticism, Textual. 4. Bible. N.T. Gospels – Criticism, interpretation, etc. 5. Bible. N.T. Acts – Criticism, interpretation, etc. 6. Manuscripts, Greek – England – Cambridge. 7. Manuscripts, Latin – England – Cambridge. 8. Cambridge University Library. I. Bible. N.T. Gospels. Greek. Codex Bezae. 1991. II. Bible. N.T. Gospels. Latin. Codex Bezae. 1991. III. Bible. N.T. Acts. Greek. Codex Bezae. 1991. IV. Bible. N.T. Acts. Latin. Codex Bezae. 1991. V. Title.
BS2548.P37 1991
226′.048 – dc20 90-40226 CIP

ISBN 0 521 40037 6 hardback

For Karen

Contents

Illustrations

Preface

Like the celebrated novel of Alessandro Manzoni (not to mention Umberto Eco's), this book begins with a manuscript, and attempts to tell a story from it. Although unlike them, it cannot tell the story of how the manuscript was found by the author, I can describe how the book came to completion.

It is the child of a twelve years' study of the Codex Bezae. The first eight of these were spent in the parochial ministry so that my study was regular but not prolonged – like Stephanus' verse divisions, it was done *inter equitandum*. Since then, the advantages of vacations and finally study leave have given me longer periods to spend on it.

During this time, a great many people have helped, encouraged, and listened in various ways. My first and deepest thanks are to Karen, to whom I dedicate this book. Matthew Black, my first teacher in textual criticism, introduced me to Codex Bezae. Dr Caroline Hammond Bammel and Dr Ernst Bammel gave me vital advice in deciding on a subject for study, and offered great encouragement. Professor Neville Birdsall has been a colleague in Birmingham from whose company and seminars I have derived much pleasure and the opportunity to try out some ideas, as has the textual criticism seminar of the Studiorum Novi Testamenti Societas. Professor T. J. Brown gave his time on several occasions to encourage my work, in typically generous fashion. My colleagues in the British Committee of the International Greek New Testament Project's Gospel of John (Bill Elliott, Keith Elliott, Lionel North, and Tom Pattie) have been stimulating and encouraging in very many ways.

My former colleagues, the Revds Jeremy Harrold and Gregory Page-Turner, were always more than generous in encouraging me in these studies, when there was always more than enough for us to be doing.

I am grateful to the British Academy for a grant which enabled me to visit Münster and Lyons in the spring of 1989; to Professor Barbara Aland and the staff of the Institut für Neutestamentliche Textforschung in Münster (particularly Klaus Witte) for their welcome and their help in working there; to the librarian and staff of the Bibliothèque Municipale de Part-Dieu, Lyons, and to those of all the other libraries I have visited in writing this book. I owe thanks also to the successive librarians of Ridley Hall, Cambridge, for the long loan of their copy of the facsimile edition of Codex Bezae. This has been the next best thing to Bentley's privilege of borrowing the manuscript itself.

A special debt is due to Mr Owen and the staff of the Manuscripts room of Cambridge University Library, particularly Mr Godfrey Waller, who have helped me in very many ways since the work began.

Cambridge University Press has now been publishing books on Codex Bezae for two hundred years. I owe my thanks to all those whose meticulous care at each stage of this book's production have maintained the scholarly standards of this tradition.

It is appropriate also to acknowledge my debt to previous researches on Codex Bezae. Of these, I single out Scrivener, for his transcription of the codex, and Yoder and Stone for their concordances, to the Greek and Latin texts respectively. Although they will rarely be mentioned by name, their use lies behind much of what follows.

To all those other people with whom I have discussed the subject of this book, and from whom I have learnt, my grateful thanks. In particular, Iain Torrance and Peter Harvey have contributed enormously to the final stages, even though our conversations have hardly ever been about textual criticism.

Several people have helped in the laborious task of trying to remove errors from this work. My father read the typescript and, from the standpoint of another discipline, suggested some clarifications. My especial thanks go to the Revd James Miller of Bury St Edmunds, who dedicated long hours to examining my typescript, in the course of which he detected a number of errors and discrepancies. In addition, he made helpful suggestions about the extent of my *apparatus criticus* and about other matters. The checking of readings in Codex Bezae was a task done only by myself. In this, as of course in everything else, the errors that remain are mine. Finally, the Revd Alistair Stewart Sykes most usefully added his eyes to mine in the examination of the proofs.

Late in 1989, this book was submitted as a doctoral thesis to the University of Leiden. I am greatly indebted to Professor M. de Jonge and Dr H. J. de Jonge, who acted as Promotor and Referent respectively. They read and commented on the text with great thoroughness. A number of pertinent and searching questions were asked at the *Promotie*, and I was subsequently able to make several improvements in detail.

In one respect, history has overtaken this book: *manuscripti Petropolitani* have had to remain in Leningrad.

Abbreviations and textual conventions

LITERATURE

Adn. ed.	Scrivener (q.v.), *Adnotationes editoris*
A.-G.	W.F. Arndt and F.W. Gingrich, *A Greek–English Lexicon of the New Testament and Other Early Christian Literature*, 2nd edition, Chicago, 1979
Aland, *Liste*	K. Aland, *Kurzgefasste Liste der griechischen Handschriften des Neuen Testaments* (*ANTF* 1), Berlin, 1963
Alands, *Text*	K. and B. Aland, *The Text of the New Testament*, translated by E.F. Rhodes, Grand Rapids and Leiden, 1987 (1981)
ANTF	*Arbeiten zur neutestamentlichen Textforschung*, Berlin, 1963ff
AUSS	*Andrews University Seminary Studies*
BBC	*Bulletin of the Bezan Club*
B.-D.	F. Blass and A. Debrunner, *A Greek Grammar of the New Testament and Other Early Christian Literature*, revised by Robert W. Funk, Chicago, 1975
Bischoff, *Palaeography*	Bernhard Bischoff, *Latin Palaeography. Antiquity and Middle Ages*, transl. Dáibhí Ó Cróinín and David Ganz, Cambridge, 1990 (Berlin, 1979)
B.-L.	M.-E. Boismard and A. Lamouille, *Le Texte occidental des Actes des Apôtres. Reconstitution et réhabilitation*, 2 vols., Paris, 1984
Cavalieri and Lietzmann	P.F. de' Cavalieri and J. Lietzmann, *Specimina codicum Graecorum Vaticanorum* (Tabulae in usum scholarum 1), Berlin and Leipzig, 1929

Cavallo, *Ricerche*	G. Cavallo, *Ricerche sulla maiuscola biblica* (Studi e testi di papirologia 2), Florence, 1967
Cavallo and Maehler, *Greek Bookhands*	G. Cavallo and H. Maehler, *Greek Bookhands of the Early Byzantine Period* AD *300–800* (University of London Institute of Classical Studies Bulletin Supplement 47), London, 1987
CC	*Corpus Christianorum, Series Latina*, Turnhout, 1954ff
CLA	E. A. Lowe, *Codices Latini antiquiores. A Palaeographical Guide to Latin Manuscripts prior to the Ninth Century*, 11 vols. plus *Supplement*, Oxford, 1934ff plus *Index*, Osnabrück, 1982. Vol. 2 exists in two editions (1935 and 1972). The edition being cited is indicated only when they differ from each other. The first numeral refers to the volume, the second to the entry number
Clark, *Acts*	A. C. Clark, *The Acts of the Apostles. A Critical Edition with Introduction and Notes on Selected Passages*, Oxford, 1933
Clark, *Primitive Text*	A. C. Clark, *The Primitive Text of the Gospels and Acts*, Oxford, 1914
CR	*The Classical Review*
CSEL	*Corpus scriptorum ecclesiasticorum Latinorum*, Vienna, 1866ff
Devreesse	Robert Devreesse, *Introduction à l'étude des manuscrits grecs*, Paris, 1954
Epp and Fee	E. J. Epp and G. D. Fee (eds.), *New Testament Textual Criticism, Its Significance for Exegesis, Essays in Honour of Bruce M. Metzger*, Oxford, 1981
ETL	*Ephemerides Theologicae Lovanienses*
Fischer, *Beiträge*	B. Fischer, *Beiträge zur Geschichte der lateinischen Bibeltexte* (Aus der Geschichte der lateinischen Bibel 12), Freiburg, 1986
Fischer, 'Das NT'	B. Fischer, 'Das Neue Testament in lateinischer Sprache', *ANTF* 5, 1–92 (= *Beiträge*, pp. 156–274) (page references are to *ANTF*)
GCS	*Die griechischen christlichen Schriftsteller*, Leipzig, 1897ff
Gignac	F. Gignac, *A Grammar of the Greek Papyri of the Roman and Byzantine Periods* (Testi e documenti

	per lo studio dell'antichità 55), Vol. 1, *Phonology*, Vol. 2, *Morphology*, Milan, 1976–81
GMAW	E. G. Turner, *Greek Manuscripts of the Ancient World*, Oxford, 1971
Harris, *Annotators*	J. R. Harris, *The Annotators of the Codex Bezae (with Some Notes on Sortes Sanctorum)*, London, 1901
Harris, *Codex*	J. R. Harris, *Codex Bezae, a Study of the so-called Western Text of the New Testament* (Texts and Studies 2.1), Cambridge, 1891
Hatch, *Principal Uncial Manuscripts*	W. H. P. Hatch, *The Principal Uncial Manuscripts of the New Testament*, Chicago, 1939
HTR	*Harvard Theological Review*
IGNT	International Greek New Testament Project
Itala	A. Jülicher (ed.), *Itala. Das Neue Testament in altlateinischer Überlieferung ... durchgesehen und zum Druck besorgt von Walter Matzkow+ und Kurt Aland*, Berlin, 1963ff
JBL	*The Journal of Biblical Literature*
JTS	*The Journal of Theological Studies*
Lampe, *Lexicon*	G. W. H. Lampe, *A Patristic Greek Lexicon*, Oxford, 1968
Legg	S. C. E. Legg, *Nouum Testamentum Graece secundum textum Westcotto-Hortianum*, Oxford, 1935 (*Euangelium secundum Marcum*) and 1940 (*Euangelium secundum Matthaeum*)
Lowe, 'A Note'	E. A. Lowe, 'A Note on the Codex Bezae', *BBC* 4 (1927), 9–14 (=*Pal. Papers* 1, 224–8)
Lowe, 'More Facts'	E. A. Lowe, 'More Facts about our Oldest Latin Manuscripts', *The Classical Quarterly* 22 (1928), 43–62 (=*Pal. Papers* 1, 251–74)
Lowe, 'Some Facts'	E. A. Lowe, 'Some Facts about our Oldest Latin Manuscripts', *The Classical Quarterly* 19 (1925), 197–208 (=*Pal. Papers* 1, 187–202)
Lowe, 'Two Fragments'	E. A. Lowe, 'Two Fragments of Virgil with the Greek Translation', *CR* 36 (1922), 154–5 (=*Pal. Papers* 1, 127–8)
Metzger, *Canon*	B. M. Metzger, *The Canon of the New Testament: Its Origin, Development, and Significance*, Oxford, 1987

Metzger, *Manuscripts*	B. M. Metzger, *Manuscripts of the Greek Bible. An Introduction to Greek Palaeography*, Oxford, 1981
M.-H. 2	J. H. Moulton and W. F. Howard, *A Grammar of New Testament Greek*, Vol. 2, *Accidence and Word-Formation*, Edinburgh, 1929
Milne and Skeat, *Scribes and Correctors*	H. J. M. Milne and T. C. Skeat, *Scribes and Correctors of the Codex Sinaiticus, including contributions by Douglas Cockerell*, London, 1938
Moulton, *Proleg.*	J. H. Moulton, *A Grammar of New Testament Greek*, Vol. 1, *Prolegomena*, 3rd edition, Edinburgh, 1908
M.-T. 3	J. H. Moulton, *A Grammar of New Testament Greek*, Vol. 3, *Syntax*, by Nigel Turner, Edinburgh, 1963
M.-T. 4	J. H. Moulton, *A Grammar of New Testament Greek*, Vol. 4, *Style*, by Nigel Turner, Edinburgh, 1976
Nestle-Aland^{26}	K. and B. Aland, *Novum Testamentum Graece*, 26th edition, 9th printing, Stuttgart, 1987
NTS	*New Testament Studies*
Oxford Latin Dictionary	*Oxford Latin Dictionary*, Oxford, 1968ff
Pal. Papers	E. A. Lowe, *Palaeographical Papers 1907–1966*, edited by Ludwig Bieler, 2 vols., Oxford, 1972
Parker, 'Dictation Theory'	D. C. Parker, 'A "Dictation Theory" of Codex Bezae', *Journal for the Study of the New Testament* 15 (1982), 97–112
Parker, 'Translation of *OYN*'	'The Translation of *OYN* in the Old Latin Gospels', *NTS* 31 (1985), 252–76
PBA	*The Proceedings of the British Academy*
PG	J.-P. Migne (ed.), *Patrologia Graeca*, Paris, 1857–66
PL	J.-P. Migne (ed.), *Patrologia Latina*, Paris, 1844–64
PSI	*Papiri greci e latini*, Florence, 1912ff
RB	*Revue Bénédictine*
Rev. Phil.	*Revue Philologique*
Ropes	J. H. Ropes, *The Text of Acts (The Beginnings of Christianity*, Part I, *The Acts of the Apostles*, Vol. 3), London, 1926
Schulz, *Disputatio*	David Schulz, *De Codice D Cantabrigiensi*, Warsaw, 1827

Scrivener	F. H. Scrivener, *Bezae Codex Cantabrigiensis, Being an Exact Copy, in Ordinary Type, of the Celebrated Uncial Graeco-Latin Manuscript of the Four Gospels and Acts of the Apostles, Written Early in the Sixth Century, and Presented to the University of Cambridge by Theodore Bezae, AD 1581*, Cambridge, 1864 (reprinted, Pittsburgh, 1978)
Scrivener, *Adn. ed.*	F. H. Scrivener, *Adnotationes editoris, ibid.*, pp. 429–47
SNTS	Studiorum Novi Testamenti Societas
Souter	Alexander Souter, *A Glossary of Later Latin to 600 AD*, Oxford, 1949
Stone, *Language*	R. C. Stone, *The Language of the Latin Text of Codex Bezae, with an Index Verborum* (Illinois Studies in Language and Literature 2–3), Illinois, 1946
Stuttgart edition	*Biblia Sacra iuxta Vulgatam Versionem*, ed. R. Weber, 2nd edition, Stuttgart, 1975
Thackeray, *Grammar*	H. St J. Thackeray, *A Grammar of the Old Testament in Greek According to the Septuagint*, Cambridge, 1909 (reprinted Hildesheim/New York, 1978)
Thompson	E. M. Thompson, *A Handbook of Greek and Latin Palaeography*, London, 1893 (reprinted Chicago, 1980)
Tischendorf	C. Tischendorf, *Novum Testamentum Graece ... editio octava critica maior*, Leipzig, 1872
Turner, *Typology*	E. G. Turner, *The Typology of the Early Codex*, Philadelphia, 1977
VC	*Vetera Christianorum*
Vogels, *Harmonistik*	H. J. Vogels, *Die Harmonistik im Evangelientext des Codex Cantabrigiensis. Ein Beitrag zur neutestamentlichen Textkritik* (Texte und Untersuchungen 36), Leipzig, 1910
Westcott and Hort	B. F. Westcott and F. J. A. Hort, *The New Testament in the Original Greek*, 2 vols., London, 1881
Wettstein	J. J. Wettstein, *Η ΚΑΙΝΗ ΔΙΑΘΗΚΗ. Novum Testamentum Graecum*, 2 vols., Amsterdam, 1751–2

Wordsworth and White	J. Wordsworth and H. J. White, *Nouum Testamentum Domini Nostri Iesu Christi Latine secundum editionem Sancti Hieronymi*, Oxford, 1889ff
Yoder, *Concordance*	J. D. Yoder, *Concordance to the Distinctive Greek Text of Codex Bezae* (New Testament Tools and Studies 2), Leiden, 1961
ZNW	*Zeitschrift für die neutestamentliche Wissenschaft*

Besides these abbreviations, works mentioned in the bibliographical discussions will be referred to subsequently within that chapter in an abbreviated form of author and short title or date.

APPARATUS

Folio and line numbers in Codex Bezae are indicated in one of two ways. F100, l.10 means Folio 100, line 10. 100/10 means the same thing. F100 means the recto, F100b means the verso. An asterisked folio number (e.g. F172b*) means that this is a supplementary leaf (the leaves of the codex are numbered consecutively on the recto in their top right-hand corner regardless of their date).

In citing witnesses, I have borrowed the following usage from Tischendorf, except that they are not given for maiuscule and minuscule manuscripts separately.

add. (addit, addunt)	adds, add
al. (alii)	others
c. (cum)	with (i.e. supported by)
cet. (ceteri)	the rest
cj. (conjecit)	conjecture
exc. (excepto, exceptis)	except
lect. sing. (lectio singularis)	singular reading
leg. (lege)	read
min. (minusculi)	minuscule Mss
mu. (multi)	many
pc. (pauci)	a few
pler. (plerique)	very many
plu. (plures)	most

Codex Sinaiticus (01) is cited as ℵ, and 028 as S. Otherwise the sigla for witnesses, including patristic citations, are those of The International Greek New Testament Project, *The Gospel of Luke*, Vol. 1, Oxford, 1984, pp. viii–xiii, although Old Latin witnesses are sometimes cited by lower-case letters without the preceding Lvt. Greek upper-case sigla for maiuscule manuscripts are in sloping type. Codex Bezae is regularly referred to by its letter (D). Its Gregory number (05) and von Soden number (δ5) are not used.

Readings of both columns of Codex Bezae are given in uncial that attempts to imitate contemporary scripts: the typeface used is New Hellenic. In Parts III and IV this uncial is used *only* for readings where that column has a reading for which I can find no other support. In chapter 5, standard upper case is used for the Greek text in the reconstruction of the exemplar, and upper-case italics for its Latin text. Throughout the book, readings of all other Greek manuscripts are given in lower case. Those of all other Latin manuscripts are in lower-case italics. In the appendices, the readings of Codex Bezae are given in standard Greek lower case. The standard Greek typeface used throughout the book is Porson.

Apart from its use in indicating a folio and line reference, an oblique stroke (/) indicates a line ending in the Codex Bezae.

The term α measurement is used to describe the size of the leaf of a manuscript; β measurement refers to the size of its written area.

Introduction

Codex Bezae is a manuscript that has generally managed to provoke strong emotions. Bentley, with the Cantabrigian fervour which has not escaped the notice of Ernst Bammel, called it 'our Beza's'. Its script has been called crude, its spelling and accuracy lamentable. The scribe has been seen as a person with too much ink in his well, the transmitter – indeed the creator – of a text which he has no business to promulgate as authentic, the Chatterton or Macpherson of the New Testament. The impression is that we have to do with a mendacious and conceivably also heretical person. The Alands, in an attempt to destroy the myth, have been equally excessive in writing that 'what the nineteenth/twentieth century has made of it is incredible'. Since text-critical emotions here run so high, one who writes at length upon the manuscript may easily feel suspected of a natural bias in favour of its text. At the very beginning, therefore, a few statements of intent and opinion, upon matters that will not form a major part of what follows, are in order.

Although some years of frequent communion have given me a peculiar affection, which would often seek to exculpate, for this manuscript, the fact is that the longer I have studied it, the more I have become convinced that its many unique readings only very rarely deserve serious consideration if one is trying to establish the best available text. Acts is the most aberrant book, a large-scale reworking having a character on which I hope to shed some light. I am not one of those who would like to see something like the Bezan text in every Greek New Testament, lectured on in every classroom and read at every lectern.

Why then has it received so much of my attention? I find it hard to answer this directly. Let me instead give some account of how I see this book in the context of modern textual criticism.

It seems to me that New Testament textual critics are often tempted to proceed far too hastily to the comparison of manuscripts, before they have found out exactly what it is that they are comparing. The first stage of our work should be to examine the individual witnesses, to assess the character of the scribe, to enquire into the nature of the tradition from which the copy is derived, and to attempt to show why this manuscript is what it is. The study of P[45], P[66], and P[75] by Colwell is a well known example of this process. In it he isolates the peculiarities of each scribe, and uses them to assess the tradition which they set out to represent. The classic studies of Martini and Zuntz carry such investigations further. Such work should make it possible to determine the character, the essential nature, of an individual witness. It should also eliminate whatever of its text has grown up in the transmission of a particular tradition.

The immediate comparison of manuscripts is bedevilled by the fact that so few very early witnesses have been recovered. Trying to relate them to each other can be like trying to set up a model of a molecule with the spheres but not the rods to connect them.

By contrast, the editor of a classical text will, unless favoured by fortune with some papyri, probably be handling a small number of medieval manuscripts. For such a one, the decision as to whether a manuscript is good or bad, and as to how accurately it represents its *Vorlagen*, will be a vital part of the task. Whatever means we may use to reconstruct the text of the New Testament, we must not forget that the same task with regard to the individual witnesses awaits us, even though the relationships between them may be much more complicated.

This study seeks to examine a single scribe and the tradition he reproduced: how he preserved, and how altered it; the form that he received, and the manner in which he altered it; the way the tradition had developed, and the way it was used in later generations.

If the evidence produced has any significance, and the conclusions set forth any cogency, then the major maiuscule manuscripts of the New Testament, far from being a subject for study so exhausted that we need to move on to the minuscules, have hardly begun to yield up their secrets.

A second belief that has moulded this book is not unrelated to the first. The text of the New Testament exists only as a number of physical representations: a chemical preparation drawn on sheets of skin which are then tied together. Our use of printed texts (all in their own ways conflate texts, derived from several manuscripts), provides a false perspective. We know that there is, or was, an original text, or a text better than any we have, which we are seeking to establish. But it does not exist physically. We have then to encounter a number of attempts to reproduce this text, all of them books that are handwritten. The point is that the individual text must be taken seriously as a physical object. Housman once complained about people who confuse textual criticism with palaeography. I do not want to do that. But I am impatient of a textual criticism that discusses variant readings but not the scribes who made them, textual history but not the manuscripts in which it is contained. It would be unwise to confuse textual criticism with palaeography and codicology. There are in fact different skills to each of these disciplines. But it is necessary to study a text in conjunction with its material representatives. Thus, for example, the *text* of Codex Bezae is affected by the way in which it is laid out on the page. I hope to shed light on the ways in which the physical characteristics of manuscripts impinge on the handing down of texts, and so perhaps to stimulate further exploration in this direction.

I find the point forcefully made by Jean Duplacy, in an article I have read since writing the last few paragraphs. In his 1965 paper 'Histoire des manuscrits et histoire du texte du NT' (*Etudes de critique textuelle du Nouveau Testament*, ed. J. Delobel, Leuven, 1987, pp. 39–54), he spoke of the need to restore to a manuscript its history: 'the place; the traditions, the influences, the sources which explain the various aspects of its composition and its contents; its destination and its purpose; the people who were involved, in one way or another, in its origins (patrons, scribes, customers, etc.); the vicissitudes of its history'. This giving back its history to a manuscript describes vividly what I have attempted here. It is an endeavour which is far more extensive than the archaeological explorations of codicology. Having begun it, I am conscious that everything about a manuscript – what is seen, what is touched, what is read – has its part to play. Such a book as this one could be many times longer, as each detail assumed a new significance in the light of further examination.

The fascination of Codex Bezae has, therefore, been not its claim to authenticity, but its suitability for the kind of investigation I am describing, the wealth of material waiting to be studied. The character of its text, the fact that it is bilingual, and the extent of its later use, all combine to make it an excellent subject for the explorations that follow.

As a result of these two points I have made, certain things are absent from this book. One (with the exception of one or two places where it is used in reference to another point of view) is the term 'Western text', with or without inverted commas.

What is more, I do not intend to attempt to describe the text of D by comparing it with other witnesses, to mark out its shape by describing other shapes around it. It must be confessed that in several later chapters, some support for variant readings will be given. But I hope that what is done there will not betray what is set out here.

In spite of appearances, this does not signal a rejection of the genealogical method. Rather, I suggest that it is false to deduce from a genealogical stemma that a manuscript represents only that single point in the tradition that is marked by B or C. The stemma does indeed show the manuscript as a point, but a point connected with earlier points, A or x or y, by lines. And the manuscript contains, to vary the image of the molecule, the lines as well as the points. I am not therefore abandoning genealogy. But it would seem to me that the best way to begin the study of any manuscript is to treat it as though it were a *codex unicus*.

If the need to study the manuscript *as* a manuscript has moulded my study of the text, the reverse is also true. In trying to understand and to describe the physical characteristics of this codex, I have tried to understand how the nature of a bilingual text has affected the way this one has been copied. Here I must acknowledge how greatly stimulating I have found the work of the late Sir Eric Turner. From his writings questions have arisen in my mind, as to why this codex has the physical characteristics we can see; what the conventions and possibilities were for the copyist of such a work; whether contemporaries or later users understood what he had been attempting to do.

The actual progress of this work followed two stages. To begin with, I worked right through the manuscript, noting all the things which are brought together at various places. In particular, I set out to examine the differences between the columns. A mass of information was accumulated. I then began to try to describe and to make sense of what I had seen.

It is often frustrating to read books which contain conclusions but no evidence, whether they are detective novels which introduce new information in the master sleuth's unmasking of the villain, or text-critical studies which tell us the writer's opinions, but neither the reasons nor the road by which they were attained. This book sets out to provide all the evidence which formed the basis for my conclusions. Since a great deal of this evidence consists in lists of things, parts of it may seem to be rather less than deathless prose. However, the reader who, as it were, only wants to find out 'who dunnit', can skip the evidence. The readers who want to use the evidence for other purposes, or who can reach better conclusions from it, have it all before them. I hope also that by setting out the evidence, I have saved other people a good deal of work.

The book will generally provide references to the folio and line in Codex Bezae, either alone or along with chapter and verse. The purpose of this is to emphasize in practice the two chief points I have already made, attracting attention towards the manuscript itself, rather than to a printed text.

There are, so far as I am aware, no grounds for establishing whether the scribe or any of the correctors of Codex Bezae were male or female. The use of masculine pronouns is simply a matter of convenience.

PART I

The palaeography

CHAPTER ONE

The codex and the hand

The precise character of the script of Codex Bezae has been a matter for some debate. The questions which arise are precisely those raised by other aspects of the manuscript. Is it from a Greek or a Latin environment, from the East or from the West?

The proper beginning of our investigation is with the fact that the manuscript is a bilingual. The particular requirements and restrictions of copying such a text, and the various influences of its antecedents, need to be recollected at every stage of examination.

In the analysis of the hand, an immediate area of confusion is in the general relationship between Greek and Latin scripts, and the unique relationship between the two columns of a bilingual copied by a single hand. That is to say, we have to separate points of contact due to the derivation of Latin from Greek scripts, and the inevitable similarity of forms produced by a particular hand.

The problem is less acute when we apply codicological analysis to the manuscript. It is therefore helpful, as well as in accord with standard practice, to begin our examination with aspects relating to book production.

THE CODEX

Bischoff, *Palaeography*; John Chapman, 'The Original Contents of Codex Bezae', *The Expositor* (VI) 2 (1905), 46–53; S. M. Cockerell, a typewritten description of the repair and rebinding of Codex Bezae, dated November 1965, kept in a pocket folder with the Ms; Hatch, *Principal Uncial Manuscripts*; Lowe, 'Some Facts'; Lowe, 'More Facts'; E. A. Lowe, 'Greek Symptoms in a Sixth-Century Manuscript of St Augustine and in a Group of Latin Legal Manuscripts', in *Didascaliae: Studies in Honor of Anselm M. Albareda*, ed. Sesto Prete, New York, 1961, pp. 279–89 = *Pal. Papers* 2, 466–74 and Plates 108–13; Patrick McGurk, *Latin Gospel Books from AD 400 to AD 800* (Les Publications de Scriptorium 5), Paris–Brussels and Antwerp–Amsterdam, 1961; G. Mercati, 'On the Non-Greek Origin of the Codex Bezae', *JTS* 15 (1914), 448–51, reprinted in *Opere minore* 3 (Studi e testi 78), The Vatican, 1937, pp. 332–5; Metzger, *Manuscripts*; Milne and Skeat, *Scribes and Correctors*; Pierre Petitmengin, 'Les Plus Anciens Manuscrits de la Bible latine', *Bible de tous les temps*, ed. C. Kannengiesser, Vol. 2, *Le Monde latin antique et la Bible*, ed. Jacques Fontaine and Charles Pietri, Paris, 1985, pp. 89–127; Turner, *Typology*; *GMAW*; H. J. Vogels, *Codicum Novi Testamenti specimina*, Bonn, 1929.

CLA in this chapter with no further reference indicates the entry for Codex Bezae, which is 2,140.

The present extent of Codex Bezae amounts to 406 leaves. These contain, in the Greek column, Mt 1.20–3.7: 3.16–6.20; 9.2–27.1; 27.12–28.20; Jn 1.1–16; 3.26–18.13; 20.13–21.25; Luke in its entirety; Mk 1.1–16.15; Ac 1.1–8.29; 10.14–21.2; 21.10–16, 18–22.10; 22.20–29; and in the Latin, Mt 1.12–2.20; 3.8–6.8; 8.27–26.67; 27.2–28.20; Jn 3.16–18.2; 20.1–21.25; Luke in its entirety; Mk 1.1–16.6; 3 Jn 11–15; Ac 1.1–8.20; 10.4–20.31; 21.2–7, 10–22.2; 22.10–20. Some of the missing material is supplied by a ninth-century restoration. Its precise extent is given in chapter 3.

The original length and contents of the manuscript are unknown. If Acts was the final book, then a projection of twenty-five leaves for Ac 22.29 to the end (reckoning 1.37 pages of Nestle-Aland[26] to a page) gives us a total number of 535 leaves. The manuscript is composed of quaternions, except for gathering λδ′, which is a ternion. Sixty-six quaternions and the odd gathering give a total of 534 leaves. Either our calculations are slightly erroneous, or the end was very compressed (smaller letters, longer lines?), or the text was considerably aberrant, or there was a final single-sheet gathering. Quaternions became the standard size of gathering in Greek codices (Turner, *Typology*, p. 62) and were so in all periods of Latin ones (Bischoff, p. 20).

The question of the original contents of the manuscript cannot be conclusively settled. It was stated by Scrivener to have been the four Gospels, the Catholic Epistles, and Acts (p. xv). But, as he realized, the Catholic Epistles are not long enough to fill the leaves missing between Mark and Acts. Ff348–9 must have contained the end of Mark. Then 349b–414 is left for the Catholic Epistles through to 3 John 11. Scrivener calculates that these will not have taken up more than fifty of the sixty-six leaves, and suggests that the scribe wrote the wrong quire number somewhere in the lost portion (for instance, MΘ instead of MZ), and that there were actually only fifty and not sixty-six leaves in the missing section. Chapman argues on historical grounds that D is unlikely ever to have contained James, 2 Peter, and possibly Jude. This leads him to enquire whether the codex contained something other than the Catholic Epistles in this lacuna. He calculates, on the basis of the number of syllables of Westcott and Hort to a Greek column, that 1 John, with *explicit* and title, will have occupied eleven and a half pages, from 399b to 410b, 2 John will have been on 411b–412b, and then 3 John. Ff349b–398b/399 will have contained between 1,618 and 1,646 lines, followed by a four-line *explicit* and title. At the rate of 11.7 syllables per line (the number in Mark's Gospel), multiplied by 1,640 as the approximate number of lines, we have a total of 19,188 syllables for the missing book. Revelation in Westcott and Hort has about 19,408 syllables. Allowing a little leeway, we have an accurate match.

This suggestion removes the need for Scrivener's *deus ex machina*. It has the weakness that we do not know how the lines of the missing leaves were written. It also assumes that the missing part contained canonical material. This is not unreasonable. According to Petitmengin, only one Latin biblical manuscript includes extra-canonical material – a fifth-century codex of the Gospels of Matthew, Nicodemus, and Thomas (Vienna, Nationalbibliothek Lat. 563; *CLA* 10,1485). On the other hand, a number of Greek manuscripts, including the Codex Sinaiticus, do contain extra-canonical books.

Clearly, we are dealing only in probabilities. But Chapman's case remains the most scientifically argued and acceptable that we have.

The quire signatures are written in Greek numerals, at the bottom right-hand corner of the last page of each quaternion. This is the position where they are generally to be found in Latin manuscripts. The scribe of D is following Latin practice, but using Greek numerals because all the left-hand pages are given over to the Greek text.

For four exceptions to the Latin rule, see Lowe, 'Greek Symptoms', p. 284 (*Pal. Papers* 2,470) and chart. The Mss are: the Justinian *Digesta* from the Laurentian Library (*CLA* 3,295), one with the same contents from Pommersfelden (Lat. Pap. 1–6, *CLA* 9,1351), a codex of Justinian from Verona (LXII; *CLA* 4,513), and Lyons 478, of Augustine's *De Consensu Evangelistarum* (*CLA* 6,777). All are in b–r uncial, and all are of the sixth century. We may also note the use of Greek numerals in at least one other Latin Ms: the Bodley Jerome *Chronicon* (Auct. T. II.26) has nine quires numbered with Roman numerals (e.g. ·VI·) and the rest with Greek, beginning at α' (e.g. ·ϛ·).

The use of Greek numbers in Latin book production is also a feature of some Mss of Cyprian's *Ad Quirinum*. Mss X O Q M T U use them for the *capitula* and *inscriptiones* of Book 1, the same and N for both in Book 2, and O Q M T U before the *inscriptiones* of Book 3. According to the editor, Q M T U share a common archetype, whilst X and N belong to a group showing the purest text, and O to a third group (*Sancti Cypriani Episcopi Opera*, Part I, ed. R. Weber, *CC* 3, p. LVIII).

A sixth-century papyrus codex of the Digests of Justinian (*CLA* S,1723) has a Greek numeral for each law.

Codex Mediolanensis of the Gospels (Milan, Bibl. Ambros. C.39.inf, *CLA* 3,313) has the Eusebian canon numbers on its margins in Greek.

The signatures of D are enclosed in a gamma-shaped bracket with a sloping vertical and a long horizontal. This also is a Latin habit (Lowe, 'More Facts', p. 60 = *Pal. Papers* 1,271).

The outer sheet of each quire is the flesh side (and of course the manuscript follows Gregory's rule in having facing pages of the same side). In spite of Turner's view (*Typology*, p. 56) there is nothing specifically Eastern about this, as the information supplied by Lowe ('More Facts') makes quite plain.

The ruling is on the flesh side, each sheet having been ruled separately before folding.

Lowe ('More Facts', p. 61 = *Pal. Papers* 1,274) states that the manuscript is ruled on the hair side, like the Codex Bobbiensis and several other manuscripts. His description in *CLA*, however, is correct. His description of the Bobbiensis is also incorrect: D. C. Parker, 'Unequally Yoked: the present state of the Codex Bobbiensis', *JTS* N.S. 42 (1991).

The rulings are especially clear on the opening sheets, and both they and the pricking may best be seen on F10. The prickings were made quite far into what was to be the written area – in F10, 16 mm in from the outer bounding line, and on F3,

26 mm in. This is, according to Lowe, found also 'in several very ancient Latin MSS' (*CLA*). The later and more general practice was for the prickings to be on the bounding lines.

The original size of the codex has been reduced by trimming (Scrivener, p. xiv). The present size is given as 220 × 260 mm (Lowe, *CLA*), 21 × 26 cm (Metzger, *Manuscripts*), 17–22.9 × 25.8–26.7 cm (Hatch), 21.5 × 26 cm (Aland, *Liste* and Alands, *Text*), 22 × 25.4 cm (Turner, *Typology*).

This size is defined by Turner as Group III in his classification according to format of parchment manuscripts, 'Large, "Square"' (*Typology*, p. 27). Square is defined, following Schubart, as admitting a proportion of breadth to height of 7 to 8 (p. 25). Other Greek manuscripts in this category are a sixth-century copy of Strabo (Vat. Gr. 2306), the Codex Vaticanus (Gr. 1209), and the LXX manuscript Codex Colberto-Sarravianus (Leiden Univ. Lib. Voss. Gr. Q.8, with leaves in Paris and one in Leningrad). D is the least square of these, and only by assuming that the sides have been cropped more than the top and bottom can we allow it precisely to meet the definition. The square format was popular with Latin scribes of the oldest period (Bischoff, p. 26), and there is every likelihood that its shape is another indication that D was produced in a Latin *scriptorium*.

The size of the written area may, in spite of immediate appearances, be defined. It will be argued (in chapter 5, p. 82) that the two bounding lines indicate what was intended to be a maximum length of line. Although it was sometimes exceeded, there is evidence that the scribe generally kept to it. Only Lowe provides dimensions of the written area, giving 145 × 185 mm. The 185 mm for height is correct. If it is not to be too fussy, I find the width to be 144 mm (though in F3 it is under 140 mm). The initial letters of new sections (see chapter 2) are written outside the bounding line.

The shape of written area approaches the square less closely than does the page size. In this respect it fails to meet the criterion demanded of an ancient Latin manuscript.

In ordinary lines, the first letter is either against or partly astride the bounding line.

The lines of writing are not upon, but through the horizontal ruled lines (with approximately a third of each letter below them).

The indentation of some Old Testament quotations (see chapter 2) is, according to Lowe, the usual practice in Latin manuscripts of the fourth and fifth centuries ('More Facts', p. 61 = *Pal. Papers* 1,272; 'Greek Symptoms', p. 282 = *Pal. Papers* 2,469). It is also found in 06.

The colophons and superscriptions are also Latin in form. Those for Matthew and John (Ff103b and 104) are typical:

ΕΥΑΓΓΕΛΙΟΝ ΚΑΤΑ
ΜΑΘΘΑΙΟΝ ΕΤΕΛΕΣΘΗ

ΑΡΧΕΤΑΙ ΕΥΑΓΓΕΛΙΟΝ
ΚΑΤΑ ΙΩΑΝΝΗΝ

and

EUANGELIUM SEC
MATTHEUM EXPLICIT
INCIPIT EUANGELIUM
SEC IOHANNEN

There are short lines (⌐¬) above and below every second or third letter. In the Greek, the first and third lines are rubricated, and the small lines are in black, whilst for the second and fourth lines the colours are reversed. The same pattern is followed in the Latin, but here it is the second and fourth lines that have the red letters. The colophon to John is the same. But at the end of Luke (Ff284b and 285) the colouring alternates between the words instead of between the lines. The form is also different:

ΕΥΑΓΓΕΛΙΟΝ·ΚΑΤ ΛΟΥΚΑΝ
ΕΠΛΗΡΩΘΗ·ΑΡΧΕΤΑΙ ΚΑΤ ΜΑΡΚΟΝ

and

EUANG SECUND LUCAM EXPLICIT
INCIPIT EUANG SECUND MARCUM

Our attention is directed to two things here: the use of a colophon describing the previous and the next book, rather than separate subscriptions and superscriptions, and the Greek forms. The comparison with other biblical manuscripts is an interesting one.

The colophons and titles of the other Old Latin Gospel books are to be found in Jülicher's *Itala*, although in fact very little information is provided, and we are not told whether it is in the form of colophon or separate sub- and superscriptions. The same is true of the information about Vulgate Mss provided by Wordsworth and White, although their information is fuller. Most useful are the detailed descriptions in McGurk. See also Lowe, 'Greek Symptoms'.

Information for Greek Mss may be gathered from Tischendorf's *Editio octava* and from Legg. Facsimiles of the colophons in ℵ and A can be found in Milne and Skeat, *Scribes and Correctors*. To collect all the available information, I have consulted the photographs of all Mss of the Gospels in Greek written before 500 (except for 071 and 0244, which were not available), from the files of the Institut für Neutestamentliche Textforschung at Münster.

The use of *explicit* (i.e. *explicitum*) and *incipit* is standard in Latin books. The forms used in Greek manuscripts are far simpler. P[4] (Fragment c) has a heading *ευαγγελιον / κατα μαθθαιον* written by a later hand on a separate piece that has then been glued onto the sheet. P[66] has the title *ευαγγελιον κατα ιωανην* (perhaps added later – see *GMAW*, p. 16) and is lost at the end. P[75] is lost at its beginning and end, but is extant between Luke and John. It has *ευαγ'γελιον κατα λουκαν* for subscription followed by *ευαγγελιον κατα ϊωανην* for title. ℵ has the subscription forms *ευαγγελιον / κατα μαρκον* (and similarly for Luke and John, this last one written on three lines, none for Matthew), and *πραξεις / αποστολων*. Its titles are *κατα μαθθαιον, κατα μαρκον, κατα λουκαν, κατα ιωαννην* (none to Acts). B (03) has *κατα μαθθαιον, κατα μαρκον, πραξεις αποστολων, ιωανου γ*, written at the beginning and end of each book. C has only one heading extant: *ευαγγελιον κατα ματθαιον*. Its surviving subscriptions are *ευαγγελιον κατα μαρκον, ευαγγελιον κατα λουκαν, ευαγγελιον / κατα ι[ωαν]νην*. W (032) has the headings *κατα μαθθα[ιον], ευαγγελιον κατα ιωαννην, ευαγγελιονκαταλουκαν, ευαγγελιον κατα μαρκον*; and the subscriptions *ευαγγελιον κατα / μαθθεον, κατα / ιωαννην, ευαγγελιον / κατα λουκαν, ευαγγελιον κατα / μαρκον* (the last followed by a prayer in another hand).

These are all the titles and subscriptions that survive from our oldest Greek Gospel manuscripts. The forms tend to expand with time (e.g. A and E have for Acts the colophon *πραξεις των αγιων αποστολων*).

The use of *ετελεσθη* and *αρχεται* in D is unique. They are simply translations into Greek of the familiar Latin forms.

The writing of subscription and title together as a single formula in the character of a colophon is also not a Greek practice, while Latin parallels can be found. P[75] has a gap of a centimetre between the sub- and superscriptions. This, although the new gospel begins on the same page, provides the closest Greek parallel to what we have in D.

The relic of a more normal Greek form is also to be found in Codex Bezae. The opening bifolium of Luke has the headings ΕΥΑΓΓΕΛ· ΚΑΤ ΛΟΥΚΑΝ and EUANG SEC LUCAN, that for Mark has ΕΥΑΓΓΕΛΙΟΝ ΚΑΤ ΜΑΡΚΟΝ and EUANG SECUNDUM MARCUM, and that to Acts ΠΡΑΞΙC ΑΠΟCΤΟΛΩΝ and ΛCTUS APOSTOLORUM. Except for the last, these titles appear only on the first page of the book. Here, by contrast, we have Latin forms imitative of the Greek. The absence of such a formula as *initium* or *incipit* is as rare in Latin as it is standard in Greek manuscripts. The Vulgate manuscript D (Trinity College Dublin 52, the Book of Armagh) has not dissimilar forms – the superscriptions *secundum Lucanum, aeuangelium secundum iohannem*, and *incipit eiusdem tertia* for 3 John (none for Matthew, Mark, and Acts). The unusual colophon to Matthew (*ΕΧΠΛΙΚΙΤ ΑΕVΑΝΓVΕΛΙWΝ ΚΑΤΑ ΜΑΤΤΗUΜ CΡΙΠΤVΜ ΑΤΚVΕ ΦΙΝΙΤVΜ ΙΝ ΦΗRΙΑ ΜΑΤΤΗΙ*; none to Mark and Luke, a more normal one after John, one to Acts of six lines now erased, and *finit amen* after 3 John) indicates that this manuscript is by no means typical of the Latin tradition. The Vulgate codex G has the title *actus apostolorum* for Acts. Otherwise, our books contain no other examples of the type found in Codex Bezae.

This simple and Greek form in Codex Bezae is likely to be the remnant of a practice that was standard further back in the tradition. We have no extensive Latin Gospel manuscripts older than the second part of the fourth century, so we cannot date the development of the now standard form, or of the emancipation of the

Latin form from Greek models. One of our oldest Old Latin manuscripts (k) shows Greek evidence in another way, with the use of *cata*:

euangelium cata / marcum exp. / incip. cata mattheum / feliciter (F41)

Similarly, the Codex Palatinus (e) has

secundum mattheum / explicit incipit / secundum iohannem (F43b)
euangelium / cata iohannem / explicit incipit / cata Lucan (F118b)

Cata was to remain common (see, to take a random example, the Echternach Gospels of the seventh or eighth centuries). However, although our information is so scanty, it is worth suggesting that this form in D, paralleled in Greek manuscripts at least from P^{66} and P^{75} on, may be the superscription of the earliest period of the bilingual tradition, when there were no established Latin formulas.

With regard to dating, the colophons are not much help. The fact that *explicit* and not *finit* is used would be regarded by Lowe as against extreme antiquity ('More Facts', p. 60 = *Pal. Papers* 1,272; see further Bischoff, p. 44). But the value of this evidence may be regarded as questionable. The material gathered by Lindsay ('Collectanea varia', *Palaeographia Latina*, ed. W. M. Lindsay, Part II (St Andrews University Publications 16), Oxford, 1923, pp. 5–10) is of no help for present purposes, relating as it does to a later period. The use of red is no more helpful for dating purposes. The alternation of red and black lines is a custom of some antiquity. It is found, for example, in the Old Latin codices Vercellensis and Bobbiensis (a k), both of the fourth century, as well as in manuscripts of the fifth and sixth centuries. In the purple manuscript Palatinus (e), silver and gold alternate in the colophons.

The ornamentation between text and colophon, described by Lowe as ropelike, also executed in red and black, is found in the Old Latin prophets fragment from Stuttgart (fifth century).

The use of red ink for the first lines of each book (first three lines in D) is often taken as another indication of great antiquity (Bischoff, p. 79).

The running titles are also, according to Mercati, of a Latin type. There is a certain variety of usage in the codex, which is worth recording in detail: see table 1.

It is hard to find any order here at all, unless in Acts the scribe uses the full title at the beginning of gatherings *ΝΑʹ* (423), *ΝΓʹ* (439), *ΝΘʹ* (463), *ΞΑʹ* (479), and on the second sheet of *ΞΒʹ* (488). Quaternion *ΝΖʹ* is missing. Also, a full Latin title on the recto is twice followed by the full Greek title on the verso (435–435b, 443–443b).

From the information that follows in tables 2 and 3, it will become clear that running titles are far less common in Greek than in Latin biblical manuscripts. It will also become apparent that the Greek running titles of D are modelled on Latin forms, particularly in the use of abbreviations.

Table 1. *Running titles in Codex Bezae*

Title	Folio
MATTHEW	
Greek	
ΚΑΤΑ ΜΑΘΘΑΙΟΝ	3b, 8b–10b
ΚΑΤ ΜΑΘΘΑΙΟΝ	4b–6b, 11b–13b, 16b, 25b, 27b–31b, 34b–35b, 38b, 40b–43b, 50b, 80b–81b, 87b
ΚΑΤ ΜΑΘΘΕΟΝ	33b, 36b–37b, 39b
ΚΑΤ ΜΑΘΘ	44b–49b, 51b–79b, 82b–86b, 88b–90b, 92b–93b, 95b, 97b–102b
None	14b, 15b
Latin	
SEC MATTHAE	4
SEC MATTHAEUM	5, 10, 12, 13, 25, 28
SEC MATTH	6, 60–5, 67–8, 70–90, 92–3, 95, 97–8, 101–2, 104
SEC MATTHEUM	8, 11, 14, 27, 29–31, 33–4, 36–45, 47–55, 57–9
SEC MATTHEU͞	35, 56
SEC MATTHEUS	46
SEC MATT	66, 69
SEC ΜΑΘΘ	99
SEC MA[ ]	103
SEC M[ ]	32
None	15, 16, 100(?)
JOHN	
Greek	
ΚΑΤ ΙΩΑΝ	113b, 116b–122b, 124b–168b, 177b–end
ΚΑΤ ΙΩΑΝΝΗΝ	114b
ΚΑΤ ΙΟΑΝ	115b
ΚΑΤΑ ΙΩΑΝ	123b
ΚΑΤΑ [ ]	104b
Latin	
SEC IOHAN	throughout, except
SEC ΙΩΑΝ	125
LUKE	
Greek	
ΕΥΑΓΓΕΛ·ΚΑΤ ΛΟΥΚΑΝ	182b
ΚΑΤ ΛΟΥΚ	183b, 189b, 194b–195b, 198b, 201b, 204b–206b, 208b–211b, 213b, 217b, 221b–224b, 230b–232b, 234b–237b, 239b–240b, 242b–246b, 249b–258b, 260b, 262b, 265b–271b, 273b, 275b–276b, 278b, 282b–284b

Table 1. (*cont.*)

Title	Folio
ΚΑΤ ΛΟΥΚΑΝ	184b–188b, 190b–193b, 196b–197b, 199b–200b, 202b–203b, 207b, 212b, 214b–216b, 218b, 220b, 225b–229b, 233b, 238b, 241b, 247b–248b, 259b, 261b, 263b–264b, 272b, 274b, 277b, 279b–281b
Latin	
EUANG SEC LUCAN	183
SEC LUCAM	184, 195–6, 236, 241, 244, 248
SEC LUCAN	185–94, 197–218, 220–35, 238–40, 242, 245–7, 249–58, 260–end
SEC LUC	237, 259
SEC LUEAM	243
MARK	
Greek	
ΕΥΑΓΓΕΛΙΟΝ ΚΑΤ ΜΑΡΚΟΝ	285b
ΚΑΤ ΜΑΡΚΟΝ	286b, 289b, 292b–293b, 295b–311b, 314b–316b, 319b, 322b, 324b–325b, 330b–331b, 333b, 335b, 340b–343b
ΚΑΤ ΜΑΡΚ	287b–288b, 290b–291b, 312b–313b, 317b–318b, 320b–321b, 323b, 326b–329b, 332b, 334b, 336b–339b, 344b–347b
ΚΑΤΑ ΜΑΡΚΟΝ	294b
Latin	
EUANG SECUNDUM MARCUM	286
SEC MARCUM	287–8, 290–312, 314, 316–17, 319–22, 325, 328–30, 334–5, 342–3, 345
SEC MARC	289, 313, 315, 318, 323–4, 326–7, 331–3, 336–41, 344, 346–7
3 JOHN	
Latin	
EPIST IOHANIS III.	
ACTS	
Greek	
ΠΡΑΞΙϹ ΑΠΟϹΤΟΛⲰΝ	415b, 423b, 435b, 443b, 458b
ΠΡΑΞ·ΑΠΟϹΤΟΛⲰΝ	416b, 422b, 426b, 429b, 431b, 433b, 444b–445b, 457b, 464b, 475b, 483b
ΠΡΑΞ ΑΠΟϹΤΟΛⲰΝ	420b, 424b, 427b–428b, 432b, 434b, 438b–439b, 442b, 446b, 455b, 461b–462b, 470b, 475b, 479b, 482b–483b, 510b
ΠΡΑΞΙϹ ΑΠΟϹΤΟΛ	417b
ΠΡΑΞ·ΑΠΟϹΤΟΛ	418b–419b, 421b, 436b–437b, 440b–441b, 456b, 460b, 463b, 466b, 476b–478b, 480b–481b, 485b–489b, 491b–492b, 495b, 499b–502b, 504b–505b, 508b

Table 1. (*cont.*)

Title	Folio
ΠΡΑΞ ΑΠΟCΤΟΛΩΝ	425b, 459b, 465b, 467b–468b, 471b–474b, 484b, 490b, 493b–494b, 496b–498b, 506b–507b
ΠΡΑΞ ΑΠΟST (*sic*)	469b
None	430b
Latin	
ACTUS APOSTOLORUM	416, 423–4, 435, 437, 439, 443, 463, 476, 479–80, 488
ACTUS APOSTOL·	417, 419–20, 431, 495
ACTUS APOSTOL	421–2, 425, 427–30, 436, 438, 440–2, 444–6, 455–62, 464–5, 467–9, 471–5, 477–8, 481, 484–7, 489–91, 493–4, 496–502, 504–8, 510
ACTUS APOSTOLOR·	418
ACTUS APOSTOLOR	432, 434, 466
ACTUS APOST	426, 482
ACTUS APOSTOLO	433
ACTUS APOST·	470
ACTUSA POSTOL	492

In table 2, the forms found in Greek manuscripts copied before 500 are again derived either from the manuscripts or from photographs at Münster. Since many of the texts are in a fragmentary condition, I attempt to indicate how much of the top margin survives.

What of the form of running title used by those few Greek manuscripts that have them? The running titles of Codex Sinaiticus have certain idiosyncrasies, which I indicate in full in table 4. The practice of alternate blank tops to the pages is not found in Paul or the Catholic Epistles, but it does recur in Revelation, in the first part of Barnabas, and in Hermas. According to Milne and Skeat (*Scribes and Correctors*, pp. 30–5), the running titles of the Gospels were added later by Scribe A, those of Acts, Revelation, Barnabas and Hermas being added later by Scribe B.

Codex Vaticanus follows consistently the rule of having *κατα* on the left, and the name of the evangelist on the right-hand page of each opening. In Acts it simply has *πραξεις* on each right-hand page. In Paul it has *προς* on the left and the name of the recipient(s) on the right.

Thus, of sixty-seven manuscripts with at least some top margin, only three – ℵ, B, and D itself – have running titles. Twenty have numbers, of page, leaf, or column. With information not available for three, the remaining forty-one have nothing at the head of the page.

A quite different situation pertains with regard to Latin New Testament manuscripts of the period. Indeed, as Lowe showed ('Some Facts', pp. 206f = *Pal.*

Table 2. *Running titles in Greek New Testament manuscripts written before 500*

The description of top margins as fully surviving does not, in the case of manuscripts extensively extant, indicate that *all* the top margins are present.

A question mark indicates that the area where a running title would probably be is missing.

The manuscripts listed are those given a date from the fifth century or earlier in Aland, *Liste*.

Manuscript	Top margin	What is written
P^{1}	all	page numbers
$P^{4}/P^{64}/P^{67}$	most	nothing
P^{6}	all	page numbers
P^{8}	all	nothing
P^{12}	some	nothing
P^{13}		column numbers
P^{15}	most	nothing
P^{16}	none	
P^{17}	none	
P^{18}	none	
P^{19}	some	nothing
P^{20}	some	nothing
P^{21}	none	
P^{22}	some	nothing
P^{23}	all	page numbers
P^{24}	none	
P^{25}	all	page no. on recto (top r.h. corner)
P^{27}	none	
P^{28}	none	
P^{29}	none	
P^{30}	none	
P^{32}	none	
P^{35}	some	nothing
P^{37}	none	
P^{38}	some	*NΘ* in middle of papyrol. verso
P^{39}	some	page numbers
P^{40}	none	
P^{45}	some	page numbers
P^{48}	none	
P^{49}	none	
P^{50}	none	
P^{51}	none	
P^{52}	some	nothing
P^{53}	none	
P^{54}	some	nothing
P^{56}	some	nothing
P^{57}	none	
P^{62}	some	nothing
P^{63}	some	page numbers
P^{65}	some	page numbers?
P^{66}	all	page numbers

Table 2. (*cont.*)

Manuscript	Top margin	What is written
P69	none	
P70	none	
P71	none	
P72	some	page or leaf number
P73	none	
P75	most	nothing
P77	none	
P78	none	
P80	none	
P81	some	nothing (?)
P82	none	
P85	none	
P86	none	
P87	none	
P88	some	nothing
P89	none	
P90	some	nothing
P91	none	
P92	some	nothing?
P93	none	
P94	none	
P95	none	
01	all	running titles (see below)
02	all	nothing
03	all	running titles (see below)
04	all	nothing
05	all	running titles (see below)
016		
026	all	nothing
029/0113	all	page numbers
032	all	nothing
048		
057	some	nothing
058	none	
059/0215	some	page numbers??
060	some	page numbers
061	none	
062	some	blank
068	none	
069	none	
071	none	
072	all	nothing?
077		
088	some	nothing
0160	none	
0162	most	nothing
0163	none	

Table 2. (*cont.*)

Manuscript	Top margin	What is written
0165	some	nothing
0166	none	
0169	most	page numbers
0170	none	
0171	some	nothing
0172	none	
0173	most	τι
0174	lost	
0175	none	
0176	none	
0181	all	nothing
0182	some	nothing (?)
0185	most	page numbers
0186/0224	none	
0189	most	page numbers
0201	some	nothing (?)
0206	most	leaf number on verso
0207	all	page numbers
0212	none	
0213	none	
0214	none	
0216	some	nothing
0217	none	
0218	none	
0219	some	nothing
0220	most	nothing (?)
0221	some	nothing
0226	none	
0227	some	nothing (?)
0228	none	
0230	none	
0231	none	
0232	most	leaf (?) numbers on verso
0236	none	
0239	none	
0240	none	
0242	some	nothing
0244		
0252	none	
0253	some	nothing
0254	some	nothing
0258	none	
0261	some	nothing
0264	none	
0267	none	
0268	some	cross above r.h. edge of text
0270	all	page or leaf number

Table 3. *Running titles in Latin New Testament manuscripts written before 500*

According to Lowe (*CLA*) these manuscripts all predate 500.

The description of top margins as fully surviving does not indicate that *all* the top margins are present.

For bilinguals, see chapter 4.

Manuscript	Top margin	What is written
Old Latin		
1 (k)	all	running titles
2 (e)	all	running titles
3 (a)	all	running titles
4 (b)	all	running titles
8 (ff²)	all	running titles
12 (h)	all	running titles
16	all	running titles
17 (i)	all	running titles
19		
21 (s)	all	running titles
22 (j)	all	running titles (not every page)
23	none	
55 (h)		
79	all	running titles on hair only
Vulgate		
N	all	running titles
Σ	all	running titles on flesh only
Leningrad, Q.V.I.12		
Munich, Clm 29270/1	none	
Vienna, Nat. Bibl. Lat. 563		

Papers 1, 199–201; 'More Facts', p. 59 = *Pal. Papers* 1, 270), their presence is nearly universal in all ancient Latin manuscripts. Table 3 shows that no New Testament Old Latin copy lacks them. Numbers, except for quire signatures, do not occur.

36 (a Gothic–Latin bilingual fragment of Luke) is dated by Fischer to the fifth century (B. Fischer, *Verzeichnis der Sigel für Handschriften und Kirchenschriftsteller* (Vetus Latina, Die Reste der altlateinischen Bibel 1), Freiburg, 1949), but Lowe considers it to be of the sixth, observing that 'The Latin script is not of the oldest type' (*CLA* 8,1200).

33, dated by Fischer to the end of the fifth century, is considered by McGurk (p. 62) to be from the sixth. In Lowe's opinion (*CLA* 5,600), it is fifth to sixth. He describes the material at the head of the pages as follows: 'No running titles except "Iohannem" in late Rustic capital on fol. 72. A chrismon stands in the centre of the upper margin of the first page of some quires (foll. 174, 182).' This rather unusual book (with a page size of 57 × 71 mm, it contains the Gospel of John on 263 folios) provides a possible exception to the rule. The question of its date illustrates that the requirement 'written before 500' should be taken as meaning 'reasonably certainly fifth- rather than sixth-century'.

In general, the running titles are written in the same script as the rest of the manuscript, but generally in somewhat smaller characters, up to the end of the fifth

Table 4. *Running titles in Codex Sinaiticus*

It is necessary to include the subscriptions to understand the running titles. An oblique stroke (\) indicates that what is written is divided between the left- and right-hand pages of an opening.

Folio	What is written
Matthew	
1	title *κατα μαθθαιον*
1b, 2	*κατα μαθθαιον*
2b–7	*κατα* \ *μαθθαιον*
7b–8	nothing
8b	*κατα*
9	*κατα μαθθαιον*
9b–15	*κατα* \ *μαθθαιον*
15b–16	nothing
16b–18	*κατα* \ *μαθθαιον*
No subscription to Matthew	
Mark	
18b	heading *κατα μαρκον*
19	blank
19b–21, 22b–23, 24b–25, 26b–27	*κατα* \ *μαρκον*
21b–22, 23b–24, 25b–26, 27b–28	nothing
28b	*κατα*
29	*μαρκον* above col. 2 (where Mark ends)
Subscription *ευαγγελ* / *λιον* / *κατα μαρκον*	
Luke	
Incipit for Luke at the top of col. 3, where Luke begins	
29b–47	nothing
47b	nothing
Subscription to Luke at end of F47b	
John	
48	*κατα ιωαννην* above col. 1
48b–59	nothing, as in Luke
59b–60, 60b–61	*κατα* \ *ιωαννην*
Subscription to John at end of F61, col. 4	
Acts	
100	running title *πραξεις*
100b–101	nothing
101b–102	*πραξεις* on right page
And so alternately blank and with *πραξεις* on right to 114	
115, 116, 117	nothing
Subscription to Acts on 117, col. 3	

century (and see Bischoff, p. 79). From then on, the use of a different script increases in popularity.

The practice of writing on every other opening is found, as well as in parts of ℵ, in the Latin manuscripts 79, Σ, and the Vulgate manuscript of Judges and Ruth Vat. Lat. 5763 (where it is on the hair only).

Running titles in Old Latin manuscripts show a certain variety. (Again, an oblique stroke \ indicates that what is written is divided between the left- and the right-hand pages of an opening.)

k has *euangel* or *euang* or *euangelu* \ *cata marc* and *euangel* or *euang* \ *cata matthe* (or *matth*, *mattheum*, *math*).

e has *secundum* \ *mattheum*, *iohannem*, *lucan*, *marcum*.

a has:
Matthew – *sec* or *sec·* or *secund* or *secu* \ *mattheum* or *mattheum·*
John – *secund* \ *iohannen* (only in some earlier pages) or *iohannem*
Luke – *sec·* or *secund·* \ *Lucanum*
Mark – *secund* \ *marcum·*

b has *sec* \ *matthaeum* (it seems: few survive), *iohannen*, *lucan*, *marcum*

The conclusion that in using running titles, the scribe of D was doing what as a Latin scribe he considered normal, seems to be inescapable. The use of abbreviations also indicates this: *sec* is a common enough Latin practice, but κατ is unique, as are the shortened names of the evangelists.

In the form of *incipit* and *explicit*, in the running titles, and in the other details of book production that we have examined, we find that Latin customs are this scribe's invariable rule. There is no evidence to suggest that he could have been trained in a Greek *scriptorium*, while there is plenty to prove his Latin habits. The belief that he shows a mixture of skills cannot be sustained in the face of this study. We are dealing with the work of a Latin copyist.

It seems unlikely that the scribe of D wrote in all the running titles of a gathering at the same time as ruling, before or after folding. To write such a variety of forms one after the other in Luke or Mark seems very improbable. It is more likely that he wrote the title of each page as he began writing on it. A manuscript where the running titles are on alternate openings (parts of ℵ, and four Latin manuscripts in Lowe's 'More Facts' (p. 59 = *Pal. Papers* 1,270)) is more likely to have had the running titles entered immediately after ruling, before folding, on the flesh side.

We come finally to the materials used by the scribe and to the finished book.

The parchment is very carefully prepared and fine. The thinnest leaves are only

$1\frac{1}{2}$ thousandths of an inch thick (Cockerell). This may be compared with the Codex Sinaiticus, whose thinnest leaf 'has large areas under 0.0015 in'; most leaves are between 3 and 6 thousandths of an inch (Milne and Skeat, p. 71). It is not surprising that there are a few lacunae in the material, around which the scribe wrote.

The ink is aptly described by Lowe as olive brown (*CLA*). The release of acid from the compound has, as in other ancient manuscripts, eaten through the parchment, leaving a stencil of many letters. As is always the case, the ink has adhered much better to the hair than to the flesh sides.

A small amount of information about the manuscript's binding came to light when it was last rebound. Cockerell wrote:

> The backs of the gatherings were so badly damaged that it was difficult to tell how the book had been originally sewn. There were 7 saw cuts in the spine, 2 of them presumably for kettle stitches; also 8 other sewing marks, making some 15 sewing marks in all. Out of these it is possible to select a sewing of 4 or 5 bands that might have been used originally.

This evidence makes it seem likely that the manuscript was originally bound as a single volume – and the beginnings of Luke and Mark are on the verso of a leaf whose recto contained the end of the previous book (a division into two would have required blank sides).

THE HAND

J. N. Birdsall, 'The Geographical and Cultural Origin of the Codex Bezae Cantabrigiensis: a Survey of the *Status quaestionis*, mainly from the Palaeographical Standpoint', *Studien zum Text und zur Ethik des Neuen Testaments* (Festschrift Heinrich Greeven), ed. Wolfgang Schrage, Berlin, 1986, pp. 102–14; Bischoff, *Palaeography*; F. C. Burkitt, 'The Date of Codex Bezae', *JTS* 3 (1902), 501–13; Cavallo, *Ricerche*; Cavallo and Maehler, *Greek Bookhands*; Edward Johnston, *Formal Penmanship and Other Papers*, ed. Heather Child, London, 1977; Stan Knight, *Historical Scripts. A Handbook for Calligraphers*, London, 1984; Lowe, 'A Note'; Jean Mallon, 'Observations sur quelques monuments d'écriture latine calligraphiés dans les cinq premiers siècles de notre ère', *Arts et métiers graphiques* 66 (1939), 37–40 (reprinted in *De l'écriture, recueil d'études publiées de 1937 à 1981*, Paris, 1982, pp. 38–42); Mallon, 'Notes paléographiques à propos de CIL II 5411', *Emerita XIII*, Madrid, 1945 (*Revista de filología española* 29, 1945, *Miscelánea Nebrija*, 1), 213–80 (reprinted in *De l'écriture*, pp. 75–109); Robert Marichal, 'L'Ecriture latine et l'écriture grecque du Ier au VIe siècle', *L'Antiquité classique* 19 (1950), 113–44; Marichal, 'L'Ecriture latine et la civilisation occidentale du Ier au XVIe siècle', in *L'Ecriture et la psychologie des peuples*, Centre International de Synthèse, XXIIe semaine de synthèse, ed. Marcel Cohen *et al.*, Paris, 1963, pp. 199–247, pp. 208f; Marco Palma, 'Per una verifica del principio dell'angolo di scrittura', *Scrittura e Civiltà* 2 (1978), 263–73.

The evidence in the externals of book production points to the scribe being one who was trained in the Latin tradition. As we have already indicated, the question of the influence upon him of Greek and Latin *scripts* has led to much confusion. The focus of this confusion has been the angle of the pen used by the scribe.

The angle of writing

It is sometimes stated that the scribe of Codex Bezae cut his pen for writing Greek. The origin of this tradition is Burkitt's 1902 article, 'The Date of Codex Bezae':

> It seems to have been the usual custom, at least until early in the sixth century, for Latin uncials to be written with a *slanting* pen, while Greek uncials were written with a *straight* pen. If the top of the page be supposed to point North, in Greek writing a line drawn from N to S will generally be thick and from W to E fine, but in Latin the thickest will be from NW to SE and the finest from SW to NE. (pp. 501f)

This opinion may be found repeated by Lowe in 1927, and by Birdsall (p. 107). Burkitt gives no support for his assertion, which seems to be a hypothesis aimed at explaining what he believed to be the facts rather than a piece of verifiable information. Since the twentieth century has discovered only evidence pointing towards the scribe having been trained in Latin practices, this particular belief has been a matter of some embarrassment. However, there are several objections to it so weighty as to bring all perplexity over a Latin scribe using a pen with a Greek cut to an end.

The first is that the cut of the pen is not the only factor to be considered. The angles at which the writing material is held in the scribe's left hand, and the pen in his right, are also significant. Their relevance was first shown by Mallon ('Observations').

Care should be taken in using the two illustrations on p.39 of the reprint in *De l'écriture*: the second figure is wrongly described in both the French and the English captions. It actually illustrates the thickness of the strokes in Script III, 'la page inclinée'.

Mallon argues that the vertical strokes are the thickest when the writing material is held at an angle, the left corner nearer to the scribe than the right. The script described by Burkitt as typically Latin would then be due to the writing material being held straight.

Mallon developed his theory in another direction a few years later ('Notes paléographiques'). Here he discusses the angle of the pen to the writing material. This was examined in more detail by Marichal (1950). He showed that when a pen is held so that a line at right angles to its axis forms an angle of 50° to the writing line (which is horizontal), the oblique stroke – NW to SE – will be thickest. If the angle is 15°, and the writing surface is tilted to the left at an angle of 35°, then the verticals will be thickest.

A chronological question also arose. Mallon suggested a connexion between writing 'la page inclinée' and the introduction of the codex. This cannot be pressed. All we can say is that such writing would not be possible on a roll, because the part already written would need to go on the floor by the scribe's left knee, forcing the part on which he was writing to go straight across his lap. Marichal (1950) argued that the 'page inclinée' style replaced the other from the third century onwards. The chronological argument was challenged by Turner (*GMAW*, p. 27), and abandoned by Mallon in the 1980 preface to his first article (*De l'écriture*, p. 38).

The whole matter has been well described and developed by Marco Palma. He regards Cavallo's definition as definitive: 'Per angolo di scrittura si intende l'angolo complementare a quello formato dalla retta passante per le punte dello strumento scrittorio con il rigo di base della scrittura, e avente quest'ultimo elemento in comune' (Cavallo, p. 4, n. 3, cited by Palma, p. 269). Palma handles also the question of the cut of the pen (p. 268, and especially p. 270).

This debate is rather unsatisfactory because of its highly theoretical character. I therefore attempted to verify Mallon's conclusions by experimenting with a square steel nib. My scribal efforts were not altogether satisfactory, but my immediate conclusions seemed to support Marichal's theory. When the paper was held at an angle, the axis of the pen was closer to being parallel to the sides of the paper, so that more of it was in contact with the paper in vertical strokes. Greater delicacy would then be required for the horizontals, where only the leading edge of the nib is writing. If the angle is too fine, the ink will not flow, and if too much pressure is applied the tip may be damaged. This is why many horizontal strokes in Codex Bezae are very faint – they are formed by the narrowest width of a lightly held pen.

Experiment also showed that, however you hold the pen and place the paper, an oblique stroke from top left to bottom right (Burkitt's NW to SE) will always be at least a little thicker than one going the other way, unless the pen is held almost at right angles to the sides of the page. To produce the opposite effect, it seemed that one would have to write with the hand resting on the page *above* the line of writing. This is why manuscripts in both styles of writing all show the first stroke of *chi* or *x* thicker than the second.

This is using an ordinary straight-ended nib. One with a slanting end would need to be held at an angle nearer to 50° to produce the effect created by a straight nib held at 15°.

At this point it seemed possible that all three factors – cut of pen, angle of writing material, and angle of holding the pen – should be taken into consideration (and see Palma, p. 271). I therefore sought the assistance of a living scribe, and found myself in a quite different world, one where the character of individual scripts was interpreted in a way that was new to me.

I am indebted to Stan Knight, of the Society of Scribes and Illuminators, for opening this world to me. It may be noted in passing that one of the most valuable features of his book is the use of photographs magnifying the size of pages in order to show details of the formation of the letters. Palaeography will be the poorer if it neglects to learn from people who are actually able to write, and who know the physical techniques necessary to produce particular shapes.

Knight draws attention to the seven pen-stroke constants listed by Edward Johnston in *Formal Penmanship* (pp. 119–21) as a guide to the essential character of any formal script. These are

> (1) the Angle of the pen (which within certain scripts may vary); (2) the Weight of the pen strokes in relation to the height of the letters; (3) the Form and structural shape of the letters; (4) the Number, (5) Order and (6) Direction of the pen strokes; and (7) the Speed at which it was written. (Introduction)

He is able to demonstrate (and see his figure 1) that a single script can be produced in several different ways, as far as angle of pen and material are concerned. Together, the cut of the pen, and the angle of pen and material, belong in the first constant, and the seven constants affect each other so that a number of different combinations can produce similar results. The recognition of each variable in a given script remains, however, important. It can help us to be more precise in studying hands. But we cannot assume that a scribe will have had only one way of cutting his pen and holding it against the paper.

A skilled scribe will have been able to achieve several different effects. For instance, the Bodleian Jerome *Chronicon* was penned by a scribe who could write three hands that we know of – that of the text, and those of the upright and the sloping marginalia.

Not all scripts require a constant angle, and it should be noted that the ancient and medieval practice of writing with only the little finger resting on the page (Bischoff, p. 38) provides greater suppleness and flexibility to the hand.

The conclusion is that the importance of the angle of writing in the formation of hands is indisputable. But the exploration of the factors responsible for a particular angle reveals a more complicated interaction than had been supposed.

One other factor needs to be discussed here: the pliability of the pen. According to Marichal (1963), 'le copiste grec emploie un calame à pointe dure et mince qui n'accuse pas les pleins, le latin un calame à pointe souple et large qui lui permet d'opposer fortement les pleins et les déliés, de donner, par conséquent, à l'écriture un relief et un rythme que le grec ne peut avoir . . .' (p. 209). But this does not advance our understanding of much more than early Latin cursive hands. Why should not different types of script – Greek and Latin – require particular cuts of point and pliabilities of pen? One would like to know of any grounds for attributing all Greek hands to one kind of pen, and all Latin to another.

However, for the present discussion, it is enough to note that the last two factors are sufficient on their own, without reference to the first, and that the boundaries are between types of script, not according to the language of the text being copied.

To return to Burkitt's theory. A second, and if possible even more fatal, objection is that examples of each type of script are to be found in both languages. Mallon provides two examples of each from Latin hands. Turner gives a Greek representative for each from the second century AD (*GMAW*, plates 13 and 28 –

Bodley Gr. Class. a. 1(P) and Cambridge Univ. Lib. Add. 5895). The two ways of writing are not confined the one to Greek, the other to Latin scripts. With this fact, the claim that the scribe of D cut his pen as would a Greek scribe falls to the ground. Even more than that, the view that all Greek scribes cut their pens differently from all Latin scribes is shown to be without foundation.

But we can do much more than show an old theory to be false. The question of the angle of writing lies at the heart of a proper understanding of the scripts of D.

Mallon, in his 1939 article, suggests an application of his theory to the study of Codex Bezae, by raising the question of the relationship between the Latin capital and uncial scripts. (In the following quotation, his Script III is Berlin P. 6757.)

> Toute explication de l'onciale, donnée à partir de la capitale, reste boîteuse, peu nette. Si, au contraire, on prend le problème par l'autre bout, c'est-à-dire à partir de l'écriture III, tout devient simple: *il suffit de conserver, tel quel, dans ses formes et ses graisses, cet alphabet de l'écriture III*, en y réintroduisant seulement les formes capitales de R et S avec les graisses de l'écriture sur papier incliné. On obtient ainsi l'alphabet de l'onciale dite 'onciale *b d*' du type du célèbre *Codex Bezae* de Cambridge.
>
> (p. 42)

The example of writing 'sur papier incliné' given as his main example is the Livy *Epitome*. This in itself is a major obstacle to the theory – the Livy *Epitome* is a *roll* and therefore would have had to go fairly straight across the lap. But the point remains that the angle is different, however it was achieved.

Mallon is therefore able to show that the Latin script of Codex Bezae can be understood within the development of Latin hands, without needing to posit particular Greek influence.

Here we are again confronted by the question of general and specific Greek influences, and need to clarify the point.

Marichal sees a general influence of Greek on Latin scripts, and follows Traube in regarding biblical uncial as the model for Latin uncial (1950, p. 129; see also 1963). To find specific Greek influences on the Latin forms of D, we will need to look for un-Latin details. It is also becoming clear that everything which *can* be explained as a Latin form *should* be taken for one.

Formation and date

It is interesting that, to many people, the overall appearance of a double page of D is Greek. There are several reasons for this. The first is that biblical maiuscule is essentially a Greek form. The second is that Latin biblical manuscripts survive in a variety of scripts. Biblical maiuscule was the preferred script for some centuries from the fourth onwards. In Latin there was no such uniformity. We are thus more familiar with the square but flowing script of D from Greek than from Latin examples.

Another reason lies in this general dependence of Latin on Greek scripts. In detail, however, such dependence is not shown by D. To understand this better, we must study the Latin hand of D more carefully, and its place within the history of Latin scripts. We cannot do better than follow Bischoff's account (pp. 72–5).

Latin uncial and half-uncial developed as calligraphic versions of cursive, the latter out of cursive minuscule ('Later Roman cursive'). Apart from the adoption of particular minuscule letters, the principal characteristic is the angle of writing. Bischoff believes that the two principal types of half-uncial both imitate Greek style. These two types are the older (Eastern) half-uncial (the script of the Livy *Epitome* and of related Mss) and its sub-division, the oblique form. Its nearest analogy in Greek scripts is the contemporary biblical maiuscule. (The point is well taken, if we compare the manuscript with which Cavallo begins his account of the canonization of biblical maiuscule (P Ryl 16), dated by him to 220–5, with the Livy *Epitome*, which also dates from the first half of the third century.) The idea for this kind of Latin hand, used from the third to fourth centuries onwards, of which the best known vertical example is the Livy *Epitome*, comes from Greek. Its origin is in the East – both the Greek writing angle and the Greek elements in the texts copied support this. Because of the considerable number of legal texts in this script (*CLA* 2,248; 8,1039, 1041, 1042; 10,1527; 11,1657), he suggests that 'the Latin law school of Berytos (Beirut) probably played a rôle, if not already in its formation then certainly in its use from the third to the fifth century' (p. 74). With regard to Codex Bezae, he writes: 'The Greek–Latin Codex Bezae ... and the Seneca manuscript written by a certain Nicianus [*CLA* 1,69] – two further calligraphic witnesses to this kind of script – also fit into the Greek framework' (pp. 74f).

The Latin column of Codex Bezae, therefore, is written in a form of half-uncial developed in the East, used most frequently in the production of legal texts, and possibly associated with Berytus.

For an account of the Greek hand, we turn to Cavallo.

He sees the history of biblical maiuscule as falling into three parts – formation, perfection, and decline. The highest point is reached with the two great codices of the entire Bible, Sinaiticus and Vaticanus. The decadence set in around the year 400, and progressed through to the script's eclipse in the ninth century. Both formation and decadence were marked by variation in the angle of writing. The decay is not constant, but is observable in the abandonment of one or another of the canonical elements (p. 73).

The uncanonical characteristics of Codex Bezae are an inconstant angle of writing (so that the right-to-left oblique strokes are of varying thicknesses), while the strokes sloping the other way tend to be the thickest. The serifs are light, and only slightly more pronounced on the thinnest horizontals. The decadence is not marked, and the manuscript is discussed amongst others, all dated before 450, which also abandon only one or two elements of the canonical script.

To Cavallo, we may add that the Greek of Codex Bezae preserves the essential squareness of biblical maiuscule, and also its simplicity of execution. Like the best examples, it is written fast.

We may now see the place of each script within its tradition. Can we come to any conclusions with regard to the basic training and expertise of the scribe?

Firstly, we note that the Greek script is an example of the most common way of writing biblical manuscripts. The Latin, by contrast, represents a fairly short-lived variation of the half-uncial form. The only other important biblical example is the Claromontane Pauline Epistles, which in fact is a very different script from that of Codex Bezae.

Secondly, a comparison of the columns shows certain Latin elements in the Greek side. Particularly noteworthy is *upsilon*, which has both its oblique strokes at the same angle to the vertical. The classical biblical maiuscule form has the first oblique stroke at a less steep angle than the second. The form in D is, in fact, a Latin Y.

The variable pen angle noted by Cavallo may be due to the influence of Latin cursive on early half-uncial, carried across into the formation of the Greek characters.

This evidence, not in itself overwhelming, is substantiated by all the codicological facts that we have already found. In chapters 6 and 7 (Part II), the evidence of the *nomina sacra* and the orthography will be shown to point in the same direction.

This may be the place to note that the presence of an asterisk for *denarius* in the Greek column can no longer be taken to be a Latin habit. See Birdsall, n. 28 (p. 108f). The use of the *anchora* for indicating omissions, on the other hand, should be taken as a Latin feature (see *CLA* 4,viiif).

There can no longer be any serious doubt that this scribe was a Latin scribe. Once this conclusion has been reached, we can give it further weight by attempting an explanation of the manuscript's appearance.

The fact that the Latin script has its closest connection with legal hands prompted Brown to the following reconstruction:

> The scribe was a specialist hack, technically competent but poorly educated, who had been engaged in the more or less exclusive copying of texts in Roman law, which he did in 'early half-uncial' somewhere in the Roman East. He sometimes had to copy some Greek as part of his job. (In a letter, quoted by Birdsall, p. 108)

The choice of such a scribe for the copying of such a bilingual text is clear: he was a person with the necessary linguistic skills. But the selection is also interesting with regard to the scripts. Apart from the aesthetic superiority of a double page with matching scripts, the way in which this scribe wrote his Latin hand will actually have made the formation of biblical maiuscule letters no hard task for him.

At the same time, we must bear in mind the fact that scribes will have had the skill to vary their hand to meet a particular need. This scribe has set out to write in such a way that the double pages form as much of a visual unity as he can achieve. There is thus an interaction between the hands.

The point has come to attempt to determine the date of the manuscript. Cavallo approaches this solely by an examination of the Greek side. He dates it to 'a little before the middle of the fifth century' (p. 75). That is to say, he places it in the first stage of the decline of biblical maiuscule, slightly later than P. Vindob. 3081 of John, P. Vindob. 36113, *PSI* 4 (both of Romans), and P. Ant. 13 (Acts of Paul and Thecla); these he dates to between 400 and 425. Manuscripts he considers to be contemporary with D are P. Vindob. G. 35779, 39209, 30135, 26782, and P. Berol. 9754.

Given the fact that the scribe of D was not trained to copy Greek, it is probably unwise to attempt to date the volume from his Greek script. On the one hand, there is the possibility that he is imitating older models; on the other, features which Cavallo regards as symptomatic of degeneration in biblical maiuscule could simply reveal a lack of expertise. The first possibility would force us to date it later than just before 450, while the second could make a much earlier date possible.

It is therefore necessary to attempt to reach a date by an examination of the Latin script.

First, the correctors. These will be examined in detail in chapter 3. It will be argued there that Corrector G could be dated as early as the fourth century. Corrector A worked some time between 400 and 440, and C and B between 400 and 450. The evidence of G is of especial significance: it will be argued that these corrections were made to the manuscript when it was newly written. The proofs of this are both palaeographical and in the nature of the corrections.

Thus a date of 400 is probably required by G, and a date before 440 by A.

Codicological evidence encourages us in a date of about 400. As we have seen, there are many early features. It will be shown in Part II that the form $\overline{\mathrm{DNS}}$ for the *nomen sacrum dominus* is found in the manuscript, but only to a limited extent. This abbreviation was becoming popular at the end of the fourth and beginning of the fifth centuries.

With regard to the Latin script, this short-lived form of early half-uncial has to stem from the end of the fourth century.

A date of either the very end of the fourth century or the very beginning of the fifth is therefore the most acceptable. It will be most convenient to speak of the manuscript having been written in 400.

Finally, a word must be added with regard to the means by which the manuscript was taken down. I have argued elsewhere that it was written by eye, rather than to dictation (Parker, 'Dictation Theory'). The evidence for this lay in the high number of readings where the copyist's eye had been distracted by groups of letters near to those he was attempting to copy. I see no reason for abandoning the conclusions stated there.

The question of *where* the manuscript was written will be left till later. In addition to the evidence of this chapter, we will need to learn more about the character of the book and its history before advancing a theory.

CHAPTER TWO

The punctuation

This section is purely descriptive. A discussion of the purpose of the punctuation will be found in the chapter on the sense-lines (chapter 5).

Examination indicates that the punctuation is somewhat different from the description given by Scrivener (pp. xviiif). Lowe's account (*CLA* 2,140, both editions) is unfortunately even less complete. Besides the fact of the sense-lines themselves, there are eight phenomena to be noticed.

1. A line projecting into the left-hand margin, with some initial letters enlarged (see below).
2. A double point, like a modern colon, found within a line (occasionally at the end), sometimes followed by an enlarged initial letter.
3. A medial point, also found within a line, but sometimes at the end.
4. A large space, sometimes followed by a large initial letter.
5. A small space.
6. A large space with a medial point in it.
7. A high point.
8. A quotation from the Old Testament indented.

The scribe also used the diaeresis and apostrophus. His practice is clearly described by Scrivener (p. xix), and need not concern us further. The use of the terms *στιγμὴ μέση* and *στιγμὴ τελεία* for the middle and high points might be taken to suggest different grammatical uses by the scribe. These are not discernible, and the terms should therefore not be used.

The definition of large and small spaces must contain a degree of subjectivity, and no criteria of measurement can be offered. In Luke it is often difficult to distinguish between the two. But a glance at the most commonly reproduced bifolium (F 205b–206) will show that there are three large spaces on F205b, and eight or nine small ones.

The initial letters merit further examination. Close investigation reveals that the scribe had certain habits in writing them.

In the Greek script B, Γ, Δ, E, H, Θ, I, Λ, O, Π, C, Y, and ω are written larger than normal. M is only slightly larger than its average size. So is T, which has a tendency for the vertical to go below the line (on F92b/4 it is written with a tail to the vertical). A is larger, with the long stroke slightly more upright than usual. K is sometimes slightly larger, sometimes the usual size (e.g. 484b/2), but with the tail of the vertical stroke longer than average, sometimes almost filling the space if it is within a line. P is written in its normal size.

In the Latin column C, D, E, G, I, M, N, S, and U are all written large. H is only a little over average (e.g. 442/11). F is its usual size, but has a tail to its vertical stroke. Q and R remain their normal size. So does P, though this letter is not written consistently when it is in the initial position (e.g. F344). A is similar to its Greek counterpart. T is written either large or ordinary, with a tendency for the vertical to go below the line.

It should also be observed that there is a difference between the two columns in the extent to which the line projects. Although exceptions could be found, it is safe to say that the Greek text has only the first letter, or most of it, projecting into the margin, whilst the Latin usually has all of the first and most of the second.

Further investigation of other manuscripts for similar features could significantly increase our knowledge of the affinities of D.

Returning to the forms of punctuation that we have listed, analysis shows us that, as in other characteristics, the codex is not consistent throughout (see table 5).

Acts is quite different from the Gospels. All but three of the spaces in it are found before F440b. Studying the Gospels, we find that in Matthew the scribe favoured the medial point, that in John he continued to use it up to about F136b (308 occurrences thus far), and then used the space more (629 from F137 to the end); that in Luke he overwhelmingly uses the space, and that in Mark he returns to the point. We find the double point used in Matthew and Mark, and the large space adopted in the other three books.

It therefore seems probable that the small space had the same function as the medial point, and the large space as the double point. The equivalence of the latter is further established by those places where they stand opposite each other in the two columns – Ff94b–95/23, 157b–158/20, 272b–273/9.

Only in Acts does the scribe use the high point. There are some points elsewhere which could be, as it were, either low high points or high medial points, but as a regular symbol it is undoubtedly confined to Acts.

The indentation of Old Testament quotations is used only sporadically. It is found in the last third of Matthew, in the opening quotation of Mark's Gospel, and in the first part of Acts.

The examples are: F68b–69/12–15 = Mt 21.5; 69b–70/6–7 = 21.13; 20–1 = 21.16; 72b–73/21–5 = 21.42; 76b–77/12–14 = 22.44; 91b–92/16–18 = 26.31; 97/22–7 = 27.9f; 285b–286/3–7 = Mk 1.2f; 417b–418/21–3 = Ac 1.20; 420b–421/32 to 421b–422/12 = 2.25–8; 422b–423/2–5 = 2.34f; 429b–430/4–8 = 4.25f; 442b–443/25–6 = 7.49; 469b–470/18–24 = 13.33; 28–9 = 13.34; 31–2 = 13.35. All but one (F97, where the corresponding part of F96b is lost) have the indentation in both columns.

Table 5. *Punctuation*

(a) Greek text

Punctuation mark[a]	Mt	Jn	Lk	Mk	Ac
1	563	164	143	154	224
2	9[b]	8	4	11–12	—
3	9.56[c]	3.45	79–81[d]	8.44	17–19
3*	17	6	—	—	—
4	1	34	76	1	6
5	10–15	5.81	11.88	20–2	5–6
6	2	5	8	—	—
7	—	—	—	—	5–6
8	6	—	—	1	8

(b) Latin text

Punctuation mark[a]	Mt	Jn	Lk	Mk	3 Jn	Ac
1	566	165	153	155	3	225
2	9	4	2	6	—	—
3	10.23	3.03	64–6	8.97	—	27–8
3*	4	4	—	1	—	—
4	—	15	47	1	—	5
5	17–23	5.71	11.46	22–5	—	16
6	2	3	4	1	—	—
7	—	—	—	—	—	2
8	7	—	—	1	—	8

Notes

[a] Punctuation marks:

1 Line projecting into the left-hand margin, with some initial letters enlarged
2 Double point, found within a line (occasionally at the end), sometimes followed by an enlarged initial letter
3 Medial point, found within a line, but sometimes at the end (see mark 3*)
3* Medial point at the end of a line. The figure is included in the total number listed under mark 3
4 Large space, sometimes followed by a large initial letter
5 Small space
6 Large space with a medial point in it
7 High point
8 Quotation from the Old Testament indented

[b] It is not always easy, particularly in Matthew, to distinguish double points *prima manu* from those added by L to indicate a new Ammonian Section. But, with one exception in Mark where uncertainty must remain, I am confident that all those I have included are original.

[c] The figures with decimal points are the average number per column for that book.

[d] Where the number is given as a range, e.g. 11–12, the approximation reflects difficulty in reading the Ms or, in the case of small spaces, uncertainty as to whether or not the scribe intended one.

Can any rationale for its use be found? The quotations from Matthew are all, except for the first (presumably) and the last, on the lips of Jesus. But equally obvious OT citations by him at 22.32, 37; 24.29, 30; 27.36 are not indented. All the quotations in Acts are from speeches, or at least from direct speech. Ac 1.20 is the only quotation in Peter's first speech. But the remaining examples are from speeches which contain other quotations that are not indented.

All the quotations are from the Psalms (nine), Isaiah (five) and Zechariah (two). One hardly dare postulate a scribe who had either a very limited knowledge of Scripture, or a drastically reduced canon. It is impossible to form any conclusion as to why this practice occurs where it does.

It should also be noted in this connection that the indentation of 333b–334/25 (Mk 13.18), which is not a quotation, is unique in the codex; and that the second part of the indented quotation at Ac 13.33 is a longer reading.

There is most punctuation in Matthew, which has on average about sixteen indications to a page, and least in Acts, which has about three. John has around twelve, Luke fifteen, and Mark eleven to twelve. Although the Greek and Latin have the same amount overall, there is a variation between the books. The Latin has more than the Greek in Matthew, Mark, and Acts, and fewer in John and Luke.

CHAPTER THREE

The secondary hands

Cavallo, *Ricerche*; Cavallo and Maehler, *Greek Bookhands*; Clark, *Acts*, pp. 173–8; Harris, *Annotators*; Hatch, *Principal Uncial Manuscripts*; Scrivener, pp. xxiv–xxix.

Broadly speaking, the correctors of Codex Bezae have been correctly identified. Although Kipling attempted to place them in groups according to their age, as *antiquissimus*, *perantiquus*, *vetus*, and *recens*, we owe the classification of the various hands to Scrivener. There is no doubt about the existence of hands A to H, and L. Apart from the physical characteristics of the scripts, each has its own textual characteristics, as we shall discover in chapter 9.

However, Scrivener's dating of some of the hands was wildly incorrect. This is partly due to the late date he gave to the manuscript itself, partly to some considerable palaeographical indiscretions. Some of these were recognized a long time ago. But in what follows we shall find others.

The chronological sequence of the hands will need to be altered. There are also many corrections which cannot be by the hands to which Scrivener ascribed them (and my revisions of his opinions will be found in appendix 2). Therefore, although Scrivener was correct in his identification of the principal hands, the task of revision is still considerable.

A particular problem in the study of these correctors is the identification of the Latin and Greek scripts of a single hand. Whilst some of these are beyond doubt (for example, the Greek hand of G or the Latin hand of J^1), others cannot be established with such certainty. But I have often accepted Scrivener's decision, and in Part III these corrections of dubious origin will be found discussed in the section devoted to the hand to which Scrivener ascribed them, with varying cautionary comments as to their authenticity.

The starting point for redating the correctors is the date of the codex itself, and known points in its history. The first we have seen to be about 400 AD. The only known point is that it was in Lyons in the ninth century.

The first stage in establishing a comparative chronology is to discover whether one corrector altered the work of others. The evidence is that

C corrected A (F457b/7)
H corrected A (137b/2, 6, and see 53b/19)
D corrected B (498b/10)
E corrected B (487b/2–3)
H corrected B (137b/9, 488b/27–8)
H corrected E (487b/2–3)
L wrote over J (150b, top outer corner)
L wrote over M² (128b, outer margin)

There are also various erasures and deletions by unidentifiable hands, and corrections by 'K' who, as we shall see, is not one hand.

We can see from these facts that A is older than C and H, that B is older than D and H, and that E is older than H. The relationships between A and B, B and C, and C, D, and E cannot be determined by this means. But it does appear that A and B are older than D and E, and that H comes later than both groups. The hands not accounted for are C, F, and G. That G was the first corrector is a matter of general agreement. I shall argue that Scrivener also placed C and F in the wrong place in the sequence. The only way to work this out is to look at each hand in turn. I shall do this in alphabetical sequence, except that I shall begin with G.

HAND G

F. C. Burkitt, 'The Date of Codex Bezae', *JTS* 3 (1902), 501–13 (505ff); F. C. Kenyon, review of the facsimile edition, *JTS* 1 (1900), 293–9, esp. p. 296; E. A. Lowe, 'Codex Bezae: The Date of Corrector G', *BBC* 5 (1928), 32–3 = *Pal. Papers* 1,275–6; Lowe, 'The Oldest Omission Signs in Latin Manuscripts. Their Origin and Significance', in *Miscellanea Mercati*, Vol. 6, Vatican, 1946, pp. 36–79 = *Pal. Papers* 2,349–80.

The dating of Hand G to the twelfth century was the worst blemish of Scrivener's edition. Kenyon, commenting that it is 'impossible to imagine' why he thought so, placed it in the sixth or seventh (p. 296). Burkitt's opinion was that there was nothing on the palaeographical side to prevent us from assigning G to any date from the fourth to the seventh centuries (p. 507). In 1928, Lowe gave a date of between 500 and 550 (*CLA* 2,140 simply calls it 'one of the earliest Latin correctors'). Yet he compares the *u* and *g* with a fourth-century papyrus letter. Lowe does nothing to weaken Burkitt's view (and Burkitt offered it believing the manuscript to have been written later than the fourth century, so that the point was academic). Burkitt also said that 'G is contemporary with Codex Bezae itself, and that it is the hand of some person in authority for whom the Codex itself was made' (p. 506). This case stands even when the manuscript is given an earlier date. We shall see that the evidence for this lies in the nature of his corrections as much as in the hand. But Burkitt's argument was substantiated with carefully adduced palaeographical evidence, both Greek and Latin, and in my opinion is to be upheld.

Today it is understandable why his most convincing parallels are with the oldest material he mentions.

The hand is not calligraphic. It is fluent in both Greek and Latin, whilst being more Latin than Greek in character.

Where G substitutes one word for another, he draws a line over both the original and the replacement (e.g. F14/31, 46/1, 51/9, 14, 54/19). The deletion of a word is shown by oblique strokes above the letters (e.g. 8/30). The substitution of one letter for another is by writing it above and generally striking through the cancelled letter with an obelus. An insertion is made by writing the letter or word above the line, beginning it above the place where it should be. The large insertion at F59b–60 is marked by *anchorae superiores* and *inferiores*. This practice is fully described by Lowe ('The Oldest Omission Signs'). It is of Greek origin, and its use here is an important indication that Corrector G worked in the earliest, part-Greek, environment of Codex Bezae. The only other Latin manuscripts found by Lowe to use the symbols are Vatic. Pal. Lat. 1631 (*saec.* IV-V), Urbin. Lat. 1154 (*saec.* V *ex.*), Naples Lat. 2 (*saec.* V), and Florence Laurenz. *PSI*, *sine numero* of the Justinian Digesta (*saec.* VI). The eleven Greek examples are, all but one, of the fourth century or earlier, the exception being from the fifth.

Deletions by any hand in the Latin text are, unlike those in the Greek, very rarely by erasure and almost always by means of point and obelus, employed both separately and together. The analogy of the substitution of letters encourages one to believe that the use of an obelus alone indicates that correction to be by G. Indeed, the fact that this symbol is used only in Matthew and the first part of John bears out the assumption. Scrivener actually gives some of these deletions by obelus as the work of G, but others he ascribes to '*s.m.*' (*secunda manus*). For consistency, I attribute them all to G.

They are at F49/3, 60/19, 68/21, 69/26, 70/16, 19, 31, 33, 78/25, 135/27, 140/27, 148/28. I have not ascribed any corrections with point *and* obelus, or point alone, to G. The alterations to Scrivener will be found in appendix 2.

HANDS A AND B

The dating of these hands to the fifth century is uncontroversial. A can be seen to be close in time to the first hand. His letters are simple, and straightforwardly Greek. The same is true of B.

HAND C

I find the dating of C to be a harder matter. His additions are either alterations of letters by the first hand, or else are squeezed neatly between the line; as a result, we have no way of knowing the natural proportions of his characters. Comparison with B gives no palaeographical justification for placing either earlier than the other. The only evidence is in the character of his readings: I will suggest in Part III that placing him before B makes better sense of the sequence.

HAND D

This hand is not remarkable for its calligraphy. The writing does not flow, and where he writes in the size of the first hand, his strokes are more vigorous than elegant. He is clearly a Greek writer, and where he writes in Latin (*est* at F494/27 and *omnes* at 505/33) he attempts to imitate the style of the first hand. He is not a professional scribe. He is a scholar making his own annotations.

His largest corrections are at F458b/22 (Ac. 10.46) and 492b/4 (18.17). In spite of the difficulty of writing over the erasure, and the fact that here too he tries to present an approximation to the first hand at least in the size of the letter, it is possible to get some idea of the hand. It sets out to be a form of biblical maiuscule somewhere between, let us say, the two examples given by Cavallo and Maehler in their plate 18 – P. Amherst 1 (Ascension of Isaiah; also Cavallo, *Ricerche*, plate 53) and *PSI* 251 (Galatians, 0176, also in Cavallo as plate 62). The first of these is dated by Cavallo and Maehler to early in the fifth century, the second to the middle of it. Although in immediate appearance our corrector may seem to be closer to the older of these two, various indications – for example, the form of *upsilon* – lead one to favour a slightly later date. The form of *mu* in F492b is not of a part with the other characters: the middle strokes are written as a single curve, whereas at F458b they are written in the two strokes of biblical maiuscule. The correction at F492b therefore furnishes safer evidence for dating the hand, since its imitation of the formal script is less successful. A date of about 450 is acceptable.

HAND E

This hand shows some variety in the forms it produces: compare the *tau* in the corrections at F419b/7, 461b/26–8, 467b/33, and 502b/25, or the *upsilon* at 143b/13 and 277b/28 with those at 458b/24 and 488b/27. Moreover, some corrections are roughly made, such as that at 480b/30. This variation makes dating difficult. It also led Scrivener into making E the source for corrections it never made.

Some of the corrections wrongly ascribed to E are quite important, so I provide the information here as well as in appendix 2. The correction *μη* at F428b/20 uses the cursive form of *eta*, whereas E elsewhere uses the maiuscule form, and the *mu* is unlike that at, for instance, 276b/9. This correction, and its Latin companion, are neither of them by E. Nor is that at F433b/13 (which writes *αρχι* as *ARXI*). The *R* and the clumsy *chi* betray that it is inserted by a Latin pen. The *xi* at 432b/4 is from the hand of B. The addition of *homini* (*sic*) at 483/16 is unlikely to be by E. Certainly it cannot be from the same hand as produced *undecim* at F420/25. And the latter looks to me to be quite unlike anything else produced by E. The *mi* added to *honibus* in 434/20 is not from E either, although it may be by the hand that wrote *homini* in 483. Note, finally, that the whole of *τουτου* (135b/30) is from E. The variation in his hand means that there is no need to assign part of the correction to D, whose *tau* is in any case quite different.

Thus Scrivener attributed a number of miscellaneous corrections to E, which in fact are not from him, and not all like each other, though those at 434/20 and 483/16 (and 428b/20?) may be by the same hand.

The date of E is not much later than that of D. The largest correction is at F461b/26 (Ac 11.26). Again, the restricted space makes it hard to be certain that this is the corrector's normal way of writing. At any rate, we have a fairly unadorned and square script. Elsewhere, the writing can be somewhat heavier (as at F135b/30), or more finicky (481b/11); at F433b/28, *upsilon* is written without lifting the pen, so that the bottom is almost looped. None of this is very consistent but, even at its least attractive, the hand is recognizable as an attempt at a maiuscule datable to the second part, and probably to the third quarter, of the fifth century.

HAND F

Kenyon, pp. 295–6.

We are fortunate in having several additions by F which are long enough to give us some idea of his hand. The best is at the foot of F163b. The style is not unlike that of H, but the overall impression is of something more cramped.

Kenyon thought that F may well have been seventh-century. But this type of sloping pointed maiuscule is rather too simple for such a late date. Following the examples provided by Cavallo and Maehler, this hand is a later form of the type best known from the Freer Gospels, showing signs of a contrast between thick and thin strokes which they find to be typical from the later fifth century onwards (see pp. 4, 42). A date of 450–500 is therefore quite possible. I would add that F cannot be far separated from H.

HAND H

The dating of H by Harris to 'cent. xii?' (*Annotators*, p. 6) is based on Scrivener's description of it as 'somewhat later than G' (p. xxvi). We have already seen that G was not eleventh-century, but Harris did not question the dating of H. Apart from general characteristics, Scrivener argued that H must be later than G because of the correction at F421b/21, where G wrote *οσφυος* in the margin, and H wrote it in the text. This argument founders on the fact that it seems incredible that the hand which wrote the two lines at the bottom of F59b could also have written *οσφυος* in the margin of 421b. The latter cannot be older than medieval. It is there, I suggest, because the correction by H was hard to read. The dating of H is further confused by the ascription to him of the addition at F198b/6–7 of *τεθραμμενος εισηλθεν*. Given the late date assigned by Scrivener, this ascription is understandable, since the words are in a fairly late hand. But they are certainly not by H: *tau* is different, and *alpha* markedly so. Comparison with the genuinely H *τι αυτος* at 488b/28, which I am about to discuss, will make the point clear.

To when, then, can H be dated? His alterations are rarely large enough to supply much evidence. Two only are of real help: F476b/17 and 488b/28. In the first, D* wrote ANECTHCEN, which H replaced with *αναστας*, keeping five of the first hand's letters and replacing E and H with *α*. At 488b/28 he added *τι αυτος* at the end of the line. Here his letters slope slightly to the right, and the bow of *alpha* is more pointed than that of *p.m.* The crossbar of *tau* has serifs, as do the tops of *upsilon*. The beginning of *sigma* is slightly hooked. The strokes are fine and the proportions good, though the letters do not slope consistently. The hand is much squarer than that of F but – as we have already noted – not altogether dissimilar. I see no reason why it need be later than 500. Indeed, it is not so very different from D.

His manner of correction is quite fastidious. At 201b/15, D* wrote ΑΠΟΚΡΕΙC; D^{B} altered this to $ΑΠΟΚΡ^{Iθ}ΕΙC$, but D^{H} changed it to $ΑΠΟΚΡ^{I}Θ^{E}IC$. He tries to leave unchanged as many letters and strokes of the first hand as he can. He places points over letters when he wishes to cancel them, rather than erase them (e.g. F469b/8, 476b/17). Although, as Scrivener on occasion accurately notes, *laxius scribit*, his work is generally neat, and he tries to match the size of letter used by the first hand.

The following corrections are not by H: 115b/22, a crude *ο*; 189b/9, the *ν* above the first *τ* in AITOYNTωN; 196b/13/column 1, where the wobbly stroke making Λ in ωBHΛ into Δ could be by anyone; 196b/23/column 1, *A* added to ICAK; 198b/6–7, already discussed; *ibid.* l. 7, E in EIωΘOC is written by the hand that provided the addition in ll. 6–7; 240b/2, in which ΠATHP is rewritten, is in a modern hand unused to writing uncials – note the *A* in three separate strokes; 314b/14, where the whole correction is by B; 432b/13 seems unlikely to be his work; 492b/18, where the strange erasure of EP in EPXOMENH cannot be definitely ascribed to any hand.

At F306b/24, according to Scrivener, this was the hand that wrote a horizontal line in the inner margin. The reason for the line is not clear. It would be interesting to know why Scrivener was so positive in his identification.

Did this hand correct the Latin? Scrivener thought that it did so twice – at F189/23 (*e* for I in PARIRET) and at 197/7/column 2 (*c* for K in KAINAN). There is no strong reason why the first should be his. The second is certainly very like his Greek *sigma*. But, as with other such corrections, a firm conclusion cannot be reached.

HAND J

According to Scrivener, J was certainly responsible for the lectionary direction at the top of F150b, for the additions at the bottom of Ff160b/161, and for *vobis* in 161/31. He also suggested that J wrote the lectionary directions in Ff185b/10, 188b/9, 191b/23 and 25. Harris rejected these last tentative identifications (*Annotators*, p. 37) and in this at least he is to be followed. Harris also (*ibid.*, p. 35) saw a note on F67b/18–20, which is by the same hand as gave us the one on 150b (see appendix 2).

We are therefore left with two marginal notes, and the additions on Ff160b–161.

Are there any grounds for attributing the notes and the additions to the same hand? Scrivener writes that 'the two lines in *sloping* uncials at the foot of Fol. 160*b* look more like J's [than F's], though not so large as the rest of his' (p. xxvi). The lines are certainly not by F; nor can I see any correspondence between the hands of the notes and the additions attributed to J. There seems to me to be no resemblance at all, either in general appearance or in detail. I suggest therefore that the lectionary note on F150b should be attributed to J, and the corrections on Ff160b–161 be attributed to J¹. The two hands consist, so far as I can tell, of these three passages alone.

J¹ gives the appearance of being more at home with Greek than with Latin – he did not complete the long addition in F161, he did not write Latin letters consistently (there are variations in the forms of *o*, *u*, and *m*), and not all his vertical strokes are at the proper angle. The Greek script has a compressed appearance. θ, ϵ and ς are all narrow, twice as high as wide. Uprights slope to the right. This is to say that, like the hand of F, it is an example of sloping pointed maiuscule; the letters are far narrower than those of F or H. But there is no reason why it need not also date from the second half of the fifth century. Looking back at the Latin column, we find some slight confirmation of this dating in the forms of *b* and *d*.

I suggest therefore that the hand be placed in the second part of the fifth century. It is older than the lectionary notes by J in F150b, which I do not think to be much older than L.

HAND K

K is, by Scrivener's own admission, something of a convenient repository for late corrections: 'I have sometimes indicated by K such very recent changes in several hands as Foll. 3*b* 33; 6*a* 27; 6*b* 22; 32*b* 17; 47*b* 27; 50*b* 13; 53*b* 4; 65*b* 1; 26; 88*b* 29; 90*b* 21; 167*b* 8' (p. xxvi). Some of these must be very recent indeed. The *iotas* at the end of 50b/13 and in 151/4 must be post-medieval, as must τῳ Σιλεα in the outer margin of 486b/1.

Fourteen 'corrections' are in fact horizontal strokes in the margin or the written area, which cannot be dated. The same applies to five places where points have been placed over letters, and three where obeli have been used.

The μ at F188b/20 is perhaps by the hand which added τεθραμμενος εισηλθεν at 198b/6–7.

HAND L

F. E. Brightman, 'On the Italian Origin of Codex Bezae. The Marginal Notes of Lections', *JTS* 1 (1900), 446–54.

It is clear that another drastic redating must be that of the annotators who supplied liturgical notes and Ammonian Sections to the Greek column. Scrivener dated these to the ninth century, Harris to the tenth. That this activity should have been carried on in Lyons at that period is highly improbable. This was not a problem to Harris, who argued that the codex was then in south Italy, probably Calabria. He believed L, who provided the Ammonian Sections and the main series of *τιτλοι*, *αρχαι* and *τελη*, to have been a Latin. The linguistic grounds for this – the intrusion of *γ* in e.g. *παρασκευγην* – are untenable (and see Gignac 1,71–5). The grammatical grounds are no better: that L uses *περι* as if it were the equivalent of *pro*. There is also *λεγη* (F501b/21) instead of *αναγινωσκε*, that is to say, *lege* in Greek dress. This, as Harris admits, is inconclusive (*Annotators*, p. 11, n. 1). He points out also the writer's ignorance of Greek, in producing such solecisms as *περι του κυριακη*, and altering J's *τη κυριακη* to *περι το κυριακη*. Further, he describes *εις την ενκηνηουν* opposite Jn 10.22 (143b) as a Latinism (*ibid.*, p. 29, n. 2). This word would be even stranger in Latin (where *encaenia* is plural) than it is incorrect in Greek. Harris produces a palaeographical argument, that L wrote not a Greek *sigma* but a Latin *G* in *ANNAGNOCMA* (F120b/23 and 121b/13 erased) and *ANNOGMA* (60b and 62b). This seems plausible until one tries to find a contemporary Latin *G* with anything like such a form. Only in a much earlier period (e.g. the first hand of d) is it likely. It seems more probable that the corrector simply wrote *sigma* where he should not have.

Moreover, and this is a decisive argument, L provided neither Ammonian Sections nor liturgical notes to the supplementary leaves. It seems inconceivable that he could have ignored them if they were part of the manuscript in his time.

What is the evidence that provides a date for L? His letters are upright and round, a fairly late form of biblical maiuscule. The shapes of his letters in the Ammonian Section numbers are (presumably intentionally) more similar to those of the first hand than are his lectionary notes and the addition of Lk 23.34a on F278b. The latter (which are more helpful for dating purposes) can be compared with, for example, the Washington manuscript of the Pauline Epistles (016), which dates from the sixth century, and is considered by Cavallo to come from the Nitrian Desert (*Ricerche*, pp. 87f, 93). But a closer analogy can be found with manuscripts of this period having a Syrian–Antiochene origin. Cavallo lists five (p. 104), the Vienna Genesis, Codex Beratinus (*Φ*, 043), N (022), Codex Sinopensis (O, 023), and Codex Rossanensis (*Σ*, 042). All of these are purple manuscripts; the New Testament ones all have a text with at least some Caesarean elements. The last of them is especially comparable to our corrector. In the collection of Cavallo and Maehler, No. 44, a manuscript of Chrysostom's *Homiliae in Matthaeum* (Cod. Guelferb. Helmst. 75a), is the most similar, not least in the form of *delta* with two knobs on the base.

A date at the end of the sixth century is therefore most probable. The analogy with these manuscripts also furnishes some evidence that Codex Bezae was in Syria at that time. We shall return to this point in a later section.

Apart from the palaeographical and historical impossibilities involved in the later date, the earlier one makes it easy to account for the irregularities of the lectionary system compared to later standards: this is an early form.

HANDS I, M, M¹, M², M³, M⁴, N, O, O²

For the *Sortes*, see F. C. Burkitt, 'Codex Bezae and the Sortes Sangallenses', *JTS* 28 (1926/7), 58–9 = *BBC* 4 (April, 1927), 6–7; Harris, *Annotators*; B. M. Metzger, 'Greek Manuscripts of John's Gospel with "Hermenaiai"', in *Text and Testimony, Essays on New Testament and Apocryphal Literature in Honour of A. F. J. Klijn*, ed. T. Baarda *et al.*, Kampen, 1988, pp. 162–9; O. Stegmüller, 'Zu den Bibelorakeln im Codex Bezae', *Biblica* 34 (1953), 15–17.

Useful lists of the annotations by these hands are provided by Harris, *Annotators*, pp. 37ff.

These are the hands which provided lectionary *αρχαι* and *τελη*, *τιτλοι*, and the *Sortes* (a collection of sixty-nine *hermenaiai*, written in the bottom margin of Mark's Gospel). Scrivener allocated them as follows:

Lectionary notes:	I (John and Luke)
	M (Matthew and Luke)
	M² (Luke)
	M⁴ (Mark and Acts)
	N, O, O² (Acts)
Τιτλοι	M¹ (Matthew)
	M² (John, Luke)
Sortes	M³ (Mark)

It is necessary to reallocate the *τιτλοι* and the *Sortes*. According to Scrivener, followed by Harris, M¹ provided *τιτλοι* for Matthew; M² supplied them for John and Luke. He thinks that M² may be the same as the hand of the *Sortes*, M³. I would suggest that M¹ was responsible for the *τιτλοι* in Matthew and for the *Sortes*; M² for the *τιτλοι* in John and Luke. M³ has therefore no separate existence. Beyond this, I wonder whether the minuscule M² and the maiuscule M¹ are not two scripts from a single pen. The forms of *τ*, *ι* with a diaeresis (e.g. Ff129b and 318b), and *ρ* are very alike.

If this is so, then the dating of this material can be made fairly precise. Harris noted that at F128b, L wrote over a *τιτλος* written by M². This observation seems to be correct. A date in the second half of the sixth century (and necessarily earlier than L) seems to be quite acceptable for both these poor and rough scripts.

The dating of the other hands is not a matter on which the present writer feels fully competent. I is the writer of two lectionary notes, on Ff130b and 197b. The script slopes unevenly, has fairly narrow letters, and poorly executed serifs. It is, I would suggest, from somewhere between 550 and 650.

The division between some of the other hands is fairly uncertain. For example, the indications of the beginning of a lection *τι πεντικοστι* at the head of F418b and *του αγιου. διονυσιου. αρεωπαγιτου* at the top of 488b seem to me to be by the same hand, not by M[4] and O respectively.

A small feature which provides circumstantial evidence is that the annotator M[4] always (since we have disposed of Scrivener's exception on F418b) provides a *τελος* to his lections. The fact that his lection beginning on F347b (Mk 16.9) has no *τελος* on the supplementary leaf 348b* suggests that he predates not only the restoration, but the *loss* of the original leaf: why should anybody want to provide an *αρχη* for a half-missing lection?

While unwilling to be too categorical on the subject of dating these several crude hands, I suggest that it is safe to say that they all fit into the period 550–650.

It should be noted that these various lectionary notes are not the haphazard uses of the manuscript that they appear to be. Only twice (M at Mt 2.1 and J at Jn 12.1) do they overlap with L. Otherwise, they are found to provide lections not given by L. The conclusion to be drawn is that they come after L. Alternatively, could it have been that L provides a professional insertion of material that had begun to be added in a haphazard fashion? Since L is later than both J and M[2], should the other lectionary annotators also be placed before L? Or, are some of the annotators before, some after L? Whichever of these may be correct, it is clear that the habit of noting lections in the manuscript was of fairly short duration – a hundred years at the most.

The fact that the Corrector M[4] provided *αρχαι* on leaves preceding ones now lost at Mk 16.9 (F347b) and Ac 8.26 (446b) suggests, as I have said, that the manuscript was at that period still not defective. The same argument is likely to apply to the *αρχη* of Hand M on F6b, though the fact that he never resumes on the other side of the lacuna makes this less certain. Moreover, there are no lectionary notes on any supplementary leaf. Thus one thing that emerges from the lectionary notes is that the manuscript is likely to have been complete (at least for the Gospels and most of Acts) until the middle of the seventh century.

SECUNDAE MANUS

It will be clear that a number of corrections which Scrivener allocated to known hands have fallen off the map. The number of corrections which can be described only by the phrase *secunda manu* is larger than Scrivener had supposed, and includes a number of hands. My phrase *secunda manu* really embraces material divided up by Scrivener into K and *s.m.* For all purposes of the present study, it may as well include the activity of hands M and O and their subdivisions. That is, it consists in deletions and erasures, sundry small corrections, and some larger ones made by a hand which can be detected either once or only very rarely, whose dates vary from the fifth century through to modern times.

It remains to add that close examination of the methods of deletion used in the

Latin text enables us to learn more about the number of hands active in correcting it.

Having suggested that the use of an obelus to delete a word is the practice of G, we are left with a variety of other usages. The most common is deletion with point above the letter and *obelus* through it (Matthew – seven times, John – four, Luke – ten, Mark – four, Acts – fifteen, total – forty). A similar usage is a point above the letter, but no obelus (seventeen times, regularly throughout the codex). There is also deletion by erasure (Matthew – one instance, John – four, Luke – three, Mark – none, Acts – thirteen, total – twenty-one). It is impossible to say more than that the erasing of letters is very probably the habit of different hands from that or those using point and/or obelus. We are safe in concluding that, besides G, there are at least two other hands in evidence. But further speculation is impossible, and we cannot identify these alterations with any of the known hands.

All these methods of deletion (point and obelus alone or together, and erasure) are found in the Greek column also.

THE SUPPLEMENTARY LEAVES

J. Chapman, 'The Original Contents of Codex Bezae', *The Expositor* (VI) 2 1905, 46–53; C. Charlier, 'Les Manuscrits personnels de Florus de Lyon et son activité littéraire', *Mélanges E. Podechard*, Lyons, 1948, pp. 71–84; L. Delisle, 'Notices sur plusieurs anciens manuscrits de la bibliothèque de Lyon', *Notices et extraits des manuscrits* 29, Part II (1880), 402; Lowe, *Codices Lugdunenses Antiquissimi*, Lyons, 1924; Lowe, 'The Codex Bezae and Lyons', *JTS* 25 (1924), 270–4 = *Pal. Papers* 1,182–6 and plates 24–5; Lowe, 'Nugae Palaeographicae', in *Persecution and Liberty, Essays in Honour of George Lincoln Burr*, New York, 1931, pp. 55–69 = *Pal. Papers* 1,315–25, esp. pp. 322–5.

The place and date at which these were added has been well established. Some writers have even put a name to the scribe. The evidence from Ado's *Martyrology*, that the manuscript was in Lyons in the ninth century, will be described in Part III.

The supplementary leaves are numbered in the facsimile edition (and on the leaves themselves) as 7*, 169*–175*, and 348*. They contain, in the Greek, Mt 3.7 *απο* to 3.16 *θ̅υ̅*; Jn 18.14 *εν* to 20.13 *κλαιεις*; Mk 16.15 *παση* to 16.20 *αμην*; and in the Latin, Mt 2.21 *qui* to 3.7 *fugere*; Jn 18.2 *iudas* to 20.1 *essent*; Mk 16.6 *crucifixum* to 16.20 *amen*.

Chapman suggested (pp. 52f) that Revelation (which, as we have seen, he believed to have come after Mark), and the Johannine epistles were not replaced because they were not needed for liturgical use. Acts, he suggests, was at that time still complete and therefore did not need restoring. Since we do not know that we still have all the restored leaves, the latter argument is worthless. As to the former, there is no evidence, and very little likelihood, of the manuscript's ever having been used liturgically in Lyons (Chapman will have accepted the received and late date for L).

The format endeavours to reproduce that of the first hand. The line endings of

F7* match those of 6b. The same is done on Ff169* and 348*. Ff169b*–175* are written in sense-lines, which are intended to be identical in the two columns. There are thirty-three lines on F169b*–170*, 170b*–171* (thirty-two in 171*) 173b*–174*, and thirty-two on 171b*–172*, 172b*–173*, 174b*–175* (thirty in 175*). Both inner and outer margins are ruled with double bounding lines. The β measurement is 151 × 180–5 mm. Unlike the body of the manuscript, there are no running titles. No quire signatures were needed.

The two columns are written in an imitation of uncial, except for the Latin colophon to Mark, which is in rustic capitals.

The two main features which enabled Lowe to recognize these leaves as produced at Lyons were the use of blue ink (and it is a quite bright blue that has kept its colour well) and the form of the interrogation mark. Blue ink is used in the Lyons manuscript 484 (414), Florus' excerpts from Augustine on the Pauline *corpus*. According to Delisle, this manuscript may have been Florus' autograph. Lowe cautiously adopts this opinion ('for part of it at least this may easily be true' – 'Codex Bezae and Lyons', p. 273 = *Pal. Papers* 1,184). Dom Célestin Charlier advanced the opinion with no hesitation at all, in giving an extended list of manuscripts in which he found the hand of Florus. Lyons 600 (517), of Jerome, is an early-eighth-century manuscript with blue ink, which was *probably* written in Lyons. A third manuscript, the Missale Gothicum (Rom. Vat. Regin. 317 (Cavalieri and Lietzmann, plate 18)), uses both red and blue ink. It was produced by the Luxeuil *scriptorium*. The interrogation mark is found in five manuscripts besides D^s: Lyons 484 (414) (already mentioned), Lyons 478 (408), F6b (a quire added to a sixth-century manuscript of Augustine), Lyons 604 (521) + Paris BN Lat. 1594 (again, a manuscript of Augustine with annotations attributed to Florus by Charlier (p. 83)), Paris Lat. 9550 (again containing material from Florus' hand), and Lyons 431 (357) (containing similar additions).

Interrogation marks were a comparatively recent innovation. The first extant examples are in manuscripts from Corbie written in the period 772–81. See further Jean Vezin, 'Le Point d'interrogation, un élément de datation et de localisation des manuscrits. L'Exemple de Saint-Denis au IXe siècle', *Scriptorium* 34 (1980), 181–96 and plate 13. Vezin lists signs that are distinctive to ninth-century Mss from Corbie, Saint-Amand-en-Pevèle, Worcester, Lyons, and Southern Italy, besides isolating a type unique to St-Denis in the same period.

The difficulties in identifying the hand of Florus are considerable. My visit to Lyons, during which I paid particular attention to manuscripts 478 and 484, was just long enough to make these difficulties obvious. If Florus was responsible for the parts of these codices attributed to him by Charlier, then he wrote a bewildering variety of hands: in the first, capitals (in red ink) for *explicit* and title and (in black) the occasional marginal note; rustic capitals (in blue ink) for the biblical text and for marginalia indicating the source in Augustine; and minuscules for the body of the text; in the second, a kind of uncial which imitates the sixth-century uncial of the original scribe, rustic capitals for title and opening lines, and marginalia in yet another hand.

While one should be reluctant to deny versatility to a scribe, the problem with attributing all these hands to Florus is that the criteria have to become so loose as to be useless. It seems to me improbable that he can have written them all. Apart from the fact that such a scholar will have had *amanuenses* to work for him, it is quite obviously in the nature of a *scriptorium* that it will produce books that are very similar in appearance.

I shall therefore leave aside the question of Florus' responsibility for the supplementary pages of Codex Bezae, and of whether the hand that wrote them is represented in other Lyons manuscripts. Another good reason for showing such caution is that the Latin supplementary leaves are written in an intentionally archaic script. This masks the form of the letters natural to the writer.

Instead, the question is to be raised as to whether the Greek and Latin columns could be by the same hand. Apart from the fact that the Greek script is larger and written with a thicker pen, none of the letters in common between the two alphabets is written in the same way. *A*, *C*, *E*, *I*, *M*, *N*, and *T* in the Latin are all different from the Greek parallel – this is surprising because the Greek is certainly not expertly written by a Greek scribe, but is a Latin imitation. The forms of the horizontal stroke over the *nomina sacra* are quite different. So are even the medial points, which in the Greek are sometimes given a tail, so that their shape approaches that of a modern comma.

In comparing the Greek additional leaves in D with Latin marginalia in other manuscripts, we encounter a problem which we have already had to face: how to identify corrections or additions made in one column with a hand known from the other. The consequence of this is that one tempting possibility – to ascribe the copying of the Greek leaves to Florus – lacks any means of being established. In favour of it is the fact that we know Florus to have learnt Greek – but we do not know how many other people in his circle shared this accomplishment.

It has never, so far as I am aware, been noticed that the supplementary leaves themselves contain corrections. The Latin equivalent of the final line of F169b* (Jn 18.25) is added to the right of ll. 32 and 33 in F170*:

dixerunt ergo ei·'
numquid et tu ex disci
pulis eius es'

The form of *d* and *l*, the joining of letters, and the absence of the peculiarly Lyonnaise interrogation mark, are manifest indications that this is not by the hand that wrote the other replacement Latin leaves. It also is of the ninth century.

The other correction is that μετα δε ταυτα, originally written both at the end of F173b* and the beginning of 174b*, is erased in F173b*/33.

In conclusion, the evidence does not permit us to be more specific than to say that Codex Bezae was certainly in Lyons in the ninth century.

The evidence we have been studying, whatever may be said about Florus, does point to one common feature of these manuscripts – a conservation movement in ninth-century Lyons. All of these manuscripts were restored at the same period. It is very clear that Lyons was important as a centre for the recovery, restoration, and publishing of ancient material. It also played a role in the preservation of Roman legal material (and Charlier claimed that we have Florus' notes in Ms Lyon 375, a commentary on the *Lex Visigothorum*). The restoration of Codex Bezae was a part of this important programme. And, while Florus' role as a copyist may be in doubt, his significance as an initiator of this programme cannot be doubted.

Another interesting piece of information which may link Codex Bezae with ninth-century France is provided by Wettstein (Vol. 1, p. 28). He cites a quotation from Druthmar, the ninth-century monk of Corbie who, in his *Expositiones in Matthaeum* (*PL* 106,4266), records that

> Vidi tamen librum Evangelii Graece scriptum, qui dicebatur Sancti Hilarii fuisse, in quo primo erant Matthaeus et Johannes, & post alii duo. Interrogavi enim Euphemium Monachum [*om.* monachum *PL*] Graecum, cur hoc ita esset? dixit mihi: in similitudinem boni agricolae, qui, quos fortiores habet boves, primo jungit.

Wettstein comments:

> Utrum vero Codicem in urbe Pictavorum, quae Aquitaniae pars erat, an in Claro Monte, an Corbejae viderit, non dicit: vidit tamen, nisi admodum fallor, hunc ipsum Codicem Cantabrigiensem, qui unus & solus omnium Codicum Graece scriptorum hunc ordinem servat.

Codex Bezae is no longer the only known manuscript to contain the Gospels in this order (see Metzger, *Canon*, pp. 249f), although it is the only one we know to have been in the south of France. Possibly against the identification with Codex Bezae is the absence of any reference to a Latin column in Druthmar's description.

CONCLUSIONS

Setting aside the hands we have included in *secunda manus*, as well as K, which is neither one hand nor early, there are a dozen to be fitted into a chronological list. From what has been said, the list will look like this:

c. 400	G
400–440	A
400–450	B
	C
450	D
450–500	E
	F
	H
	J[1]

550–600	J
	M^1/M^2
	L
550–650	I
	M
	M^4
	N
	O
	O^2
830–50	supplement

Within this, I would suggest, partly on the basis of evidence to be demonstrated in Part III, that the sequence was in fact G A C B D E H F J^1 J M^1/M^2 L. The correctors divide into three groups; the first, consisting of G, A, C, and B, worked in the first part of the fifth century; the second (D, E, H, F, and J^1) came in the later part of the century; the third came more than fifty years later, in the second part of the sixth. At about this period, or rather later, came the annotators.

This represents my opinion of the order and dates of the correctors. It forms the groundwork for the important task of studying the textual influences of the various hands, and provides a framework for reconstructing the history of the manuscript's life. These are subjects for future chapters.

CHAPTER FOUR

Towards the codicology of a bilingual codex

An analysis of the physical characteristics of bilingual manuscript traditions has yet to be made. Such an undertaking would be a valuable contribution to our knowledge of ancient manuscripts. At present we can hardly advance beyond seeking for the correct questions to be asked. Are there links between the different groups of bilinguals – for instance between those in Greek and Coptic and those in Greek and Latin? Can particular sizes of book be discerned? Can lay-outs on the page, rules with regard to use of scripts for running titles, colophons, and quire signatures? Are there different practices for bilinguals written for different purposes or according to their contents? How is a copyist's writing style affected by the adjacent scripts? What are the typical corruptions of a bilingual tradition? In what ways may it be superior to a monolingual one? Is there any continuity between ancient, Carolingian, and Renaissance Graeco-Latin manuscripts? The analysis of colophons and running titles which we undertook in chapter 1 enabled us to place the scribe of Codex Bezae within a Latin copying tradition. Can such studies be undertaken elsewhere?

It is impossible here to undertake a full-scale study of all bilingual manuscripts. However, some attempt to compare Codex Bezae with other bilinguals is desirable. Different though it is from most other biblical manuscripts known to us, we have no justification for assuming that its scribe's contemporaries will have seen it as so very different. It is certainly not without genealogy, and we must seek for clues to the sources of its character. We begin with non-biblical Graeco-Latin manuscripts. First I shall provide a list of those of which I know, and then give some tabulated details. It should be noted that the phrase non-biblical does not precisely apply to one item (no. 6). However, this text is not a manuscript of the New Testament either, and is better placed here.

NON-BIBLICAL GRAECO-LATIN MANUSCRIPTS

The manuscripts prior to the ninth century are gathered from *CLA*. Otherwise, my source is Georg Goetz, *Corpus Glossariorum Latinorum*, 7 vols., Leipzig, 1888–1901, supplemented by Henri Omont, 'Notice du Ms. Nouv. Acq. Lat. 763 de la Bibliothèque Nationale, contenant plusieurs anciens glossaires grecs et latins, et de quelques autres manuscrits provenant de Saint-Maximin de Trèves', *Notices et extraits des manuscrits de la Bibliothèque Nationale et autres bibliothèques*, Vol. 38, Paris, 1903, pp. 341–96, esp. pp. 342f, 346, 349 (description), 372–83 (transcription).

A. Bataille, 'Les Glossaires gréco-latins sur papyrus', *Recherches de papyrologie* 4 (1967), 161–9; Lowe, 'Two Fragments'; A. Wouters, 'An Unedited Papyrus Codex in the Chester Beatty Library Dublin containing a Greek Grammar and a Graeco-Latin Lexicon of Four Pauline Epistles', *Actes du XVe Congrès International de Papyrologie*, Vol. 3, *Problèmes généraux* (*Papyrol. Bruxelles* 18), 1979, 97–107; Wouters with J. M. Robinson, 'Chester Beatty Accession Number 1499. A Preliminary Codicological Analysis', in *Miscellània papirològica Ramon Roca-Puig*, ed. Sabastià Janeras, Barcelona, 1987, pp. 297–306. See further the bibliographies in *CLA*.

The texts are arranged in four groups in table 6: Greek texts with a Latin translation, Latin with a Greek translation; thirdly, writing exercises; the fourth group contains the materials listed by Goetz (one of his manuscripts, Harley 5792, is also in *CLA*, but I have omitted it from the first group). Three papyrus fragments described by Goetz, on the other hand, are placed under their *CLA* classification. The parchment texts of the second group are placed before those on papyrus. Otherwise they are in the order in which they are to be found in *CLA*, followed by the material from Goetz and Omont. I have not included Pap. Oxy. 3315, a fragment from the first or second century consisting of Latin words with Greek transcriptions.

In the hope of discovering a pattern, I have collected information about these texts, generally on the basis of Lowe's descriptions, in table 7. Only the oldest of Goetz's manuscripts (those prior to the eleventh century) are included here. Some of the manuscripts in British libraries (as well as no. 11) I have examined personally.

On the whole, the results are disappointing. However, reflection does produce some conclusions.

The Graeco-Latin manuscripts are all, except for the eighth-century examples, on papyrus (including one roll). Absolutely no conclusions can be drawn about the comparative measurements of these few damaged specimens. There is no preferred lay-out in this group: we find the Latin on the left and the Greek on the left, and in two instances the Latin (or at least a Latin summary) preceding the Greek text. The smaller number of manuscripts in this than in the second group reflects the needs of the Eastern empire where they have been preserved.

Turning to the second group, we see that there are more parchment manuscripts in the list. There is also a clearer preference for placing the original Latin in the left column. The only possible exception is no. 26, in which it is unclear which way round the glossary is intended.

None of the examples is calligraphic. All are very ordinary tools. In many the standards of writing and of knowledge are not high; in some they are very low.

The only constant between the papyrus and parchment texts of the first groups is the preference for two columns to the page.

What were these texts for? The certain answer is that they were teaching aids. Lowe regularly describes them with phrases like 'doubtless a school book'. They were cribs, dividing up the phrases and verses of Latin writers into tiny units of one

Table 6. *List of non-biblical Graeco-Latin manuscripts*

In groups A, B, and C the number in parentheses following the item number is the *CLA* catalogue number.

A GRAECO-LATIN TEXTS

1 (2,225) Manchester, Rylands Pap. 476: *Chronicon Graeco-Latinum*
2 (3,291) Florence, Laurenziana *PSI* 848: *Aesopica Graeco-Latina, Ps.-Dositheus* (fragment)
3 (5,699) Paris, Sorbonne, Inst. de Papyrol. Pap. Reinach 2140: *Glossarium*
4 (8,1171) Cologne, Hist. Archiv. W 352* + Göttingen, Univ. Bibl. App. Dipl. 8C + 8D: *Glossarium*
5 (9,1656) New York, Pierpont Morgan Lib. Pap. G.26: Babrius, *Fabulae* (XI, XVI, XVII)
6 (S,1683) Dublin, Chester Beatty Collection Pap. Ac. 1499: Paradigms; glossary for selected *lemmata* in Rom., 2 Cor., Gal., Eph.; juridical glosses
7 (S, 1731) Marburg, Staatsarchiv Hr 2, 2: *Glossarium*
8 (S,1738) Oxford, Ashmolean Mus. Pap. Oxy. 2194: *Litterae Graeco-Latinae* (part of a letter)
9 (S,1780) Ann Arbor, Univ. of Michigan Pap. 457 (Inv. 5604*b*, verso): Aesop (verso of a roll – recto is a legal fragment, dating from *saec.* I-II)

B LATINO-GREEK TEXTS

10 (2,137) Cambridge Univ. Lib. Add. Ms 5896: *Lexicon Aeneidos*
11 (3,306) Milan, Ambrosiana Cimelio Ms 3, foll. 113–20: Virgil, *Aeneis* I (parts), with Greek version
12 (5,697) Paris, Mus. du Louvre, Pap. Egypt. 7332: *Grammatica Latino-Graeca* (fragments)
13 (10,1522) Vienna, Nat. Bibl. Pap.-Sammlung L24: Virgil, *Aeneis* V. 673–4, 683–4, with Greek version
14 (10,1525) Vienna, Nat. Bibl. Pap.-Sammlung L27: *Glossarium Latino-Graecum*
15 (10,1570) Cairo, Mus. of Egyptian Antiquities Pap. Fuad 5: Virgil, *Aeneis* III. 444–68, *cum versione Graeca*
16 (11,1651) El Cerrito Western Baptist College, California, Allen Pap. s.n.: Virgil, *Georg.* I. 229–36 (the upper script of this palimpsest is a Sahidic version of the Wisdom of Solomon 11.4–15)
17 (2,224) Manchester, Rylands Pap. 61: *Cicero in Catilinam* II. 14, 15 *cum versione Graeca*
18 (2,226) Manchester, Rylands Pap. 477: *Cicero in Q. Caecilium Divinatio* (§§33–7 *init.*, 44–6) *cum versione et scholiis Graecis*
19 (2,227 + 3,367 + 10 p. 38) Manchester, Rylands Pap. 478 + Milan, Univ. Cattolica del Sacra Cuore Pap. Med. 1 + Cairo, Mus. of Egyptian Antiquities Pap. 85644 A + B: Virgil, *Aeneis* (parts of Book I) *cum versione Graeca*
20 (3,290) Florence, Laurenziana *PSI* 756: *Interpretamenta Aeneidos*
21 (5,696) Paris, Mus. du Louvre, Pap. Egypt. 2329: *Glossarium Latino-Graecum*
22 (5,698) Paris, Sorbonne, Inst. de Papyrol. Pap. Reinach 2069: *Glossarium Latino-Graecum* (S-U)
23 (10,1519) Vienna, Nat. Bibl. Pap.-Sammlung G30885 *a* + *e*: Cicero, *Orat. in Catilinam* 1, 6.15f, 7.17f, 8.19f
24 (11,1652) New York, Pierpont Morgan Lib., P. Colt 1: Virgil, *Aeneis* I, II, IV (parts). (Illustrated in Cavallo and Maehler, plate 46b; *they* date it to the first half of the seventh century.)
25 (S,1791) London, Egyptian Exploration Soc. Pap. Oxy. 2624: *Glossarium*

C *Exercitationes scribendi*

26 (S,1681) Cambridge Univ. Lib. Add. Ms 5902 (Pap. Oxy. 1315)
27 (S,1705) London, Egyptian Exploration Soc. Pap. Ant. 1 (fragment 1 verso)
28 (S,1755) Paris, Sorbonne, Inst. de Papyrol. Pap. Bouriant 2249

D MANUSCRIPTS LISTED BY GOETZ (SUPPLEMENTED BY OMONT)

Where Goetz's Latin place name may be ambiguous, it is retained.

I Pseudophiloxenus

29 Paris, BN Lat. 7651, *saec.* IX
30 Paris, BN Lat. 7652, *saec.* XVI (copy of 29)
31 Leiden, Cod. Voss. misc. lat. 1 pars 5, *saec.* XVII (copy of 29)

Table 6. (*cont*)

32 Paris, BN Lat. 7653, *saec.* XVI
33 Leiden, Scaliger 25, *saec.* XVI
34 Leiden, Scaliger 61, *saec.* XVI
35 Berne 189, *saec.* XVI

II Pseudocyril

36 London, BL Harley 5792, *saec.* VIII, copied in Italy or France
37 Laudunensis 444, *saec.* IX*ex*., written in Gaul
38 Rome, Lib. of the Oratorians, Vallicellianus B 31, *saec.* XV
39 Saint-Flour (Aedilium Floe. Eccles.) Bibl. mun. Cod. CCXIX, *saec.* XV
40 Florence, Laurenziana 92, *saec.* XV/XVI
41 Florence, Laurenziana 57, 16, *saec.* XV/XVI
42 Madrid, Escorial Σ.I.12, *saec.* XV
43 Paris, BN Lat. 2320A, *saec.* XV/XVI
44 Paris, BN Gr. 2627, *saec.* XV/XVI
45 Paris, BN Gr. 2628, *saec.* XV*ex*.
46 Cambridge Univ. Lib. Kk V.12, *saec.* XVI.
47 Naples, Bibl. Naz. II.D.34, *saec.* XV

III Glossae Servii Grammatici

48 London, BL Harley 2773, *saec.* XII
49 Leiden, Perizonianus Q 72, written by I. F. Gronovius, and copied from 48
50 Leiden, Scaliger 63, written by Carolus Labbaeus, and copied from a lost codex Puteanus
51 Leiden, Cod. Ruhnkenii 5, *saec.* XVII (copy of 50)
52 Leiden, Burmannorum Q°.5.X, copied in 1600

IV Idiomata

53 Naples, Bibl. Naz. IV.A.8, *Charisii idiomata*, *saec.* VIII
54 Paris, BN Lat. 7530, *saec.* VIII

V Glossariolum

This is contained in Cod. Laud. 444 (no. 37 above).

VI Hermeneumata Pseudodositheana

Hermeneumata Leidensia
55 Leiden, Cod. Voss. Gr. Q.7, *saec.* X
56 Saint-Gall 902, *saec.* X
57 London, BL Harley 5642, *saec.* X, copied at Saint-Gall
58 Munich, Bayerische Staatsbibl. Lat. 601, *saec.* X, also copied at Saint-Gall?
59 Erfurt, Amplonianus F 10, *saec.* IX
60 Paris, BN Lat. 7683, written by Salmasius
61 Paris, BN Lat. 6503, *saec.* IX
62 Leiden, Scaliger 61 (copy of previous item)

Hermeneumata Monacensia
63 Munich, Bayerische Staatsbibl. 13002, written in 1158
64 Munich, Bayerische Staatsbibl. 22201, written in 1165
65 Munich, Bayerische Staatsbibl. 27317, *saec.* XV
66 Heiligenkreuz 17, *saec.* XII
67 Naples, Bibl. Naz. Gr. II.D.35, *saec.* XV/XVI
68 Munich, Bayerische Staatsbibl. Gr. 323, *saec.* XVI

Table 6. (*cont*).

Hermeneumata Einsidlensia
69 Einsiedeln 19 (124), written in 1503
70 Einsiedeln 683 (Greek part only), written in 1518
71 Paris, BN Lat. 3049, written by Georgius Hermonymus Spartanus
72 Naples, Bibl. Naz. Gr. II.D.35 (see no. 67)
73 Florence, Laurenziana Ashburnham 1439, *saec.* XV

Hermeneumata Montepessulana
74 Montpellier H 306, *saec.* IX
75 Montpellier H 143, *saec.* XVI, a copy of no. 74

Smaller collections
76 Brussels 1828–30, *saec.* X
77 Rome, Vatican 6925, *saec.* X
78 Berne 688, *saec.* XIII

Glossae Vaticanae
79 Rome, Vat. Pal. 1773, *saec.* X
80 Rome, Vat. Pal. 1774, *saec.* XIII
81 Cambridge Univ. Lib., Gale O.5.34, *saec.* XII/XIII
82 Oxford, Balliol 155, *saec.* XIV
83 Leiden, Cod. Voss. 24
84 Berne 236 (*saec.* X)

VII Hermeneumata medicobotanica

Glossae Casinenses
85 Casino 69, *saec.* IX

Hermeneumata Senensia
86 Siena F V 8, *saec.* X/XI

Hermeneumata codicis Vaticani
87 Rome, Vat. Reg. Chr. 1260, *saec.* X

Hermeneumata Bernensia
88 Berne 337, *saec.* XI
89 Oxford, Bodl. Laud. misc. 567, *saec.* XII
90 Cambridge, Corpus Christi College?
91 Rome, Vat. 4417, *saec.* X/XI
92 Paris, BN Lat. 11218, *saec.* IX

VIII Glossaria
93 Paris, BN Nouv. Acq. Lat. 763, Ff34v–42v, *saec.* IX
94 *ibid.*, F147v, *post saec.* IX

Table 7. *Detailed comparison of non-biblical Graeco-Latin manuscripts*

No.[a]	Origin	Date[b]	Material	α measurement (cm)	β measurement (cm)	Folios
A Graeco-Latin texts						
1	?	IV-V	papyrus	106+ × 121+	?	1 frg.
2	Egypt?	V-VI	papyrus	105 × 103 now	lower mgn 40	1 frg.
3	?	V	papyrus	190 × 190	*c.* 140 × ?	
4	Byzantium?	VI	papyrus	233 × 322	180–92 × 250–5	3
5	Egypt	III-IV	pap. roll		Lat. 140–70 × ?; Gr. 115–20 × ?	
6	Egypt	IV	papyrus	*c.* 136 × *c.* 168	*c.* 114 × *c.* 148	52 (13)
7	Fulda	VIII *ex.*	parchmt	232 × *c.* 275	190 × 208	1
8	?	V	papyrus	100+ × 246+	?	1
9	Egypt?	III[1]	pap. roll	50+ × 128+	?	1 frg.
B Latino-Greek texts						
10	Byzantium	V	parchmt	140 × 253	95–105 × 176	1
11	East	VI[2]	parchmt (palimps.)	174 × 268	135 × 200	4
12	Egypt	V-VI	parchmt	*c.* 200 × 240?	*c.* 130 × ?	2
13	?	V	parchmt	?	*c.* 120 × ?	
14	East?	V	parchmt	?	?	
15	Egypt	IV-V	parchmt	270? × 305?	225? × *c.* 215	1
16	East	V	parchmt			
17	Egypt?	IV	papyrus	172 × 177	122+ × ?	1
18	?	IV–V	papyrus	200 × 290	120 × 180	2
19	?	IV	papyrus	240 × 360	160 × 260	3
20	Egypt	V	papyrus	300 × 180	240 × ?; inner mgn 40	1 frg.
21		VI	papyrus	120 × 293		1
22	found at Oxyrynchus	III	verso of pap. roll			12 frg.
23	Egypt	IV-V	papyrus	300? × 400		3 (4 frg.)
24	Egypt?	V *ex.*?	papyrus	200 × 275	135–40 × 190–200	
25	Egypt?	II[2]	papyrus			
C *Exercitationes scribendi*						
26	Egypt	V	papyrus	145 × 123	/	1 frg.
27	?	IV-V	papyrus	190 × *c.* 210	/	3 frg.
28	?	II-III	papyrus	*c.*155 × *c.*110	/	1 frg.
D Manuscripts listed by Goetz (supplemented by Omont)						
29		IX	parchmt	215–20 × 270–5		219
36	Italy/France	VIII	parchmt	215 × 293	160 × 232	271
37	France	IX *ex.*	parchmt	230 × 292		318
53						
54		VIII				
55		X	parchmt	220 × 260		42
56		X	parchmt			
57	Saint-Gall	X	parchmt			47
58	Saint-Gall?	X	parchmt			
59		IX	parchmt			
61		IX	parchmt	238 × 338		
74		IX	parchmt	165 × 230		220
76		X	parchmt			
77		X	parchmt			F67–8
84		X	parchmt			
85		IX				
86		X/XI				
87		X				
92		IX				Ff39v–41v
93	Trèves	IX	parchmt	160 × 250		Ff34v–42v

[a] See table 6.

[b] The superscript numbers indicate the first or second half of the century.

Table 7. (*cont.*)

No.[a]	Columns	Lines	Greek script	Latin script	Language on left	Quire signatures
A Graeco-Latin texts						
1	—	—	unc.	early h-unc.	?	—
2	2	8+	unc. (could be *saec.* III)	early h-unc. (roundish)	Latin?	
3		15+	unc.	early h-unc.	Latin	
4	2	39–40	unc.	unc.	Greek	
5		22+		curs.	Lat. of each fable over Gr.	
6	1/3–4	27–31/29–33	cp. Cairo Menander?	early h-unc. (mixed)	Gr. and Lat. words/ alternate	
7	2	20		Anglo-Saxon min.		
8	1	9+	unc.	early/late h-unc.	Lat. of each over Gr.	?
9	?			curs.		
B Latino-Greek texts						
10	2	38?	square unc.	early b-r unc.	Latin	—
11	2	30	unc., very like the Lat.	mixed h-unc.	Latin	—
12	2	23+	unc.	b-r unc.	Latin	
13	2	9+	unc.	unc.	Latin	
14	2	18+	unc.	early h-unc.	Latin	
15	2 pairs of 2	25–6	d/δ, n/ν identical	curs.	Latin	
16	2	21+	unc.	unc.	Latin	
17	2	18+	unc.	early h-unc.	Latin	
18	2	21–2		early h-unc.	Latin	
19	2	*c.* 36	unc.	early h-unc.	Latin	
20	4	60?	unc. (could be *saec.* IV)	h-unc.	cols (l.-r.) Lat.-Gr.-Lat.-Gr.	
21		29	written in Lat. letters	curs. min.		
22	8	up to 23 surv.		curs.	continuous	
23	2 double cols.?	*c.* 50?		early h-unc.	Latin	
24	2	26	unc.	early h-unc.	Latin	top l. cnr, leaf 1, in Gr.
25				curs.	Latin (tr. of Gr.?)	
C *Exercitationes scribendi*						
26	/	/	unc.	capitalis and h-unc.		
27	/	/	rustic capitals (*sic*)	early h-unc./rustic caps.		
28	/	/	?	ancient curs.	Gr. below	
D Manuscripts listed by Goetz (supplemented by Omont)						
29	2	34–8	inexpert	unc.	Greek	Greek
36	2					q+Rom. num.
37						
53						
54						
55	2		unc.	min.	Greek	
56						
57						
58			Lat. letters			
59						
61						

In the measurements, the width is placed first (for a justification of this procedure, see Turner, *Typology*, chapter 2 and especially p. 14). The number of folios given is the extant number. A plus sign after the number of lines indicates that these are the number extant in a mutilated copy. A query indicates the number suggested by an attempt at reconstruction. A dash or question mark alone in any column indicates that the information cannot be

Table 7. (*cont.*)

Ruling	Bounding lines	Running titles	Punctuation	Abbreviations	Other notes	No.[a]
						1
			none			2
					cp. *CLA* 2,246	3
none	none	heading in Lat.		≥ = *con*, p = *prae*		4
						5
none	none	none	: betw. words		Latin influenced by Greek	6
						7
/	/	?	// betw. Gr. and Lat.	none	cp. *CLA* S,1782: both scripts unusual	8
					verso of the roll	9
flesh	double, l. of cols.	none	: once	q·, ϗ	*p.m.* and *s.m.* corrections; zigzag border to *explicit*	10
hair, from centre, all leaves tog.	double	—	: and ; betw. words			11
			new § projects into l. mgn		red for new word to be declined	12
?			?			13
?						14
no description in *CLA*					lost: no facsimile	15
					cp. *CLA* 2,206	16
						17
						18
						19
			—	—	each line a word or short phrase	20
					barbarous spelling	21
			spaces betw. Gr. and Lat. words		recto accounts of transport by water	22
			very short lines		cp. *CLA* 2,224	23
			first word projects		quaternions; pap. recto outside matching sides	24
						25
						26
						27
						28
hair	double on l. of col.	none	> if cols. too close tog.	↪ for final *n*/*m*		29
hair						36
						37
					corrected *saec.* XVI/XVII	53
						54
						55
						56
						57
					corrected *saec.* X/XI	58
						59
						61

recovered. No entry indicates that I have not been able to gather the information. An oblique stroke indicates that the column entry is inapplicable to this manuscript.

Abbreviations particular to this table: betw., between; cnr, corner; curs., cursive; frg., fragmentary; h-unc., half-uncial; l., left; mgn, margin; min., minuscule; palimps., palimpsest; pap. roll, papyrus roll; parchmt, parchment; r., right; surv., surviving; tog., together; tr., translation; unc., uncial

Table 8. *Non-biblical Graeco-Latin manuscripts listed by century*

	Manuscript groups[a]			
saec.	A	B	C	D
II	1	1		
III	1	1	1	
IV	1	2		
V	4	9	2	
VI	2	3		
VII				
VIII	1			3
IX				7
X				9
XI				4
XII				5
XIII				3
XIV				1
XV				6
XVI				15
XVII				3

[a] Group A, Graeco-Latin texts; B, Latino-Greek texts; C, *Exercitationes scribendi*; D, Mss listed by Goetz (supplemented by Omont).

or two words (e.g. no. 11), so that the student could find the meaning of each. The division of the literary texts and their translations into sense-lines is a feature that they have in common. The glossaries were clearly produced for similarly practical purposes.

Besides their palaeographical interest, these texts shed some light on Graeco-Roman culture. The Latin writers represented are Virgil (eight manuscripts, of which seven are of the *Aeneid*) and Cicero (three manuscripts).

It is not without interest to list the manuscripts by century, as in table 8. Nine of the manuscripts in the second group are dated by Lowe to the fifth or sixth centuries although, from the Greek script, at least one could be put back into the fourth. The reason for the high number of Latino-Greek manuscripts of the fifth century will be a matter for discussion in chapter 15.

If any typical features emerge from this exploration, it is of a school text, very probably of Virgil, with two columns to the page and the Latin on the left, each hexameter spread over several lines, written with no concern about beauty.

Item no. 6 provides a bridge between our two groups of bilinguals. The first part of this codex contains Greek verb conjugations. The second is a lexicon to Paul, formed from a distinctive Greek text and a Latin one of a pre-Vulgate type not unrelated to that found in the Codex Claromontanus. Amongst them are legal phrases with a translation. Most of the codex, some at least of whose quires were formed by folding a large sheet of papyrus, is blank. According to Wouters, it was written by a Greek anxious both to improve his knowledge of his own language, and to learn some Latin.

BIBLICAL MANUSCRIPTS

Turning to biblical manuscripts, I have confined my explorations (table 9) to New Testament manuscripts of which one language is Greek.

There are New Testament manuscripts in other pairs of languages, including Coptic–Arabic, Syriac–Arabic, and so forth. For information on Copto-Arabic fragments of the Old Testament, see W. Grossouw, *The Coptic Versions of the Minor Prophets. A Contribution to the Study of the Septuagint* (Monumenta Biblica et Ecclesiastica 3), Rome, 1938. A Graeco-Arabic fragment of Deuteronomy in Greek and Arabic is amongst the most recent (1975) finds in the monastery of St Catherine on Mount Sinai. The uncial fragment 0205 is not listed here, since it is actually a Coptic text whose scribe accidentally began by copying a Greek text. I am indebted to J. I. Miller for his guidance here, and with regard to other Coptic matters. I do not include ℓ925, of which the Greek is only certain transliterated headings such as *Kuriachi Pempii ystera apo to Pascha*. I am not sure why this manuscript is included in Aland's *Liste*. Nor do I include ℓ1354, which is conceivably a Graeco-Coptic manuscript. A parchment leaf from Qasr Ibrim contains Jn 20.11–18 in Greek on one side and an Old Nubian version of Mk 11.1–10 on the other (G. M. Browne, 'The Sunnarti Mark', *Zeitschrift für Papyrologie und Epigraphik* 66 (1986), 49–52). There does not appear to be enough evidence to define it as a bilingual according to the present frame of reference. It should be noted that there are also Christian bilingual texts which are not biblical (as well as no. 6 from our first list), for example the Graeco-Coptic *Gloria in excelsis* from the Codex Scheide.

Of these bilingual manuscripts, I have been able to examine 05, 08, 010, 012, 070 (with the London fragments and microfilm of the leaves in Vienna), 086, 0200, 0203, 0204, 9^{abs}, 694, ℓ311, and ℓ1994. I have also studied microfilm of all the other Graeco-Latin manuscripts except 628, and of the Graeco-Coptic manuscripts (except those officially designated lectionaries) at the Institut für Neutestamentliche Textforschung in Münster. Groups B and C clearly merit separate investigation such as cannot be undertaken here. But we may use them to gain some idea of the pattern of distribution through the centuries. This is shown in table 10.

The Coptic manuscripts provide evidence of a strong tradition of bilingual copying over a period of eight centuries. They include six papyri, ranging in date from the fourth to the eighth centuries. The papyrus and maiuscule manuscripts (I have not examined the lectionaries) divide into three groups, each with its own distinctive format.

P^2, P^6, P^{62}, 086, 0100, 0129, and 0260 have alternating blocks of Greek and Coptic. In P^6 the Greek comes first, and the sections of Coptic contain longer passages of text. In 0260 the Coptic comes first, and again there seems to be more of it than of the Greek. In 0129 also the Greek comes first.

T, 070, 0164, 0177, 0184, 0204, 0239, and 0299 all have two columns to the page,

Table 9. *List of bilingual New Testament manuscripts*

A Graeco-Latin manuscripts

1 $\mathrm{D^{ea}}$ (05) Codex Bezae
2 $\mathrm{D^{suppl}}$
3 $\mathrm{D^{P}}$ (06) Codex Claromontanus
4 $\mathrm{D^{abs1}}$ Codex Sangermanensis (Tischendorf's $\mathrm{E^{P}}$)
5 $\mathrm{D^{abs2}}$
6 $\mathrm{E^{a}}$ (08) Codex Laudianus
7 F (010) Codex Augiensis
8 G (012) Codex Boernerianus
9 *Δ* (037) Codex Sangallensis
10 0130
11 0230
12 $\mathrm{9^{abs}}$
13 16
14 17
15 79
16 130
17 165
18 620
19 628
20 629
21 694
22 866b + 1918
23 1269
24 ℓ1289

Note on 1918: this manuscript is not described as bilingual in Aland, *Liste*. But it is the same codex as 866b. In fact it has the Latin as far as F5, l. 8 (Rev. 17.7, *admiratione magna*); thereafter one column is blank.

B Graeco-Coptic manuscripts

25 $\mathrm{P^{2}}$
26 $\mathrm{P^{6}}$
27 $\mathrm{P^{41}}$
28 $\mathrm{P^{42}}$
29 $\mathrm{P^{62}}$
30 $\mathrm{P^{96}}$
31 T (029) + 0113 + 0125 + 0139
32 070 + 0110 + 0124 + 0178 + 0179 + 0180 + 0190 + 0191 + 0193 + 0194 + 0202
33 086
34 0100 + 0195 + ℓ963
35 0129 + 0203 + ℓ1575
36 0164
37 0177
38 0184
39 0200
40 0204
41 0236
42 0237
43 0238
44 0239
45 0260
46 0275
47 0299
48 ℓ143
49 ℓ961
50 ℓ962
51 ℓ964a
52 ℓ964b
53 ℓ965
54 ℓ1353
55 ℓ1355
56 ℓ1602
57 ℓ1604
58 ℓ1606
59 ℓ1607
60 ℓ1614
61 ℓ1678
62 ℓ1739
63 ℓ1741
64 ℓ1994

C Graeco-Arabic manuscripts

65 0136 + 0137
66 0278
67 211
68 609
69 ℓ6
70 ℓ255
71 ℓ311
72 ℓ762
73 ℓ804
74 ℓ937
75 ℓ1023
76 ℓ1331
77 ℓ1343
78 ℓ1344
79 ℓ1746
80 ℓ1773

For 0278, see Linos Politis, 'Nouveaux manuscrits grecs découverts au Mont Sinaï', *Scriptorium* 34 (1980), 5–17, esp. p. 10 and plate 4b, and B. Aland, 'Die neuen neutestamentlichen Handschriften vom Sinai', *Bericht der Hermann Kunst-Stiftung zur Förderung der Neutestamentlichen Textforschung für die Jahre 1982 bis 1984*, Münster, 1985, pp. 76–89, esp. p. 81. For a thorough study of ℓ6, see H. J. de Jonge, 'Joseph

Table 9. *(cont.)*

Scaliger's Greek–Arabic Lectionary', *Quaerendo* 5 (1975), 143–72. For another Greek–Arabic lectionary now at Leiden, see the same writer's 'Een recente aanwinst onder de Nieuwtestamentische tekstgetuigen in Nederland (Leiden, Bibliotheek der R.U., Ms. Or. 14.239)', *Nederlands Theologisch Tÿdschrift* 31 (1977), 2–7, and J.J. Witkam, *Catalogue of Arabic Manuscripts*, Vol. 3, Leiden, 1985–6, pp. 336–48.

D Greek–Old Church Slavonic manuscripts
81 525
82 2136
83 2137

E Graeco-Armenian manuscript
84 256

F Graeco-Turkish manuscript
85 1325
The Turkish of this last manuscript is written in Greek letters.

Trilingual manuscripts of the New Testament seem to be very few in number. There are only 460 (Greek–Latin–Arabic), and ℓ1605 + ℓ1993 (Coptic–Greek–Arabic). Another part of this second example seems to be preserved as Vienna Nat. Bibl. K II 346 (see the account by de Jonge, *Quaerendo* 5 (1975), p. 157).

Table 10. *Bilingual New Testament manuscripts listed by century*

saec.	Manuscript groups[a]			
	A	B	C	Others[b]
IV	2	3		
V		3		
VI	2	7		
VII		5		
VIII		6		
IX	6	3	2	
X	1	4	3	
XI		3	3	1 (Gr-Arm)
XII	1	1	2	
XIII	2	2	6	
XIV	5		2	
XV	5			1 (Gr-OS)
XVI	1		1	2 (Gr-OS)
XVII				
XVIII				1 (Gr-Tk)

[a] Group A, Graeco-Latin Mss; B, Graeco-Coptic Mss; C, Graeco-Arabic Mss.
[b] Gr-Arm, Graeco-Armenian; Gr-OS, Greek–Old Church Slavonic; Gr-Tk, Graeco-Turkish.

those on the recto in Coptic and those on the verso in Greek. 0275 is the precise opposite of this, with two Greek columns on the recto and two Fayyumic on the verso.

P^{41}, P^{42}, 0236, and 0237 have the Greek in the column on the left and the Coptic in the one on the right, be there one column on the page (P^{42}) or two (the others). 0238 probably also belongs here, but its lay-out is difficult to reconstruct. It is likely to have had a single column to the page.

Thus the Coptic copying tradition had two formats (the first and second groups) not paralleled in Graeco-Latin manuscripts. The implications of this will be explored later.

The evidence of the Graeco-Latin documents does not point to a sustained tradition (see table 11). Apart from the three great uncials and the tiny fragment 0230 of the early period, we have nothing before the Carolingian era. There is another gap, then a further revival in the Renaissance. Compared to the glossaries (see table 6), they are also very few in number.

The accompanying table of information about the Graeco-Latin biblical manuscripts (table 11) is laid out like the previous table (7), and the same symbols are used, although some of the right-hand columns contain different information. I have not sought to provide information from the Renaissance manuscripts for all columns.

Plates of 05, 06, and 08 are easily found. Some of the others are less commonly photographed, and so I include here a list, indicating the folio illustrated. For minuscules, Hatch = W. H. P. Hatch, *Facsimiles and Descriptions of Minuscule Manuscripts of the New Testament*, Cambridge, Mass., 1951; Metzger = *Manuscripts*; Tischendorf = C. Tischendorf, *Monumenta sacra inedita (Nova collectio)*, Leipzig, 1855ff; Vogels = H. J. Vogels, *Codicum Novi Testamenti specimina*, Bonn, 1929.

D^{suppl}: Facsimile edition of D (all); Lowe, *Pal. Papers* 1, plate 24 (Latin, part of F169*)
F: Vogels, plate 23 (F22); Hatch, plate L (F77)
G: The facsimile, edited with an introduction by Alexander Reichardt, *Der Codex Boernerianus*, Leipzig, 1909; Vogels, plate 25 (F23); Metzger, plate 28 (F23)
Δ: Vogels, plate 24 (F294b–295); Hatch, plate LXV (page 153)
0130: Tischendorf, Vol. 3 (1860), plate II
0230: *CLA* S,1694 (all; and see bibliography p.67 below)
17: Hatch, plate XCV
165: Metzger, plate 40 (F100b); Cavalieri and Lietzmann, plate 38 (F100b)

It was argued in chapter 1 that the use of running titles was evidence for the Latin origin of Codex Bezae. The evidence from the other bilinguals complicates the matter. 06 has them, but 08 does not. In the Carolingian period, only 012 and 037 have them. Given the clear way in which Latin scribes prefer to include them, this is surprising. It suggests a Greek influence on this aspect of book production in Graeco-Latin bilinguals. If so, then the likelihood of Codex Bezae being Latin, and particularly unsusceptible to Greek influence, is strengthened.

The story of the later medieval and Renaissance manuscripts is not least one of unfinished beginnings, in text or illumination (the latter is not rare in monolingual manuscripts). 16 has the Latin to the bottom of F130 (Mk 11.13), for part of F194

Table 11. *Graeco-Latin manuscripts of the New Testament*

See table 7 for an explanation of abbreviations and conventions.

In addition, the following abbreviations are used: aft., after; bef., before; bibl., biblical; s.-ll., sense-lines.

No.	Origin	Date	Material	α measurement	β measurement[a]	Folios
D (05)	see chapter 15	*c.* 400	parchmt	220 × 260	140–5 × 185	415
D^{suppl}	Lyons	IX	parchmt	220 × 260	151 × 180–5	10
D (06)	S. Italy? Sardinia?	VI (V Lowe)[b]	parchmt	192 × 250	138 × 150	533
D^{abs1}	Corbie	IX	parchmt	275 × 360	224 × 270–5	176
D^{abs2}	Corbie	X *ex.*	parchmt	220 × 368	72 (Gr.)/63 (Lat.) × 267	6
E (08)	Sardinia	VI-VII	parchmt	218 × 272	*c.* 160 × 200	227
F (010)	Reichenau	IX	parchmt	185 × *c.* 230	144 × 165	136
G (012)	Saint-Gall	IX	parchmt	185 × 239	125 × 170	99
Δ (037)	Saint-Gall?	IX	parchmt	182–6 × 225	130–45 × 180	195
0130	Reichenau?	IX	parchmt (palimps.)	180 × 260	163 × 201	6
0230	?	IV-V	parchmt	?	*c.* 132 × *c.* 160 (Dahl)[c]	1 frg.
9^{abs}	Milan	XV (bef. 1461)	paper	200 × 290		118
16		XIV	parchmt	252 × 316		361
17	Paris?	XV (aft. 1476)	parchmt	210 × 309		353
79		XV	parchmt	120 × 165		208
130		XV	paper	211 × 284		229
165	Rhegina	1291/2	parchmt	204 × 304		214
620		XII	parchmt	130 × 185		150
628		XIV	parchmt	187 × 247		16
629		XIV	parchmt	121 × 171		265
694		XV	paper	213 × 296		211
866b/1918		XIII/XIV	parchmt	168 × 260		4
1269		XIV *ex.*	paper	207 × 279		126
ℓ1289		1544	parchmt	135 × 200		18

[a] The β measurements of D^{abs2}, F, Δ and 0130 were reached by calculation from the photographs, and are therefore open to correction.
[b] *CLA* 5,521.
[c] N. A. Dahl, '0230 (= *PSI* 1306) and the Fourth-century Greek–Latin Edition of the Letters of Paul', in *Text and Interpretation. Studies in the New Testament Presented to Matthew Black*, ed. E. Best and R. McL. Wilson, Cambridge, 1979, pp. 79–98.

(Lk 5.21–4), and again from Ff194 – 329 (Jn 1.1–12.17). The set of miniatures is incomplete. 694 has the Latin only to F5b, l. 6 (Mt. 3.11), from F59 to 59b (Mk 1.1–24), and for a leaf and six lines giving the first fourteen verses of John. The initial letters of these Latin beginnings were all left for an illuminator who never supplied them. The Latin column of 1918 stops at F5, l. 8 (Rev. 17.6). ℓ1289 has

Table 11. (*cont.*)

No.	Cols.	Lines[a]	Greek script	Latin script	Language on left	Quire signatures	Ruling
D (05)	1	33	bibl. unc.	'b-d' unc.	Greek	bottom r. cnr. last fo., in Gr.	flesh
D[suppl]	1	30–3	unc.	unc.	Greek		flesh
D (06)	1	21	bibl. unc.	'b-d' unc.	Greek		flesh, each fo. separately
D[abs1]	2	31	(strange) unc.	unc.	Greek	bottom 1st fo., Lat. nums.	
D[abs2]	1	42	Western unc.	min.	Greek	none	
E (08)	2	24–6	late bibl. unc.	'b' unc.	Latin	none	flesh
F (010)	2	27–8	unc.	Carolingian min.	Lat. outer col. on each fo.	only quires 13–16	flesh
G (012)	1	20–6	unc.	min.	interlinear	top l. cnr. 1st fo., Lat. nums.	
Δ (037)	1	17–29	(poor) unc.	min.	interlinear		
0130	2	22	unc.	unc.	Lat. outer col. each? leaf		
0230	1	4 extant 19–24		rustic caps.	Greek	—	flesh
9[abs]	2	20–1			Greek		
16	2	26			Greek		
17	2	25			Greek		
79	2	26+			Latin		
130	2	26			Latin		
165	2	33			Greek		
620	2	32			Greek		
628	2	32			Lat. outer col. each leaf		
629	2	27			Latin		
694	2	33+			Greek		
866b/1918	2	46			Greek		
1269	2	30+			interlinear		
ℓ1289	3	13			Greek		

[a] The number of lines given for interlinears indicates the number of lines of Greek.

only the Greek after F9b, with the rest of the right-hand pages blank except for transliterations of lectionary headings; strangely, at these places the Greek is left blank. 629 is also lacking some of its illuminated letters (F1, Ac 1.1 – Latin but not Greek – and F79b, Jas. 1.1). Wherever the Latin fails in these manuscripts, one column continues blank – a clear indication that the whole of the Greek was written first. The scribe of 694 accidentally wrote his Greek in the right instead of the left column of F202b.

Why are these manuscripts incomplete? Was the problem of needing to keep the columns more or less in step so distracting that scribes could not stick to their mechanical task of copying? This seems not unlikely, and suggests that the ninth-century 0130 may have been a failure for the same reasons. By contrast, it may be that the practice of our oldest bilinguals, where one scribe copied both columns –

Table 11. *(cont.)*

Bounding lines	Running titles	Punctuation	Line division	Rubrication	Other notes	No.
single	yes	none	s.-ll., equal betw. cols.	1st 3 lines of each book; parts of colophons		D (05)
double	no	normal	tries to follow D	none	blue ink; interrogation mark	D^{suppl}
	generally	none	sense-lines	1st 3 lines of each letter; OT quotations		D (06)
single?	no	none	as 06		2 scribes (first – Ff1–68)	D^{abs1}
double	no	none	as 06			D^{abs2}
single	no	none	short s.-ll.	1st 3 lines of the book	Ff36, 39, 43 not matched flesh	E (08)
double	no	none	equivalent, not s.-ll.	initials; 1st line of each epistle		F (010)
single	yes	words separated	regular line length	yes	scribe Irish	G (012)
	yes	none		initials (several colours used)		Δ (037)
double	?	Gr. cols. regular				0130
double (inner mgn)	?		sense-lines	?	writing betw. 2 lines	0230
					scribe Bartholomaeus Melzios	9^{abs}
						16
					scribe Georgios Hermonymos	17
						79
						130
					scribe Abbot Romanos	165
						620
						628
						629
						694
						866b/1918
						1269
						ℓ1289

and in my opinion, copying only a small section of each column at a time – was more successful.

None of these manuscripts is written in sense-lines. One (1269) is an interlinear, the Latin gloss written above. In the rest, an attempt is made to keep approximate equivalence, certainly for the contents of a page, but not from line to line. The Greek column is sometimes slightly wider. In 9^{abs}, 16, 165, 620, 694, 866b, the Greek column is of even width, the Latin more irregular, sometimes with a blank line to keep step with the less concise Greek. 130 and 629 are the opposite of this. It is the irregular column which will have been written later, keeping step with the first. This is borne out by the fact that 130 and 629 both have their Latin on the left, whilst in the others it is on the right. Gregory believed the Latin of 79 to be older than the Greek. This manuscript, with 17, has both columns regular in appearance.

628 has a format unique among the late manuscripts. It would be interesting to explore the possibility that it has some connection with 010 and 0130.

The Carolingian manuscripts show some experimentation. This, I suggest, indicates that they had no tradition of bilingual copying to follow. Only the texts which are derived from an old model (D^{suppl}, D^{abs1}, D^{abs2}) have the Greek on the left. Saint-Gall favours interlinears. Reichenau has the Latin in the outer column of each page.

One wonders whether 0130 is not another Reichenau manuscript. There are seven surviving leaves of this palimpsest. The inner, Greek, column is present throughout. But the Latin was supplied on only one of the leaves, that containing Lk 1.64–71 (a recto). The final line is clearly visible, the rest has been erased. It seems strange that only this passage, the *Benedictus*, has had its Latin supplied (compare the example of the minuscule 16). It should be emphasized that there is no question of the rest of the Latin being absent because it has been erased; it was quite certainly never written. This unfinished manuscript provides clear evidence that, at least on occasion, the whole of the Greek was copied before any Latin was supplied.

There has been a considerable amount of study of these Carolingian manuscripts, generally with regard to the relationship between 010 and 012.

See particularly W. H. P. Hatch, 'On the Relationship of Codex Augiensis and Codex Boernerianus of the Pauline Epistles', *Harvard Studies in Classical Philology* 60 (1951), 187–99 and H. J. Frede, *Altlateinische Paulus-Handschriften*, Freiburg, 1964 (Vetus Latina: Aus der Geschichte der lateinischen Bibel 4), pp. 81–5. For a description of F, see M. R. James, *The Western Manuscripts in the Library of Trinity College Cambridge. A Descriptive Catalogue*, Cambridge, 1900, entry 412 (pp. 544–6).

Since 010 has a Vulgate, and 012 an Old Latin text, the relationship cannot be one of direct copying, or derivation from a common exemplar. According to Hatch they are 'cousins' – that is, they are descended from a common archetype through, he prefers to believe, two intermediate copyings. One wonders whether the relationship is even that close. A similar theory of descent from a single manuscript is held by Frede.

Examining the Augiensis, one is struck by the fact that, as Richard Bentley long ago wrote in the margin of F35:

> Vide pag. 39. Defuit folium in Autographo: nam utrobiq, et hic et 39: et 94 par et [*pariet*?] spatium / Nec vero exscriptus est ex Cod. Claromontano: quia et iste et Germanensis utroq, loco integer est. RB.

That is to say, the Greek column lacks 1 Cor. 3.8–16 (twenty-nine complete lines of the Latin), 6.7–14 (thirty-five lines), and Col. 2.1–8 (thirty-one lines); it ends finally at Philem. 20 (thirteen lines of the Latin complete the epistle), after which Hebrews is copied with the same page lay-out, but in Latin only. Therefore, the Latin and Greek text cannot have been companions from the beginning – the codex is derived from a damaged Greek, but a whole Latin archetype. If the Greek *is* descended from the Claromontan bilingual tradition, the Latin (Vulgate anyway!) has clearly no part in it.

We learn from the omissions that F does not preserve the lines of its archetype. If each omission were due to the loss of one leaf in an ancestor, then that manuscript would have had different numbers of lines on each side of those leaves. The number of lines on the lost pages would have been variously thirteen, fourteen, fifteen, sixteen, seventeen, and eighteen. Apart from the improbability of such fluctuation in the number of lines on a page, even seventeen or eighteen would be a surprisingly small number, lower even than the Claromontanus. Rather – and the regular line length of F bears this out – the average length of its line is longer than that in the archetype, which may have been written in sense-lines.

In passing, we may note that Scrivener wondered whether there were two scribes for F. Although the appearance of some leaves that happen to be misplaced (inserted after F102) is dramatically different from those around them (this is to speak of the Greek script – the Latin is more regular throughout), one may in fact observe a steady progression in the Greek writing which shows it all to be the work of one hand. The most instructive example is *Υ*. It begins in a normal Greek style, then a form more like a modern lower-case *y* takes over, to be succeeded in a short while by a form with no lower extension, more akin to *V*. And at about F37b the scribe adopts a character where the lower extension is almost horizontal to the line below the first stroke.

Frede has also discussed the two copies of the Claromontanus, the Codex Sangermanensis (*Paulus-Handschriften*, pp. 34–49), and the Meringenhausen leaves (pp. 47f), as well as the Leningrad lectionary.

For the Corbie script, not discussed by Frede, see Lowe, 'A New Fragment in the B-Type', *Palaeographia Latina* 5 (Oxford, 1927), 43–7 = *Pal. Papers* 1,229–32 and plate 26, with many references; Bischoff, *Palaeography*, p. 106.

Frede goes on to argue that these Pauline bilinguals represent two branches of a single tradition. The one branch is represented by 06 and its copies, the other by 010 and 012. The archetype (Z), a bilingual set out in sense-lines, was written in about 350.

From the point of view of our present purposes, it is instructive to note how this bilingual Pauline tradition has been treated. The first branch has one column to the page. The second has two quite different lay-outs – F has two columns (and the inner one always Greek), G is interlinear. F has imported a different Latin text. The Greek texts of F and G have many differences from that of 06, as well as between each other. Thus these early medieval bilinguals present two different extremes – the one preserves the ancient tradition in an accurate copy, the other has a quite different appearance.

More recently, Dahl has argued that 0230 also is a member of this group of manuscripts.

Dahl, '0230 (= *PSI* 1306)' (bibliographical details in the notes to table 11); see also Bischoff, p. 58 and n.33; H.J. Frede, *Epistula ad Ephesios* (Vetus Latina 24/1), Freiburg, 1962, p. 14*; Lowe, *CLA* S, 1694; G. Mercati, *PSI* 13,1 (1949), 87–102 and plate VI. Against Mercati's view that the Ms had two columns to the page (followed by Aland, *Liste* and Alands, *Text*), Lowe argues forcefully that there was only one.

On the basis of very meagre evidence, Dahl concludes that the Greek represents 'a normal Egyptian text', but that the Latin 'is slightly in favour of a connection between the fragment and the other bilinguals' (p. 88).

Dahl goes on to argue that the original colometry of the archetype Z is best preserved in a sixth-century Gothic–Latin palimpsest of part of Romans, now at Wolfenbüttel (Herzog-August-Bibliothek 4148; *CLA* 9,1388; in Old Latin nomenclature, variously known as Guelferbytanus, gue, w, and 79). In this he is picking up a hint from Corssen. This manuscript, Dahl continues, contains four sets of vertical lines on each leaf, marking the positions for the beginning of sections, *cola*, and *commata* in each of the two columns. He suggests that the archetype Z had some such system, perhaps rendered even more sophisticated by further lines for indented Old Testament citations (marked in Guelferbytanus by the *dipla*). The need to simplify such a lay-out, he claims, explains the differences between the descendants of Z. All this conjecture takes us too far too rapidly. The fact is that the evidence from 0230 is too meagre for any conclusions to be drawn. And Dahl's arguments from format are unsound: for example, that the double bounding lines indicate that Old Testament quotations were indented as in Claromontanus. As to the archetype, there is no reason for attributing to it the sum total of the characteristics of its descendants. There is no evidence that any ancient Graeco-Latin bilingual was so complicated in its lay-out.

Turning to our surviving ancient examples, we again find an absence of unanimity. E has two columns to the page with the Latin on the left and the Greek on the right. The other three have one column, the Latin on the recto.

As to script, the Latin of 0230 is almost unique amongst early Christian and biblical manuscripts: the only other such text written in rustic capitals is the tiny Old Latin fragment of John now at Aberdeen (Univ. Lib. Pap. 2a; *CLA* 2,118). It should, however, be added that two corrections in this script are to be found in the Laudian Acts (Ff84, 92b), and that Vatic. Lat. 3806, Ff1–2 (*CLA* S,1766) is part of a Canones Evangeliorum in a late (*saec.* VI) form of the same script: Petitmengin (see bibliography p. 7) presumes that the rest of the manuscript will have been written in uncial (p. 96, n. 49). Rustic capitals were often used for supplementary material for centuries after they had passed out of use as a standard hand.

The Greek of 0230 shows the Coptic *M*, and there can be little doubt that it was copied in Egypt. Mercati could not be certain that the Greek and Latin are not from different scribes.

The other three manuscripts also have unusual Latin hands. Two are in so-called b-d uncial, though they actually have less in common than has sometimes been supposed. The fourth is in b uncial, influenced by Greek and probably written by a Greek scribe (Cavallo, *Ricerche*, p. 105; *CLA* 2,251).

The three main examples all show the use of red ink for the first three lines of a book. This represents ancient Latin practice in general, and is certainly not a distinguishing feature of bilinguals.

Two have single bounding lines, two have double. Running titles are not found in E.

Only in the use of sense-lines are the oldest New Testament Graeco-Latin bilinguals consistent.

The lack of consistency in all other respects, even among so few examples, suggests that there was no strong tradition of specialism in copying Graeco-Latin biblical texts. The need will have arisen only rarely, and then the scribe employed will have been whoever could be found to have the necessary competences. This explains the lack of agreement, the way in which the general features of book production simply reflect those current at the time, and the fact that such untypical hands were used for writing these texts.

However, there must have been a tradition of some kind. There will have been a reason for the ways in which the earliest copies were produced, and their descendants will have imitated them. It seems very probable indeed that the biblical texts, or some of them, were modelled on the typical bilingual Virgil that we have described. The contrast with the Graeco-Coptic manuscripts written in blocks, which we discussed earlier, supports this: there was no similar precedent for Coptic copyists to follow, so they created a format based on the use of church lections in two languages, the one followed by the other. In the codices where pairs of columns are written in the same language, the Copts created another format.

To return to the example of the bilingual Virgil: of surviving examples, the Laudian Acts approaches closest to this, with its Latin on the left, its two columns to the page, and its very short sense-lines of just a couple of words. Other copyists realized that the Latin had been on the left in the secular text because it was the original, and therefore wrote the Greek on the left of their productions. The implications for Codex Bezae of this relationship between the secular and biblical texts will be discussed in chapter 5.

Another comparable lay-out is Origen's *Hexapla*. We know from the Ambrosian and Genizah fragments of the Psalms that each line contained only a couple of words. This was for the purpose of easy comparison between the columns, as well as because of the physical restraints of having so many columns on a page. But whether this precedent can have had any effect on bilingual book production must be regarded as questionable. How many scribes will have had a sight of even a partial copy, let alone the original?

Some of the questions with which we began have received some kind of preliminary answer. The background to Codex Bezae is certainly not a sustained tradition of expertise in this kind of copying. What we have already learned about the scribe agrees with this conclusion. The wider world of secular and school texts is no further away than the world of legal documents. The importance of these findings will emerge more fully later (see particularly chapters 5 and 15).

PART II

The scribe and the tradition

In this second part of the book, we turn from an analysis of the codex and the hands that wrote in it, to examine the details of the way in which the scribe copied down the texts he had received. The purpose is twofold: to find out about the forms in which he received them, and to discover his ways in preserving them. We are not going to be examining variant readings, but are pursuing further the questions of lay-out with which we were concerned in Part I, and combining with them study of the presentation and the orthography. The three main subjects are the division of the text into sense-lines, the forms of the *nomina sacra*, and the spelling. Variations in the last two of these have long been known; the examination of the punctuation will help us to interpret the evidence more accurately. We shall be able to find out much about the *Vorlagen* of D, and about how the scribe departed from them.

CHAPTER FIVE

The sense-lines

We have seen sense-lines to be a regular feature of Graeco-Latin bilingual manuscripts. They facilitate the scribe's keeping the two texts in step with each other, and the reader's comparing the columns. Another way of achieving this was to write one column evenly, and the other in lines of corresponding content but uneven length. Yet another was to write fewer lines in one column than the other, without exact correspondence between lines. A fourth was to provide an interlinear translation.

Table 11 in chapter 4 shows that New Testament manuscripts written in sense-lines include the Laudian Acts (08) and the Claromontanus of Paul (06). The second method is exemplified by 9^{abs} (Ms Bodl. Lyell 95): the Greek column is of constant width, whilst the Latin has lines of uneven length, each of which has the same *contents* as its Greek equivalent. For the third method, see ℓ311 (Cambridge Univ. Lib. Add. Ms 1879.13), a Graeco-Arabic text. There is a column of each text to a page, and in the fragments which contain parts of both, the proportions are as follows: F1 has ten Greek lines, six Arabic Ff1b, 2b, 3b have eleven Greek and seven Arabic; Ff2 and 3 have eleven Greek, six Arabic. Best known examples of interlinear texts include the Graeco-Latin Δ (037), the Lindisfarne Gospels written in Latin with a later Anglo-Saxon gloss (BM Cotton. Nero D. iv), and the Pauline Ms 010 (Codex Augiensis).

TERMINOLOGY

D. de Bruyne, *Préfaces de la Bible latine*, Namur, 1912; Devreesse, pp. 61f; *GMAW* p. 19; Charles Graux, 'Nouvelles Recherches sur la stichométrie', *Rev. Phil.* 2 (1878), 97–144; G. B. Gray, *The Forms of Hebrew Poetry*, Oxford, 1915; J. R. Harris, *Stichometry*, London, 1893; F. G. Kenyon, 'The Western Text in the Gospels and Acts', *PBA* 24 (1938), 287–315, esp. pp. 310f; J. A. Robinson, *Euthaliana* (Texts and Studies 3.3), Cambridge, 1895; J. K. Suicer, *Thesaurus Ecclesiasticus*, 2nd edition, Amsterdam, 1728; H. B. Swete, *Introduction to the Old Testament in Greek*, Cambridge, 1914, pp. 344–50; Thompson, pp. 78–81; C. H. Turner, 'St Cyprian's Correspondence', in *Studies in Early Church History. Collected Papers*, Oxford, 1912, pp. 97–131, esp. p. 103.

At least three words have been used to describe the manner in which the text of D and similar manuscripts is divided into lines. Scrivener calls them *στιχοι* (pp. xviif.). He is followed by Clark (*Acts*, pp. xxvii–xli and *passim*). Kenyon claimed that this was a wrong use of the word, and his opinion has been generally accepted. The evidence is worth reviewing.

There is no doubt about the meaning of *στιχος*. First it was a line of verse (see Liddell and Scott). It then came to represent, in Kenyon's definition, a 'unit of measurement of fixed length' in prose. This length was shown by Graux to be equivalent to the average Homeric line, calculated as between thirty-four and thirty-eight letters. That a *στιχος* was the same length as 'the average hexameter' is confirmed by Harris (p. 15) who adds what one would expect, that the measurement is by syllables, not by letters. The division of a text into *στιχοι* provided both a check on the length of a copy, and a means of reckoning the scribe's remuneration. The Cheltenham list of Cyprian's writings makes it clear that the equivalent length (a Virgilian hexameter of sixteen syllables) provided the measure of Latin texts (Turner, p. 103).

Thompson states that the term 'was also applied to the lines or short periods into which certain texts were divided in order to facilitate reading: in other words, sense-lines' (p. 81). He does not, however, provide any examples of the word being used in this way. The nearest we have is Suidas –

> *κῶλον: μόριον λόγου ἐκ δύο ἢ καὶ πλειόνων μερῶν συνιστάμενον· τὰς συλλαβὰς γὰρ τέμνουσι καὶ τὰ κῶλα τῶν νοημάτων.* [Δ] *Κῶλος οὖν ὁ ἀπηρτισμένην ἔχων ἔννοιαν στίχος.*
> (*Suidae Lexikon*, ed. Ada Adler, Part III, Leipzig, 1933, p. 172, l.21; see also Part III, p. 26, l.18)

What we have here is a description of the length of a *κωλον* – that it corresponds to a *στιχος*, a fixed length, which also forms a grammatical unit.

Devreesse compiles an impressive collection of evidence to show that the type of line division we are discussing is properly called *στιχηδον* or *στιχηρον*. He concludes:

> (1) L'écriture *στιχηδον* ou *στιχηρον* est identique à l'écriture *per cola et commata*; (2) elle est en rapport avec l'écriture en forme de vers adoptée pour les Prophètes et les livres 'poétiques' de l'Ancien Testament; (3) elle a été utilisée pour la transcription de Démosthène et de Cicéron; (4) elle n'a du vers que l'apparence extérieure; (5) alors que l'écriture à pleine ligne ne laissait nul repos à l'oeil et demandait un gros effort d'attention, l'écriture *στιχηδον* aidait la lecture et facilitait par son ordonnance l'intelligence des textes. On pourrait ajouter qu'entre cette disposition des lignes et l'évaluation de l'étendue des écrits par stiques, il n'existe quelquefois aucune connexion. (p. 63)

Devreesse totally rejects the use of *στιχος* as a name for these lines written *στιχηδον*, and none of his authorities use it in this way. Those cited by Scrivener, taken direct from Suicer (Vol. 2, col. 1033), refer to the line division of the poetic and prophetic books of the Old Testament (the first edition of 1682 is identical). To these references we may add Origen's scholion on Ps. 118.1 (LXX): see Gray, p. 12, n. 1.

It must therefore be concluded that Scrivener and others were confused by the apparent similarity of the words στιχος and στιχηδον. Only the adverb can be used correctly of the lines in Codex Bezae.

The second description is that the manuscript is copied *per cola et commata*, κατα κωλα και κομματα. This is an acceptable description. But I shall not use it. Since the scribe was a Latin, only the Latin phrase would be apposite. But its usage in the Latin tradition carries as strong a connection with the poetical books of the Old Testament as στιχος does. The purpose there of *cola et commata* is described by Jerome in his Preface to Isaiah – *nos quoque utilitate legentium providentes, interpretationem novam novo scribendi genere distinximus* (de Bruyne, p. 123). The purpose in a bilingual is different. It is to facilitate comparison, whether in lectionary use or in study.

Moreover, the *very* short sense-lines often typical of bilinguals are often not even κωλα or κομματα, which have a precise definition. Quintilian, writing on composition:

> At illa series tris habet formas: incisa, quae κομματα dicuntur, membra, quae κωλα, περιοδον quae est vel ambitus vel circumductum vel continuatio vel conclusio.
> (*Institutio oratoria*, ed. L. Radermacher (Teubner edition), Leipzig, 1971, 9.4.22)

Neither of these terms is precisely applicable. I propose to adopt the third possibility and to use English. These lines written στιχηδον will be called sense-lines.

THESIS

My main interest in this section is with exploring what can be found out about the ancestors of D, in particular its exemplar, and in examining how the scribe of D worked.

This will not involve abstruse and confusing computations of average lengths of lines in ancestors. Clark, *Primitive Text*, provides the best example of the pitfalls of this approach. Kenyon's comments (pp. 301–7) say all that is necessary. The attempts by P. Gächter ('Codex D and Codex Δ', *JTS* 35 (1934), 248–66) to prove that a 'pre-Δ Ms had become an ancestor of D' (p. 265) merits similar criticism. The justice of such claims is much that of the Chuzzlewits to be a very ancient family, on the grounds that they undoubtedly descended in a direct line from Adam and Eve. Harris (*Codex*, chapter 23) proceeds more cautiously and helpfully. The most useful study is Clark, *Acts*, pp. 178–81, although his figures are not always reliable.

The central argument will be that in the Gospels the sense-lines of D are not those of its exemplar, and that in Acts they are. This is in direct contradiction to previous writers. Scrivener states that 'Codex Bezae, as well the Latin as the Greek pages, *was copied from an older model similarly divided in respect to the lines or verses*' (p. xxiii, his italics: see also pp. xviif.). And Harris agrees: 'there is no reason to doubt the accuracy of Scrivener's statement' (*Codex*, p. 242).

There is one passage which I put first, as in my opinion conclusive. At F89b/32–3 the scribe found that he had omitted material. He therefore washed out these two lines and, having inserted the missing line 32, rewrote them as 89b/33 and 90b/1. The first time, he wrote

ΠΡΟC ΤΟΥC ΑΡΧΙΕΡΕΙC ΚΑΙ ΕΙΠΕΝ ΑΥΤΟΙC
ΤΙ ΘΕΛΕΤΑΙ ΜΟΙ ΔΟΥΝΑΙ

The second time, he wrote

ΠΡΟC ΤΟΥC ΑΡΧΙΕΡΕΙC
ΚΑΙ ΕΙΠΕΝ ΑΥΤΟΙC·ΤΙ ΘΕΛΕΤΕ ΜΟΙ ΔΟΥΝΑΙ

I conclude that the exemplar was written like this –

προς τους αρχιερεις
και ειπεν αυτοις
τι θελετε μοι δουναι

The scribe of D reduced these three lines to two, putting a different pair together the second time from the first. It also appears that the medial point is used to indicate the end of a sense-line in the exemplar. It is curious that Scrivener discusses this correction (p. xxiii) without appreciating its significance.

By studying the punctuation, the places where the line endings differ in the two columns, and the breakdown of the sense-line system in part of the codex, we shall be able to discover the format of the manuscript from which the scribe was copying, and the method in which he altered it.

Examination of the various Pauline bilinguals provides analogous evidence of alterations to sense-lines. H. J. Vogels ('Der Codex Claromontanus der paulinischen Briefe', in *Amicitiae Corolla: A Volume of Essays Presented to J. R. Harris*, ed. H. G. Wood, London, 1933, pp. 274–99) compares the manuscripts in order to reconstruct the sense-lines of the archetype (e.g. 1 Cor. 9.20, p. 291). Dahl (for his article, see p. 63) argues cogently that the scribe of the Claromontanus sometimes writes two or even three of his exemplar's sense-lines as one of his own lines (p. 93).

THE BREAKDOWN OF THE SENSE-LINE SYSTEM

We begin with the way in which the lines of D are least like those of its exemplar.

Scrivener (pp. xviif) describes some of the odder ways in which the lines of D divide the text up. His account of the changing practice of the scribe as his work progressed may be amplified.

Separation of article and noun

Matthew: 48b/25–6: ΠΑΝΤΑC ΤΟΥC / ΚΑΚΩC ΕΧΟΝΤΑC. Compare F49, OMNES MALE / HABENTES.
John: 127b/23–4: ΤΗΝ / CΑΡΚΑ
132b/11–12: ΤΟΥC / ΕΛΛΗΝΑC

141b/4–5 to the end of the Gospel: twenty-six instances
Luke has eighty-five, scattered evenly throughout the book.
Mark has one each on Ff290b/31–2, 291b/9–10, 309b/32–3, and 310b/1–2.
Acts has two: 436b/14–15 and 458b/1–2.

Preposition, article and noun

When the article is preceded by a preposition, the scribe has a rule: when breaking the three words over two lines, he always ends the line after the article, not after the preposition.

Matthew: 15b/25–6: ΕΙϹ ΤΟ / ΤΑΜΙΟΝ
61b/18–19: ΑΠΟ ΤΗϹ / ΓΑΛΕΙΛΑΙΑϹ
John: 104b/32–3: ΕΚ ΤΟΥ / ΠΛΗΡѠΜΑΤΟϹ ΑΥΤΟΥ
125b/30–1: ΕΚ ΤΟΥ / ΟΥΡΑΝΟΥ:
127b/23–4 onwards: thirty-one instances
Luke: seventy-four in all
Mark: 285b/5–6 and 334b/6–7
Acts: no examples

In contrast to Scrivener, I find not forty-nine but sixty-one places where a line ends with the article.

Separation of preposition and noun (no article)

John: 159b/21–2 (cp. F160)
Luke: 185b/11–12 and sixteen further occurrences
Mark: 289b/18–19 (not 290); 291b/18–19 (not 292); 299/4–5 (not 298b); 319/14–15 and 22–3 (neither 318b)

In the earlier part of the codex, these line divisions are associated with discrepancies between line endings in the two columns. This is true of the examples at Ff48b/25–6, 61b/18–19, 125b/30–1, and 132b/11–12.

Line division in Luke contains almost every possible violation of the principles of transcribing a text *στιχηδον*. We find separation of a conjunction and its following phrase; separation of noun or participle from adjective, pronoun, or demonstrative; separation of verb and adverb; separation of two related nouns, and so forth. Division of words in half is also more common in Luke.

To give some idea of the frequency of the phenomena, I have noted the following number of occurrences, taking them in the order given above: in the Greek, thirty-eight, sixty, nine, twelve. Division of words in two: fifteen times in the Greek, nine in the Latin. These last divisions are correctly made (compare the anomalous examples given in Gignac, 1,327–9).

The information here collected leads to the conclusion that the scribe altered his way of working twice, once at round about F127b–128, and once either at the very beginning of Mark, or in its opening leaves.

The explanation that is closest to hand is that the scribe became aware of the need to save space. If he was altering the lay-out from that of his exemplar, then he will have found it difficult to compute in advance the number of quaternions that he needed. But a calculation based on his own first fifteen gatherings (Ff1–120) may have shown that he needed to compress his material more. With an original length of 534 leaves, Codex Bezae already has more leaves than any other extant New Testament uncial, though D^{P} has 533. (The size of Cassiodorus' Lesser Pandect (636) and his Codex Grandior (760 folios) was remarkable.) A review of the space needed for Mark to Acts may have indicated that he no longer needed to compress the material so much.

However, the further evidence we will find makes it uncertain whether the scribe actually did save very much parchment. It will be suggested that the abandonment of the short sense-lines of the exemplar was not for the sake of producing a convenient book, or for economic reasons.

It might be that the two changes represent ones in the character of the exemplar. For the two points at which the scribe changed his practice correspond closely to the change in punctuation from the medial point to the space and back again (see chapter 2).

THE EVIDENCE OF THE PUNCTUATION

It will have been observed, in the first example which I gave, that the point written by the scribe after AYTOIC on the second occasion corresponds to the ending of the line that he expunged. The conclusion that a point indicates the end of a line in the exemplar seems inescapable. That the first copying did not include a point after APXIEPEYC warns us not to expect every sense-line ending in the exemplar to be so indicated.

Evidence to support this suggestion is found at places where the line endings of the two columns do not tally. Sometimes a point is found in one after the word which ends the line in the other. The first example that occurs is F30b/13–14

ΔΙΑ ΤΟ ΟΝΟΜΑ ΜΟΥ·Ο ΔΕ ΫΠΟΜΕΙΝΑC ΕΙC ΤΕΛΟC
ΟΥΤΟC CωΘΗCΕΤΑΙ

=F31/13–14

PROPTER NOMEN MEUM·QUI AUTEM SUSTINEBIT
IN FINEM·HIC SALVUS ERIT

The rest are

Matthew: F50b–51/4–5; 53b–54/23–4; 57b/16–17=58/16; 57b/27–8= 58/26–8 *bis*; 71b–72/24–5: 75b–76/2–3.
John: 116b–117/14–15; 119b–120/20–1; 125b–126/30–1 (double point on the

Table 12. *Punctuation at disparate line endings*

	Point	Space	Total
Matthew	8	—	8
John	10	4	14
Luke	2	11	13
Mark	21	4	25
Acts	4	1	5
Total	45	20	65

Greek side); 128b–129/13–14; 132b–133/9–10; 133b–134/30–1; 136b–137/9–10; 153b–154/25–6; 157b–158/25–6; 180b–181/24–5.
Luke: 241b–242/3–4; 252b–253/27–8.
Mark: 297b–298/15–16, 23–4; 298b–299/31–2; 301b–302/3–4; 306b–307/8–9, 14–15, 15–16; 308b–309/4–5, 20–1; 310b–311/3–4; 313b/23–4=314/22–3; 313b/32=314/31–2; 314b–315/12–13; 316b–317/20–1; 321b–322/2–3; 335b–336/29–30; 338b–339/23–4, 24–5; 340b–341/15–16; 341b–342/11–12; 344b–345/31–2.
Acts: 425b–426/17–18 (where a word has dropped out in the Latin); 426b–427/15–16; 430b–431/9–10; 444b–445/24–5.

Use of a space, adopted from John onwards, has the same function. The evidence is less extensive.

John: F135b–136/17–18; 155b–156/21–2; 158b–159/28–9; 181b–182/12–13.
Luke: 203b–204/23–4; 208b–209/21–2; 215b–216/11–12; 216b–217/22–3; 223b–224/14–15; 226b–227/10–11; 235b–236/2–3; 238b–239/24–5; 261b–262/3–4; 263b–264/5–6; 283b–284/27–8.
Mark: 289b–290/18–19; 319b–320/22–3; 335b–336/24–5; 339b–340/26–7.
Acts: 490b–491/28–9.

These statistics, collected in table 12, reflect the changing practice of the codex, as we noted it in chapter 2.

The majority of the remaining discrepancies in line endings between the columns consists in those where neither divides at a break in the sense.

On these grounds, I suggest that the argument for medial points and small spaces both representing a line division in the exemplar is well established.

In describing the punctuation (chapter 2) I suggested that the double point and large space serve the same function. By analogy with the use of a single point and small space to indicate a line ending, they may indicate a new paragraph or section.

These are marked also by lines projecting into the left-hand margin. Perhaps, although this must remain conjecture, all divisions represented in our codex by the projecting line, the double point, and the large space, were marked in the exemplar by the projecting line.

Not all the evidence fits this hypothesis. Three double points in Matthew are unlikely to represent a new paragraph (F14b/11; 84/26; 94/1). The same, with a lesser certainty, applies to 79b–80/28 and 95/23. The use of the symbol on Ff14b and 94 is particularly baffling. The absence of an enlarged initial letter (where it is one that the scribe regularly enlarges) at these places suggests that the double point has some other function here.

Reference to the table of punctuation symbols (table 5 in chapter 2, p. 33), shows that there is far less use of them in Acts. If the punctuation is the result of the scribe's alterations to the lay-out of his exemplar, then the conclusion must be that he has altered that of Acts very little. It has therefore come to him in a different form from that of the Gospels.

But the objection must be raised: if punctuation indicates a change from the sense-lines of the exemplar, and the sense-lines of Acts are not changed, then there should not be any punctuation in Acts at all. It would be over-confident to assert that the sense-lines of Acts are never altered by our scribe. They may occasionally have been – categorical assertions are not possible.

But a closer look at the punctuation of Acts suggests that he may have inherited the punctuation we find there. This is probably true of the high point, which is not used elsewhere. A great many of the other indications come after names of places, individuals, or groups. A number of others separate two very short phrases.

Punctuation after names: F417b–418, 419b–420, 424b–425, 425b, 427b–428, 434b, 435b–436, 436b, 438b–439, 440 (except for the third indication), 440b–441, 443b, 457, 465, 468 (two out of three), 473b–474, 489
Between two short phrases: 418b, 445b/16, 468/30, perhaps 476
Point at the beginning of a line: 493/32
Point at the end of a line: 477b/25, 27; 497b/26
Other punctuation: 437b–438/12; 441/24 (?); 500b/33; 501b/13

Along with the observation that the high point is found only in this book, this shows that in Acts the punctuation is used differently from the Gospels. Since we have put forward reasons to show that the punctuation in the Gospels is used by the scribe for his own purposes, the conclusion that the punctuation he used for Acts was that of his exemplar is hard to avoid. But we can go still further.

It seems to me in using the manuscript, although this remains an impression, that the pages early in Acts are on the whole more covered than those later on. It is certainly true that most of the punctuation is in the early part of the book. And this punctuation is almost always, as we have just seen, either between very short phrases, or after (rarely before) proper names. The appearance is of the briefest sense-lines being joined together. One-word lines still exist in Acts (e.g. F422b–423/16, 29; 444b/24), as elsewhere. I suggest that at an earlier stage in the transmission, the bilingual text of Acts also existed in very short lines. By the time that it reached D, the lines had become longer units. The occasional punctuation sign is a relic of this process.

Clark (*Acts*, p. 179) lists lines of one or two words. His figures are:

	Mt	Jn	Lk	Mk	Ac
One word	3	1	0	1	11
Two words	71	5	5	37	70

This supports the theory that the text of Acts was also once in very short lines. The other implications of this evidence will be explored in the final chapter of this part.

In adopting the use of similar symbols in changing the punctuation of the Gospels, the scribe of D follows the precedent and custom of the bilingual tradition.

There is no difference in Acts between the large and the small space. Thus, in the list of nationalities in 2.9–11 (F419b–420/7–15), the medial point and spaces of various sizes are all used. This variance in scribal practice underlines the fact that Acts has been transmitted differently from the Gospels, even if the sense-lines were once of a similar character.

The scribe did not always use a point or a space – in fact there are many pages where he more often did not, or used them in only one column. It is not possible to reconstruct every line of the exemplar, certainly not on the basis of punctuation alone.

Having given this evidence that the Gospel exemplar had different sense-lines from the extant codex, we can move on to material which substantiates it and gives us a more detailed picture of the scribe at work.

DIFFERENCES BETWEEN THE COLUMNS IN LINE DIVISION

Equivalence between the columns is the essential feature of sense-lines in a bilingual manuscript, and the scribe of D did his best to maintain it. Discrepancy is rare. To make what we are discussing quite clear, let us take the first example that occurs, at F8b–9/3–4. The Greek has

ΚΑΙ ΪΔΟΥ ΦѠΝΗ ΕΚ ΤѠΝ ΟΥΡΑΝѠΝ ΛΕΓΟΥCΑ
ΠΡΟC ΑΥΤΟΝ CΥ ΕΙ . . .

The Latin has

ET ECCE VOX DE CAELIS DICENS AD EUM
TU ES . . .

The line division occurs at a different place in the text in each column. The number of such discrepancies is –

Matthew	21
John	34
Luke	33
Mark	47
Acts	5
Total	140

This list includes neither divided words (e.g. CON / SERVO, F62/9–10), nor discrepancies caused by variant readings between the columns.

Occurrences are spread evenly throughout the codex, except for a gap of thirty-five folios in Acts (445b–490, *desunt* 447–454b), and there is no observable trend. It seems that in Mark less care was taken, but even here we are talking about only forty-seven out of something over 2,000 lines.

The categorizing of these discrepancies goes together with the exploration of how the scribe went about altering the sense-lines. In undertaking the latter, we need to be aware of an important underlying question: upon which column was he concentrating? There are two ways he could have gone to work. Either he did it as he went along, dividing up the Greek, and then casting his eye across to that column as he copied the Latin; or he marked the exemplar in advance. In the latter case, he could have marked either column first, and then marked the other to correspond. I have already suggested that the reason why so many Renaissance bilinguals were left incomplete was that the task of adjusting a Latin column to an already completely written Greek text was too difficult. It therefore seems to me that whichever of the two practices he adopted, the scribe of D worked by copying fairly short blocks of each text alternately.

In what follows, it will become clear that, although a codex written in sense-lines does not have a *fixed* length of line, it does have a *maximum* length of line (see p.10 above). Codex Bezae is ruled with inner and outer margins, the same two lines serving both the recto and the verso of each leaf. As we have seen, it has a β measurement of 144 by 185 mm. Although he occasionally writes a line longer than 144 mm, the scribe's intention is not to exceed it. When he does so, he sometimes writes the last letters below the line (e.g. 13b/33; 44b/33; 114/30), sometimes writes them smaller (e.g. 135b/16), sometimes uses abbreviations (horizontal stroke for final M or N, ligature N), and sometimes abandons equivalence and starts a new line.

Let us return to the example on F8b–9.

ΛΕΓΟΥCΑ ΠΡΟC ΑΥΤΟΝ and its Latin equivalent should all be on one line. The reason that they are divided in the Greek is that there was no space left on the line. This then is the first reason for a discrepancy.

Other places where this happens in Matthew are 32b–33/22–3; 50b–51/4–5; 75b–76/2–3; 90b–91/13–14. In each of them the Latin ends at a pause in the sense.

The second group is where the Latin runs out of space. There is only one such in Matthew – 30b–31/13–14.

In most of the remaining discrepancies in Matthew, the Latin runs on further than the Greek, failing to end the line in the same place. This provides the third group of discrepancies. For instance, at F28b–29/16–17 we have

ωCTE ΕΚΒΑΛΕΙΝ ΑΥΤΑ·ΚΑΙ ΘΕΡΑΠΕΥΕΙΝ
ΠΑCAN NOCON ·...

and

UT EICIANT EOS·ET CURARE OMNEM
LANGUOREM·...

This is likely to be caused by forgetfulness.

It comes also at F30b–31/23–4; 53b–54/23–4; 58b–59/6–7; 71b–72/24–5; 74b–75/2–3; 93b–94/4–5.

The fourth group consists of lines where the Latin has run on, and by so doing has preserved a sense-line that is broken up in the Greek. There are no examples of this in Matthew.

In the fifth group it is the Greek that runs on further than the Latin, breaking up the next sense-line of the exemplar. In Matthew this happens only at F61b–62/18–19.

The sixth group is of discrepancies in which each column seems to break up a sense-line, but does so differently (in Matthew, 29b–30/18–19; perhaps 39b–40/8–9; and 48b–49/25–6).

The seventh and final group is where a whole sense-line of the exemplar is written on a different line in each column. This is caused by various confusions, including an omission further up the page, undetected and leading to inequivalence between the columns and transposition. In Matthew the instances are found at 13b/25 = 14/24–5; 39b–40/7–8; 57b/16–17 = 58/16, followed by 57b/27–8 = 58/26–8.

Turning to the Gospel of John, we find that the evidence suggests the scribe was slightly more concerned with preserving the Latin sense-lines than the Greek.

Group 1: 116b–117/14–15; 121b–122/2–3; 125b–126/30–1; 128b–129/13–14; 132b–133/9–10, 11–12; 136b–137/9–10; 149b–150/31–2; 154b–155/28–9; 158b–159/27–8, 28–9; 181b–182/12–13
Group 2: 113b–114/30–1
Group 3: 119b–120/19–20; 120b–121/21–2; 135b–136/9–10; 141b–142/1–2, 20–1; 155b–156/21–2; 157b–158/25–6; 160b–161/7–8; 180b–181/24–5

Group 4: 128b–129/11–12; 132b–133/19–20; 135b–136/17–18; 143b–144/4–5; 159b–160/21–2; 160b–161/15–16
Group 5: 127b–128/20–1; 133b–134/30–1; 134b–135/9–10
Group 6: 122b–123/24–5
Group 7: ?117b–118/32–3?; 119b–120/20–1

In Matthew we saw that the Greek alone ended at a break in the sense nine times, and the Latin alone six times. In John, by contrast, there are eight instances of the former, and twenty-two of the latter.

The same tendency may be recognized in Luke. In this Gospel, the principle of writing in sense-lines is, as we have seen, gradually abandoned as its copying progresses. But the frequency of discrepancy in line endings between the columns has not increased proportionately. It appears that maintaining equivalence between the columns was more important than presenting the text in units of sense.

Group 1: 208b–209/21–2, 31–2; 223b–224/14–15; 241b–242/3–4; 252b–253/27–8; 263b–264/16–17; 273b–274/29–30; 283b–284/27–8. On F241b, the medial point after ΟΥΧΙ in l. 4 indicates that, in spite of the sense, this is how the exemplar ended a line. This may suggest that at least some of the sense-lines of Luke were already in some disarray – or at least, not uniformly perfect – in the exemplar.
Group 2: 193b–194/32–3; 221b–222/14–15; 234b–235/5–6
Group 3: 182b–183/18–19; 183b–184/15–16; 208b–209/32–3; 226b–227/10–11; 235b–236/2–3; 281b–282/22–3
Group 4: 238b–239/24–5; 239b–240/1–2; 280b–281/4–5; perhaps 215b–216/11–12 and 281b–282/14–15
Group 5: 203b–204/23–4; 257b–258/28–9; 261b–262/3–4; 263b–264/5–6
Group 6: 200b–201/30–1; 216b–217/22–3; 242b–243/4–5; 248b–249/26–7; 250b–251/7–8; 253b–254/24–5; 259b–260/14–15
Group 7: no examples

The greater number of discrepancies in Mark is accounted for by the large first group (the Greek running out of space). That the scribe was getting into the habit of filling up his lines is corroborated by, for instance, F305b. This is an unusually well covered verso, with no fewer than seven lines projecting into the inner margin.

Group 1: 285b–286/11–12; 289b–290/18–19; 297b–298/15–16, 23–4; 301b–302/3–4; 306b–307/14–15, 15–16; 310b–311/3–4; 313b/23–4=314/22–3; 319b–320/22–3; 321b–322/2–3, 3–4; 328b–329/16–17; 336b–337/27–8; 337b–338/1–2; 339b–340/26–7; 340b–341/15–16; 341b–342/11–12
Group 2: 327b–328/23–4; 344b–345/2–3

Group 3: 306b–307/8–9; 308b–309/4–5, 20–1; 310b–311/12–13; 314b–315/7–8; 316b–317/20–1; 324b–325/29–30; 325b–326/5–6; 327b–328/9–10; 335b–336/29–30; 338b–339/23–4; 344b–345/31–2; 345b–346/17–18
Group 4: 298b–299/31–2; 319b–320/6–7
Group 5: 325b–326/2–3; 335b–336/24–5
Group 6: 291b–292/18–19; 298b–299/4–5; 318b–319/14–15, 22–3; 325b–326/6–7; 339b–340/5–6; 341b–342/7–8
Group 7: 314b–315/13–14; 338b–339/24–5; and possibly 305b–306/12–13

The material from Acts may be quickly described. This is in itself significant.

Group 3: 430b–431/9–10; 444b–445/24–5
Group 5: 426b–427/15–16
Group 6: 425b–426/17–18. Here in fact the Latin has run on.
Uncertainty over the translation of ἂν may account for the discrepancy at 491b–492/28–9

The absence of any discrepancies caused by miscalculations of the space needed for a given line must be taken as further evidence that the scribe is simply reproducing the lines of his exemplar. The only five discrepancies he makes are all caused by carrying on too far on one line.

I have suggested elsewhere ('Dictation Theory') that the cause of a number of errors in the Latin text of Acts was the influence on the scribe of a similar group of letters in the context. Where these letters stand directly above or below each other in the codex, then we have further evidence that this is where they were in the exemplar. Examples I gave include F427/5–6 and 431/40–1.

There are two ways in which this imitation of the exemplar in Acts is significant. First, we find that in copying Acts the scribe had a simpler task. We may therefore expect, with one less distraction, fewer errors of a casual nature. Second, the Acts of the Apostles was handed down to the scribe of D in a physically different form from that in which he received the Gospels. It is thus the product of a different bilingual tradition. With its comparatively long lines, it is not like, to take the obvious example, the Laudian Acts, which is little more than a Glossary.

What we have been doing is to try to divine the mental processes by which the scribe produced the sense-lines that are before us. We may fill out the picture by adding a number of other suggestions, even referring again to examples which I have already listed.

The discrepancy at F122b–123/24–5 may, like that at 491b–492, be caused by uncertainty about the word ἂν.

There are a number of places where what I have described as the Latin line being carried on too far could be intended to reduce the length of the next line.

Some examples are F31/23–4; 59/6–7; 72/24–5; 120/19–20; 121/21–2; 142/1–2; 158/25–6; 184/15–16; 216/11–12; 227/10–11; 282/22–3; 307/8–9; 309/20–1; 317/20–1; 326/5–6; 339/23–4; 345/31–2; 431/9–10; 445/24–5.

The same may apply where the Greek runs on, at 61b/18–19; 133b/30–1; 261b/3–4; 426b/15–16, and where neither column ends with a sense-line at 250b–251/7–8; 253b–254/24–5; and 425b–426/17–18.

It is thus more common for the scribe to think ahead in transcribing the Latin column than for him to run out of space. Why he should prefer to cause a discrepancy by anticipation rather than by miscalculation is not at all apparent. It suggests that he was thinking about the sense-line equivalence, and occasionally correcting the planned sense-lines as he actually wrote them. It may be that he marked at least one column of his exemplar in advance. The fact that in the whole codex, the Latin line runs on fifty-one times, and the Greek only ten, encourages us to believe that only the Greek column was marked, so that the scribe had to look back at it to find the line ending as he copied the Latin; something which on occasion he forgot to do.

It is highly unlikely that the exemplar itself was without such discrepancies between the columns, and one should be aware of the possibility that a difficulty in D is caused by one. At F241b–242/3–4, the manuscript has

ΑΝΘΡΩΠΟΥϹΤΟΥϹΕΝΟΙΧΟΥΝΤΑϹΪΕΡΟΥϹΑΛΗΜ
ΟΥΧΙ·ΛΕΓΩΔΕΫΜΕΙΝΟΤΙΕΑΝΜΗΜΕΤΑΝΟΗϹΗΤΑΙ

and

HOMINESQUIINHABITANTHIERUSALEMNON
DICOAUTEMUOBIS QUODSINPENITUERITIS

Perhaps the negative was wrongly placed with the proper name in both columns of the exemplar. The scribe of D, running out of space after ΪΕΡΟΥϹΑΛΗΜ, wrote ΟΥΧΙ on the next line, duly setting a point after it.

It is worth concluding this section by repeating that these discrepancies are extremely infrequent. Both this fact, and the evidence we have been gathering, demonstrate the careful way in which the scribe of D altered the lay-out of his exemplar in the Gospels. But along with this care goes the curious breaking down of the sense-line system to which we have already referred.

REPETITIONS, TRANSPOSITIONS, AND OMISSIONS

We already have two means at our disposal for determining the line lengths of the exemplar of D. There is a third available, the examination of the text for errors due to a miscopying of these lines. Three types of error merit study, to discover whether or not they are illuminating.

Repetitions

There are five places in the manuscript where a word is repeated at the end of one line and the beginning of the next.

(a) 152b/21–2 (Jn 12.29)
ΑΛΛΟΙΕΛΕΓΟΝΟΤΙ
ΟΤΙΑΓΓΕΛΟCΑΥΤΩΛΕΛΑΛΗΚΕΝ

(b) 201/26–7 (Lk 4.42)
ABIITINDESERTUMLOCUMET
ETTURBAEQUAEREBANTEUMETBENERUNT

(c) 227b/8–9 (Lk 10.11f)
ΓΕΙΝΩCΚΕΤΕ ΟΤΙΗΓΓΙΚΕΝ Η
ΗΒΑCΙΛΕΙΑΤΟΥΘΥ ΛΕΓΩΔΕΫΜΕΙΝ

(d) 259b/33–260b/1 (Lk 18.43–19.1)
ΪΔΩΝΕΔΩΚΕΝΔΟΞΑΝΤΩΘΩ ΚΑΙ
ΚΑΙΕΙCΕΛΘΩΝΔΙΗΡΧΕΤΟΤΗΝΪΕΡΕΙΧΩ
=260/33–261/1
VIDENSDEDITGLORIAMDEO ET
ETINTRANS...

(e) 278b/2–3 (Lk 23.23f)
ΚΑΙΚΑΤΙCΧΥΟΝΑΙΦΩΝΑΙΑΥΤΩΝ ΚΑΙΤΩΝ
ΤΩΝΑΡΧΙΕΡΕΩΝ ΕΠΕΚΡΕΙΝΕΝΔΕ

Each repeated word is likely to have been the beginning of a line in the exemplar (and note especially the repetition at Ff259b–261, where both new columns take up the beginning of the line already begun).

Transpositions

Scrivener (p. xxiii) gives six instances of dislocation which he thinks indicate the sense-lines to be identical with those of the exemplar. Each time the scribe missed a line and then added it lower on the page, indicating the correct sequence with Greek numerals in the left margin. On three occasions he also made a partial correction. This helps us to see the stages of the error. Three are due to homoioteleuton, two to similar but more complicated circumstances.

F220/7–8, 17 (Lk 8.44f) is the most interesting example. I suggest that the exemplar was written

ACCEDENSTETIGIT
TUNICAMEIUS
ETCONFESTIMSTETIT
PROFLUVIUSSANGUINISEIUS
IHSAUTEMSCIENS

The scribe first copied this as

ACCEDENSTETIGITPROFLUVIUMSANGUINIS
EIUSIHSAUTEMSCIENSQUAEEXIVIT

His eye jumped from the letters *STETIGIT* to *STETIT*, omitting two lines of the exemplar. He even altered the ending of *PROFLUVIUS* to make it the object. He then saw that this was wrong, and expunged PROFLUVIUMSANGUINIS, substituting the sense-line *TUNICAMEIUS*, and then went on. After a few lines, he noticed that the Latin was a line ahead of the Greek, and realized that he had missed out a line. The ink was now dry, so he had recourse to the expedient of placing numerals in the margin.

At 209/22–3, 28–9 (Lk 6.37) spaces in the columns suggest that the exemplar stood as

NOLITEIUDICARE
UTNONIUDICEMINI
NOLITECONDEMNARE
UTNONCONDEMNEMINI
DIMITTEETDEMITTEMINI
DATEETDABITURVOBIS
MENSURAM...

The scribe's eye jumped from *IUDICEMINI* to *DEMITTEMINI*.

The error on F233/19–20, 23 (Lk 11.26) is not explicable as a visual error. It seems to be more of a mental leap. The omitted words form a line in both exemplar and copy.

At 264/24–5, 27 (Lk 19.47) the scribe first wrote

POPULIQUAEREBANTQUIDFACERENTEI

and then replaced the last three words with EUMPERDEREEUM. That is, his eye jumped from *QUAEREBANT* to *INVENIEBANT*. According to Scrivener, the one word would have been more or less directly under the other. If the exemplar ran

ETPRIMIPOPULI
QUAEREBANTEUM
PERDEREEUM
ETNONINVENIEBANT
QUIDFACERENTEI

then the mistake might be somewhat harder to make.

At 276/30–2 (Lk 22.68) the exemplar had, according to Scrivener, two lines ending in *-ERONON*, and the scribe omitted the second. Spaces in the two columns indicate sense-lines in the exemplar something like

ADILLEDIXITILLIS
SIVOBISDIXERO
NONCREDETIS
SIINTERROGAVERO

NONRESPONDETISMIHI
AUTDIMITTETIS
AMODOAUTEM . . .

The omission would then be either by homoioteleuton (*NON*[1] . . . *INTERROGAVERO*) or by homoiarcton (*CREDETIS* . . . *NON*[2]).

Finally, the dislocation at 504/18–19 and ? (Ac 21.6) is harder to assess, since the transposed line is no longer extant. But it seems clear that again it was parablepsis that was to blame, the two lines ending in *INVICEM* and *INNAVEM*. The scribe first wrote

ETCUMSALUTASSEMUSINNAUEM
REUERSIUEROQUISQUEADSUA

INNAUEM was expunged and replaced with INUICEM, and the Greek numerals Α and Γ put in the left margin. Since I am arguing that the sense-lines of Acts are the same as those of the exemplar, there is no difference between my understanding of the error here and Scrivener's.

Only one example is easier to explain according to Scrivener's theory (F264). It is of course in the nature of parablepsis that a group of similar letters anywhere in sight can catch the eye, so that there is no wholly unambiguous evidence for any theory here, except that the example on F220 shows the scribe getting into difficulties as he alters the sense-lines.

Although these are by no means all the examples of transposition in the codex, they are all the ones shown by numerals in the margin. Others may be the result of different influences on the text. Two readings which appear relevant at first sight (Mk 2.26; 10.25) are more likely to be harmonizations (Clark, *Primitive Text*, p. 54; for Mk 2.26, see Vogels, *Harmonistik*, p. 73). The reversal of the second and third beatitudes (Mt 5.4f) is also unlikely to be due to mechanical error. The text of Mt 17.12–13 involves the transposition of what may have been a sense-line in the exemplar – the Greek column has a point after ΑΝΘΡΩΠΟΥ (F56b/13). But, attested by the Latin column and other Old Latin manuscripts (a b c e ff[1] ff[2] g[1] r[1] – some admittedly later than D), the reading is more likely to have come down to D through the tradition.

Omissions

We turn to passages where there is omission in only one column. The evidence of the other may indicate more clearly what the exemplar was like, and whether the omission was of a single line of it. In fact, most such omissions in D are of only single words, and just four examples are helpful.

At F250b/29–30 (Lk 16.7), the Greek omits the equivalent of

TUAUTEMQUANTUM
DEBES ADILLEDIXIT

Short sense-lines in the exemplar would be

ΕΠΕΙΤΑΤΩΕΤΕΡΩΕΙΠΕΝ
ΣΥΔΕΠΟΣΟΝΟΦΕΙΛΕΙΣ
ΟΔΕΕΙΠΕΝ
ΕΚΑΤΟΝΚΟΡΟΥΣΣΙΤΟΥ

The scribe's eye went back to the wrong ειπεν.

At F275b/19 (Lk 22.61) ΜΗΕΙΔΕΝΑΙΜΕ in D is a harmonization to v. 34. The Latin omits this. It could be a place where the two columns represent different texts, but if the Latin had omitted by *saut du même au même*, then the words could have constituted a sense-line in the exemplar. Note the long space after them in the Greek.

A good case can also be made from 311b/24 (Mk 8.11): d omits the equivalent of CYNZHTEINCYNAYTω. Points in the text suggest that the exemplar had

ETCOEPERUNT
CONQUIRERECUMILLO
QUAERENTESABILLO

Finally, in 313b/20 (Mk 8.31) a rendering of ΚΑΙΑΠΟΚΤΑΝΘΗΝΑΙ is omitted in the Latin. The Greek line is here identical to that of the exemplar. The scribe was confused by the succession of lines beginning with *et*.

More instructive than some of the preceding readings are the four occasions where the scribe later added in a smaller hand material which he had at first omitted.

At F51b–52/27 he added the line

ΜΗΠΟΤΕΕΚΛΥΘωCINENΤΗΟΔω

and its equivalent. Did the ending of the previous line, θελω, confuse him? This is likely to have been a line of the exemplar.

On the very next bifolium (52b–53/4–5) there is a longer insertion, to the end of one line and below it. It runs

·Ζ̅·CΦΥΡΙΔΑCΠΛΗΡΕΙC
ΟΙΔΕΑΙCΘΙΟΝΤΕCΗCΑΝ·ΤΕΤΡΑΚΙCΧΙΛΙΟΙΑΝΔΡΕC

The Latin corresponds, with a medial point after ERANT. The first line, along with what was written already, cannot have been a single line in the exemplar, since the total number of letters is forty-seven in the Greek and fifty-one in the Latin. These are so far above the average as to be too long for the page, whatever the lay-out. I suggest therefore that the insertion represents three lines of the exemplar.

At 262b–263/16, there is a single added line in each column. The Greek runs:

ΕΦΟΝΟΥΔΕΙCΑΝΘΡωΠωΝΕΚΑΘΙCΕΝ·ΚΑΙΛΥCΑΝΤΕCΑΓΑΓΕΤΕ

The Latin corresponds, even to the medial point. Here, two lines seem to have been omitted. With forty-four lines in the Greek, it fits on one line only because it is written so small. Thus, again, the exemplar cannot have had the same format as the copy, for there would not have been enough room for so long a line.

The restoration at F314b–315/1–2 again uses the medial point:

·OCΔAN
AΠOΛECEIAYTHN

Again the Latin is identical. The use of other points in the passage enables us to reconstruct the lines of the exemplar as

ΟΣΓΑΡΑΝΘΕΛΗ
ΤΗΝΨΥΧΗΝ(Ε)ΑΥΤΟΥΣΩΣΑΙ
ΑΠΟΛΕΣΕΙΑΥΤΗΝ
ΟΣΔΑΝΑΠΟΛΕΣΕΙΑΥΤΗΝ
ΕΝΕΚΕΝΤΟΥΕΥΑΓΓΕΛΙΟΥ
ΣΩΣΕΙΑΥΤΗΝ

Three omissions corrected by G complete the survey.

At 14/16 he adds *facit eam moechari*, the equivalent to the Greek line ΠOIEI AYTHN MOIXEYΘHNAI. The scribe had omitted a sense-line of the Latin.

At 37/17 he supplies the words *harundinem quassatam*, omitted in both columns. Significantly, he places them to the right of the previous words, separated from them with a medial point.

His largest correction, at the foot of Ff59b–60, supplies the missing passage as

εσταιδεδεμμεναεντοισουρανοισ
καιοσααλυσητεεπιτησγησεσται (the second *εσται* erased)

and

eruntligataincaelis
etquaecumquesolueritisinterramerunt (the second *erunt* erased)

I shall argue (in Part III) that Corrector G had access to the exemplar of D. His line division here may reflect that of the older manuscript. His use of the point in the first example shows him imitating the method of the first hand.

THE RECONSTRUCTION OF THE LINES OF THE EXEMPLAR

The length of sense-lines that these investigations have found in the exemplar is typically short, consisting of perhaps two or three words. F79 of the codex preserves examples of this. But longer lines also existed – the passage at F59b–60 which we have just studied suggests that at least on occasion the lines could represent the *parallelismus membrorum* of the text's poetic diction.

It remains to try to reconstruct a longer passage of the exemplar. By studying bifolia that contain many of the indications we have collected, it is possible to do this. For Matthew I take F64b–65/17–27. Using the evidence of both columns, I suggest that the Greek column of the exemplar was laid out as follows.

ΟΜΟΙΑΓΑΡΕΣΤΙΝ
ΗΒΑΣΙΛΕΙΑΤΩΝΟΥΡΑΝΩΝ
ΑΝΘΡΩΠΩΟΙΚΟΔΕΣΠΟΤΗ
ΟΣΤΙΣΕΞΗΛΘΕΝ
ΑΜΑΠΡΩΪ
ΜΕΙΣΘΩΣΑΣΘΑΙΕΡΓΑΤΑΣ
ΕΙΣΤΟΝΑΜΠΕΛΩΝΑΑΥΤΟΥ
ΣΥΜΦΩΝΗΣΑΣΔΕ
ΜΕΤΑΤΩΝΕΡΓΑΤΩΝ
ΕΚΔΗΝΑΡΙΟΥΤΗΝΗΜΕΡΑΝ
ΑΠΕΣΤΕΙΛΕΝΑΥΤΟΥΣ
ΕΙΣΤΟΝΑΜΠΕΛΩΝΑΑΥΤΟΥ
ΚΑΙΔΙΕΞΕΛΘΩΝ
ΠΕΡΙΩΡΑΝΤΡΙΤΗΝ
ΕΥΡΕΝΑΛΛΟΥΣΕΣΤΩΤΑΣ
ΕΝΤΗΑΓΟΡΑΑΡΓΟΥΣ
ΚΑΚΕΙΝΟΙΣΕΙΠΕΝ
ΫΠΑΓΕΤΑΙ(-ΕΤΕ?)ΚΑΙΫΜΕΙΣ
ΕΙΣΤΟΝΑΜΠΕΛΩΝΑ
ΚΑΙΟΑΝΗΔΙΚΑΙΟΝ
ΔΩΣΩΫΜΕΙΝ
ΟΙΔΕΑΠΗΛΘΟΝ

Twenty-two lines of the exemplar have been compressed into eleven by the copyist.

Reconstruction of a passage in John, which has less punctuation, is not so easy. In Luke the observation of spaces between words is more hazardous than noting medial points. But I suggest that behind F212b–213/9–25 is an ordering in the exemplar that goes like this.

ΑΠΕΛΘΟΝΤΩΝΔΕ
ΤΩΝΑΓΓΕΛΩΝΪΩΑΝΟΥ
ΗΡΞΑΤΟΛΕΓΕΙΝΠΕΡΙΪΩΑΝΟΥΤΟΙΣΟΧΛΟΙΣ (two lines?)
ΤΙΕΞΗΛΘΑΤΕ
ΕΙΣΤΗΝΕΡΗΜΟΝΘΕΑΣΑΣΘΑΙ
ΚΑΛΑΜΟΝ
ΫΠΟΑΝΕΜΟΥΣΑΛΕΥΟΜΕΝΟΝ
ΑΛΛΑΤΙΕΞΗΛΘΑΤΕΕΙΔΕΙΝ
ΑΝΘΡΩΠΟΝΕΝΜΑΛΑΚΟΙΣΪΜΑΤΙΟΙΣΗΜΦΙΕΣΜΕΝΟΝ (two lines?)
ΪΔΟΥΟΙΕΝΙΜΑΤΙΣΜΩΕΝΔΟΞΩ

ΚΑΙΤΡΥΦΗΔΙΑΓΟΝΤΕΣ
ΕΝΤΟΙΣΒΑΣΙΛΕΙΟΙΣΕΙΣΙΝ
ΑΛΛΑΤΙΕΞΗΛΘΑΤΕ
ΕΙΔΕΙΝΠΡΟΦΗΤΗΝ
ΝΑΙΛΕΓΩΫΜΙΝ
ΚΑΙΠΕΡΙΣΣΟΤΕΡΟΝΠΡΟΦΗΤΟΥ
ΟΤΙΟΥΔΕΙΣΜΕΙΖΩΝ
ΕΝΓΕΝΝΗΤΟΙΣΓΥΝΑΙΚΩΝ
ΠΡΟΦΗΤΗΣ
ΪΩΑΝΟΥΤΟΥΒΑΠΤΙΣΤΟΥ
ΟΥΤΟΣΕΣΤΙΝ
ΠΕΡΙΟΥΓΕΓΡΑΠΤΑΙ
ΪΔΟΥΑΠΟΣΤΕΛΛΩ
ΤΟΝΑΓΓΕΛΟΝΜΟΥ
ΠΡΟΠΡΟΣΩΠΟΥ
ΟΣΚΑΤΑΣΚΕΥΑΣΕΙ
ΤΗΝΟΔΟΝΣΟΥ

Twenty-seven lines have become seventeen.

THE SUPPLEMENTARY LEAVES

The method used by the ninth-century restorers provides a vivid commentary on our discussions of the sense-lines. Clearly, the fact that the columns were not both written by the same scribe makes precise comparison impossible. However, the goal and the means to it are very similar to those of the first hand.

F7* matches the lines of F6b exactly. F7b* is written in far longer lines, with the result that after eighteen such, the restorer has to finish the page with thirteen short ones so as not to leave a blank space. This method is like that of ℓ311, which we mentioned above (p. 73). F169* follows the lines of 168b, except that ΙΗΜ goes into l.16 instead of 15.F175b* is only partly matched to F177: ll.1–8 are equivalent, and so are 20–5. The others are a phrase apart, each with two phrases to a line.

The main addition, where both columns are provided (Ff169b*–175*), is also intended to match the original. The first two double pages have thirty-three lines on them (by error only thirty-two in 171*), and the others have between thirty and thirty-three (see chapter 3, p. 46, for details). The last sixteen lines of 174b* are very short, the last two consisting in the word *σκο* / *τιας*. This was again because the restorer did not want to leave blank parchment. The written area of the leaves has a height of about 5 mm less than that of D*. The horizontal measurement (of which the lines are clearly to be seen on F171b* in the facsimile) is 14 cm (14.5 including the space for projecting initial letters). This also is about 5 mm less than that of the original hand.

The use of initial letters projecting into the left margin (used only in the Greek, except for 348b*/col. 2) also imitates D*.

The format of the addition at the end of Mark is quite different. F348*, certainly, matches 347b line for line. But in 349* a format of two columns to the page is adopted, with the Greek on the left and the lines equivalent. This format was adopted so as to get the end of Mark onto a single leaf. There is a parallel with the change in the first hand at Ff196b–197, from which the restorer may have taken the idea.

Within the addition Ff169b*–175*, the sense-lines generally match. The exceptions parallel what we have seen in examining the original text. F169b*/28 is two lines in the Latin. The copyist never noticed that he was a line out, and the Latin simply omits the equivalent of l.33 in the Greek (his omission was corrected by another hand). The Latin parallel to F170b*/18–19 is one line. As a consequence, F171* has only thirty-two lines.

F171b*/8–9 *αυτου / τη κεφαλη* = 172*/9 *capiti eius.*

In F172*, l.17 = 173*/17–18, and 25–6 = 26, where the copyist noticed that he was a line out.

Some eccentricities in line division are also parallel to the original scribe's. At F170b*/26–7 he wrote *τοις / ιυδαις* (*sic*), at 172b*/10–11 *οι αρχϊε / ρεις*, and at 348b*, col. 1/7–8 *λαλη / σωσιν*.

Μετα δε ταυτα was originally written at the end of F173b*, then erased, so that it comes only in its proper place at the beginning of F174b*. The error (carrying on too far on one line) parallels some of those we saw in the first hand. F174b*/30–2 to 175b*/1 has *πρωι σκοτιας / ετι ουσης*, while the Latin equivalent is all on F175*, reduplicating *essent* on F177/1.

The content of the sense-lines is not obvious. One would expect to find the copyist dividing the text *per cola et commata* according to Latin tradition. But he does not do this. The *cola et commata* are, approximately, marked by medial points in the Latin text though, if this is what they are, he knew a system with shorter lines than the standard we know from Wordsworth and White and the Stuttgart edition. *If* they indicate the *cola et commata*, then the medial points have a similar function to that in the rest of the codex – to indicate a different division from the one adopted. At any rate, the division is not into the standard lines of the Latin Bible. It seems most likely that one of the scribes acquainted himself with the practice of the first hand, and divided the text in a way that he felt to be consonant with this. It is likely that it was the scribe of the Greek column who did this.

These leaves show us a scribe handling the problems of a bilingual text, and both accepting and adopting the form handed down to him. Because we can see both the form and the product where the supplementary leaf parallels the first hand, the conclusions we drew about the first hand can be substantiated by the comparison.

THE FORMAT OF THE EXEMPLAR

One important question remains: with such short sense-lines, can the exemplar have been similar to D in having one column to the page? For this to be the case, its α measurement will have to have been much smaller. The alternative is that the lay-out of the columns was different. Since the α measurement of New Testament codices of the period is fairly constant, it seems more probable that it had two columns on the page, and a β measurement similar to that of the Laudian Acts. Codex Bezae itself preserves such an arrangement on Ff196b–197, where the Lukan genealogy of Jesus is presented with two columns to the page, the Greek on the left and the Latin on the right. The β measurement and number of lines are the same as in the rest of the manuscript, but the position of the columns is likely to reproduce that of the exemplar.

CONCLUSIONS

The reconstruction of the exemplar of Codex Bezae we have reached is of a codex with, for the Gospels, two columns to the page, Greek on the left and Latin on the right. It was written in short sense-lines. In Acts it had one column on each page, and longer lines. Paragraphs were begun with a line projecting into the left margin. The greater part of John, and all of Luke, had a further characteristic which cannot yet be determined.

The evidence which we gathered in chapter 4 sheds light on this development in the textual tradition of Codex Bezae. We saw how Graeco-Latin bilinguals, especially of Virgil, were written with the hexameters divided into short phrases, each on a line with the Greek equivalent beside it. In biblical manuscripts, this lay-out is paralleled by the Laudian Acts. This primitive form of bilingual text is the source of format for the Gospel exemplar of Codex Bezae, and no doubt also for that of its predecessors as far back as the formation of the bilingual tradition.

In copying Acts, the scribe of Codex Bezae followed the lines of the exemplar. In copying the Gospels he altered them. The lines of the exemplar are sometimes indicated by punctuation. The places where the line endings in the columns are not the same indicate a slightly greater concern with the Latin text than with the Greek. Along with this, the creation of longer lines is an important stage in the emancipation of the Latin version from the Greek text. It no longer exists as little more than an aid to understanding the Greek, or as a translation to be read after it. It is becoming authoritative in its own right.

Any consideration of textual variants in D needs to take into consideration the lay-out of the exemplar. It may be possible to recognize certain readings or types of readings as errors peculiar to such a type of manuscript. One is able also to find readings in D which are the result of the scribe's alterations to the lay-out handed down to him.

The text of Acts also once existed in very short sense-lines but, from its state in the exemplar, we have evidence that the Bezan text is an amalgam of disparate elements. The evidence separates Acts from the Gospels, and Matthew and Mark from John and Luke.

In the division of sense-lines, as in other matters, the scribe of D was far more careful than has sometimes been supposed. We are not dealing with an eccentric, but with a scribe handling a particularly specialized scribal tradition.

The most important point, one that is foundational to all further study, is that we are demonstrably dealing with a tradition and not with a single aberrant manuscript. It is not permissible to regard the text of D as coterminous with the Codex Bezae, nor to confuse the functions of redactor and copyist.

CHAPTER SIX

The nomina sacra

Clark, *Acts*, pp. 205f; Lowe, 'A Note', esp. *Pal. Papers* 1,226f; Metzger, *Manuscripts*, pp. 36f (with extensive bibliography); A. H. R. E. Paap, *Nomina Sacra in the Greek Papyri of the First Five Centuries AD. The Sources and Some Deductions*, Leiden, 1959; C. H. Roberts, *Manuscript, Society and Belief in Early Christian Egypt*, Oxford, 1979; L. Traube, *Nomina Sacra: Versuch einer Geschichte der christlichen Kürzung*, Munich, 1907; C. H. Turner, 'The *Nomina Sacra* in Early Christian Latin Mss', *Miscellanea Francesco Ehrle*, Vol. 4, Rome, 1924, pp. 62–74.

Detailed studies of the *nomina sacra* are ready to hand, and the scope of this chapter need be no more extensive than to describe the practices found in Codex Bezae and to evaluate their significance for this particular manuscript tradition. Although a few words will be devoted to their wider implications, the reader will easily be able to set them within the context of the conclusions of Traube, Paap, and others.

It has seemed worthwhile to check through every occurrence of the words which are candidates to be *nomina sacra*. This has revealed the care taken by the scribe in his copying. In wider terms of the explanations of readings often made from alleged misrecognition of *nomina sacra* as something else, note that occasionally the line above the letters is omitted (half a dozen times in the Greek and a couple in the Latin) and that none of the transcriptional errors we find could mislead a subsequent copyist (Mk 1.27 ΠΝΕΥΝΑ; 5.8 Ο ΙΗΥ (*ο ιηυς* Corrector A); Ac 5.9 ΠΝ; in the Latin, at Mt 17.19 and Lk 3.21 the scribe wrote IHS before correcting himself to IHU).

THE GREEK FORMS

There are eight words treated in the Greek text as *nomina sacra*: *θεος*, *'Ιησους*, *κυριος*, *πατηρ*, *πνευμα*, *σταυρος*, *σταυροω*, and *χριστος*. The reading ΛΟΝ for *λογον* at Ac 13.5 (F466b/7) is, in my opinion, the accidental omission of a syllable.

θεος

The usual form ($\overline{θς}$, $\overline{θν}$, $\overline{θυ}$, $\overline{θω}$) appears in every instance of the word in the singular, without exception. The plural is always in full.

There is a considerable confusion in the text of Acts between ΘΕΟC and ΚΥΡΙΟC.

Ἰησους

ΙΗC, ΙΗΥ, ΙΗΝ is the totally regular usage. ΪΗCΟΥΝ is written at Ac 7.45, where the reference is to Joshua son of Nun.

Κυριος

The abbreviation is uniformly the contraction ΚC, ΚΕ, and so on. There is no attempt to confine its use to the Divine Name and those places where Jesus is so addressed. We thus find, for example, that the various *κυριοι* of the Matthaean parables are honoured with the *nomen sacrum*. The word is written in full only at Mt 13.27; Lk 16.5, 13 (these are in the singular: there is no abbreviation available for the plural).

Πατηρ

This word is generally written in full. But the abbreviation is also used, at the following places:

ΠΑΡ: Jn 12.26; 14.28; 15.1
ΠΡΑ: Jn 5.45; 14.28, 31; 16.3; 20.17 (*bis*)
ΠΡC: Mt 11.27; 13.43; 18.10; 26.29; Jn 4.12; 5.43; 15.26; Lk 2.49; 9.26
ΠΡΟC: Jn 6.65
ΠΡΙ: Jn 4.21

The vocative is always written in full. ΠΑΡ, ΠΡΑ, ΠΡΟC, and ΠΡΙ appear only in John, and ΠΡC is found in the first three Gospels. Even in John, the word is written *plene* on the vast majority of occasions.

	Mt	Jn	Lk	Mk	Ac
Full form	51	113	46	18	9
Contracted	4	14	2	—	—
Plural forms	2	5	7	—	22

Πνευμα

We find the forms ΠΝΑ, ΠΝC, and ΠΝΙ. On three occasions (Mk 5.13; Ac 19.12, 13) ΠΝΑ represents the plural *πνευματα* (nominative and accusative).

ΠΝΕΥΜΑΤΑ in full appears at Mt 12.45; Lk 11.26; Ac 8.7. The genitive and dative plurals are always written in full.

When we look in detail at the singular forms and their occurrence, it is clear that there is no consistent practice. Both the contraction and the full form are used, regardless of whether the Spirit of God is meant or not. One can discover why this is so by looking at each book separately.

Matthew at least is consistent. On no occasion is any singular case of *πνευμα* written in full. This includes the four places where the reference is not to the Spirit of God.

In John our scribe writes ΠΝΕΥΜΑ in full twice. At both 4.24 and 20.22 the reference is to God. He also writes ΠΝΕΥΜΑΤΙ at 11.33, where Jesus is described as being troubled in his spirit. On the remaining twelve occasions, the word is contracted. This includes 13.21, where the reference is again to Jesus' spirit.

In Luke we find the word written *plene* fifteen times, and contracted thirteen. There are some signs that the division reflects the use of the word by the evangelist.

	Divine	Other
Full form	7	8
Contracted	9	4

There is thus a very slight attempt in Luke to preserve a distinction between the divine and the ordinary reference. But since the full form is commoner, even though the word is more often than not used of the divine, it seems that the scribal practice reflected is moving either from or towards the absence of the contracted form. In view of the position in the other books, it may be shown that the movement is *towards* the contracted form. That is, the full form had once been the rule in Luke, but is now being supplanted by the abbreviation – usage is becoming uniform throughout the manuscript.

Mark is quite different. Although the reference is to the Spirit of God on only six occurrences, it is abbreviated every time but once (ΠΝΕΥΝΑ [*sic*], 1.27).

We find the same in Acts. Used sixty-five times in the singular, it is written in full only at 6.5, where the Holy Spirit is meant.

We thus find that Matthew, Mark, and Acts, share the same practice. Luke is ranged against them in its preference for the full form, whilst the position of John is uncertain. Table 13 summarizes these findings.

Σταυρος

Σταυρος is written in full on each of its five occurrences in Matthew and two in Luke. In Mark it is once written in full (15.21) and three times contracted – ϹΤΡΝ (8.34) and ϹΤΡΥ (15.30, 32).

Table 13. *Forms of Πνευμα*

	Contracted			Full form		
	Divine	Other	Plural	Divine	Other	Plural
Mt	10	4	—	—	—	2
Jn	11	1	—	2	1	—
Lk	9	4	—	7	8	5
Mk	6	14	1	—	1	1
Ac	62	2	2	1	—	2
Total	98	25	3	10	10	10

Σταυροω

The same pattern is found with the verbal form. In Matthew, Luke, Acts, and three times in Mark (15.20, 24, 27), it is written in full. On its other three appearances in Mark, it is contracted –

15.13 $\overline{\text{CTPN}}$ for *σταυρωσον*
15.14 $\overline{\text{CTN}}$ for *σταυρωσον*
15.15 $\overline{\text{CTH}}$ for *σταυρωθη*

Χριστος

The use of the abbreviations is unbroken. The forms that appear are $\overline{\text{XPC}}$, $\overline{\text{XPE}}$ (Mt 26.68), $\overline{\text{XPN}}$, and $\overline{\text{XPY}}$.

THE LATIN FORMS

The Latin text has as *nomina sacra*: *Christus, Deus, Dominus, Iesus, Pseudochristus*, and *Spiritus*.

Christus

The form is uniformly $\overline{\text{XR}}$–. We have $\overline{\text{XRS}}$, $\overline{\text{XRM}}$ (none in Mark), $\overline{\text{XRI}}$ (none in John or Luke), and $\overline{\text{XRO}}$ (none in John, Luke, or Mark).

Deus

The usage here is more complicated. The forms of contraction are $\overline{\text{DS}}$, $\overline{\text{DM}}$, $\overline{\text{DI}}$, and $\overline{\text{DO}}$. But, except for the nominative, the word also has a line above it when it is

Table 14. *Forms of* Deus

	Mt	Jn	Lk	Mk	3 Jn	Ac	Total
Nom.: $\overline{\mathrm{DS}}$	10	14	16	14	—	59	113
DEUS	1	2	—	—	—	—	3
Acc.: $\overline{\mathrm{DM}}$	9	9	26	4	1	17	66
$\overline{\mathrm{DEUM}}$	—	2	—	—	—	—	2
$\overline{\mathrm{DUM}}$	—	—	—	—	—	3	3
Gen.: $\overline{\mathrm{DI}}$	7	—	—	16	—	37	60
$\overline{\mathrm{DEI}}$	19	23	66	14	—	—	122
DEI	2	—	—	—	—	—	2
Dat./Abl.: $\overline{\mathrm{DO}}$	1	—	1	1	—	20	23
$\overline{\mathrm{DEO}}$	1	14	8	—	—	2	25

written in full. The pattern is worth showing in full – see table 14. (The figures given by Clark, *Acts*, are not always identical to mine; the differences are slight.)

There are no contractions available for the plural forms.

In Matthew the preferred forms are $\overline{\mathrm{DS}}$, $\overline{\mathrm{DM}}$, $\overline{\mathrm{DEI}}$.
In John and Luke they are $\overline{\mathrm{DS}}$, $\overline{\mathrm{DM}}$, $\overline{\mathrm{DEI}}$, $\overline{\mathrm{DEO}}$.
In Mark and Acts they are $\overline{\mathrm{DS}}$, $\overline{\mathrm{DM}}$, $\overline{\mathrm{DI}}$, $\overline{\mathrm{DO}}$.

In fact, $\overline{\mathrm{DEI}}$ for the genitive is preferred in Mark up to 9.1 (thirteen times out of seventeen), but $\overline{\mathrm{DI}}$ from 9.47 onwards (with the exception of 12.17, where the combination with $\overline{\mathrm{DO}}$ as the very next word suggests that the full form may have been used to avoid confusion).

The conclusion to be drawn is that, in Matthew, John, Luke, and the first half of Mark, the preferred forms are the contractions for the direct cases, the full form with *linea superscripta* for the oblique; while from Mk 9.47 to the end (presumably) of the codex, the contraction is used for all the cases.

There are two possible explanations for this, both of which shed light on the earlier history of the text. The first is that the activity of two separate scribes is indicated, one copying the first half of a predecessor of D, the other the second. The second explanation is that an incomplete revision, which finished in the middle of Mark, has taken place. A combination of the two explanations is also possible.

There is further evidence pointing to revision: traces of a preference for $\overline{\mathrm{DI}}$ remain in Matthew, which would then have been in line with Mark and Acts.

The appearance of $\overline{\mathrm{DUM}}$ in Acts is also a vestige of an earlier practice.

Dominus

The variety here is even more intriguing (table 15). The reading $\overline{\mathrm{DUM}}$ in Acts is an error for $\overline{\mathrm{DNM}}$, and I have included it under that in the summary table. For the

Table 15. *Forms of* Dominus

	Mt	Jn	Lk	Mk	Ac	Total
(a) Detail						
Nom.: DMS	18	7	27	9	—	61
DNS	2	—	—	—	20	22
Voc.: DME	17	35	28	3	—	83
DNE	5	—	—	—	10	15
DOME	—	—	1	—	—	1
Acc.: DMN	4	—	—	2	—	6
DOM	—	8	11	—	—	19
DNM	2	—	1	—	16	19
DUM	—	—	—	—	1	1
Gen.: DMI	8	2	24	3	1	38
DNI	1	—	—	—	39	40
Dat./Abl.: DMO	5	2	9	4	—	20
DNO	1	—	—	—	12	13
(b) Summary						
DMS form	52	46	88	21	1	208
DNS form	11	—	1	—	98	110
DOM form	—	8	12	—	—	20
In full	5	—	2	—	4	11

form DOME, compare the Brescian fragment of Cyprian, which has *domo* once. The full form occurs only where the word has a secular reference, representing an attempt, or the vestiges of one, to confine the abbreviation to its proper use. It is wholly successful only in Acts.

With the exception of the suspension DOM used in John and Luke, the forms are those of contraction. Of the contractions, DMS is the older form. It was supplanted by the form in *n* during the period from which Codex Bezae comes.

The forms favoured in Matthew and Mark are DMS, DME, DMN, DMI, and DMO.

In John and Luke they are the same, except that DOM is preferred to DMN.

In Acts they are DNS, DNE, DNM, DNI, and DNO.

This would be easier to understand were the Gospels in the order we take as normal.

Acts can be seen to be from a different tradition, in which the new form in *n* has totally supplanted the older form.

There are signs of the newer form having begun to take over in Matthew.

Iesus

The forms are uniformly IHS, IHM, IHU, with the exception that the accusative IHN, imitative of the Greek, occurs at three places (Jn 12.9; Lk 5.12; Ac 2.32). In

Table 16. *Forms of* Spiritus

	Mt	Jn	Lk	Mk	Ac	Total
(a) Detail						
Nom.: full	—	1	4	—	1	6
SPS	5	6	7	7	20	45
Voc.: full	—	—	—	1	—	1
SPE	—	—	—	2	—	2
Acc.: full	1	—	—	—	2	3
SPM	3	3	3	5	20	34
Dat./Abl.: SPIRITU	1	1	6	—	1	9
SPIRITO	—	—	2	—	—	2
SPIRITUI	—	—	2	1	—	3
SPU	6	4	2	5	6	23
SPO	1	—	1	1	14	17
(b) Summary						
Full	2	2	14	2	4	24
Contracted	15	13	13	20	60	121
Dat.-Abl. *u*	7	5	8	5	7	32
Dat.-Abl. *o*	1	—	3	1	14	19

view of the rare and haphazard nature of this, it may be presumed to be inadvertent.

As in the Greek, the word is written in full at Ac 7.45.

Pseudochristus

The form PSEUDOXRI is used at Mt 24.24, the only occurrence of this word in the manuscript. The Greek text has ΨΕΥΔΟΧΡΕΙϹΤΟΙ in full.

Spiritus

In the usage here too there is a certain lack of uniformity. There are four contractions used – SPS, SPE, SPU, and SPO (table 16).

It will be seen that Acts, in contrast to the Gospels, prefers the dative and ablative in *o*.

With regard to the use of contraction, it will also be seen that it is clearly preferred in every book but Luke, where the full and contracted forms are found with equal frequency. It is impossible that an incomplete revision can have led to this, since the forms also occur equally often in the first four chapters, where sixteen of Luke's uses of the word are to be found. Rather, we see here a book where the development towards the contraction is half complete.

There is absolutely no attempt to limit the use of the *nomen sacrum* to the Spirit of God.

CONCLUSIONS

The study we have undertaken sheds light on three areas: the stage of development represented by the codex itself; the habits of the scribes of its *Vorlagen*; and the *nomina sacra* themselves.

The stage of development evinced by the manuscript

The conservatism of D in its use of the *nomina sacra* is noted by Paap (p. 120). The Greek text is not very far from that early stage when *θεος, 'Ιησους, κυριος*, and *χριστος* were the only ones, even though by 400 AD there were some fifteen of them. Besides the original four, for which the use of the contraction is virtually uniform, there are a mere four words in the process of becoming *nomina sacra* – *πατηρ, πνευμα, σταυρος*, and *σταυροω*. It is clear that only comparatively recently has *πατηρ* been added to this select list. *Πνευμα*, on the other hand, has nearly reached the status of the original four.

The Latin text seems, at first glance, to be at the same stage. *Spiritus* is at exactly the same point as *πνευμα* (single forms of the former are abbreviated 121 times, and written in full twenty-four; of the latter are contracted 123 times, in full twenty). But in fact, there is a great variety of usage in the Latin column, whereas the Greek is far more consistent in the forms of abbreviation. Moreover, there is no sign of the forms $\overline{I\Sigma}$, $\overline{X\Sigma}$, $\overline{Y\Sigma}$, and others, which had by now become the regular contractions. It is clear that in the Greek column, the scribe of D is imitating practices totally archaic for the year 400.

The Latin text, by contrast, presents the contemporary situation. Although the position of *spiritus* could be compared to that of *πνευμα*, there is no real similarity overall. For although it is pretty certain what words may be treated as *nomina sacra*, there is plenty of uncertainty as to how they should be represented. We see on the pages of Codex Bezae the issue of the moment in the development of the *nomina sacra* – the shift from the older *deus* and $\overline{dms}$ to $\overline{ds}$ and $\overline{dns}$. In contrast to the fossilized Greek habits, the Latin reflect contemporary scribal practices. This substantiates the belief that the manuscript had a Latin scribe.

The earlier copyings of the separate books

No two books agree on every single usage, as will be seen from table 17. The majority practice of each book is taken as typical. Only those words for which there is a difference of usage are included.

Luke is the most primitive of the five books. This may be gathered from the fact that it is the only one not to use the contractions for *πνευμα* and *spiritus*. It best

Table 17. *Synoptic table of the* nomina sacra

Mt	ΠΝΑ	CTAYPOC/-OⲰ	DS/DEI	DMS/DMN	SPS/SPU
Jn	ΠΝΑ	CTAYPOC/-OⲰ	DS/DEI	DMS/DOM	SPS/SPU
Lk	ΠΝΕΥΜΑ	CTAYPOC/-OⲰ	DS/DEI	DMS/DOM	SPIRITUS/SPU
Mk	ΠΝΑ	CTPN etc.	DS/DEI	DMS/DMN	SPS/SPO
Ac	ΠΝΑ	CTAYPOⲰ	DS/DI	DNS/DNM	SPS/SPO

preserves the stage at which only four *nomina sacra* were in existence, in Greek and Latin.

Acts, by the same criteria, is the least primitive. By percentage, it is the book most in favour of contracting *πνευμα* and *spiritus*, and it has the most modern system of contraction for *dominus* – the *dns* type. Yet even here the number of the *nomina sacra* remains traditionally small.

For Matthew, the Greek and Latin texts must be taken separately. For while the Greek practices are consistent, with the exception of the four appearances of ΠΡC, the Latin is extremely confused. DEUS, DEI, and DEO go alongside DS, DM, DI, and DO, while *dominus* is abbreviated according to two different systems. SPU and SPO both appear. It may be concluded that Matthew has borne the brunt of successive attempts to introduce new usage, before scribes settled down to copy exactly what was before them.

As for John, the customs in the Latin are fixed, vacillating only in the full and contracted forms of *spiritus* and *spiritu*. In the Greek there is a greater diversity, in the use of ΠΝΕΥΜΑ and ΠΝΑ, and in its erratic predilections for the contractions of *πατηρ*.

We come finally to Mark. This is the book where we detected a change in the middle. In the Greek, the customs are reasonably consistent. As in Acts, scribal practice sets its face resolutely against any contracting of *πατηρ*, here outdoing even Luke in fidelity to ancient tradition. But the text is very nearly as thoroughgoing in preferring to contract *πνευμα*, and has been well on the way to adding *σταυρος* and *σταυροω* to the *nomina sacra*. It is equally consistent in abbreviating *spiritus*, and is the only book to have a uniform set of contractions for *dominus*. Besides the indications of one partial revision, the overall pattern is of a book that has been carefully revised.

It is clear from these observations that the four Gospels and Acts had been subjected to revisions of varying degrees of thoroughness and according to various sets of rules. The revision of *σταυρος* and *σταυροω* may have happened recently, if we argue that the contraction was disappearing under pressure from the custom of the rest of the codex. It is also possible that the rare appearances of contractions for *πατηρ* in Matthew to Luke are the result of haphazard, partly unconscious changes made at several points.

In spite of differences over many details, the five books are in a measure of agreement as to which words are *nomina sacra*. The tradition is not dramatically divided.

Light on the *nomina sacra*

A general point is that there is no thorough attempt anywhere to confine the use to places where the text refers to the sacred. The practice has become almost as much shorthand as a genuine indication of *nomina sacra*.

We see clearly in this bilingual tradition how much the Latin forms depend on the Greek. This dependence is no doubt heightened by the visual unity of the page, seen in the similarity of the lettering of the *nomina sacra*. It is clear even in the work of a Latin scribe.

In attempting to identify the stages of revision of the *nomina sacra* within the tradition to which Codex Bezae belongs, we have at the same time provided a very vague commentary on their chronology. Thus, we can see how the forms for σταυρος and σταυροω, adopted by an earlier copyist of Mark, were at a later date abandoned so that they nearly dropped out. We can see how a marked preference for the full form of *deus* was accompanied by an indifference as to how *dominus* was abbreviated, and how both πνευμα and *spiritus* could be written in full and by contraction an almost equal number of times in one Gospel.

To conclude: a study which seeks too much information from the *nomina sacra* is of questionable value. One must remain more than doubtful as to whether they convey any theological information. But they do betray something of a manuscript's antecedents and of its scribe's own habits. The very fact that Codex Bezae contains the vestiges of various systems is a witness both to the scribe's fidelity to the details of his exemplar, and to the longevity of such minutiae. There is no reason to doubt that the scribe of D contributed something of his own preferences to an already complicated situation. Examples of this may be the occasional abbreviation of πατηρ, some of the changes with regard to πνευμα and *spiritus*, and the use of $\overline{\text{DNS}}$ in the Gospels.

Particularly significant for our study is the discovery that the *nomina sacra* are at different stages in the two columns: the Latin traditions are changing and developing, whilst those in the Greek remain static and archaic. Clearly, we have to do with a scribe whose work has made him aware of the customs of other Latin scribes, but who is not influenced by contemporary Greek practice. This provides another indication as to the circumstances out of which the codex was made.

CHAPTER SEVEN

The orthography

F. Blass, *Euangelium secundum Lucam sive Lucae ad Theophilum liber prior, secundum formam quae videtur Romanam*, Leipzig, 1897, p. vif; Blass, *Philology of the Gospels*, London, 1898, p. 75f; C. M. Martini, *Il problema della recensionalità del codice B alla luce del papiro Bodmer XIV* (Analecta Biblica 26), Rome, 1966, pp. 86–122.

There are older studies that describe the spelling of our manuscript at some length. Scrivener (pp. xxxf) and Harris (*Codex*, pp. 16–30) in particular based their theories of its origins on their interpretation of the orthography. Today's far more advanced knowledge of the documents of the period spares us the need to repeat the exercise. Stone has produced a full and very valuable study and word list of the Latin column. He examined the morphology as well as the phonology. He concluded that the phonology of the manuscript presents few irregularities. The simple fact is that the Latin column is full of spellings typical of Late Latin. Stone's findings may easily be summarized.

The vowel changes are 'relatively few, and are regular' (p. 17). *a* remains constant. *is* > *es* (e.g. *omnes* for *omnis*) is very common. *e* > *a*, *e* > *ae* and *es* > *is* are all common. Less frequent are *e* > *i* (ten occurrences), and *i* > *e* (eleven). *e* > *o*, *i* > *ei*, *o* > *ae*, *u* > *e*, all occur once. *o* > *u*, *u* > *i*, *u* > *o* and *u* > *y* are all rare. Of the diphthongs, *ae* > *e* is common; *ae* > *a* is found once, and *oe* > *oi* twice. There are three instances of syncope and four of added vowels.

Of the consonantal shifts, the most common are *b* > *u* and *u* > *b*. *d* and *t* at the ends of words are regularly confused. Other changes include *b* > *p* (four times), *c* > *g* (six), *g* > *c* (eight), *m* > *n*, especially before labials (very often), omission of final *m* and *n* before *p*, *n* superfluous and *n* dropped, *nc* > *n*, *ph* > *f*, *qu* > *c*, *r* dropped before *s*, *s* added at the beginning of a word, *t* inserted between *s* and *r*, dropping of final *t*, addition and omission of *h*. Stone notes *mittunc* for *mittunt* (Mt 9.17) as rare, and *d* > *c* (Lk 7.19) and *d* > *ct* (Lk 21.22) as unattested elsewhere.

A similar study of the Greek column has not been undertaken. The comments of Scrivener (p. xlvi) are still valuable. He observes that there is 'little or no difference between the practice of Codex Bezae and the other oldest manuscripts'. His full description merits repetition in full:

> Its *itacisms* . . . are actually fewer than in Cod. ℵ and one or two more, and the errors of transcription, especially in the Greek, are not by any means so numerous. The principal vowel changes, as usual, are *ει* for *ι*, *ε* for *αι*, and *vice versa*: *υ* is put for *οι* chiefly in *σοι* and the various forms of *ανοιγω*, *υ* and *η* are transmuted principally in the cases of *ημεις* and *υμεις*: itacisms so harsh as *κε* for *και* John vii. 47; Acts xviii. 2; *ε* for the article *αι* Luke iii. 5; *σοι* for *συ* John vii. 52; *ετεραι* for *εταιρε* Matth. xxii. 12; xxvi. 50 (not xx. 13) are not at all frequent. The changes so very common in later writing between *ο* and *ω*, *ε* and *η* are rare (such as *εξηλθη* Matt. xii. 43; cf. John vi. 3): those between *ει*, *η* and *ι* (even *ηασεν* Matth. xxiv. 43), *ου* and *ω* (in the third person plural of verbs) are more familiar. The accommodation of spelling to pronunciation in *νγ*, *νκ* and *νχ* for *γγ*, *γκ* and *γχ*, e.g. *ηνγικεν* Matth. iii. 2; *ανγελον ibid.* xi. 10; xiii. 39 (not *v.* 41); *ανκιστρον* xvii. 27 (so Luke ii. 28 *ανκαλασ*); *εσπλανχνισθη ibid.* ix. 36 (not xiv. 14), especially the last, occurs perhaps more often than in other copies; but the orthography presents no other peculiarity worth notice.

The forms *ϋμειν* and *ημειν* are certainly more common than *ϋμιν* and *ημιν*, and occur throughout the manuscript. The most recent work in the area of Hellenistic Greek phonology, that of Gignac, bears out Scrivener's conclusion that there is 'no other peculiarity worth notice'.

Martini concluded that D was more systematic in its orthography than either P[75] or B. This was in his study of Luke; it would be interesting to know whether this is true throughout the Gospels and Acts.

The fact that the Latin spelling is far more obviously influenced by contemporary pronunciation than the Greek, is a further demonstration of two facts. First, the scribe was a Latin speaker – he wrote the Latin as he would hear it, but the Greek as he saw it. Second, the manuscript was copied by eye, and not to dictation. If the latter, then the Greek would show far more signs of the speech of the day if the reader knew Greek well, and far more impossible combinations of sounds if he did not. The premise of these observations is that the orthography of the manuscript is the product of the scribe. In the case of the Latin column, this seems very likely, though we cannot rule out the possibility that it is shared with the exemplar. But the kind of corrections made by G who, we will suggest (p. 128), knew the exemplar, seems to support the view that at least a good deal of the Latin spelling comes into the tradition through the scribe of D. The Greek, with which he is less familiar, and which he does not read out loud to himself with a strongly Hellenistic accent, will in this respect be closer to the text of the exemplar. But we should note that in the correction at Ff89b–90b with which we began our examination of the sense-lines (see p. 76), he first wrote ΘΕΛΕΤΑΙ, then ΘΕΛΕΤΕ. Of course, we have no way of knowing which spelling was in the exemplar.

Beyond the consistent spelling of the scribe, there is the possibility of finding variations between the orthography of different parts of the manuscript. The evidence which prompts us to explore this was first discovered by Ernst Lippelt, a student of Friedrich Blass. Blass presented the argument in his edition of Luke, and popularized it in *Philology of the Gospels*.

Blass' account is as follows:

> The name of John has in Greek two spellings, one with one *N* and another with two. I do not doubt that the former is the right one . . . But in a later age there crept in much irregularity in the doubling of the liquid consonants . . . Now the Vaticanus B, than which there is no more trustworthy witness in all matters of spelling, nearly always gives *'Ιωάνης*, whilst the Cantabrigiensis D has both spellings, but more frequently that with double *N*. The order of the books contained in D is this: Matthew, John, Luke, Mark, Acts. In the first two, the spelling with double *N* has a very large predominance . . .; but in the third Gospel, that of Luke, the writer of a sudden adopts the opposite principle . . . This of itself would perhaps not be very astonishing; but when he comes to Mark, he falls back to his first spelling . . . Last comes the second part of Luke, and again he changes . . . That this definite inconsistency, and at the same time consistency, cannot have been effected by mere chance is quite evident . . .
>
> (*Philology of the Gospels*, pp. 75f)

Blass drew two conclusions from these facts (from which I have for the present omitted the figures). The first, that 'we must acknowledge in the writer of D a degree of care which hitherto seemed to be alien from him' (p. 76), deserves greater recognition than it has yet received. It is supported by what we have learned in the two preceding chapters.

His second conclusion was that the 'archetype' of D (does he mean the archetype or the exemplar?) had Luke last of the four Gospels, so that the two books of Luke were together. It follows from this that 'the archetype (or one of the archetypes) of D united in itself parts coming from different sources, one part of which consisted of the two books of Luke written by one scribe' (p. 77).

The final suggestion is scarcely tenable. Had Blass gone on to compare the practice of the Greek and Latin columns, he would not have made it. The time has come to set out the information, according to my examination, which provides two pieces of evidence not noted by Lippelt (table 18). My figures do not include the colophons and titles.

The idea that the bilingual Luke–Acts is derived from a single scribe is not acceptable, since Acts has a peculiarity not shared by Luke. Whereas in Luke the single *ν/n* form is found in both columns, in Acts the Greek has the single and the Latin the double liquid.

But the evidence certainly suggests that the manuscript as we have it represents either a rearrangement of the order of books in a *Vorlage*, or a copying of separate volumes – or possibly both.

Blass goes on to suggest that the earlier order was Matthew–

Table 18. *The spelling of the name John*

	IΩANNHC	IΩANHC	IOHANNES	IOHANES
Mt	22	2	24	—
Jn 1.1–5.33	4	—	7	—
5.36–end	—	7	4	3
Lk	1	27	3	25
Mk	23	2	24	1
Ac	2	21	22	1

John–Mark–Luke–Acts. This order for the Gospels is that given in the list of books placed between Philemon and Hebrews in the Codex Claromontanus. Its origin is generally regarded as being the Alexandria of about 300 AD.

See, most recently, Metzger, *Canon*, pp. 230, 296f, 310f, and references.

However, this evidence on its own cannot be used to establish very much. It seems at least as likely that the order could have been Matthew–Mark–John–Luke. We then have together all the block that prefers the doubled letter.

This order is found in the Curetonian Syriac, the Cheltenham Catalogue (also known as the Catalogus Mommsenianus, it may have had its origins in North Africa in about 360), and the Latin Gospel Commentary of Pseudo-Theophilus of Antioch, which was written in Gaul round about the year 500 (Metzger, *Canon*, pp. 231, 296f, 311f; for Pseudo-Theophilus, see H.J. Frede, *Kirchenschriftsteller, Verzeichnis und Sigel* (Vetus Latina 1/1), Freiburg, 1981, s.v. Ps-THl).

There is no direct evidence for Blass' claim that the order with Luke last is intended to place Luke's two books together. In the Catalogus Mommsenianus, Paul's letters come between the Gospels and Acts, and the list in the Codex Claromontanus places them even further apart, with all the epistles it regards as canonical, and Revelation, between them.

There are no grounds for assuming that the former order, whatever it may have been, was in the exemplar of D. If our scribe could preserve the distinction, so could another, and the difference may be of great antiquity.

The possibilities might be multiplied considerably by positing two scribes, copying different gospels in one of anything up to twenty-four different orders (though only nine are found in the existing lists and Gospel books).

At this point the need to find more evidence of a similar kind becomes pressing, and is the object of the present chapter. Unfortunately, I have been able to find very little material analogous to that available for the word *Ιωανης*. The requirements are very exact.

Αβρααμ is written *Αβρααμ'* in John (nine times), and twice thus in Acts. In table 19 I include the evidence from the Latin column only to show that it tells us nothing.

Table 19. *The spelling of the name Abraham*

	ΑΒΡΑΑΜ	ΑΒΡΑΑΜ'	ABRAHAM	ABRAAM
Mt	1	—	1	2
Jn	1	9	10	1
Lk	16	—	14	2
Mk	1	—	1	—
Ac	5	2	8	—

Table 20. *The numeral twelve*

	ΔΩΔΕΚΑ	Numeral	DUODECIM	Numeral
Mt	3	10	5	8
Jn	4	2	5	1
Lk	2	11	3	10
Mk	—	13	1	12
Ac	1	3	1	3

Table 21. *The numeral seven*

	ΕΠΤΑ	Numeral	SEPTEM	Numeral
Mt	6	2	7	1
Lk	5	1	5	1
Mk	—	8	3	5
Ac	2	2	3	1

One other fact calls for attention: the writing of numerals in full or as a number. The most common numeral is twelve (table 20); the next most frequent is seven (table 21). Eight is written in full in both columns every time (it comes in John and Luke). So is ten, except for its only place in Mark (it is found also in Matthew, Luke, and once in Acts). No other numeral comes more than once or twice.

It is possible that a full study of various other details such as are found in Martini's work on P^{75} and B would yield further evidence to support what we have found.

The conclusion to this chapter must be left to the next, where we will try to draw together all that we have learnt here and in the rest of Part II.

CHAPTER EIGHT

The Codex Bezae and its ancestors

In Part II we have studied the sense-lines, the *nomina sacra*, and the orthography (chapters 5–7), in an attempt to learn more about the manuscript tradition that lies behind D. The third of these chapters yielded very little fresh evidence, but what we *have* found enables us to interpret more coherently the evidence from the other two chapters. We therefore begin the conclusion to this part by taking up the implications of what we learnt about the orthography.

We direct our attention first toward the Gospels.

John has two peculiar features in its Greek side. First, the use of the apostrophe after *Αβρααμ*; second, the change in chapter 5 from the double form to the single in the writing of *Ιωανης*, which, it should be noted, is only partly shared by the Latin column. This change makes it possible that an earlier manuscript could have had the Gospels in the order Matthew–Mark–John–Luke. Although the agreement between the columns could be chance, it is more likely to indicate that this earlier manuscript was a bilingual. It could be that a copy of John had been written at some stage, either by two scribes, or from two exemplars, the change coming in the middle of chapter 5. This could have occurred at any stage in the history of the transmission. (Since all the occurrences of Abraham in the Fourth Gospel come in chapter 8 onwards, the use of the apostrophe does not help us.) But it is worth noting that the middle of John 5 is not far off the midpoint of a text with the books in the order Matthew–Mark–John–Luke: Matthew, Mark, and the beginning of John constitute about 163 pages of Nestle-Aland[26], and the rest of John and all of Luke comes to 155 pages. It is therefore not inconceivable that the change in spelling stems from a bilingual *Vorlage*, which had the Gospels in this order, and which was copied by two scribes who divided their work at this point.

Although it seems a strange place to divide the copying, the reason will have been that it was calculated as being the beginning of a new quire. The division of the Bible between the scribes of the Sinaiticus was generally dictated by just such considerations. See Milne and Skeat, *Scribes and Correctors*, pp. 29, 94–112.

Whether this manuscript was the exemplar of D cannot be determined on this evidence alone. If we return to the description of the punctuation, it will be recollected that the medial point is used in Matthew, John up to about F136b (middle of chapter 8), and Mark, and that small spaces are used in the rest of John and all of Luke. The double point is used in Matthew and Mark, and the large space in John and Luke (see chapter 2). In the chapter on the sense-lines (chapter 5) we noted that in the second half of John and in Luke, the exemplar had a further characteristic that cannot be determined. It may therefore be suggested that the manuscript which had the Gospels in the order Matthew–Mark–John–Luke was actually the exemplar of D, and was the work of two copyists. Whatever the precise reason that led the scribe of D to switch from medial points to spaces when he did, it must owe something to the differences between the two scribes of this manuscript. I would suggest that the scribe of the first half wrote a medial point at the ends of his lines, and that our scribe imitated him.

This is the point at which to note that, having reached these conclusions and written this section, I was gratified to discover that over eighty years ago, Dom John Chapman argued precisely the same case with regard to the order of Gospels in the exemplar ('The Order of the Gospels in the Parent of Codex Bezae', *ZNW* 6 (1905), 339–46). His grounds were the use of points and the spellings of the name John.

A difficulty with this theory is that the precise points of change in John between the spellings of *Ἰωανης* (5.33–6, F121b–122) and the types of punctuation (middle of chapter 8, F136b) are not identical. But as a matter of fact, the spelling with one *nu* at 5.36 is the only one before chapter 10. Given that the spelling *Ἰωανης* comes twice in Matthew, and that the Latin of 5.36 has *Iohannes*, the use here could be chance. The change accords as closely as we dare hope.

This difficulty, however, raises another problem. The further into John we move the hypothetical division of labour, the more unequal the two parts become. A change of scribe somewhere in chapter 8 adds about fourteen or fifteen pages to the first scribe, and takes them away from the second, giving us a proportion of something like 178 against 140. The multiplication of hypotheses to account for this discrepancy is to be resisted.

The explanation of the distinctive sense-lines of John and Luke is presented differently by Clark (*Acts*, p. 180):

> Scrivener has some curious remarks upon the differences of the *στίχοι* in various parts of *D*. He notices that in Mt. they usually coincide with some pause in the sense, that in Jn. the dissolution of verses becomes much more marked, and that in Lk. 'an entire breaking up of the stichometry becomes rather the practice than the exception' (p. xviii). His explanation is that 'in course of time the ancient *στίχοι* were gradually dissolved by successive transcribers'. This does not account for the archaic condition of the *στίχοι* in Mt., which is not likely to have been less frequently transcribed than Jn. and Lk., or for the return to regularity in Mk. and Acts. A more natural

> suggestion would be that the Greek of Jn. and Lk. in *D* is drawn from a different source, i.e. from a MS. not divided into sense-lines, and that the *στίχοι* as found in *D* were arranged by an unskilful person who did not understand the ancient system.

It needs to be asked whether the breakdown of the sense-lines in John and Luke, which we have attributed to the scribe of D's planning of his work and calculations of space, actually goes back further. It must be supposed that the two scribes of the exemplar will have had to copy the lines as they found them in *their* exemplar, or no point of division between their labours could have been arranged in advance. This is to suppose that they worked simultaneously. If, on the other hand, the second scribe began work when the first had finished, then the objection does not apply.

If the treatment of the sense-lines by the second scribe of the exemplar differs from that by the first, then this could account for the marked disintegration tat we find in D, in John and particularly in Luke. Such an explanation is probably weightier than the suggestion that it concerned his use of space: the sense-lines of John and Luke were already on their way to dissolution before the scribe of D began work.

Clark seems to have assumed that there were two Greek manuscripts of the Gospels, both written in sense-lines, albeit of differing characters, from which the Greek column of the bilingual tradition was compiled. This theory has to be rejected. According to all the evidence that we have collected, the sense-lines were formed at the time that the bilingual tradition was created. The separate Greek and Latin sources for this will have been written normally.

At this point we are clearly pushing the little evidence we have to its limits. Our account sets its verbs in the indicative rather than the subjunctive because it can be expressed more clearly and cogently by this means. As we continue, a possible conditional construction is implicit.

The distinctive features that we observed in the orthography of Acts have a bearing on our discovery that the sense-lines in the exemplar of D were of a different character in Acts from those in the Gospels. It is now possible to suggest that Codex Bezae is derived from two exemplars, one containing the Gospels and one containing the Acts of the Apostles.

If this is so, then the evidence of the previous chapters begins to fall into place. The exemplars had one great difference between them. That of the Gospels was written in two columns to the page, with very short sense-lines. Acts had only one column to the page, and longer lines. The scribe calculated that he would save space by adopting the Acts format in the Gospels. It will also have been easier to join sense-lines than to set himself the task of creating, or recreating, short sense-lines in Acts, particularly since, as I have suggested, the Acts format suited the needs of the day better than did that of the Gospels.

The most confusing evidence that we have examined in this part of our study is

Table 22. *The* nomina sacra

Mt	ΠΝΑ	CTAYPOC/-OΩ	DS/DEI	DMS/DMN	SPS/SPU
Mk	ΠΝΑ	CTPN etc.	DS/DEI	DMS/DMN	SPS/SPO
Jn	ΠΝΑ	CTAYPOC/-OΩ	DS/DEI	DMS/DOM	SPS/SPU
Lk	ΠΝΕΥΜΑ	CTAYPOC/-OΩ	DS/DEI	DMS/DOM	SPIRITUS/SPU
Ac	ΠΝΑ	CTAYPOΩ	DS/DI	DNS/DNM	SPS/SPO

that from the *nomina sacra*. Does the theory that we have outlined help us to understand the forms of the abbreviations?

In table 22 I set out the evidence for differences between the books that we have already collected (p. 105 above), in the postulated order of the exemplar. This evidence marks out Acts as different from the Gospels. It also separates Matthew and Mark from John and Luke (this distinction, of course, can be applied only to the Latin column): Matthew and Mark have the accusative of *dominus* as DMN, whilst John and Luke have DOM. Matthew and Mark also show traces of a genitive of *deus* as DI.

There is a small amount of evidence that does not fit into my argument. We noted that in Mark, the form DEI was preferred as far as 9.1, and DI from 9.47 onwards. In addition, the numerals present a problem. Here, Mark stands out in having the numeral for seven, while Matthew and Luke prefer the word in full. The preference for the numeral of twelve is constant, except for John which prefers the word. I have no explanation for any of this.

It can be suggested that, these exceptions apart, all this could be taken as further evidence for an exemplar produced by two copyists: the scribe of Matthew and Mark prefers *dei* to *di*; the other scribe has a different set of preferences. But it should be observed that they do not agree together – John prefers the abbreviated, Luke the full forms of *πνευμα* and *spiritus*. The figures are

	πνα	*πνευμα*	*sps*	*spiritus*
John	12	3	13	2
Luke	13	15	13	14

The second scribe of the exemplar could have been introducing the abbreviation for these two forms, not used in his own exemplar.

Such a reconstruction assumes that the form found near the end (for instance, D in Mark or SPIRITUS in Luke) is what the exemplar had, the scribe having given up altering it to his own preference. An alternative would be to argue that the nearer he got to the end, the less trouble a scribe would take to copy precisely (*sicut navigantibus proximus est portus, sic et scriptori novissimus versus*), so that he reverts t his normal practice. If this were so, then the exemplar would have had DEI in Mark and SPS in Luke. However, this alternative explanation fails to meet the facts: Matthew and Mark solidly prefer the accusative DMN, John and Luke as unwaveringly show DOM. Moreover, the fact that Matthew shows the greatest variety of forms of the *nomina sacra* indicates that generations of scribes have begun by substituting the forms they prefer, and then reverted to copying that which they had before them.

The picture that emerges is of two exemplars. The first contained the Gospels, in the order Matthew, Mark, John, and Luke. It was written by two scribes: one of them copied Matthew, Mark, and the first part of John; the second wrote the rest of the codex. It had two columns to the page, one Greek and one Latin, and was in very short sense-lines. The other exemplar contained the Acts of the Apostles. It is impossible to decide whether it also contained those epistles of which we only have one recto. This manuscript had one column to the page, and longer lines. The scribe of D altered the lay-out of the Gospels to accord with that of his Acts manuscript, and changed the order of the Gospels. The reason for the second alteration is not at all clear.

The order of the Gospels found in D itself is shared with only a few Greek, some versional manuscripts, and the testimony of a few writers.

Gregory, *Prolegomena* (=Tischendorf, Vol. 3); M.J. Hunter, 'The Vernacular Scriptures', Part I, 'The Gothic Bible', in *The Cambridge History of the Bible*, Vol. 2, Cambridge, 1969, Chapter 9; Metzger, *Canon*; P.E. Pusey and G.H. Gwilliam, *Tetraeuangelium Sanctum iuxta simplicem Syrorum versionem*, Oxford, 1901; W. Wright, *Catalogue of Syriac MSS. in the British Museum*, London, 1870–72; T. Zahn, *Geschichte des NT Kanons*, 2 vols., Erlangen, 1890.

The two principal Greek witnesses are the fifth-century Washington Codex (W), and the tenth-century Codex Monacensis (X). Other attestation is somewhat vaguely described by Metzger as 'several of the older Greek minuscule MSS' (p. 296). These are 594 (Gregory, p. 137), and 055 (formerly 309 in Tischendorf's numeration; cited as such by Zahn, p. 370 and n. 1; see also Gregory, p. 524). There is also the manuscript referred to as 256 in Tischendorf's numeration (Moscow, Sanctae Synodi 138); this is described in the *Prolegomena* as a ninth-century 'comm in Mt Ioh Lc Mc cum textus fragmentis'. It is not included in the Aland catalogue.

The available information about 594 is not consistent. Gregory, *Prolegomena*, is the authority for its inclusion in this list. According to the Aland catalogue, it contains Matthew and Luke, with lacunae. The manuscript is of the fourteenth century, and is Venice, Bibl. di S. Lazzaro 1531.

The next group of evidence is from three versions.

First there are some Peshitta Syriac manuscripts. They are listed by Zahn (*Geschichte*, n. 2) as numbers LXXXIX (*saec.* VI or VII) and XCVI (*saec.* VI) in Wright (Add. Mss. 12141 and 17715, = 34 and 10 in Pusey and Gwilliam). Zahn also draws attention to numbers XCVII and XCVIII (Add. Mss. 14467 and 17224 folios 43–57). None of these Syriac manuscripts contains the four Gospels:

LXXXIX has Matthew and John, followed by Luke in several hands, one of the eleventh century and another representing two leaves from Add. Ms. 12137 (Wright's LXXV), which is a manuscript of Matthew, Luke, and John. Number XCVI consists of Matthew, John, Hebrews, Jude, and Acts. XCVII has parts of Mt 7–17 on Ff1–8, and of Jn 8–20 on Ff9–15. XCVIII has Mt 1.7–6.25 on Ff43–54 and Jn 20.25–21.25 on Ff55–7. The reconstruction of book sequences from such materials is uncertain enough to reduce the weight of this evidence considerably, at least until the manuscripts have been examined to find out what can be established.

The Old Latin manuscripts a b e f ff² q also have the D order. They provide the widest geographical and temporal evidence for its use.

It is found in one other version – the Gothic: that is to say, the Codex Argenteus. This manuscript dates from the beginning of the sixth century. According to Hunter, Matthew and John are descended from Ostrogothic, Luke and Mark from Visigothic originals (p. 344). A question may therefore arise as to whether this order reflects Ulfilas' own preference. But it must be added that the view advocated by Hunter does not seem to have won general support amongst experts on the subject. It may be possible simply to say that the order in the Gothic version is due to the influence of Old Latin codices.

There are several other testimonies to this order.

J. B. Cotelier, *Patres Apostolici, editio altera*, 2 vols., Amsterdam, 1724; C. L. Feltoe, *Διονυσιου Λειψανα. The Letters and Other Remains of Dionysius of Alexandria*, Cambridge, 1904, Letter XIV, pp. 91–105; J. B. Lightfoot, *The Apostolic Fathers*, Part II, 2nd edition, 3 vols., London, 1889.

The third of the Latin fragments attributed to Polycarp, describing the way in which each Gospel begins, discusses them in this sequence.

The fragment is rejected by Lightfoot as spurious (Vol. 1, p. 473; Vol. 3, pp. 419–22). They were contained in a manuscript (now lost, according to Lightfoot) of a catena, possibly composed by John the Deacon. The catena cites from an otherwise unknown work by Victor of Capua, the *Responsiones*, which gives the alleged quotations from Polycarp. Certainly this ascription is far from sure, and their rejection by Lightfoot is to be followed. We are left with a source for the Gospels in this order that dates from at least the first part of the sixth century, when Victor was writing.

Another witness is the Apostolic Constitutions, II. 57 (Cotelier, Vol. 1, p. 265), where part of the liturgy is described:

> *διάκονος ἢ πρεσβύτερος ἀναγινωσκέτω τὰ εὐαγγέλια, ἃ ἐγὼ Ματθαῖος, καὶ Ἰωάννης παρεδώκαμεν ὑμῖν, καὶ ἃ οἱ συνεργοὶ Παύλου παρειληφότες κατέλειψαν ὑμῖν Λουκᾶς καὶ Μάρκος.*

It is also found in Dionysius of Alexandria's Letter to Basilides. In discussing the correct hour at which the Paschal Fast should end, Dionysius examines the time at which, according to the Gospels, the women come to the tomb:

> *καὶ ὀψὲ CABBÁTWN, ὡς ὁ Ματθαῖος εἶπε καὶ ΠΡWÍAC ἜTI CKOTÍAC OŸCHC, ὡς ὁ Ἰωάννης γράφει· καὶ ὌΡΘΡΟΥ ΒΑΘÉΟC ὡς ὁ Λουκᾶς· καὶ ΛÍΑΝ ΠΡWÌ ἈΝΑΤΕÍΛΑΝΤΟC ΤΟΫ ἩΛÍΟΥ, ὡς ὁ Μάρκος.* (Feltoe, p. 96)

He goes on to discuss the accounts in more details, following the same order (pp. 97–100). Finally, we have the passage in Druthmar which we encountered in chapter 3. It will be recalled that Druthmar had seen a Greek Gospel manuscript said to have belonged to Hilary, with Matthew and John placed first. Zahn prefers to regard this reference as support for the order Matthew–John–Mark–Luke (p. 369, n. 3).

The earliest evidence is that from Dionysius. After that, it seems to be an order that emerges in the fourth century, and is most popular in the West. Did the scribe of D alter the order of his exemplar to that which he considered to be the new standard? The oldest Latin manuscript support apart from D is from codices copied in North Italy – a b e. Codex Argenteus also has North Italian origins. Although it would be hard to find such influence on the other manuscripts which support this order, it is tempting to find here some Italian influence on D.

Beyond reconstructing something of the character of the two exemplars, can we trace the tradition any further back? The *nomina sacra* give us a few clues. We have suggested that the second scribe of the exemplar was introducing abbreviations for πνευμα and *spiritus*, which *his* exemplar had in full. This, with the general agreement between Matthew and Mark, would indicate that the Gospel exemplar of D was itself copied from a manuscript containing Matthew, Mark, Luke, and John, in that order. It leaves us with a manuscript showing a considerable variety of practices:

Matthew and Mark	πνα	*ds* / *di*	*dms* / *dmn*	*sps*
John	πνα	*ds* / *dei*	*dms* / *dom*	*sps*
Luke	πνευμα	*ds* / *dei*	*dms* / *dom*	*spiritus*

This manuscript presents us with a good many questions. The grandparent, as it were, of D, it would presumably be of some antiquity. If it were bilingual, could its Latin column have been a compilation of several books?

The complicated and very provisional conclusion that we have reached may be set out diagrammatically (figure 1). The earliest stages are very clearly the most tentative. This reconstruction can be further tested in later chapters. Here it remains to note that it leaves Codex Bezae as the third-generation manuscript of its bilingual tradition of the Gospels. This pushes the origins of the tradition well back in time.

It is also clear that the Latin has its origins outside the bilingual tradition. These points can be explored in greater detail when we come to study the texts of the two columns, and the differences between them.

By contrast with the Gospels, the evidence suggests that the tradition of the Acts text is less ancient. We have the more modern form of DNS. We have also the fact that the spelling of *John* is different in each column. Codicological considerations provide further support. According to Turner, 'the double-column scheme

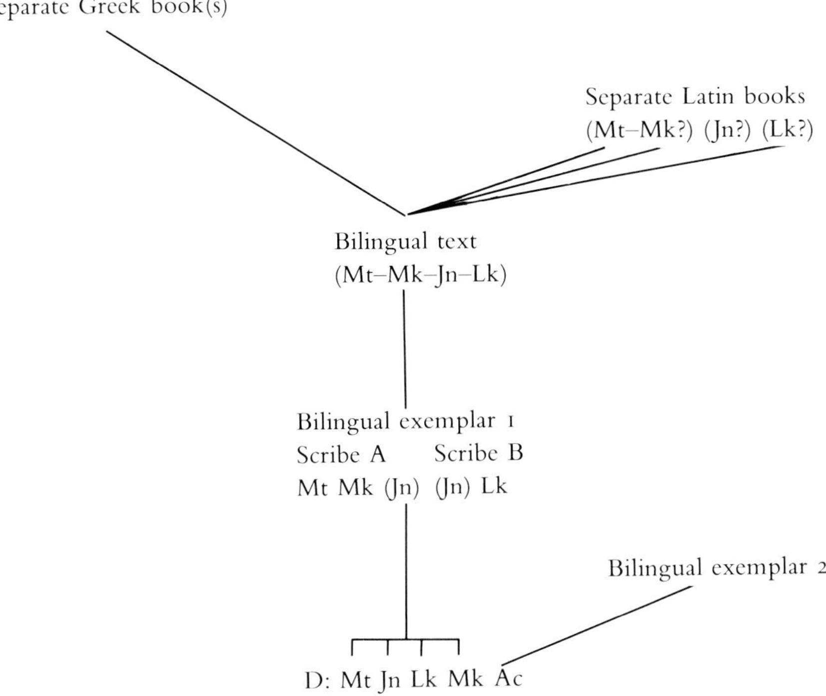

Figure 1 Ancestry of the Codex Bezae

reproduced in many parchment codices is an old-fashioned one' (*Typology*, p. 36). According to Lowe ('Some Facts', p. 207 = *Pal. Papers* 1,201), the preference for two columns on the page is also a mark of antiquity in Latin manuscripts. Thus, by contrast with the traditional double-column lay-out of the Gospel exemplar, that of Acts has a more modern single-column format.

An important aspect of these conclusions is that the bilingual tradition of D is shown to be several copyings old. Codex Bezae is not a creation out of nothing, nor is its Latin text a new version. The scribe is a copyist, and not a reviser nor a creator nor a translator. This must be recognized in any attempt to understand the text and its history. Indeed, it is necessary to appreciate this, or one will scarcely understand the whole earlier history of the New Testament text. Our reconstruction of these several copyings will be the presupposition for the explorations of Part IV.

Having tried to find evidence that will enable us to trace the tradition back, we turn now to the correctors, and seek to follow it forwards in time.

PART III

The correctors

CHAPTER NINE

The corrections

Fischer, 'Das NT', pp. 208–19; Harris, *Annotators*; Scrivener, pp. xxiv–xxix.

Observation of the correctors shows us a variety of ways in which a bilingual tradition was treated over several centuries. This can give us an insight into the transmission of the tradition which lies behind D. In studying the correctors, we are observing the bilingual text developing. We are also able to find indications of the early use and history of the manuscript. Apart from this, it is to be hoped that some more generally applicable insights into the correcting of manuscripts may be gained.

We shall therefore be examining three main questions: what kind of alterations each corrector made; how these affected the relationship between the columns; and what other texts were known to him.

With regard to the relationship between the columns, the received wisdom is that the column in which a corrector wrote was the one that concerned him. This is not necessarily the case. If, for example, all his corrections were to the Greek column, but invariably brought it into agreement with the Latin where formerly they had disagreed, then it could be argued that his interest was in the latter and in justifying its text. This instance is in fact hypothetical. But we cannot follow Bonifatius Fischer in dividing the early history of D into three stages. According to him the first, including its copying and Corrector G, was bilingual; the second, lasting till 800, was purely Greek; and the third purely Latin (p. 40).

In this chapter, we will study each corrector in turn. I shall anticipate my arguments by placing them in what I hope to show to be their correct sequence. We begin by discovering the degree of activity shown by each (table 23).

The most striking fact about table 23 is that nearly one half of the total number of corrections is to the text of Acts. All the eight oldest correctors devoted more of their attention to it than to any one Gospel. Moreover, a high proportion of the corrections in Acts are textually significant – almost a quarter, as compared to between one-seventh and one-fifth for the Synoptists, and just under 30 per cent

Table 23. *The activity of the correctors*

Corrector	Mt	Jn	Lk	Mk	Ac	Total
G	224	7	—	—	55	286
A	21	27	35	36	56	175
C	22	12	15	14	74	137
B	42	46	53	29	161	331
D	28	14	17	11	97	167
E	2	9	6	3	45	65
H	14	7	11	4	52	88
F	2	5	—	—	23	30
J^1	—	2	—	—	—	2
L	—	—	2	—	—	2
K	25	16	11	2	14	68
s.m.	68	50	67	57	235	477

Secunda manus is a way of grouping all corrections not attributable to any of the known hands.

Table 24. *Corrections to each column*

Col.	Mt	Jn	Lk	Mk	Ac	Total
Greek	207	160	193	148	698	1406
Latin	239	32	24	8	106	409
Both	2	3	—	—	8	13
Total	448	195	217	156	812	1828

for the Fourth Gospel. It is clear that this text of Acts proved as problematical in antiquity as it does today.

A second table (24) will show us how many corrections were made to each column. Reference to the table of corrections by G (table 25) will show that almost all corrections to the Latin text are by him. Most of the others are by unidentifiable hands.

The very low number of corrections made to both columns at once is worthy of note. This, coupled with the fact that each corrector made almost all of his corrections in only one column, prompts us to wonder how much Codex Bezae was ever used as a bilingual book.

The majority of alterations that we are going to encounter are not of great significance. For instance, most of those by G are of spelling errors, particularly betacisms. Many Greek corrections are of interchanged vowels or readily identifiable copying errors. The characteristics of such activity are distinctive to each corrector, and we will attempt to describe them.

Questions of the hands and dates of the correctors were treated in chapter 3. With the exception of the additions by L, the annotators will not be examined in this chapter. Suggestions as to the allocation of corrections and other corrections to Scrivener's notes are to be found in appendix 2. A word is needed about the textual evidence supplied in this chapter. Earlier notes included a full *apparatus criticus* to each correction. But it became clear that, for the most part, the reader would be better off with a simple list of corrections. Reading through this in the company of a good *apparatus* will allow readers to interpret my evidence more easily. Exceptions to this are Correctors B and D, which need to be treated somewhat more fully. Where evidence is cited, either in the listing of variants or by way of conclusion, I have used a number of sources. I used Legg for Matthew and Mark, the International Greek New Testament Project volumes for Luke, and B.-L. (sometimes) for Acts. But my main source has been Tischendorf, whose abbreviations I have used (they are given in the list of abbreviations), sometimes as a rough guide to the kind of support a reading enjoys.

CORRECTOR G

F.C. Burkitt, 'The Date of Codex Bezae', *JTS* 3 (1902), 501–13, esp. pp. 505–12; F.G. Kenyon, Review of the facsimile edition, *JTS* 1 (1900), 293–9, esp. pp. 295–7; E. A. Lowe, 'Codex Bezae: The Date of Corrector G', *BBC* 5 (1928), 32–3 = *Pal. Papers* 1,275–6.

Table 25. *Corrections by Corrector G*

Col.	Mt	Jn	Lk	Mk	Ac	Total
Latin	223	7	—	—	54	284
Both	1	—	—	—	1	2

The pattern of Corrector G's work is shown in table 25. The corrections to John are in Ff116, 118, 135, 140, and 148. All corrections to Acts are in Ff416–28 (1.1–4.15). This last section represents the most intense activity by any corrector.

For the greatest part, these corrections are orthographical. Attention to betacisms is pre-eminent: *b* to *v* forty-two times (eight in Acts), and *v* to *b* thirty-six times (three in Acts). There are four changes of *n* to *m*, two insertions of *m* in *temptare*, and an insertion of *n*. There are twenty-four other consonantal alterations, including sixteen involving *h* (six of *c* to *ch*). He makes over forty vowel changes, including

e to *i* – ten times
e to *ae* – fourteen times
i to *e* – seven times
ae to *e* – four times

The others are *o* to *u*, *u* to *o*, *e* to *a*, *a* to *e*, and *i* to *ii*.

For the rest, we have insertion of a missing syllable seventeen times, correction of the ending thirty-five times, and correction of other nonsense twenty-one times. Twice the line is added over a *nomen sacrum*. These account for 231 of his corrections. We are left with thirty-two significant corrections in Matthew, and twenty-three in Acts, which deserve listing.

Matthew 3.16 (8/30): ET BAPTIZATUS EST d*; *et baptizatus* d^G^; deest D
5.32 (14/16): OM d*; *facit eam moechari* d^G^; ποιει αυτην μοιχευθηναι D
5.37 (14/31): ETIAM ETIAM d*; *est est* d^G^
5.41 (15/8): MILIUM UNUM d*; *mille passum* d^G^; μειλιον εν D
6.2 (16/5): FACITIS d*; *facis* d^G^; ποιης D
9.28 (28/21): ETIAM d*; *credimus* d^G^; ναι D
10.36 (32/25): *homines* d*; *hominis* d^G^; του ανθρωπου D
12.20 (37/17): OM d* D*; · *harundinem quassatam* d^G^; καλαμον συντετριμμενον D^F^
13.51 (46/1): *etiam* d*; *intelleximus* d^G^; ναι D
15.18 (51/9): *communicant* d*; *coinquinat* then *coinquinant* d^G^; ΤΑ ΚΟΙΝWΝΟΥΝΤΑ D*·K; τα κοινουντα D^D^
The correction is repeated (with the right ending first time) at v. 20 (l. 14).
15.36 (53/2): DISCIPULI d*; *disc. autem* d^G^; οι δε μαθηται D
16.16 (54/19): SALVATORIS d; *viventis* d^G^; ΤΟ CWZONTOC D*; του σωζοντος D^A^; του ζωντος D^H^
16.17 (54/23): PATER d*; *pater meus* d^G^; ο πατηρ μου D
16.23 (55/13): OM d*; *sunt* d^G^
17.25 (58/15): *etiam* d*; *facit aut prae[stat]* d^G^; ναι D cet.
The final letters of this note in the outer margin were lost when the leaves were subsequently trimmed.
18.18 (59b–60): In the Greek, G has added ↑ after γης[1] (the anchora having been wrongly placed twice, first after the initial Λ in ΛΕΛΥΜΕΝΑ, then before it), with the addition supplied in the lower margin –

εσται δεδεμμενα εν τοις ουρανοις
και οσα αν λυσητε επι της γης↓

(The second line originally ended γης εσται↓, which he then corrected.)

To the Latin, he adds ↑ after the first *terram*, and in the lower margin writes

erunt ligata in caelis
et quaecumque solueritis in terram↓

(originally *terram erunt*↓).
18.25 (61/15): NON HANTE EO d*; *non habente autem eo* d^G^; μη εχοντος δε αυτου D
ibid. (61/18): RESTITUI d*; *restituere* d^G^; ΑΠΟΘΗΝΑΙ D*; αποδοθηναι D^A^
19.8 (63/8): DIMISIT d*; *permisit* d^G^; επετρεψεν D
19.9 (63/12): EXCEPTA RATIONE d*; *excepta causa* d^G^; παρεκτος λογου D
20.13 (66/22): TE NOCUI d*; *tibi nocui* d^G^; αδικω σε D
20.25 (67/30): *eorum* d*; *earum* d^G^; αυτων D
ibid. (67/31): EORUM d*; *earum* d^G^; αυτων D
21.16 (70/19): ETIAM d*; OM d^G^; ναι D
22.12 (75/4): *hoc* d*; *hic* d^G^; ωδε D
22.35 (76/29): ET DICET DICENS d*; *et dicens* d^G^; και λεγων D
23.4 (77/27): *enim* d*; OM d^G^; γαρ D*; OM D^s.m.^
25.25 (87/27): OM d*; *est* d^G^
25.34 (88/22): PRAEPARATUM EST VOBIS REGNUM d*; *praep. vobis regnum* d^G^; την ητοιμασμενην υμειν βασιλειαν D
26.42 (93/18): ABIIT d*; *abiens* d^G^; απελθων D

27.31 (99/28): DUXERUNT d*; *et dux.* d^G; *απηγαγον* D*; *και απηγ.* D^B
Acts 1.3 (416/8): PRAESENTIAM d*; *repraesentavit* d^G; *παρεστησεν* D
1.6 (416/26): *restituere* d*; *restitues* d^G; ΑΠΟΚΑΤΑCΤΑΝΕΙC D
1.11 (417/11): *qui* d*; *quid* d^G; *τι* D
1.15 (418/1): *in diebus his* d*; *in diebus autem his* d^G; *εν δε ταις ημεραις ταυταις* D
ibid. (417b/3): To the Greek: ΓΑΡ D*; *δε* D^G
To the Latin: PRAETEREA d*; *autem* d^G
1.20 (418/21): *eorum* d*; *eius* d^G; *αυτου* D*
1.21 (418/24)
EORUM QUI VENERUNT NOBISCUM VIRORU͞ d*
ex his viris qui convenerunt nobiscum d^G
των συνελθοντων ημειν ανδρων D
2.2 (419/6): ECHO d*; *vox* d^G; *ηχος* D
The d^G reading is in the margin, without the p.m. version being cancelled.
2.30 (422/21): DE FRUCTUM DE PRAECORDIA d*; *de fructum praecordia* d^G;
de fructu praecordia $d^{s.m.}$; ΚΑΡΔΙΑC D*; *οσφυος* D^H
2.38 (423/20): ACCIPITE d*; *accipietis* d^G; *λημψεσθαι* D
2.46 (424/13): PER DOMOS IDIPSUM d*; *per domos in idipsum* d^G;
ΚΑΤΟΙΚΟΥCΑΝ ΕΠΙ ΤΟ ΑΥΤΟ D*; *κατοικους επι το αυτο* $D^{s.m.}$
The readings of Codex Bezae and its correctors are unlike those of any other text.
3.3 (424/29): RESPICIENS OCULIS SUIS ET VIDIT d*; *resp. oc. suis vidit* d^G; ΑΤΕΝΙCΑC ΤΟΙC ΟΦΘΑΛΜΟΙC ΑΥΤΟΥ ΚΑΙ ΙΔΩΝ D
3.4 (424/33): INTUITUS ... ET DIXIT d*; *intuitus ... dixit* d^G;
ΕΜΒΛΕΨΑC ... ΚΑΙ ΕΙΠΕΝ D*; *εμβλεψασ ... ειπεν* $D^{s.m.}$
3.11 (425/21)
EXEUNTE AUTEM PETRUM ET IOHANNEN d*
exeunte autem petro et iohanne d^G
ΕΚΠΟΡΕΥΟΜΕΝΟΥ ΔΕ ΤΟΥ ΠΕΤΡΟΥ ΚΑΙ ΪΩΑΝΟΥ D
3.13 (426/4)
CUM IUDICASSET ILLE DISMITTERE EUM VOLUIT d*
cum iudicasset ille dismittere eum d^G
ΤΟΥ ΚΡΕΙΝΑΝΤΟC ΕΚΕΙΝΟΥ ΑΠΟΛΥΕΙΝ ΑΥΤΟΝ ΘΕΛΟΝΤΟC D*
κρειναντος εκεινου απολυειν αυτον $D^{s.m.}$ (G?)
3.17 (426/17): OM d*; *scimus* d^G; *επισταμεθα* D
3.26 (427/14): *suscitavit* d*; *suscitans* d^G; *αναστησας* D
4.6 (428/1): *caifas* d*; *caiafas* d^G; ΚΑΪΦΑC D
ibid. (*ibid.*): IOATHAS d*; *ionathas* d^G; ΪΩΝΑΘΑC D
4.7 (428/3): OM d*; *et* d^G; *και* D
ibid. (*ibid.*): CUM STATUISSET d*; *cum statuissent* d^G; *στησαντες* D
4.9 (428/10): BENEFACIO D*; *beneficio* d^G; *ευεργεσεια* D
ibid. (*ibid.*): HOMINEM INFIRMUM d*; *hominis infirmi* d^G

These corrections are eloquent in the story they tell. The longest, the insertion at Mt 18.18, has two clauses written in two sense-lines. Comparison with the punctuation of the first hand (point before OCA AN and QUAECUMQUE, line ending at OYPANOIC and CAELIS) indicates a similar division of these parallel clauses in the two hands. Moreover, his line division is identical in the two columns. The implication is that the corrector had to hand, certainly a bilingual manuscript written in sense-lines, and probably the exemplar of D itself. This is further substantiated by his use of a medial point in F37/17 (Mt 12.20) between the end of the line and his addition.

It is rare for d^G to adopt a Latin rendering that departs from the text of the Greek column. We have only Mt 5.41; 15.18, 20; 16.16; 23.4; 27.31; Ac 1.21; 3.3; 4.6 (*caiafas*) – nine variants. There is also Ac 2.30, where the alteration to the Greek text creates a difference with d. On the other hand, differences between the columns are removed at Mt 6.2; 10.36; 15.36; 16.17; 18.25; 25.34; 26.42; Ac 1.3, 6, 11, 15 (first correction), 20; 2.30 (Latin correction), 46; 3.17, 26; 4.6 (*ionathas*), 7 (both corrections) – a total of nineteen. Where he adds to both columns, his text is identical in each. The material that we have gathered also shows that, when he alters the Latin text to improve the style, he does not generally do so in such a way as to create a difference between the columns. To put it differently, his better readings are drawn from a versional tradition that is closely related to Codex Bezae. Again, the implication is that he was using the exemplar.

One of the purposes of his activities in Acts is to remove discrepancies between the columns. This is an example of the kind of revision that had already taken place in the Gospel ancestors of Codex Bezae. Just as in that stage the revision was done most effectively in Matthew, so G's work on the Gospels deals only with the first of them. His brief but intense contribution to Acts would have moulded a copy taken from Codex Bezae in such a way that careful study would have revealed revision in chapters 1–4.

This corrector was far more than that remover of betacisms who was so repugnant to Scrivener. We see him improving both the accuracy of the version (the nineteen corrections that adopt the same text as that in the Greek column), and its style. The use of *etiam* for *ναι* is distasteful to him (see also Burkitt, pp. 509f). He prefers to pick up the verb in the question – Dicit Iesus creditis? Dicunt ei Credimus (Mt 9.28); Intellexisti haec? Dicunt ei Intelleximus (13.51). At 17.25 he gives a fuller comment on the rendering: Magister vester non praestat tributum. Et dicit – *etiam* won't do, and he writes *facit* in the margin, then *aut*, as a better idea strikes him, *praestat*. At 21.16 he placed deletion marks over *etiam*, but failed to insert his alternative. At 19.9 he replaces *ratione* for *λογου* with *causa*. He smooths out incongruencies of participle and main verb (Mt 3.16; 25.34; 26.42; Ac 3.3, 4 (these two both participle + *et* + main verb); 3.26). He suggests *vox* rather than *echo* for *ηχος* (Ac 2.2). We observe the Latin tradition of Codex Bezae being moulded and improved.

G is also a genuinely bilingual user of the codex. This is shown not only by the fact that he uses both columns, but also by his preference for readings that are common to both. Where both D and d present nonsense, it is rare for him to correct only the Latin. The only exception is Mt 12.20. That is, once his orthographic and stylistic corrections to the Latin are set aside, he shows equal interest in both columns.

Whether G knew other Old Latin texts, and what, if he did, they were like, is virtually impossible to determine. The data are too slight, and the relationship between the witnesses too involved. But several exact agreements with h (Ac 3.4, 17; 4.7) and near-agreements (3.3, 11) may be worth noting.

The picture that emerges is of a corrector who handled the volume when it was still new. A problem arises, in that he corrected in only 117 bifolia. That Acts should have merited particular attention is understandable, and he worked conscientiously through its opening folios, before giving up. That he can have been the official diorthotes may be discounted on the grounds of his script and of the character of the corrections. Burkitt suggests that he was the bishop of the Latin-speaking community for which D was produced. It is clear that Burkitt has in mind the example of Victor of Capua and his Codex Fuldensis. Although an episcopal ductus has no *character indelibilis* that we may recognize it, the suggestion does justice to the confidence that the corrector shows, whilst allowing for the intermittent nature of his activity. Burkitt's description is thoughtful and imaginative, and is worth repeating:

> (1) G's language was Latin.
> (2) Yet he knew Greek, and where he adds a line of Greek (Matt. xviii. 18) he writes it with an assured hand.
> (3) He pays no attention to the traditional Latin Bible.
> (4) His handwriting is that of a scholar, not of a professional scribe, and he makes corrections where he chances to have been reading. (p. 511)

As to Burkitt's third point, it is certain that there was no 'traditional' Latin Bible in 400, certainly not of Acts. The fourth point is open to question, although it is possible that he took a sample Gospel and a sample section of Acts to examine the manuscript – as it were a primitive Claremont Profile Method.

G's freedom in altering the Latin text shows, according to Burkitt, that the Greek side of D 'was Holy Scripture; the Latin side was merely a "crib", if one may be allowed to use the word' (*ibid.*). This expresses the nature of his alterations very vividly. The Greek column is corrected to give sense and a reliable original, the Latin to follow the Greek and to be tolerable Latin. The context of such work will have been a Latin community that still used the Greek in its services, and knew sense from nonsense, but which also expected a written Latin version which was at once faithful as a translation and recognizable as Latin.

The vital conclusion to be drawn from the fact that G knew the exemplar of D is that, where his corrections are not stylistic, they are to be regarded as a more authoritative witness to tradition than are those of the first hand. It is a very great pity that he did not revise the entire manuscript.

In his work, there is no sign that G is ill at ease with the peculiarities of Codex Bezae. Again, this is a sign that he knew the text it came from, and accepted its authority. No other corrector was to be so comfortable with the text of D as this one was.

CORRECTOR A

Table 26. *Corrections by Corrector A*

Col.	Mt	Jn	Lk	Mk	Ac	Total
Greek	20	26	35	36	53	170
Latin	1				2	3
Both	—	1	—	—	1	2

There is no pattern of alteration by Corrector A of the Greek text to or from the Latin (table 26). The majority of corrections which bring it into agreement with the Latin are also ones where D* has a reading that is either unique or poorly attested. Such are Mt 11.12; 13.21; Lk 22.13; Mk 12.42; Ac 2.15; 6.2; 7.41, 60; 12.19; 15.7. The more interesting of these are

Acts 2.15 (419b/32)
ΟΥϹΗϹ ωΡΑϹ ΤΗϹ ΗΜΕΡΑϹ ·Γ· D*
εστιν γαρ ωρα ·γ· της ημερας D^A d
7.41 (441b/29): ΑΠΗΓΑΓΟΝΤΟ D*; *ανηγαγον* D^A d
The D* reading needs the addition of such a word as either *προς* after it (cp. 1 Cor. 12.2), or *θυσιᾳ*, in order to make sense. The corrector shows no knowledge of any such reading.
12.19 (464b/28): *αποκτανθηναι* D*; *απαχθηναι* D^A; OBDUCI d

The Greek support for all these corrections is so general that there are no grounds for assuming any interest on the corrector's part in the Latin column. As to his Greek text, it is clear that he is not comparing D with a close antecedent, for the example at 7.41 shows him removing nonsense by adopting an alternative text, rather than restoring the reading of the Bezan tradition. Beyond this, we cannot deduce anything about the text he knew.

There is little more to be gleaned from corrections that bring about a difference from the Latin text. These are Mt 19.22; Jn 5.13; 7.9; 8.40; 11.10; Lk 9.25; 23.56; Ac 1.16, 23; 5.22; 13.39. One or two tell us a little more about him.

Matthew 19.22 (63b/17): *ακουσας ο νεανισκος* D* d; *ακουσας ου νεανισκος* D^A
The D^A text is a clumsy attempt to read *ακουσας ουν ο νεανισκος* ('inepto modo', as Tischendorf remarks in his apparatus).

John 7.9 (130b/2): *αυτος* D*; *αυτοις* D^A; *ipse* d
Luke 9.25 (222b/23)
ΑΝΘΡΩΠΟΝ ΚΕΡΔΗϹΑΙ ... ΑΠΟΛΕϹΑΙ D* d
ανθρωπος εαν κερδηση ... απολεση D^A
The reading of the first hand is harmonization to par. Mk 8.36. The correction, which is also a harmonization (this time to par. Mt 26.36), has only versional support in the IGNT apparatus – the rest of the Latin evidence, the Old Syriac, the Armenian, and the Ethiopic. It cannot be decided whether the corrector is acting out of his own recollection of Matthew, or on the authority of a Greek manuscript known to him. Note that at Mk 8.36 also D harmonizes (though not in the word order) to Matthew (Vogels, *Harmonistik*, p. 95).
23.56 (280b/28): *ητοιμασαν* D* d; *ητοιμασεν* D^A
This 'correction' makes no sense and merely corrupts the text.
Acts 13.39 (470b/9): *ηδυνηθητε* D* d; *ηδυνηθημεν* D^A
The same is true of this reading.

At several places, both *p.m.* and A differ from d.

Acts 1.3 (415b/10): ΤΕϹϹΕΡΑΚΟΝΤΑ ΗΜΕΡΩΝ D*; *τεσσερακοντα δι ημερων* D^A; POST DIES QUADRAGINTA d
11.9 (459b/30): *εγενετο* D*; *εγενετο δε* D^A; *respondit vero* d
This correction is a mixture of the other variants. Did A fail to notice the *εγενετο*?
18.26 (493b/4)
ΚΑΙ ΑΚΟΥϹΑΝΤΟϹ ΑΥΤΟΥ ΑΚΥΛΑϹ ΚΑΙ ΠΡΙϹΚΙΛΛΑ D*
ακουσαντες δε αυτου ακ. και πρ. D^A
ET CUM AUDISSENT EUM AQUILAS ET PRISCILLA d
The D* reading seems to take the whole clause as a genitive absolute, in spite of the endings of the nouns, and is a corruption of *και ακουσαντες* ... (cp. d).

At several places where the Latin is not extant, we have significant alterations to the Greek text.

Matthew 6.10 (16b/7): add. *ως* post *θελημα μου*
John 1.6 (104b/9)
ΠΑΡΑ ΚΥ ΗΝ ΟΝΟΜΑ ΑΥΤΩ · ΪΩΑΝΝΗΗΝ (or ΪΩΑΝΝΕΝ ?) D*
παρα θυ ονομα αυτω · ϊωαννης D^A
Κυριου and *ϊωαννην* are both peculiar to D. Hν is read by ℵ* W^s sy (c).
Mark 16.11 (347b/18): In the unique D reading ΚΑΙ ΟΥΚ ΕΠΙϹΤΕΥϹΑΝ ΑΥΤΩ, the final word has been changed to *αυτη*. The bigger variant, of participle (and subordinate clause) followed by *και* and a finite verb – a regular phenomenon in D – has not been altered (compare the correction at Ac 5.22, and see further on Corrector B, below).
Acts 20.38 (502b/23): add. *ω ειρηκει* post ΛΟΓΩ. The whole text of D is different here. The correction is a partial conflation with the standard text.

This hand also made corrections to the corresponding place in both columns. The first of these is at F121b/122, l.20 (Jn 5.32). The first hand read Η ΜΑΡΤΥΡΙΑ ΜΟΥ and TESTIMONIUM. This was altered by A to *η μαρτυρια αυτου* and *testimonium eius*.

The other correction is at F421b/422, l.22 (Ac 2.30): the whole line has been placed within angled brackets to show that it should be omitted. The attribution of this to Corrector A must remain uncertain.

We find three corrections to the Latin column attributed to this hand: F32/4 – *magis* for MACIS; 439/16 – *regis* for REGAE; and 463/30 – *producere* for PRODOCERE. None of these is significant.

The remaining corrections to the Greek text are either orthographic, or deal with first-hand readings which are clearly scribal error, such as the omission of *τι* in F228b/25, or *ου* in 439b/33, or do not affect the sense for purposes of comparison with the Latin text.

In correcting vowel shifts we find that Corrector A most often makes ones involving *ει* and *ι*:

ι to *ει*: twenty times (all initial letters; five are *ις* to *εις*, thirteen are to parts of *εἶδον*).

αι to *ε*: once

ω to *ο*: three times

ο to *ω*: once

Movable *nu* is inserted twice (before ΛΑΓΩΝ at 261b/19), ΟΥΚ becomes *ουχ'* before ΟΥΤΟC at 302b/1, and ΟΥΧ *ουκ* before ΗΔΥΝΑΤΟ at 303b/22.

There is a nonsense correction at 469b/1 – the insertion of *ι* between ΪΝΑ and ΕΙC. The definite article is inserted seven times, and a missing syllable is supplied nineteen times.

In most of the remaining readings, it is a casual error of D* which is corrected (for Mt 16.16 and Jn 8.40, see the section devoted to Corrector H). In many others, D* is unique, and D^{A} adopts the only variant. About a dozen merit closer attention.

Matthew 6.18 (16b/28): ΚΡΥΦΙΑ D*; *κρυφαιω* D^{A}
23.24 (78b/20): *τυφλοι* D*; *τυφλοι οι* D^{A}
John 9.29 (141b/12): ΟΤΙ ΘC ΑΜΑΡΤΩΛΩΝ ΟΥΚ ΑΚΟΥΕΙ D*; add. *ο* ante ΘC D^{A}
This is likely to be a grammatical correction made without reference to the other texts.
Mark 8.10 (311b/22): ΜΕΛΕΓΑΔΑ D*; *μαγαιδα* D^{A}
8.35 (314b/1): *την ψυχην αυτου* D*; *την ψυχην εαυτου* D^{A}
11.32 (327b/5): ΦΟΒΟΥΜΕΝ D*; *φοβουμεθα* D^{A}
φοβουμεθα is a harmonization to par. Mt 21.26. D* is simply a mistake for that (the active being obsolete in the Hellenistic period), perhaps caused by ΕΙΠΩΜΕΝ in the line above. Is A again correcting the grammar on his own initiative?
14.33 (338b/29): ΑΚΗΔΕΜΟΝΕΙΝ D*; *αδημονειν* D^{A}
Acts 5.36 (434b/12): *προσεκληθη* D*; *προσεκλειθησαν* D^{A}
8.17 (445b/23): *επετιθουν* D*; *επετιθεσαν* D^{A}
See M.-H. 2,202. D^{A} rejects the intrusion of the thematic ending.
10.25 (456b/12): D* has *προσκυνεω* with the accusative, as at Mt 4.10; Jn 4.22 (bis), 23; 9.38;

Lk 4.8. D^A rejects it here, in a longer reading. Compare Corrector C, who adds *αυτον* after *προσκυνουντας* at Jn 4.24.

13.29 (469b/1): ΕΤΕΛΟΥΝ D*; *ετελεσεν* D^A

Intrusion of the strong aorist is discussed by Gignac, 2,332 (§3). The corrector may perhaps have intended the third person plural.

15.34 (479b/18): *αυτους* D*; *προς αυτους* D^A

B.-L. gives a cross-reference to 21.4, where ℵ B C H P and most other manuscripts have *αυτου*, A E L and others *αυτοις*, Lvt (d e) and other versional evidence *προς αυτους*. D is lost.

16.16 (482b/10): *πυθωνα* D*; *πυθωνος* D^A

17.26 (488b/33): *προτεταγμενους* D*; *προσταγμενους* D^A

The high proportion of singular readings shown by D^A is quite striking. So too is the eclectic nature of his other readings. He cannot be associated with any single known text, including that represented by D. It seems that he regularly acts out of grammatical principles. This latter is more significant, if we observe the proportion in his total number of corrections. Out of 176, forty-seven correct itacisms, seventeen correct endings of verbs or nouns, twenty-five correct consonants, and nineteen insert an omitted syllable – amounting to 108.

This corrector is not much concerned with text. His main aim is to tidy up D* as he finds it. However, the fact that he seems to prefer to do this without reference to other manuscripts, suggests that his attitude to textual matters accords with that of the text which he is correcting. He is, let us say, more concerned with what he thinks the reading should be, than with external evidence for it.

CORRECTOR C

Table 27. *Corrections by Corrector C*

Col.	Mt	Jn	Lk	Mk	Ac	Total
Greek	22	12	15	14	73	136
Latin	—	—	—	—	1	1

One feature of this corrector is that his activity is spasmodic (table 27). There is only one correction between F48b (Mt 15.1) and 77b (Mt 23), and there are none between F229b (Lk 10) and 285b (Mk 1), nor between 319b (Mk 10) and 347b (Mk 16). Acts contains more than half of his corrections. Fourteen of those made to Matthew are in Ff3b–48b, after which his enthusiasm wanes a trifle.

Compared to the hands A and B, this one has no interest in correcting itacisms. He deals with only five, all in the *ε/η/ι* range (191b/22, 285b/15, 319b/26, 429b/18, 455b/7). Two of his corrections (100b/20 and 423b/30) introduce itacism. They involve the same vowels.

He inserts many definite articles, no fewer than twenty-nine. D* is unique in all but a few of these readings. The insertion at 16b/28 is an alteration to the correction by D^A. The sequence is ΚΡΥΦΙΑ D*, *κρυφαιω* D^A, *τω κρυφαιω* D^C. One of these readings (77b/29) is a correction that makes the Greek column different from the Latin. Some others will also come in the list of significant textual variants.

A syllable omitted by D* is replaced sixteen times. Movable *nu* is inserted four times. The spelling ЇѠΑΝΗϹ is once altered to the double *nu* form (463b/33). There are ten other small corrections such as the insertion of omitted letters or replacement of wrong consonants.

Insertion of the article: F10b/27, 12b/5, 16b/28, 28b/1, 34b/32, 42b/33, 77b/29, 81b/1, 102b/25, 191b/21, 210b/33, 285b/13, 347b/2, 423b/21, 425b/18, 429b/27, 443b/3, 444b/2, 17, 457b/19, 458b/20, 459b/22, 23, 464b/9, 473b/5, 17, 476b/21, 494b/3, 495b/1
Insertion of an omitted syllable: 4b/16, 6b/6, 118b/19, 141b/16, 147b/32, 152b/10, 217b/22, 227b/17, 229b/4, 308b/9, 28, 319b/4, 415b/17, 471b/8, 489b/9, 508b/26
Insertion of movable *nu*: 463b/1, 465b/16, 473b/33, 475b/12
At 431b/10 the missing word *προς* is restored to the text.
Other small corrections: 15b/24, 92b/26, 198b/17, 218b/4, 226b/32, 285b/26, 422b/23, 435b/26, 457b/4, 486b/25.

These corrections amount to one half of the total number.

The single correction to the Latin text attributed to this hand is at F436/14 (Ac 6.1):

DISCUPIUNTUR d*; *dispiciuntur* d^C

The attribution to C has to remain questionable. The error in d* is due to misrecognition.

An analysis of the more significant readings of this hand betrays a movement away from the Latin-related base of the Greek text.

Corrections that remove a discrepancy with the Latin	13
Corrections that introduce a discrepancy with the Latin	21
Corrections that do neither	35

We shall take each group in turn.

Corrections that remove a discrepancy with the Latin

Matthew 5.19 (12b/5): ΟϹ D*; *οσ αν* D^C; QUICUMQUE d
John 6.50 (127b/15): *ινα* D*; *ινα εαν* D^C; *ut si* d
21.18 (180b/33): ΟΠΟΥ ϹΥ ΘΕΛΕΙϹ D*; *οπου συ ου θελεις* D^C; *ubi tu non uis* d

Luke 4.18 (198b/13): απεσταλμαι D*; απεσταλκεν μαι D^C; *misit me* d
8.36 (218b/17): ΛΙΩΝ D*; ληγαιων D^C; *legion* d
Acts 2.43 (423b/4): OM D* (τερατα next word); τε D^C; ETIAM d
3.3 (423b/30): EINAI D*; εισειεναι D^C; INTROIRE d
3.16 (425b/12–13)
ΤΟΥΤΟΝ ΘΕΩΡΕΙΤΕ ΚΑΙ ΟΙΔΑΤΕ / ΟΤΙ ΕСΤΕΡΕΩСΕΝ D*
τουτον ον θεωρ. κ. οιδατε εστερεωσεν D^C
HUNC QUEM UIDISTIS ET SCITIS CONSOLDAUIT d
4.14 (427b/30): OM D*; τε D^C; QUOQUE d
4.25 (429b/5): καινα D*; κενα D^C; INANIA d
10.33 (457b/5)
παρακαλων ελθειν προς ημας D*
παρακαλων ελθειν σε προσ ημας D^C
ROGANDO VENIRE TE AD NOS d
ibid. (457b/7): ΔΟΥ D*; ἴδου D^A; ουν D^C; *ergo* d
Whilst Tischendorf and Wettstein (Vol. 2, p. 520) take the D* reading as an error for ιδου, Scrivener (*Adn. ed.*) reads it as δ' οὐ.
14.16 (473b/33): KATA D*; παντα D^C; *omnes* d

Corrections that introduce a discrepancy with the Latin column

Matthew 9.17 (26b/23): ΤΗΡΟΥΝΤΑΙ D*; συντηρουνται D^C
Servo is used by Lvt (a b d h k q), *reservo* by Lvt (c), and *conservo* by the remaining Lvt Mss and by Lvg.
19.3 (61b/24): λεγουσιν D*; λεγοντες D^C; DICUNT d
Here the text of D*/d requires a break after AYTON, which may have been present in the exemplar as the end of a sense-line.
23.16 (77b/29): λεγοντες D*; οι λεγοντες D^C
27.53 (100b/20): ΕΦΑΝΗСΑΝ D*; ενεφανεισαν D^C; PARUERUNT d
27.56 (100b/31): ιωσηφ D*; ιωσητος D^C; *ioseph* d
John 4.24 (115b/32): προσκυνουντας D*; +αυτον D^C; *adorantes* d
15.5 (160b/25): ποιειν D* d; +ουδεν D^C
15.7 (160b/31): OM D* d*; υμιν D^C
Again the sense of D*, such as it is, depends on the division into sense-lines. By the omission, ΚΑΙ ΓΕΝΗСΕΤΑΙ is placed with v. 8. d* was later corrected by J.
17.11 (166b/18): +εν τω κοσμω post ΕΓΩ D^C
The whole sentence is one that in Greek is unique to Codex Bezae, being a reduplication of the beginning of v. 12, with an added initial ΕΓΩ (variation in the two forms of the Latin translation of the phrase indicates that it is a genuine translation of this corrupt Greek text). There is variation between the manuscripts in v. 12:
εν τω κοσμω A C³ Θ pler. Lvt (f q)
OM ℵ B C* D L W 1 pc. Lvt (cet.)
ibid. (166b/19): ο D*; ους D^C; QUOD d
Luke 1.34 (184b/30): μαρια D*; μαριαμ D^C

Acts 3.1 (423b/21)
ΕΠΙ ΤΗΝ ѠΡΑΝ ΕΝΝΑΤΗ ΤΗ ΠΡΟϹΕΥΧΗ D*
επι την ωραν της προσευχης την ενατην D^C
AD HORAM NONAM ORATIONIS d
5.32 (433b/30): *και το πνευμα* D* d; *και το πνευμα δε* D^C
7.21 (439b/20): *αυτη* D*; *αυτον εαυτη* D^C; (SIBI d)
10.20 (455b/17): *αναστα* D*; *αναστας* D^C; SURGE ET d
10.33 (457b/8)
ΕΝѠΠΙΟΝ ϹΟΥ ΑΚΟΥϹΑΙ ΒΟΥΛΟΜΕΝΟΙ D*
ενωπιον του θεου παρεσμεν ακουσαι D^C
IN CONSPECTU TUO AUDIRE VOLUMUS d
10.38 (457b/22): ΟΝ ΕΧΡΙϹΕΝ D* d; *ον εχρισεν αυτο* D^C
10.40 (457b/33): *αυτω ενφανη* D* d; *αυτω μεν φανη* D^C
Kipling thought that the correction read *αυτον ενφανη*. But the added letter is undoubtedly *μ*, and the loss of the second part of the *ω* is simply the result of the ink flaking.
15.15 (477b/15): *ουτως* D* d; *τουτω* D^C
17.1 (485b/21)
ΚΑΙ ΚΑΤΗΛΘΟΝ ΕΙϹ ΑΠΟΛΛѠΝΙΔΑ ΚΑΚΕΙΘΕΝ D*
κατηλθον και εις απολ. κακειθεν D^C
και την απολ. ηλθον cet.
This is an attempt to soften the grammar of D (ΔΙΟΔΕΥϹΑΝΤΕϹ ... ΚΑΙ ΚΑΤΗΛΘΟΝ).
17.16 (487b/23): *αυτου* D*; *αυτους* D^C

Corrections that cannot be compared to the Latin

Matthew 9.10 (25b/9): ϹΥΝΕΚΕΙΝΤΟ D*; *συνανεκειντο* D^C
12.25 (36b/33): *στησεται* D*; *σταθησεται* D^C al.
15.1 (48b/29): ΠΡΟΕΡΧΟΝΤΑΙ D*; *προσερχονται* D^C; ACCEDUNT D
27.66 (101b/28): *ησφαλισαν* D*; *ησφαλισαντο* D^C
The middle of this verb was used for the active in the NT period, according to A.-G. The active is cited by Lampe, *Lexicon*, although the middle was clearly predominant.
John 20.21 (177b/32): *αποστελλω* D*; *πεμπω* D^C
Luke 2.39 (191b/21): *πολιν* D*; *την πολιν* D^C
ibid. (*ibid.*): *εαυτων* D*; *αυτων* D^C
4.17 (198b/10): ΑΠΤΥΞΑϹ D*; *αναπτυξας* D^C
9.33 (223b/17): ΠΟΙΗϹѠ D*; *ποιησωμεν* D^C; FACIO d
Mark 1.11 (285b/30): *ευδοκησα* D*; *ηυδοκησα* D^C
4.31 (297b/3): *μεικροτερον εστιν* D*; *μεικροτερος μεν εστιν* D^C;
MINOR EST = *μικροτερος εστιν* d
There are two variants here – the ending of *μικροτερος*, and whether *εστιν* should be included (in several possible places) or omitted.
7.21 (309b/15): *κακοι* D*; *οι κακοι* D^C
9.36 (317b/21): ΑΝΑΚΛΙϹΑΜΕΝΟϹ D*; *εναγκαλισαμενος* D^C
10.3 (319b/12): *ετειλατο* D*; *ενετειλατο* D^C

Acts 1.20 (417b/22): Η D*; εστω D^C
3.11 (424b/24): ΤΗ CΤΟΑ Η D*; τη στοα τη D^C; PORTICUM QUI d
4.12 (427b/24): Ο ΔΕΔΟΜΕΝΟΝ D*; το δεδομενον D^C; QUOD DATUM EST d
4.30 (429b/19): γενεσθαι D*; γινεσθαι D^C
4.32 (429b/27): καρδια D*; η καρδια D^C
D^C does not add η before ψυχη.
8.6 (444b/16–17)
ωC ΔΕ ΗΚΟΥΟΝ ΠΑΝ ΟΙ ΟΧΛΟΙ / ΠΡΟCΕΙΧΟΝ ΤΟΙC ΛΕΓΟΜΕΝΟΙC ΫΠΟ ΦΙΛΙΠΠΟΥ [ ] (ΕΝΙΖΟΝΤΟ ??) D*
προσειχον δε οι οχλοι τοις λεγομ. υπο φιλ. ομοθυμαδον D^C
INTENDEBANT AUTEM OMNIS TURBAE / HIS QUAE DICEBANTUR A PHILIPPO UNANIMO d
ωC ... ΟΧΛΟΙ in D* is bracketed by the corrector.
8.21 (446b/5): η καρδια D*; η γαρ καρδια D^C; deest d
10.45 (458b/20): ΤΟΥ ΠΝC ΑΓΙΟΥ D*; του πνς του αγιου D^C
11.28 (462b/3): μεγαν D*; μεγαλην D^C
12.15 (464b/10): Ο ΔΕ ΕΛΕΓΟΝ ΑΥΤΗ D*; οι δε προς αυτην D^C
Tischendorf and (hesitantly) Ropes both thought that the first hand of D read οι, not ο. But the *iota* is certainly secondary. B.-L. give no justification for their selection of D^C as the authentic 'Western' text.
13.1 (465b/25): εν οις D*; εν οις ην και D^C; IN QUO d
14.10 (473b/5): μεγαλη φωνη D*; μεγαλη τη φωνη D^C
ibid. (473b/9): ΑΝΗΛΑΤΟ D*; ανηλλατο D^C
15.2 (475b/29): οπως κριθωσιν επ αυτοις D*; οπως κριθωσιν επ αυτων D^C;
UT IUDICENT SUPER EOS d
15.7 (476b/21): στοματος D*; του στοματος D^C
15.15 (477b/15): CΥΝΦωΝΗCΟΥCΙΝ D*; συνφωνουσιν D^C; CONSONAT d
16.25 (483b/13)
ΚΑΤΑ ΔΕ ΜΕCΟΝ ΤΗC ΝΥΚΤΟC D*; κατα δε το μεσονυκτιον D^C
CIRCA MEDIAM VERO NOCTE d
ibid. (483b/16): ΔΕCΜΟΙ D*; δεσμιοι D^C
17.17 (487b/29): ΠΑΡΑΤΥΧΟΝΤΑC D*; παρατυγχανοντας D^C
17.27 (489b/5): ΟΝ ΑΦ ΕΝΟC D*; ων αφ ενος D^C
17.28 (489b/6): ΕΝ ΑΥΤΗ D*; εν αυτω D^C

These sixty-nine readings are for the most part in agreement with the majority of manuscripts collated for the critical editions. Only a couple of dozen betray special influences, but they are enough for these influences to be taken seriously.

Corrector C has ten singular readings:

Mt 27.53	ενεφανεισαν
56	ιωσητος
Jn 17.11	εν τω κοσμω
Mk 4.31	μεικροτερος μεν εστιν

Ac 10.38	ον εχρισεν αυτο
40	αυτω μεν φανη
12.15	οι δε προς αυτην
13.1	εν οις ην και
14.10	ανηλλατο
17.27	ων αφ ενος

Several of these may be partial corrections where the corrector forgot to make the whole alteration necessary. At Mt 27.53 the D* reading of the second aorist ΕΦΑΝΗCΑΝ may have prompted the corrector's reading, which is the second aorist of ἐμφαινω rather than of ἐμφανιζω (Gr. cet.). 'Εμφαινω is not found in the New Testament or early Christian literature, and occurs only twice in the Septuagint (Ps. 79 (80).2; 2 Macc. 3.16). Ac 10.38 is another incomplete correction, and the strange appearance of *μεν* in v. 40 is also likely to be one. Is the reading at Ac 12.15 a correction towards the majority text, which simply failed to add the verb? Yet, as it stands, it is a good Lukan idiom.

Other corrections may be attempts to improve passages where the corrector accepted a longer variant in D, but was dissatisfied with it in detail. Ac 13.1; 14.10; and 17.27 are all of this kind. Jn 17.11 may belong here. But he must have known the variant form from ℵ B D in verse 12 – did he intend to correct that, and inserted the phrase in the wrong place?

Of the remaining singular readings, Mt 27.56 *ιωσητος* is a harmonization to parallel Mk 15.40, and Mk 4.31 seems to take *μικροτερος* as the beginning of a new clause.

With the possible exceptions of Mt 27.56; Mk 4.31; and Ac 12.15, there is no evidence that the corrector knew a strikingly distinctive text that is otherwise lost. But there are signs that he was willing to use his own judgement in correcting the text.

There is a small group of readings which could suggest that the corrector was sensitive to the character of Codex Bezae, and not unaware of its Latin affiliations. These are the readings with only Latin support – *ινα εαν* at Jn 6.50 (*ut si* Lvt (a aur b c d f ff^2 q r^1)) and *συ ου* at 21.18 (*quo tu non vis* Lvt (aur b c d e f ff^2 q)) – and those with significant Latin support at Mt 5.19; Ac 4.14; 10.33, 45. It may be that the last of these is simply stylistic, and that at Jn 21.18 he was concerned only with the glaring omission of *ου*, and did not realize that it was connected with the intrusion of *συ* at an early stage in the tradition – or he would have corrected it by altering *συ* to *ου*. The readings at Mt 5.19 and Ac 4.14 may have been in a Greek copy known to him. We are left with two readings. Ac 10.33 could also be a stylistic correction. If not, it is either an almost unique indication that he knew another Greek text similar to D, or else a reading similar to that remarkable one at Jn 6.50. There it seems hard to deny either that he was influenced, directly or indirectly, by a text similar to that of the Old Latin manuscripts which share the reading; or that the reading of the Latin column influenced his opinion of the Greek text. We will be able to form a better judgement on this when we have looked at other groups of readings.

Apart from these few examples, the majority of corrections at readings where the evidence is split follow the *Koinē* text. Three are with the Alexandrian – Ac 4.14 (*τε* ℵ A B E pc.); 10.45 (*του πνευματος του αγιου* B 181); 11.28 (*μεγαλην* ℵ A B pc.). Two of these we have just cited as possible evidence of the influence of Latin texts. (I am not suggesting that they can have been affected by both.) Is the third (11.28) a correction out of the corrector's own sense of good grammar? (See M.-H. 2,123f for the gender of *λιμος*.) If this is so, then there is no evidence except for 4.14 and 10.45 that this corrector knew any text at all like that of ℵ B. This strengthens the possibility that the readings at 4.14 and 10.45 are due to Latin influence.

There are eight readings with the *Koinē* against the B ℵ text – Jn 17.11; Lk 2.39 (*την πολιν*); Mk 1.11; 4.31; Ac 2.43; 4.32; 5.32; 14.10.

Finally, two readings agree with a smaller group of Greek manuscripts. At Mt 5.19 Corrector C reads *ος αν* with 33 71 471 (and d). At Ac 15.2 he has *οπως κριθωσιν επ αυτων* with 614 (the *apparatus* in Ropes is wrong in citing 614 for *αυτοις* with D*). This also could be an independent stylistic correction (see Ac 24.21; 25.9).

A tentative profile of this corrector has three features. Firstly, many corrections are his own stylistic improvements. Secondly, the Greek text known to him was of a *Koinē* type that cannot be more closely defined. The third feature is that, Greek though he seems to be, he was occasionally influenced by elements with Latin affiliations. This is unexpected, and goes against what has generally been believed of the Greek correctors of Codex Bezae. It is clear that it would be going beyond the evidence to claim that he knew any Latin texts. This, with the chance agreement with 614, a manuscript which apparently has a number of agreements with D in the central chapters of Acts, leads us after all to be able to define the text of Corrector C as Byzantine, with a number of quite distinctive readings.

The description I have just given of 614 comes from a talk by Dr C. D. Osburn, at the Conference on New Testament Textual Criticism, held in Birmingham in September, 1987, in which he described the collating of manuscripts of Acts in which he is at present engaged.

The overall trend of the correctors suggests that, slight though the Latin influence is, it might be safer and might present a more plausible account if this hand be placed between A and B; that is, at a fairly early stage in the history of the manuscript, before the more considerably different text of B was imposed upon it.

CORRECTOR B

H. and K. Lake, *Codex Sinaiticus Petropolitanus*, 2 vols., Oxford, 1911–22: Introduction by K. Lake (the two volumes contain the same introductory material; I cite the NT volume (1911)); Milne and Skeat, *Scribes and Correctors*, pp. 40–50; J. A. Robinson, *Euthaliana* (Texts and Studies 3.3), Cambridge, 1895.

Table 28. *Corrections by Corrector B*

Col.	Mt	Jn	Lk	Mk	Ac	Total
Greek	41	46	53	29	160	329
Both	1	—	—	—	1	2

With Corrector B we find the most significant attempt to alter the character of the text, in the nature as well as in the extent of its activities (table 28).

First we note his effect on the sense-lines. His preference is to add at the end of one line a word (such as a copula) omitted at the beginning of the next. This is easier and neater from his point of view. But the effect is that a manuscript copied from D would show a further deterioration in the sense-lines.

Secondly, this corrector was quite often careless in the way he did his work, and consequently left the possibility for new error. A replacement letter is generally written above the line, without that of the first hand being deleted. Such are F39b/14 (*α* over *ει* in *εστηκεισαν*), 159b/2 (*ε* over *ιν* in *εστιν*). But beyond this, there are a number of corrections that actually present a wrong spelling:

137b/11: ΑΛΗΘΕΙΑΝ → *λαλειαν*
29: ΑΤΕΙΜΑΖΕΤΕ → *-εται*
146b/13: ΚΟΙΜΑΤΑΙ → *κεκοιμαται*
158b/12: ΛΕΙC → *λεγις*
162b/12: ΜΕΜΕΙCΗΚΑCΙΝ → *εμεμεισ-*
179b/27: ΗΛΑΤΟ → *ηλλατο*
217b/20: ΔΑΙΟΜΑΙ → *δαιομε*
29: ΛΕΓΙѠΝ → *λεγαιων*
264b/24: ΕΞΑΠΕΙΛΑΝ → *εξαπεστιλαν*
416b/6: ΑΠΗΡΘΗ → *αιπηρθη*
420b/20: ? → *αποδεδιγμενον*
433b/25: ΔΟΞΗ → *δεξεια*
437b/23: ΜΕΤѠΚΗCΕΝ → *μετωκεισεν*
444b/28: ? → *εξειστων*
471b/9: ΕΠΙΔΗ → *επιδη δε*
10: ΚΡΕΙΝΑΤΕ → *κρεινεται*
496b/25: ΓΕΝΟΜΕΝΟΙ → *γειν-*

The addition of *και* at the end of 251b/31 creates dittography. The reading *ειποντες* for ΕΙΠΑΝ in 422b/11 (Ac 2.37) is a mistake. So also are 16b/32 (Mt 6.19: + *και* before ΚΛΕΠΤΑΙ), 159b/27 (Jn 14.25: *μενει* for ΜΕΝѠΝ, later corrected back by another hand) and 217b/19 (Lk 8.28: + *και* after ΦѠΝΗ ΜΕΓΑΛΗ instead of before it).

The itacisms just listed are mostly confusions of ι with ει. All concern the letters α, ϵ, and ι. By contrast, most of Corrector B's successful vowel corrections are of ο, υ, and ω.

ο to ω: ten times (including the word *ναζορηνος* in various cases corrected to *ναζωρ-* four times)
ου to ω: four times
ω to ο and υ to οι, as well as similar corrections, occur
ι to ει: three times
ϵ to η: twice
also η to ει, ϵ to η, αι to ϵ, etc.

Another clear proclivity of this scribe is to insert the definite article. He does this nearly as often as C, twenty-seven times. In eighteen of them, D* is unique, and in three others its support is very slight (Lk 15.6; Ac 19.26; 21.11). The addition of *το* before ΠΛΗΘΟϹ at Ac 21.22 is peculiar to D^B, and may reflect an excess of zeal. In several other examples we find readings which increase our knowledge of B.

Mark 15.12 (343b/17): ΒΑϹΙΛΕΙ D*; *τω βασιλει* D^B; *βασιλεα/τον βασιλεα* cet.
The correction is a modification of the text before him, perhaps encouraged by his recollection of the article from other manuscripts.
Luke 15.22 (249b/12): *στολην* ℵ A B D* K* L P W *Θ Π* al.; *την στολην* P^75 D^B E G H K^2 M pler.
Acts 7.8 (438b/10): *ιακωβ* ℵ A B C D* pc.; *ο ιακωβ* D^B H P al. pler.
Compare *ο ιακωβ* earlier in the verse.

In each of these last two readings, D^B provides early support for what was to become the dominant reading. They are in sharp contrast to that at Mk 15.12, and show him correcting D* against other models, although the manuscript support here is not altogether typical of what we will find elsewhere.

Further enthusiasms of this corrector are the insertion of movable *nu* (twelve times – Scrivener also notes this, though he gives only ten instances), insertion of a missing syllable (eighteen times), and the very frequent correction of single letters, including ν or ς missed out in endings (and three times he adds ν in *ιωανης* – twice in Luke and once in Acts).

Scrivener isolated two places where this corrector altered both columns. They are to be approached with some care.

Matthew 13.13 (40b/41, l.24): ΛΑΛΕΙ and LOQUOR D*; *ελαλει* and *loquebat* D^B; *λαλω* Gr. cet. and *loquor* Lat. cet.
This is unusual. Note the mistake in the Latin (it should be *loquebatur*), and the unique reading that he has produced. Is he thinking of Mk 4.33f (not strictly parallel, but in the

same pericope)? There we have τοιαυταις παραβολαις πολλαις ἐλαλει αὐτοις . . . Since the Latin correction has been erased, some doubt as to the identity of its author must be voiced. But it must also be said that such an alteration could hardly have arisen in the minds of two separate correctors.

Acts 13.10 (466b/467, l.27)
ΚΑΙ ΡΑΔΙΟΥΡΓΙΑС ΫΙΟΙ ΔΙΑΒΟΛΟΥ D*; ET FALSI FILI DIABOLE d*;
και πασης ραδιουργιας ϋιε διαβολου D^B cet.; *et omnes falsi fili diabole* D^B
This does not bring the columns into agreement. Since the correction at Mt 13.13 is very hard to read, we have no comparison by which to determine whether this is the Latin hand of B (assuming he had one). We can only say that the two corrections here in Acts look similar.

In analysing the material corrections made by B, I shall categorize them in terms of their relation to the Latin column. But it will become clear that this is not a concern of his. The following places, where D* is clearly in casual error, will not be further studied: Mt 21.16; Jn 6.30; 8.43; 12.47; 15.5, 8; Lk 12.34; 15.20; Mk 6.35; Ac 2.9, 17; 5.4; 7.21, 26; 8.9; 10.34.

We begin with corrections that share the reading of d.

Matthew 3.16 (8b/2): *εις* D*; *επ* D^B; *super* d
Par. Mk 1.10 has *εἰς*. The harmonization in D* has been removed.

Such a correction of a typical D reading – and a harmonization has every claim to be called that – may be seen time and again. In readings that agree with d we have also

Matthew 21.3 (68b/8): ΕΧΕΙ ΧΡΕΙΑΝ D*; *χρειαν εχει* D^B; *opus habet* d
John 8.43 (137b/9): *αληθειαν* D*; *λαλειαν* D^B; *loquellam* d
Acts 2.8 (419b/5): ΤΗΝ ΔΙΑΛΕΚΤΟΝ ΗΜѠΝ D*; *τη ιδια διαλεκτω ημων* D^B; PROPRIA LINGUA NOSTRA d
7.30 (440b/16): ΠΛΗСΘΕΝΤѠΝ ΑΥΤѠ ΕΤΗ D*; *πληρωθεντων ετων* D^B; INPLETIS ANNIS d
Πιμπλημι is used instead of *πληροω* in D at Lk 1.20 and 24.44 also (and in the latter place is corrected by B).
12.19 (464b/28): *αποκταθηναι* D*; *απαχθηναι* $D^{A.B}$; OBDUCI d
B is here following the correction made by A, and simply altering the way the change is made.
14.22 (474b/27): ΕΛΘΕΙΝ D*; *εισελθειν* D^B; *introire* d
18.2 (490b/8): ΑΥΤѠ D*; *αυτοις* D^B; *ad eos* d
19.19 (495b/25): OM D*; *δε* D^B; *autem* d
21.19 (505b/3): ѠС D*; *ων* D^B; *quae* d

Besides these, there are six further readings of considerable interest. The first is Lk 7.2 (210b/9). Here D* has ΤΙС; D^B replaced this with *παις*, equivalent to *puer* in d. All other Greek witnesses have *δουλος* (= *servus* in the rest of the Latin material). *Παις* is found in parallel Mt 8.5. The D* reading is a corruption of *παις* caused by the preceding word *τινος*.

At Ac 6.15 (437b/6), D* read HTENIZON ΔΕ ΑΥΤΩ ΠΑΝΤΕC, which was changed to ατενισαντες εις αυτον απαντες by D^B. The text of all other Greek manuscripts is ατενισαντες εις αυτον παντες. Two points are worth noting here. The first is the reading απαντες. The second is that, by not removing KAI before ΕΙΔΟΝ, D^B has produced the same construction as the Latin – a participle followed by και and a finite verb. Although this construction particularly typical of D may be due to incomplete revision, the further evidence of απαντες suggests that B was using a Greek text similar to that which lies behind d.

The reading at Ac 17.12 (487b/2, ΑΝΔΡΕC D*; και ανδρες D^B d) is part of a bigger variant in Codex Bezae. In the absence of any other evidence, it seems that the correction is authentic to the Bezan tradition.

Acts 19.39 (498b/10) is more complex:
ΕΝ ΤΩ ΝΟΜΩ ΕΚΚΛΗCΙΑ D*
εν τω νομω εκκησιας D^B d (IN LEGEM ECCLESIAE)
εν τω εννομω εκκλησιας D^D
εν τω εννομω εκκλησια cet
Both D* and D^D are half-way between the two main variants (unless ΕΚΚΛΗCΙΑ in D* is just a slip). The genuine variant to the dominant text is given by D^B and d.

The first three corrections all indicate that the corrector had access to a Greek text with readings similar to those of a Greek *Vorlage* of d. The same could be argued of the fourth. But the reading is more likely to be of a type which we will meet again, where he simply makes sense out of the text of D as he finds it, without reference to other models.

In the last two readings the corrector adopts a variant found in only part of the rest of the tradition.

Matthew 18.14 (59b/13): ημων D* pc.; υμων ℵ D^B W f^1 al. Lvt Lvg; μου B Θ 078 f^{13} pler.
Acts 6.10 (436b/21): ΕΠ D*; υπ D^B E; OM cet.

Apart from these corrections, there are considerably more where the corrector takes the Greek out of agreement with the Latin. There are also important corrections where the Latin is lost, and others which do not affect the relationship between the columns. For convenience, we will take these groups together.

First, there are a number where a distinctive D reading is eliminated. In all of these D*/d is almost or totally alone, and D^B goes with the only other variant.

Matthew 2.16 (5b/19): ΔΙΕΤΕΙΑC D*; διετους D^B; *bimatu* d
4.16 (9b/18): εν χωρα σκεια D*; εν χ. και σκ. D^B
The variant reflects a division amongst LXX manuscripts at Isa. 9.2.
5.36 (13b/28): ποιειν D; ποιησαι $D^{B.D}$; *facere* d
11.8 (32b/27): μαλακοις D* d; εν. μαλ. D^B
24.8 (80b/31): οδυνων D*; ωδινων D^B
27.31 (98b/28): OM D* d; και D^B

John 6.63 (128b/25): OM D* d; και D^B
Luke 4.27 (199b/11): ναιμας D*; ναιμαν D^B; *naemas* d
Mark 1.22 (286b/26): ουχ D* d; και ουχ D^B
Acts 2.22 (420b/20): ημας D* d; υμας D^B
5.16 (432b/4): δε D* d; δε και D^B
5.28 (433b/15): ιδου D* d; και ιδου D^B
5.31 (433b/25): τη δοξη D*; τη δεξεια D^B
5.39 (434b/31): μηποτε θεομαχοι D*; μηπ. και θεομ. D^B
6.9 (436b/17): OM D* d; και ασιας D^B
8.7 (444b/23): χωλοι D* d; και χωλοι D^B
15.27 (478b/28): ταυτα D* d; τα αυτα D^B
16.33 (484b/9): ΕΛΥCΕΝ D* d; ελουσεν D^B

Readings of this type where d is lost are

Matthew 6.14 (16b/15): εαν D*; εαν γαρ D^B
Acts 8.24 (446b/12): περι D*; υπερ D^B
8.28 (446b/30): αρματος D*; αρμ. αυτου D^B
20.35 (502b/15): των λογων D*; τε των λογ. D^B
22.6 (508b/20): ΑΠΟ D*; εκ D^B
22.26 (510b/24): OM D*; γαρ D^B

Alterations which do not affect the translation are at

Acts 4.34 (430b/6): ΚΑΙ ΦΕΡΟΝΤΕC D*; εφερον D^B
17.12 (487b/2): ελληνων D*; ελληνιδων D^B
19.19 (495b/29): ΕΥΡΟΝ D*; και ευρον D^B
20.2 (498b/21): ΧΡΗCΑΜΕΝΟC D*; παρακαλεσας αυτους D^B
21.11 (504b/2): ΑΝΕΛΘΩΝ ΔΕ D*; και ελθων D^B
21.19 (505b/2): ΟΥC ΑCΠΑΜΕΝΟC ΔΙΗΓΕΙΤΟ ΕΝΑ D*; και ασπ. αυτους εξηγειτο καθεν D^B

Much more can be discovered in places where the evidence is more evenly split, or where there are three or more variant readings. These need to be examined in greater detail, with more manuscript evidence than has hitherto been provided.

Particularly striking is the high number of agreements with the text of Codex Sinaiticus, especially the C group of correctors.

Matthew 5.48 (14b/31): ΕΝ ΟΥΡΑΝΟΙC D*; εν τοις ουρανοις pler. d; ουρανιος ℵ B D^B al.
19.28 (64b/7): καθισεσθε D* al.; καθησεσθε ℵ B C D^B al.
21.42 (72b/25): υμων D* d f^1 f^{13} al.; ημων D^B cet.
John 1.15 (104b/30): ειπον D* pler.; ειπον υμιν D^B Lvt (f) Lvg; ειπων $ℵ^a$ B* C*
8.41 (137b/6): ουκ εγεννηθημεν B $D^{*.H}$; ου γεγεννημεθα P^{75} $ℵ^c$ C D^B pler.; εγεννημεθα ℵ* (see p. 158 below)
14.17 (159b/2): εστιν P^{66*} B* D* W al. d; εστε D^B = εσται P^{66c} $P^{75vid'}$ ℵ A B^c pler.
15.21 (162b/3): εις υμας P^{66} $ℵ^c$ B D* al.; υμιν A D^B pler.; OM ℵ*
15.22 (162b/6): ΕΙΧΑΝ D*; ειχον A D^B pler.; ειχοσαν ℵ B L pc.

15.24 (162b/11): The variants and their attestation are, for our purposes, identical with v. 22.
16.13 (163b/20): οσα ℵ B D* al.; οσα αν A D^B Θ pler.
21.7 (179b/27): ΗΛΑΤΟ D*; ηλλατο D^B; εβαλεν εαυτον cet.
Luke 2.13 (189b/9): ουρανου B* D* d; ουρανιου ℵ A B^{corr} D^B cet.
10.11 (227b/5): ΗΜΕΙΝ D* = ημιν P^{75} A B C al. d; υμιν ℵ D^B Θ al.
19.29 (262b/11): βηθανια ℵ* B D*; βηθανιαν ℵ^c D^B cet.
Mark 3.3 (291b/17): εξηραμενην D* pler.; εξηραμμενην D^B; τω την ξηραν ℵ B C* al.
4.12 (295b/14): ΑΦΕΘΗCΟΜΑΙ D*; αφησω D^B; αφεθησεται/αφεθη ℵ B C cet.; DEMITTAM d
9.1 (314b/15): τινες ωδε των εστηκοτων B D* (TINE); τινες των ωδε εστηκοτων ℵ A C D^B pler.
For the question of the attribution of this correction, see I. A. Moir, 'The Reading of Codex Bezae (D-05) at Mark ix. 1', *NTS* 20 (1974), 105; H. Greeven, 'Nochmals Mk ix. 1 in Codex Bezae (D, 05)', *NTS* 23 (1977), 305–8.
14.31 (338b/20): EAN MH ΔΕΗ D* = εαν με δεη ℵ* C W Θ pler.; εαν δεη με ℵ^c A B D^B L N al.
Acts 1.26 (418b/9): αυτων D* E al. plu. d; αυτοις ℵ A B C D^B
2.36 (422b/7): OM αυτον D* d; αυτον post κυριον ℵ A B C D^B al.; αυτον post χριστον E P al.
2.37 (422b/11): ΕΙΠΑΝ D*; ειποντες ℵ D^B 614; ειπον cet.
2.42 (423b/1): ΤΗ ΚΛΑCΙ D* = τη κλασει ℵ* A B C d; ϗ τη κλασι D^B = και τη κλασει ℵ^c E P pler.
3.24 (426b/7): Ο ΕΛΑΛΗCΕΝ D*; οι ελαλησαν ℵ D^B; οι επροφητευσαν C^2; οσοι ελαλησαν cet.; QUODQUOD LOCUTI SUNT d
B.-L. (Apparatus, ad loc.) suggest that the corrupt D* reading is due to οσοι being omitted, as attested by Lvt (p*) sy(p) Cop (G67 sah) eth, and then ο being supplied through Latin influence – *quodquod* standing, as is common, for *quotquot*. The restoration by D^B is with ℵ alone – a striking reading.
6.11 (436b/24): λεγοντες ℵ A D*; λεγοντας B C D^B E H L P pler.
7.26 (440b/1): ΤΟΤΕ D* d; τη δε E P pler.; τη τε ℵ A B C D^B H al.
7.33 (440b/28): ΟΥ D*; εφ ω ℵ A B C D^B 81; εν ω E H P pler.
εν ω is harmonization to Exod. 3.5 LXX. D* is unidiomatic, and we find D^B following ℵ (B).
8.9 (444b/28): ΕΞΕCΤΑΝΕΝ ?? D* (cj. Tischendorf); εξειστων D^B = εξιστων E H P pler.; εξιστανων P^{74} ℵ A B C pc.
8.27 (446b/28): OM P^{74vid} ℵ* A C* D*; ος P^{50} ℵ^c B C^2 D^B E H L P cet.
8.28 (446b/30): καθημενος P^{50} D* pc.; και καθημενος ℵ A B C D^B E H L P cet.
11.18 (460b/26): ΕΔΟΞΑΝ D*; εδοξασαν P^{74} ℵ B D^B al.; εδοξαζον A E H L P pler.
13.46 (471b/9): ΕΠΙΔΗ D* = επειδη ℵ* B 431; επιδη δε D^B = επειδη δε ℵ^c A E* L P pler.; επει δε P^{45} P^{74} C E^c al.
The original reading επειδη was corrupted to επει δε, and followed by the conflation επειδη δε.
14.19 (474b/9): OM D* d; δε C D^B E al. (and see further B.-L.); OM the whole phrase ℵ A B H L P pler.

15.4 (476b/5): ΠΑΡΕΔΟΘΗϹΑΝ D*; παρεδεχθησαν P^{74} ℵ A B D^B Ψ 33 81 pc.; απεδεχθησαν pler.
17.25 (488b/29): Ο ΔΟΥϹ D*; δους H pc.; διδους ℵ B D^B cet.
This is part of a bigger variant.
19.27 (496b/26): κινδυνευει D* d pler.; κινδυνευσει D^B Lvg; κινδυνευσι ℵ
ibid. (496b/30): Η D*; ην D^B cet.
This also is within a longer variant.
20.35 (502b/13): ΠΑϹ [ ] (πασι ?) D*; και παντα C D^B al.; παντα cet.
21.24 (505b/22): ΞΥΡΩΝΤΑΙ D*; ξυρησονται P^{74} ℵ B* D^B E P al.; ξυρησωνται A B^3 C H L pler.
21.31 (506b/24): και ζητουντων D* Lvt (d gig); ζητουντων δε D^B H L P pler.; ζητουντων τε ℵ A B E pc.; ζητουντων P^{74} Lvt (p)
21.32 (506b/28): εκατονταρχας ℵ A B D* E pc.; εκατονταρχους D^B H L P pler.

The high proportion of agreements with the Sinaiticus and the C group of correctors amounts in fact to twenty-five of these forty readings (table 29).

Table 29. *Agreements between Corrector B and the Codex Sinaiticus and the C group of its correctors*

	With ℵ	With $ℵ^c$	With neither
Gospels	7	3	8
Acts	12	3	7
Total	19	6	15

The degree of agreement with $ℵ^c$ is in fact very high, because D^B never agrees with ℵ* against $ℵ^c$. That is to say, the readings in which it agrees with the first hand of ℵ it also shares with the c correctors. Its total number of agreements with $ℵ^c$ is therefore twenty-five. In Acts the proportion of agreements is rather higher than it is in the Gospels.

There is also an interesting number of agreements in the text of Acts between D^B and the ninth-century Codex Porphyrianus (P^a, 025). These amount to eleven out of a possible twenty-one. Four of these are shared with ℵ as well, and three more with $ℵ^c$. 025 in Acts was described by von Soden as being *K* with some *I* readings. It is described by the Alands (*Text*, p. 111) as 'Category V' ('Manuscripts with a purely or predominantly Byzantine text' (p. 156)). The point here is that the text of D^B shows a slightly greater influence of what were to become *Koinē* readings than we find in ℵ, although it should also be noted that, in these variants, ℵ P twice agree against D^B. Generally, the agreement between $ℵ^c$ and D^B is shared with the bulk of later manuscripts (but note Mk 14.31). Although this could be taken to weaken the force of a claim for any affinity between them, it is the fact of the number of agreements with ℵ and $ℵ^c$ that bears weight.

The group of C correctors to the Sinaiticus is very fully described by Milne and Skeat. They allocate the corrections to (in chronological order) C^a, C^{Pamph}, C^{b1}, C^{b2}, C^{b3}, C^c and C^{c*} (pp. 46–50). Of these, only C^a and C^{b2} made any corrections in the Gospels and Acts. The date of the whole group has yet to be authoritatively determined.

> The latest date suggested is the seventh century, the earliest is the fifth. Sir Frederick Kenyon and Professor Hunt agree in regarding the sixth century as possible, but the former is inclined to accept the seventh as equally possible, while the latter is more disposed to favour an early date. (Lake, p. xii, col. 2)

Milne and Skeat record these two extremes, observing only that 'lack of comparative material enforces caution upon whosoever would decide between the two dates' (p. 65). One may add that Kenyon's tendency seems to have been towards dating manuscripts too late. The absolute *terminus ante quem* is the fall of Caesarea to the Arabs in 638. It should also be noted that all the A and B correctors, who were regarded by Lake and his predecessors as 'probably belonging to the fourth, and certainly not later than the fifth century' (p. xx, col. 2), are shown by Milne and Skeat to be the work of *scribes* A and D (pp. 40ff). There is therefore less obstacle to moving the date of the C correctors forward into the fifth century.

If the date of these corrections is still uncertain, their provenance may be fixed with an unexpected degree of certainty. The evidence is set out fully by Lake. The colophons to Ezra and Esther, written by C^{Pamph}, state that the corrector used a *παλαιοτατος λιαν* manuscript that had been corrected against Origen's *Hexapla* by Pamphilus, in about the year 309. Pamphilus lived in Caesarea. There is, as Lake admits (pp. xi–xii), no proof that this manuscript was still in Caesarea when C^{Pamph} used it. However, he refers also to the close connection in the Pauline epistles between $\aleph^c$ and H^{Paul} (015). This latter manuscript has a colophon stating that it had been corrected against a codex from Pamphilus' library in Caesarea, that had been written by him.

The attempt to link the genuine Euthaliana with Caesarea is difficult and complicated, but Robinson concluded that 'A Euthalian codex . . . was brought to Caesarea, and there corrected by MSS in the great library: the MS used to correct the Pauline Epistles being one written by the hand of Pamphilus himself' (*Euthaliana*, p. 36).

015, which is of the sixth century, thus provides evidence of a manuscript of Pamphilus still at Caesarea.

The character of the divisions of ℵ and B in Acts, and their relation to the Euthalian system (Robinson, pp. 36–43; Ropes, pp. xli–xliv), concerns the origin of ℵ, and not $\aleph^c$. However, the nature of the chapter divisions added to Isaiah by $\aleph^{c.c}$ might repay examination.

It should be added that scholarly discussions on this subject are often imprecise or misleading (e.g. S. Jellicoe, *The Septuagint and Modern Study* Oxford, 1968, pp. 181f). The Esther colophon gives Pamphilus' own note, and the relation to the *Hexapla* is made quite clear: there is no justification for confusion. To achieve perfect clarity in writing on the Euthaliana, on the other hand, is virtually impossible.

There is circumstantial evidence, therefore, that the Sinaiticus was in Caesarea at some point in the fifth to the sixth centuries. The arguments in favour of its having been copied there are strong.

The implication of this for our study of Corrector B is that there is evidence to suggest that Codex Bezae may also have been in Caesarea, or somewhere susceptible to Caesarean influence, at an early stage in its life, perhaps during the fifth century. Certainly D^B used a text with strong Caesarean associations.

This text was one which was based heavily on the ℵ text, yet in a modified form. The point that D^B never agrees with the first hand of ℵ *against* the C correctors must be given full weight. This modification belongs to a wider move towards what was to become the standard text of later centuries, and has certain elements in common with it – the D^B text might be described as ℵ+ℵ^c+P.

But this is not the whole character of Corrector B. We have already noted several places where his alteration seemed to reflect a text not dissimilar from that of D* or d. Examples of this are rare, though we must not forget that on occasion his emendations are to a longer text found only in D. In addition to those noted already, the longer text of D at Jn 7.39 is a good example: D* read ΤΟ ΠΝΑ ΑΓΙΟΝ ΕΠ ΑΥΤΟΙϹ, which D^B altered to *το πνα το αγιον επ αυτους*.

We saw also that there are corrections which amount to conjectural emendations – alterations to the text of D to make sense of it, without reference to other manuscripts. In these readings we sometimes see new variants coming into existence, and can observe how a free text such as that of D continues to generate new readings, even in careful hands.

Luke 5.5 (201b/17–18)
ΟΥ ΜΗ ΠΑΡΑΚΟΥϹΟΜΑΙ D* d; *ου μη παρακουσομεν* D^B; *χαλασω το δικτυον* ℵ A B pler.; *non praeteribo* d; *non intermittimus* Lvt (e)
χαλασομεν and *χαλασωμεν* are also attested in the manuscripts.
His source could be a Greek manuscript with a text like that reflected in the Palatinus. I suggest that it is more likely that he is emending on the basis of ΕΛΑΒΟΜΕΝ in the line above.
Mark 14.56 (340b/30–1): ΕΨΕΥΔΟΜΑΡΤΥΡΟΥΝ ΕΛΕΓΟΝ D*; FALSUM TESTIMONIUM DICEBANT d; *εψευδομαρτυρουν και ελεγον* D^B; *λεγοντες* 118 157 209; *λεγοντες οτι ηκουσαμεν αυτου λεγοντος* 244; *εψευδομαρτυρουν* cet.
Acts 7.11 (438b/19)
ΕΦ ΟΛΗϹ ΤΗϹ ΑΙΓΥΠΤΟΥ D*; *εφ ολης της γης αιγυπτου* D^B
εφ ολην την γην αιγ. P45 P74 ℵ A B C; *εφ ολην την γην αιγ.* E H P al. pler.
super omnem terram aegypti d e
8.23 (446b/9)
ΗΝ ΓΑΡ ΠΙΚΡΙΑϹ ΧΟΛΗ ΚΑΙ ϹΥΝΔΕϹΜΩ D* (deest d)
εις γαρ πικριαν χολης και συνδεσμον D^B
εις γαρ χολην πικριας και συνδεσμον cet.
His correction to the clearly impossible D* text has produced a new variant.

8.27 (446b/29): ΪΕΡΟΥCΑΛΗΜ D* (deest d); εν ιερ. D^B L; εις ιερ. pc.
D^B has supplied the wrong preposition, agreeing by chance with L.
17.8 (486b/21): ΑΚΟΥCΑΝΤΕC D*; ακουσαντα D^B; ακουσαντας cet.
D reads ΤΟΥC ΠΟΛΙΤΑΡΚΑC ΚΑΙ ΤΟΝ ΟΧΛΟΝ instead of *τον οχλον και τους πολιταρχας; ακουσαντας ταυτα* was then wrongly taken with *και λαβοντες* at the beginning of v.9, and became ΑΚΟΥCΑΝΤΕC ΤΑΥΤΑ. D^B is aware that this is wrong, and corruptly emends ΑΚΟΥCΑΝΤΕC to agree with *οχλον*.
22.28 (510b/29)
ΚΑΙ ΑΠΟΚΡΙΘΕΙC Ο ΧΕΙΛΙΑΡΧΟC ΚΑΙ ΕΙΠΕΝ D* (deest d)
και αποκριθεις ο χειλιαρχος ειπεν αυτω D^B
απεκριθη δε (or *τε* or OM) *ο χιλιαρχος* cet.
D^B's emendation removes the construction of a participle followed by *και* and a finite verb.

It is to be concluded that Corrector B had three sources for his corrections – a text which represents the ℵ text modified by $ℵ^c$ and other elements, a text with readings similar to D*/d, and his own wit. The remaining question is of the relationship between the first two of these. Several possible situations could be envisaged.

One is that he made use of two manuscripts, each representing one of these two sources. The other is that he used a single manuscript, which contained readings of both these types. There seem to be no grounds for establishing either of these possibilities as more likely than the other, although it seems to me that the first is preferable.

Can we draw any more precise conclusions, then, about the relation of this second manuscript to D? We are bound to ask whether it could even have been the exemplar. In favour of the possibility is the fact that removal of mistakes of an obvious nature accounts for a high proportion of B's corrections, though not as high as those of G. If this were so, then we would be bound to ascribe as high an authority to B's alterations as we have given to those by G. However, we do not have strong grounds for placing B so early, and the change in textual preference shown by the corrector's other manuscript (according to my suggestion) makes it unlikely that he can have been so close to D*.

With this corrector, we can see Codex Bezae moving out of an environment in which its text is accepted as the tradition, into a freer one where an eclectic atmosphere prevails. This is not to claim that this represents a change of place for it. A change in atmosphere and a lively interest in different traditions is amply attested.

CORRECTOR D

An even greater proportion of this hand's corrections are to Acts. Apart from the beginning of Matthew (twenty corrections up to F60b), he shows little interest in

Table 30. *Corrections by Corrector D*

Col.	Mt	Jn	Lk	Mk	Ac	Total
Greek	28	13	17	11	96	165
Latin	—	1	—	—	1	2
Both	—	—	—	—	1	1

any of the Gospels (see table 30). Forty-six of the corrections to Acts are from F493b onwards (in ten Greek columns).

Let us deal first with the corrections in which he touched the Latin text. The correction to both columns is at F493b/494, ll. 27–8 (Ac 19.2):

λαμβανουσιν τινες D* sah sy (h^mg) = ACCIPIUNT QUIDAM d; εστιν and *est* D^D (though QUIDAM is not deleted) Gr. cet. Lat. cet.

The pressing question here is why the Latin should suddenly have become for him important enough to be worth altering along with the Greek. Other corrections of equal or greater significance do not receive the same treatment. The question remains intriguing and insoluble.

The corrections to the Latin column only are

F148/28 (Jn 11.32): VIDES d; *videns* d^D aur f Lvg; *et vidit/-et/-isset* Lvt (pler.)

There is proper uncertainty as to whether this single letter *n* can be attributed to a particular corrector. It is not altogether like his *n* on the facing verso, l.14, although the first vertical and its relation to the oblique stroke are certainly similar. The correction is merely orthographic.

F505/33 (Ac 21.18): ERANT AUTEM d*; *omnes erant autem* D^D; *et . . . omnes* Lvt (gig); *et omnes* Lvg (T); *omnesque* Lvg (cet.)

Corrections to slips of the pen and other minor errors by Corrector D show a slightly different pattern from those of the first three correctors. There are eighteen corrections of vowels, fourteen of consonants, movable *nu* is inserted seven times, a missing syllable nine, the article also nine: endings are corrected in fifteen places.

Correction of vowels: ω to ο four times; ε to α three times; ϋ to η and ο to α twice; ο to ω, υ to οι, η to υ, οι to υ, α to ι, ε to ι, ε to ει, ει to αι, and η to αι once each. Consonantal corrections include δ to τ twice, τ to δ, θ to τ, τ to θ, κ to χ once, and ν to νν in IѠANHC twice (417b/28, 493b/2).
Movable ν is inserted at F247b/31, 259b/27, 315b/21, 417b/10, 495b/18, 31, 498b/15, always before a consonant except at 495b/18 (see Gignac, 1,114).
With the insertion of the article, D* is unique each time, except for 156b/21 (Jn 13.27) and 497b/2 (Ac 19.28), where it has slight support.

There are a number of other miscellaneous corrections –

156b/21: κ to ϛ
188b/28: ΧΑΡΑ to χωρα
209b/23: ΚΑΛΕΙ to λαλει
498b/5: ΟΙ ΚΑΙ to και οι
19: ΑΠΟCΠΑCΑΜΕΝΟC to απασπασαμενος (the first πα later deleted by points over it)
500b/5: ΠΑΡΕΛΑΒΟΜΕΝ to παρεβαλομεν
16: ΠΡΟC ΑΥΤΟΥC to προς αυτοις
505b/13: N in EN erased but not the E

We turn now to the rest of his corrections.

Matthew 5.36 (13b/28–9): ΠΟΕΙΝ D*; ποιησαι D^{B.D}; FACERE d
10.28 (31b/3): CΦΑΞΑΙ D*; αποκτιναι D^D = αποκτειναι cet.; *occidere* d
12.34–5 (37b/32): ΛΑΛΕΙ ΑΓΑΘΑ ΑΓΑΘΟC D* d; λαλει ο αγαθος D^D cet.
12.39 (38b/13): COI D*; αυτη D^D d cet.
15.11, 18, 20 (49b/22, 24, 50b/9, 14, 16)
κοινωνι . . . κοινωνει . . . κοινωνει . . . τα κοινωνουντα . . . κοινωνει D*.K
κοινοι . . . κοινοι . . . κοινοι . . . τα κοινουντα . . . κοινοι D^D cet.
Communicare is used by d.
17.5 (55b/20): ΕΠΕCΚΙΑΖΕΝ D* d; επεσκιασεν D^D cet.
Compare par. Lk 9.34 (-ιαζεν P75 ℵ B pc., -ιασεν P45 A C D W Θ pler.).
18.20 (60b/1): ΟΥΚ ΕΙCΙΝ ΓΑΡ D*; ου γαρ εισιν D^D d cet.
21.24 (70b/17): OM D* al d; ον D^D cet.
24.38 (83b/19): ΤΗC ΗΜΕΡΑC D*; της ημερας ης D^D; ης ημερας cet.; *in eum diem* d
John 12.40 (153b/20): στραφωσιν P66 P75vid ℵ B D* 33; επιστραφωσιν A D^D pler.
13.36 (157b/14): ΜΟΙ CY D*.s.m.; μοι συ νυν D^D; μοι νυν ℵ B pler.; TU ME d
15.13 (161b/11): ινα P66 ℵ* D* Θ d; ινα τις ℵc A B D^D cet.
15.19 (161b/28): ΗΤΕ D*; ουκ εστε D^D cet.; ERATIS d
16.23 (164b/21): εαν B C D* L; οτι εαν D^D; οτι αν ℵ A pler.
16.32 (165b/11): και ℵ A B C* D* L 33 d; και νυν P22vid P66 C3 D^D pler.
Luke 23.46 (279b/31): παρατιθημι D* W Ψ; παρατιθεμαι P75 ℵ A B C K al.; παρατιθεμι D^D; παραθησομαι pler.
Although the editions (e.g. Tischendorf, IGNT), following Scrivener, take the D^D reading to be παρατιθειμι, the letter which they read as ι is just part of the poorly erased η. The corrector is trying to introduce the P75 ℵ B reading.
Mark 1.9 (285b/25): ΤΗΝ ΪΟΡΔΑΝΗΝ D*; τον ιορδ. D^D pler.
13.31 (335b/2): ου B D*; ου μη D^D cet.
15.11 (343b/14): ΤΩ ΟΧΛΩ D*; τον οχλον D^D cet.; *turbas* d
Acts 1.17 (417b/10): ος ελαχε D*; και ελαχεν D^D d cet.
1.24–5 (418b/5): ΑΝΑΛΑΒΕΙΝ D*; ενα λαβειν D^D d pler.
According to B.-L., ενα λαβειν stood in the exemplar of D. I see no reason why this should be so.

2.18 (420b/8): ΚΑΙ ΕΓΩ D*; καιγε D^D cet.
2.30 (421b/19): ΕΙΔΩΝ D*; ειδως D^D cet.
5.24 (433b/4): ΓΕΝΗΤΑΙ D*; γενοιτο D^D pler.; FIERET d
5.26 (433b/10): ηγαγον D* d (DEDUCEBANT); ηγεν D^D al.
5.36 (434b/14): διελυθη D*; ανηρεθη D^D cet.; INTERFECTUS EST d
7.33 (440b/27): λυσον D* pler.; λυσαι D^D 618
7.43 (442b/8): ΕΠΙ ΤΑ ΜΕΡΗ D^{*vid}; επ εκεινα D^D cet.; *in illas partes* d
8.20 (446b/1): ΑΡΓΥΡΙΟΝ D*; το αργυριον σου D^D cet.; deest d
10.46 (458b/22)
D* is illegible. B.-L. conjecture ΔΟΞΑΖΟΝΤΩΝ for μεγαλυνοντων.
γλωσσαις και μεγαλυνοντων D^D cet.
LINGUIS ET MAGNIFICANTES d
11.1 (458b/32)
ΤΟΙϹ ΑΠΟϹΤΟΛΟΙϹ ΚΑΙ ΤΟΙϹ ΑΔΕΛΦΟΙϹ ΟΙ D*
τοις αποστολοις και τοις αδελφοις τοις D^D
οι αποστολοι και οι αδελφοι οι d cet.
There is also a correction later in the passage by D^E.
12.2 (462b/17): μαχαιρα B^3 D* pler.; μαχαιρη ℵ A B* D^D 81
13.8 (466b/19): ΕΤΟΙΜΑϹ D*; ελυμας D^D cet.; *etoemas* d
13.20 (468b/1): ΕΩϹ D*; μετα ταυτα ως D^D pler.; ως P^{74} ℵ A B C al. d
13.47 (471b/13): ΕΝΤΕΤΑΛΚΕΝ D*; εντεταλτε ημιν D^D = εντεταλται ημιν pler.; DEDIT NOBIS d
14.15 (473b/24): ΦΩΝΟΥΝΤΕϹ D* d (VOCIFERANTES); λεγοντες D^D pler.
17.27 (489b/3): αυτο D* d IR; αυτον D^D cet.
17.30 (489b/17): ΠΑΡΪΔΩΝ D*; περϊδων D^D 463; OM P^{74vid} pc.; υπεριδων cet.
Neither παροραω nor περιοραω is found elsewhere in the New Testament.
ibid. (489b/18): ΙΝΑ ΠΑΝΤΕϹ D* d; παντας ℵ A B D^D E pc.; πασι pler.
17.34 (489b/28): ΕΚΟΛΛΗΘΗϹΑΝ D*; κολληθεντες D^D cet.; CUM ESITASSENT d
18.6 (490b/22): ΕΤΙ ΤΑϹϹΟΜΕΝΩΝ D^{*vid}; αντιτασσομενων D^D pler.; RESISTENTIBUS d
18.15 (491b/30): ζητημα P^{74} D* pler. d; ζητηματα ℵ A B D^D E al.
18.16 (491b/33): απελυσεν D*; απηλασεν D^D cet. d
18.17 (492b/1): ΑΠΟΛΑΒΟΜΕΝΟΙ D*; επιλαβομενοι D^D cet.; ADPRAEHENDENTES d
ibid. (492b/4)
Τ[ ]Ω ΓΑΛΛΙΩ[ ]ΕΝ D*
και ουδεν τουτων τω γαλλιωνι εμελεν D^D cet. (εμελλεν ℵ pler.)
TUNC GALLIO FINGEBAT EUM NON VIDERE d
19.6 (494b/6): επ αυτοις D*; επ αυτους D^D cet.; SUPER EOS d
19.10 (494b/21–3)
Ε[Ω]Ϲ ΠΑΝΤΕϹ ΟΙ ΚΑΤΟΙΚΟΥΝΤΕϹ ΤΗΝ ΑϹΙΑΝ [Η]ΚΟΥϹΑΝ ΤΟΥϹ ΛΟΓΟΥϹ ΤΟΥ ΚΥ ΪΟΥΔΑΙΟΙ ΚΑΙ ΕΛΛΗΝΕϹ D*

ωστε απαντας τους κατοικουντας την ασιαν ακουσαι τον λογον του κυ ϊουδαιους τε και ελληνας D[D]
ωστε παντας etc. c. D[D] cet.
ITA UT OMNES QUI HABITANT ASIAM AUDIRENT VERBA DNI IUDAEIQUE ET CRAECI d
19.11 (494b/24): *δε* D* pc.; *τε* D[D] cet.
19.15 (495b/10)
ΤΟΤΕ ΑΠΕΚΡΙΘΗ ... ΕΙΠΕΝ D*; *τοτε απεκριθη ... και ειπεν* D[D]
TUNC RESPONDENS ... DIXIT d; *αποκριθεν ... ειπεν* cet.
19.20 (495b/31): ΕΠΛΗΘΥΝΕ D*; *επληθυνετο* D[D]; *ισχυεν* pler.;
CRESCEBAT ET CONVALESCEBAT d
D* has been influenced by 12.24, as has D[D]. But the Latin column has not (at 12.24 it reads AUGEBATUR ET MULTIPLICABATUR).
19.39 (498b/10): ΕΝ ΤΩ ΝΟΜΩ ΕΚΚΛΗCΙΑ D*; *εν τω νομω εκκλησιας* D[B]; *εν τη εννομω εκκλησιας* D[D]; IN LEGEM ECCLESIAE d; *εν τη εννομω εκκλησια* cet.
20.1 (498b/18): ΠΑΡΑΚΕΛΕΥCΑC D* [vid]; *παρακαλεσας* ℵ A B D[D] E pc.; OM H L P pler.
ibid. (498b/19): ΑΠΟCΠΑCΑΜΕΝΟC D*; *απασπασαμενος τε* D[D]; *ασπασαμενος* cet.
20.4 (498b/28): ΒΕΡΥΙΑΙΟC D*; *βεροιαιος* A² B D[D] al.; BERYENSIS d
ibid. (498b/31): ΔΟΥΒΕΡΙΟC D*; *δερβαιος* D[D] cet.; DOVERIUS d
20.18 (500b/18): ΕΦ ΗC D*; IN QUA d; *αφ ης* D[D] pler.
20.24 (501b/5–6)
ΛΟΓΟΝ ΕΧΩ ΜΟΙ ΟΥΔΕ ΠΟΙΟΥΜΑΙ ΤΗΝ ΨΥΧΗΝ ΜΟΥ D*
λογου ποιουμαι την ψυχην P⁴¹ ℵ* B C D[D]
λογον εχω ουδε ποιουμαι την ψυχην P⁷⁴ ℵ[c] A pc.
λογον ποιουμαι ουδε εχω την ψυχην μου E H L P al. pler.
CURA EST MIHI NEQUE HABEO IPSAM ANIMAM d
ibid. (501b/9): ΟΝ D*; QUOD d; *ην* D[D] cet.
20.27 (501b/20): ΗΜΙΝ D*; *ϋμιν* D[D] d cet. (with variations in the position of the word)
20.31 (501b/33): ΔΕ D*; *και* D[D] cet.; *ac* d
20.38 (502b/24): ΜΕΛΛΕΙ COΙ D*; *μελλουσιν* D[D] cet.; deest d
21.1 (502b/27–8)
ΚΑΙ ΕΠΙ[Β]ΑΝΤ[Ε]C ΑΝΗΧΘΗΜΕΝ ΑΠΟCΠΑCΘΕΝΤΩΝ ΔΕ ΗΜΩΝ D*
ως δε εγενετο αναχθηναι ημας αποσπασθενθας απ αυτων D[D] cet. (with variations between p.m. and s.m. of ℵ A B)
deest d
21.2 (502b/33): ΦΥΝΕΙΚΗΝ D*; *φοινεικην* D[D] = *φοινικην* cet.; deest d
21.12 (504b/10): ΠΑΡΑΚΑΛΟΥΜΕΝ D*; *παρεκαλουμεν* D[D] d cet.
21.21 (505b/11)
ΤΟΥC ΚΑΤΑ ΕΘΝΗ ΕΙCΙΝ ΪΟΥΔΑΙΟΙC D*
τους κατα τα εθνη παντας ϊουδαιους D[D] cet.
QUI IN GENTIBUS SUNT IUDAEOS d
ibid. (505b/13): ΜΗΤΕ ΕΝ ΤΟΙC ΕΘΝΕCΙΝ ΑΥΤΟΥ D*; *μηδε ε* [sic vid.] *τοις εθεσιν*

αυτους D^D; *μηδε τοις εθεσιν* cet.; NEQUE GENTES EIUS AMBULANT d
Tischendorf notes that *εθνεσιν* is a common error in the manuscripts.
21.24 (505b/25): ΑΛΛ ΟΤΙ ΠΟΡΕΥΟΥ D*; *αλλα στοιχεις ς* D^D; SED AMBULANS d

By far the majority of these significant corrections are in Acts – there are nine in Matthew, seven in John, one in Luke, three in Mark and forty-eight in Acts. Forty-two of them alter the relationship between the two columns. In eleven (nine from Acts), the correction agrees with the Latin text. In eighteen (ten from Acts), it disagrees with it. And in thirteen (ten in Acts), both the first hand and the corrector show a different text from the Latin. This random pattern indicates that the corrector was interested only in the Greek text.

Further examination shows that this corrector knew a good text. Most of his alterations (forty-three in fact) are with all, or nearly all, other Greek manuscripts. He has a reading otherwise unattested in only twelve (including Ac 7.33 and 17.30 *περιδων*, where there is support from 618 and 463 respectively). Apart from these, where the Greek evidence splits, he generally follows the ℵ B text – Lk 23.46; Ac 5.26; 12.2; 17.30 *παντας*; 18.15; 20.1 *παρακαλεσας*; 20.4 *βεροιαιος* (not with ℵ); 20.24 *λογου ποιουμαι την ψυχην* (not with $ℵ^c$). He disagrees with them only at Jn 12.40; 16.32 (but with C^3); Ac 13.20. In each place, one or both of D*/d agrees with ℵ B. At Jn 16.23 he follows ℵ A pler. against B C pc.

The character of this group of corrections seems therefore to be straightforward. We have a picture of a corrector who, as his reading of Acts progresses, becomes more and more concerned with the character of the text he is studying, and eventually goes to some trouble to alter it. In spite of his fading interest in Matthew, this is very different from, for instance, G, whose activity is all at the beginning of the codex and the beginning of Acts. Moreover, some of D's corrections at the end of Acts are very extensive, on one occasion consisting in the recasting of three lines of the manuscript.

In correcting the Gospels and the first part of Acts, he generally makes use of the most widely attested text. Towards the end of Acts he comes out more strongly in favour of a more specific type of text. This suggests a scholar with some breadth of learning. The fact that his writing is not always of the neatest ('rude changes' is Scrivener's phrase (p. xxv)) might be taken as support for this – he is a scholar, not a scribe.

The milieu of this corrector may not be far removed from that of Corrector B: Corrector B is closest to $ℵ^c$; D to ℵ B (02). Besides suggesting a degree of continuity between the two, this evidence strengthens the suggestion that C preceded B.

CORRECTOR E

The proportion of E's corrections that are to Acts is yet larger even than that of D (table 31). Besides the numerical bias, almost all of his corrections to the Gospels are more trivial than those to Acts.

Table 31. *Corrections by Corrector E*

Col.	Mt	Jn	Lk	Mk	Ac	Total
Greek	2	9	6	3	45	65

Again, we first examine the lesser corrections. We have insertion of a missing syllable nine times; insertion of a missing consonant three times; insertion of movable *nu* once (F482b/12 – before a consonant).

Correction of vowels is found eight times – once each ε to ει, ε to ι, ε to αι, η to ει, ι to η, ο to ω, ο to ου, οι to ω. Correction of a consonant occurs twice: ζ to σ and τ to θ.

An aorist ending is altered at 471b/22 (ΠΑΡѠΤΡΥΝΟΝ to -υναν); and at 487b/14 ΚΑΤΑCΤΑΝΟΝΤΕC is changed to καθιστωντες.

The article is inserted at five places in Acts. D* is unique in omitting it at three (470b/22, 480b/9, 485b/28). At 433b/27 (Ac 5.31) D^E is accompanied only by the twelfth-century manuscript 3 in reading αφεσιν των αμαρτιων. At 480b/30 (Ac 16.4) the addition of των before αποστολων is in a longer reading found only in D.

Finally, at 160b/6 the *nomen sacrum* ΠΑΡ has been altered to πηρ.

The following are the larger corrections by this hand.

John 4.38 (117b/3): OM D* d; ο D^E
8.26 (135b/30): τον κοσμον D*; τουτον τον κοσμον D^E
14.28 (160b/6): ο πατηρ D*; ο πατηρ μου D^E
Mark 5.30 (300b/15): την δυναμιν εξελθουσαν απ αυτου D* d; την δυν. την εξελθ. απ αυτου D^E
7.11 (308b/20): ΜΟΥ D*; εξ εμου D^E d
Acts 2.9 (419b/9): ΪΟΥΔΑΙΑΝ ΚΑΙ D* d; ϊουδ. τε και D^E
5.15 (431b/31): ΚΑΤΑ ΠΛΑΤΕΙΑC D* d; και εις τας πλατειας D^E
5.26 (433b/10): ΜΕΤΑ ΒΙΑC D* d; ου μετα βιας D^E
5.32 (433b/28): εσμεν μαρτυρες P^{74vid} ℵ D*; εσμεν αυτου μαρτυρες D^E; IPSI TESTES SUMUS d
7.34 (440b/30): του λαου D* d; του λαου μου D^E
8.3 (444b/5): CYNKOMICANTEC D*; συνεκομισαν τε D^E; CONPORTAVERUNT·QUAE d* (-*que* $d^{s.m.}$)
11.7 (459b/26): αναστα D*; αναστας D^E d
11.26 (461b/26–8)
CYNEXYΘHCAN ΟΧΛΟΝ ΪΚΑΝΟΝ ΚΑΙ ΤΟΤΕ ΠΡѠΤΟΝ ΕΧΡΗΜΑΤΙCΕΝ ΕΝ ΑΝΤΙΟΧΕΙΑ ΟΙ ΜΑΘΗΤΑΙ ΧΡΕΙCΤΙΑΝΟΙ D*
συναναχυθηναι τη εκκλησια ϗ διδαξαι οχλον ϊκανον χρηματισται πρωτως εν αντιοχεια τους μαθητας χρειστιανους D^E
COMMISCERE ECCLESIAM ET TUNC PRIMUM NUNCUPATI SUNT IN ANTIOCHIA DISCIPULOS CHRISTIANOS d

13.17 (467b/27): ΔΙΑ ΤΟΝ ΛΑΟΝ D* d; και τον λαον D^E
13.19 (476b/33): την γην των αλλοφυλω D*; αυτοις την γην αυτων αλλοφυλω D^E
15.29 479b/2): The addition found in D and some minuscules contains a correction by E: ΜΗ ΠΟΙΕΙΝ D*; μη ποιειντai D^E scil. μη ποιειτε
15.35 (479b/23): ΚΑΙ ΜΕΤΑ D* d; μετα και D^E
16.9 (481b/11): ανηρ μακεδων τις D* d; ανηρ μακ. τις ην D^E
16.11 (481b/20): νεαπολιν D*; νεαν πολιν D^E
17.12 (487b/2)
ΕΛΛΗΝΩΝ ΚΑΙ ΤΩΝ ΕΥϹΧΗΜΟΝΩΝ D*
ελληνιδων κ. των ευσχ. ϛ D^B d
ελληνιδων γυναικων των ευσχ. ϛ D^E
17.23 (488b/18): ΔΙΙϹΤΟΡΩΝ D*; PERSPICIENS d; αναθεωρων D^E
17.26 (489b/1): κατα οροθεσιαν D*; και τας οροθεσιας D^E d
17.27 (489b/5): ΗΜΩΝ D* d; + υπαρχων D^E
20.18–19 (500b/20–1)
ΗΝ ΠΑΝΤΟϹ ΧΡΟΝΟΥ ΔΟΥΛΕΥΩΝ ΤΩ ΚΩ D*
τον παντα χρονον εγενομην δουλευων τω κω D^E
FUI PER OMNE TEMPORE SERVIENS DNO d
20.27 (501b/19): τω αναγγειλαι D*; του μη αναγγειλαι D^E d
20.38 (502b/25): ΤΟ ΠΡΟϹΩΠΟΝ D*; + αυτου D^E; deest d
21.13 (504b/15): ΘΟΡΥΒΟΥΝΤΕϹ D*; CONTURBANTES D; συνθρυπτοντες D^E

There is nothing particularly distinctive about this text. Its influence on the Greek is to increase the number of places where it diverges from the Latin column: six corrections agree with the Latin, and twelve differ from it.

Fifteen corrections are in common with all or nearly all other manuscripts. Three (Ac 5.15; 16.9, 11) are in common with ℵ B against the majority text. One (Ac 5.32) is with E H L P against ℵ B. One (Jn 14.28) is with ℵ*ᶜ and most other manuscripts. One (Ac 8.3) is with Ee. One (Jn 8.26) is with the majority of Old Latin manuscripts and no other Greek witnesses. Four (Mk 5.30; Ac 11.26; 13.19; 17.27) are unique.

We cannot be precise about the kind of text known to Corrector E. The low proportion of unique readings suggests that he preferred to be safe and follow manuscript evidence when he made a correction. It may be that he consulted more than one manuscript in correcting Acts. The agreement with Old Latin manuscripts at Jn 8.26 is surely coincidence.

The character of the hand makes it impossible that he could have been a professional scribe.

Scrivener, who believed that E was responsible for *ARXI* at Ac 5.27 (433b/13), wrote of the 'Latin *R* betraying his nation' (p. xxv). Harris (*Annotators*, p. 10) expanded on this somewhat. A Latin corrector working almost exclusively on the Greek text would be valuable support for Harris' theory that the Greek text has been Latinized. It would also indicate that the manuscript was in Latin hands in about 700, and thus damage Fischer's scheme. In fact, neither that correction, nor those to the Latin attributed to E by Scrivener, can have been by him. There is absolutely no reason for thinking him to have been anything other than a Greek speaker.

CORRECTOR H

We have here another corrector whose enthusiasm came in bursts – twelve corrections up to Matthew 21, then only two until John 4, none from John 8 to Luke 1, then only two between Luke 7 and Mark 3, and none in Mark after 6.50 (or possibly even 5.6). Apart from a gap between chapters 8 and 11, H's activity in Acts is more sustained (see table 32).

Table 32. *Corrections by Corrector H*

Col	Mt	Jn	Lk	Mk	Ac	Total
Greek	14	7	9	4	52	86
Latin	—	—	2?	—	—	2?

Just over half of H's corrections, forty-eight in fact, are orthographic or minor. There are seventeen corrections of vowels, ten of consonants, one insertion of the article, seven corrections of forms, and fourteen corrections of nonsense.

Corrections of vowels: ι to ει four times; ο to ω three times; α to ε and η to ε twice; ω to ο, υ to ο, ε to α, ε to η, η to υ once each. For the reading of D* at 45b/32 (ΕΝΑΡΓΟΥCΙΝ), compare the confusion of ενεργης with εναργης at Heb. 4.12 B, which is also reflected in Latin Mss at 1 Cor. 16.9 (Lvt (d e f g) Lvg) and Philem. 6 (Lvt (d e f) Lvg).

Of consonants: θ to τ five times; δ to τ three times; φ to π and κ to γ once each.

Insertion of article: 69b/5, where D* alone omits it.

Corrections of forms include: 11b/15 ΑΛΑ to αλας (αλας *bis* ℵ, and see A.-G. *s.v.*); 81b/18 ΕCΤΩC to εστος with ℵ B* F G H L V Δ Π al., and at 137b/9 the restoration of D*'s original εληλυθον, where D^B had read εληλυθα.

Twenty-six of these corrections are to the Gospels, showing that his corrections to Acts are of a weightier character.

We turn to his remaining corrections.

Matthew 16.4 (52b/19): ζητει σημιον D*; σημιον ζητει D^H d (SIGNUM QUERIT d*; signum quaerit d^G)
16.16 (53b/19): ΤΟ CΩΖΟΝΤΟC D* d*; του σωζοντος D^A; του ζωντος D^H d^G
John 7.4 (129b/22): ΕΝ ΠΑΡΗCΙΑ ΑΥΤΟ D*; εν παρησια αυτος D^H

8.40 (137b/2): ΗΚΟΥϹΕΝ D*·H d; ηκουσα D^A
8.41 (137b/6): ουκ εγεννηθημεν D*·H d; ου γεγεννημεθα D^B
Mark 4.31 (297b/3): Ο ΟΤΙ ΑΝ D*; ος οταν D^H
Acts 1.6 (415b/26): ΤΟΥ ΪϹΡΑΗΛ D*; τω ισρ. D^H
Wordsworth and White cite an important note from Bede on this: 'non *huius israel* sed *huic israel* et sicut in gr. manifestum est ubi τῷ 'Ισρ. et non τοῦ 'Ισρ. scriptum est'.
2.30 (421b/21): ΚΑΡΔΙΑϹ D* d (PRAECORDIA); οσφυος D^H
2.32 (421b/27): ΤΟΥΤΟΝ ΟΥΝ ΙΗΝ D*; τουτον τον ιην D^H
5.28 (433b/19): εκεινου D*; τουτου D^H d (*huius*)
7.3 (437b/18): ΑΠΟ D*; εκ D^H
7.29 (440b/12): ΟΥΤΩϹ ΚΑΙ ΕΦΥΓΑΔΕΥϹΕΝ D*; ADQUE ITA PROFUGIT d; εφυγεν δε D^H
7.49 (442b/25): ΜΟΥ P74 D* d (MEUS); μοι D^H
This variant reflects that in the citation – Isa. 66.1 LXX: μου] μοι ℵ A.
8.7 (444b/20): ΑΠΟ or ΠΑΡΑ ΠΟΛΛΟΙϹ D* d (A MULTIS); πολλοι D^H
This is part of a variant that extends from the beginning of the verse.
12.22 (465b/10): φωναι D* d; φωνη D^H
12.25 (465b/18): ΑΠΕϹΤΡΕΨΕΝ D*; ὑπεστρεψαν D^H d (REVERSI SUNT)
ibid. (465b/20): ΤΟΝ ΙΩΑΝΗΝ D*; και ιωανην D^H; IOHANNEN d
13.1 (465b/28): ΚΑΙ ΤΕΤΡΑΡΧΟΥ D* d; του τετρ. D^H
13.6 (466b/10): ΚΑΙ ΠΕΡΙΕΛΘΟΝΤΩΝ ΔΕ ΑΥΤΩΝ D*; διελθοντων δε αυτων D^H; CUM PERGRESSI FUISSENT d
ibid. (466b/14): ΒΑΡΪΗϹΟΥΑ (or -ΑΝ?) D*; BARIESUAM d; βαριησουν D^H
13.27 (468b/28): ΤΑϹ ΓΡΑΦΑϹ D* d; και τας φωνας D^H
See also the correction by D^F to this verse.
13.31 (469b/9): ΠΛΕΙΟΝΑϹ D*; πλειους D^H
All other manuscripts have πλειους, but the whole sentence is differently cast in D. A corrector (H?) has changed ΑΝΑΒΑΙΝΟΥϹΙΝ earlier in the verse to αναβασιν by placing points over ΙΝΟΥ.
14.20 (474b/16): ΤΩΝ ΜΑΘΗΤΩΝ ΑΥΤΟΥ D* d; των μαθ. αυτον D^H
ibid. (474b/19): [ ] D*; συν D^H d
I suspect that D* may have read και.
15.7 (476b/17): ΑΝΕϹΤΗϹΕΝ ΕΝ ΠΝΙ ΠΕΤΡΟϹ ΚΑΙ ΕΙΠΕΝ D* d; αναστας πετρος ειπεν D^H
15.12 (477b/7–8): ΒΑΡΝΑΒΑΝ ΚΑΙ ΠΑΥΛΟΝ ΕΞΗΓΟΥΜΕΝΟΙ D* d; βαρναβα και παυλου εξηγουμενων D^H
15.17 (477b/24): ΠΟΙΗϹΕΙ D*; ο ποιων D^H (and cp. Amos 9.12 LXX); *faciens* d
16.22 (483b/4): ΤΟΤΕ D* d; και D^H
17.11 (486b/32): εχει D*; εχοι D^H
17.12 (487b/2–3)
ΕΛΛΗΝΩΝ ΚΑΙ ΤΩΝ ΕΥϹΧΗΜΟΝΩΝ ΑΝΔΡΕϹ ΚΑΙ ΓΥΝΑΙΚΕϹ D*
ελληνιδων και των ευσχ. ϗ ανδρες και γυναικες D^B d
ελληνιδων γυναικων των ευσχ. ϗ ανδρες και γυναικες D^E
ελληνιδων γυναικων των ευσχ. ϗ ανδρων ουκ ολιγοι D^H

The following line, ΙΚΑΝΟΙ ΕΠΙCΤΕΥCΑΝ, has been enclosed within brackets by someone.

17.18 (487b/33): *θελη* D*; *θελοι* D^H
17.25 (488b/28–9)
ΠΡΟCΔΕΟΜΕΝΟC / ΟΤΙ ΟΥΤΟC Ο ΔΟΥC D* d
προσδ. / ουτος διδους (or *προσδ. / οτι ουτος διδους*) D^B
προσδ. τι αυτος / ουτος διδους D^H
18.20 (492b/15): ΤΕ D* d; *δε* D^H
ibid. (*ibid.*): *αυτων* D* d; *αυτον* D^H
18.21 (492b/19): ΑΝΑ[ ]Ω D*; REVERTI d; *ανακαμψω* D^H
ibid. (492b/20): ΤΟΥ ΕΦΕCΟΥ D*; *της εφ.* D^H
19.33 (497b/18): ΚΑΤΕΒΙΒΑCΑΝ D*; *προεβιβασαν* D^H
19.37 (498b/3): *θεαν* D*; *θεον* D^H

There are a number of interesting things about these corrections. First is the re-adoption of the first hand's readings at Jn 8.40, 41. The move away from the Bezan text by Correctors A and B has been reversed. With this belongs the higher proportion of corrections which share the text supported by the Latin column – there are seven which are like this, and eleven which show a different text from that in the Latin (in the remaining six it differs from both columns). This presents a contrast with, for example, our next corrector – F.

There are also four unique readings (Jn 7.4; Ac 13.6; 17.12, 25). The first three are partial corrections which make a hybrid between D and the majority reading. The fourth would be called a conflation of the two, except for the reading *τι*.

Most of the corrections (twenty of them) are into agreement with all or nearly all other manuscripts. Only at Ac 8.7 does Corrector H follow ℵ A B C against later texts. In four other places he adopts a later text against the ℵ B type (Ac 13.6 *βαριησουν* with A H L P al.; 19.33 with H L P pler.; 18.20 *αυτον* with L pc.; 19.37 with E^2 P pler.). The third of these enforces the conclusion that this corrector's text had a distinctive character.

I suggested (in chapter 3) that H worked in the fifth century. The textual evidence bears this out, and also suggests a break with what follows. The codex is not in the purely Byzantine milieu in which Corrector F lived. His origins and peculiarities are closer to the manuscript's original setting, closer in text though not in time than hands A and B. It is to be concluded that H predates F, though not by very much – their hands are not, as we have seen, wholly dissimilar. H comes after D, and is about contemporary with E.

CORRECTOR F

The character of Corrector F's changes is totally different from anything we have so far encountered. None of them is orthographic. Again the main concern is with Acts (table 33).

Table 33. *Corrections by Corrector F*

Col.	Mt	Jn	Lk	Mk	Ac	Total
Greek	2	5	—	—	23	30

Matthew 12.20 (36b/18): ΟΥ ΚΑΤΙΑΞΕΙC D*; *καλαμ[ον] συντετριμμενο̄ ου κατεαξει* D^F

The final two letters of *καλαμον* have rubbed away through being near the gathering.

27.13 (97b/2–3): ΤΟCΑ ΚΑΤΑΜΑΡΤΥΡΟΥCΙΝ CΟΥ D* d; *ποσα σου καταμαρτυρουσιν* D^F

John 14.7 (158b/5–6)

γνωσεσθαι D*; *εγ*[ ] D^F

εγνωκειτε αν A C^3 pler.; *αν ηδειτε* B C* al.

Kipling thought that D^F read *εγνωκειτε αν*, and this is how Tischendorf records it (as does the eighth edition of K. Aland's *Synopsis Quattuor Evangeliorum*, Württemberg, 1973, but not Nestle-Aland[26]). The word, which was added at the end of the line, without ΓΝΩCΕCΘΑΙ in 1.6 being erased, has itself been erased, and cannot now be read. Only *ε*, *γ*, and a vertical which could be the first stroke of *ν*, are visible.

15.9 (161b/1): *ϋμας ηγαπησα* D* d; *ηγαπησα ϋμας* D^F

16.4 (162b/26): OM D* d; *αλλα* D^F cet.

16.18 (163b/33–4): ΤΙ ΕCΤΙΝ ΤΟΥΤΟ D* d; *ελεγον ουν τουτο τι εστιν ο λεγει το μικρο[ν] ουκ οιδαμεν τι λαλει ελε.* D^F

Τουτο τι εστιν is also read by A *Γ Δ Λ Π** 068 pler.; *το* is omitted by B L *Υ* 121 pc.; *ελε.* – which is apparently what it reads (*scil. ελεγον*) – forms a bridge to the first line of F164b, where D reads

ΤΟ ΜΕΙΚΡΟΝ ΟΥΚ ΟΙΔΑΜΕΝ Ο ΛΕΓΕΙ

Ο λεγει is read only by D*, whilst B omits these two words. The final reading of D^F is therefore a glorious conflation, where D* simply omitted *ο λεγει* after *εστιν* and put it in the place of *τι λεγει*.

16.25 (164b/26): OM D*; *αλλ'* D^F

Acts 2.13 (419b/22): ΔΙΕΧΛΕΥΑΖΟΝ ΛΕΓΟΝΤΕC D* d; *διαχλευαζοντες ελεγο̄* D^F

2.31 (421b/23): OM D* d; *προειδως ελαλησεν περι της* D^F

2.33 (421b/31): ΥΜΕΙΝ D*; *τουτο ο ϋμεις* B D^F

2.45 (423b/10–12)

ΚΑΘΗΜΕΡΑΝ ΠΑCΙ / ΤΟΙC ΑΝ ΤΙC ΧΡΕΙΑΝ ΕΙΧΕΝ / ΠΑΝΤΕC ΤΕ D* d

καθημεραν πασι καθο / *τι αν τις χρειαν ειχεν καθημεραν* / *παντες τε* D^F

καθημεραν belongs at the beginning of v. 46. D^F has again produced a conflation.

5.36 (434b/15): OM *διελυθησαν* D*; OM *διελ. και* d; *διελυθησαν και* D^F

Note that there is a correction earlier in the verse, from ΔΙΕΛΥΘΗ to *ανηρεθη*, made by D^D.

6.1 (435b/14–15): ΚΑΘΗΜΕΡΙΝΗ D*; *τη. καθ.* D^F

7.38 (441b/16–17): ΛΑΛΟΥΝΤΟC D*; *του λαλ.* D^F

7.52 (443b/1): ΕΚΕΙΝΟΙ D* d; οι πατερες ϋμ ω D^F
10.26–7 (456b/14–15)
ϢC ΚΑΙ CΥ / ΚΑΙ ΕΙCΕΛΘϢΝ ΤΕ ΚΑΙ ΕΥΡΕΝ D*
και συνομιλω αυτω εισηλθεν και ευρεισκι D^F
11.20 (461b/5): ελληνας D* d; ελληνιστας D^F
11.25 (461b/23): ΠΑΡΕΚΑΛΕCΕΝ D*; +αυτον D^F
The correction occurs in a longer reading of D. It seems probable that the omission of ως earlier in the verse is also due to F.
12.13 (464b/4): FORIS d; ΤΟΥ [ ] D*; του πυλωνος D^F
Scrivener rejects the opinion of Wettstein, that D* read εξω. Instead, he queries whether the D^F reading replaces another word, or is a rewriting of the same one. Nothing more can be seen in the manuscript.
13.27 (468b/27): ΑΥΤΗC [ ] ΤΑΙC D*; EIUS NON INTELLEGENTES d; αυτων τουτον αγνοουντες D^F
According to von Soden, αγνοουντες represents the $I^{\alpha 1}$ text (*Die Schriften des Neuen Testaments*, Vol. 2, Berlin, 1913, apparatus, ad loc.).
13.28 (468b/32)
ΚΡΕΙΝΑΝΤΕC ΑΥΤΟΝ ΠΑΡΕΔϢΚΑΝ ΠΕΙΛΑΤϢ D*
ητησαντο πιλατον ανερεθην κρειν. αυτον παρεδ. πειλ. D^F
F's addition was placed in brackets by a later hand.
13.45 (471b/3): ΤΟΙC ΛΟΓΟΙC D*; τοις λογοις τοις D^F
14.17 (474b/5–6): ΚΑΡΔΙΑC D*; τας καρδ. D^F
15.35 (479b/23): ΤΟΥ D*; του κυ D^F
19.29 (497b/3)
CΥΝΕΧΥΘΗ ΟΛΗ Η ΠΟΛΙC ΑΙCΧΥΝΗC D*
επλησθη η πολις της συγχυσεως ℵ* A B
επλησθη ολη η πολις της συνχυσεως D^F d (REPLETA EST TOTA CIVITAS CONFUSIONEM)
Discussion of this fascinating variant (with a fuller apparatus) will be left to a later section (chapter 13). Here, we must be content to note that D^F gives a version which is a conflation of the ℵ* B A and D* readings.
20.24 (501b/11): ΘΥ D*; του θυ D^F
20.26 (501b/16–17)
ΑΧΡΙ ΟΥΝ ΤΗC CΗΜΕΡΟΝ ΗΜΕΡΑC D*
διο μαρτυρομαι ϋμειν εν της σημερον ημερα οτι D^F
PROPTER QUOD HODIERNO DIE d
20.36 (502b/18): τα γονατα D*; +αυτου D^F; deest d
21.18 (505b/1): ΗCΑΝ ΔΕ ΠΑΡ ΑΥΤϢ D* d; παρεγενοντο D^F
22.6 (508b/18–19)
ΕΝΓΙΖΟΝΤΙ ΔΕ ΜΟΙ ΜΕCΗΜΒΡΙΑC ΔΑΜΑCΚϢ D*
ενγιζ. δε μοι μεσημ. τη δαμ. D^B
εγενετο δε μοι πορευομενω ϗ ενγιζοντι τη δαμασκω περι μεσημβριαν D^F
deest d

This corrector has a habit of conflating readings. We see it at Jn 16.18; Ac 2.45; 13.28, 45; 19.29. Also, his typical correction is an extensive one, and generally occurs at a place where there is a single alternative text to that of D. Of his twenty-nine decipherable corrections, sixteen are with all other manuscripts (Mt 12.20; 27.13; Jn 15.9; 16.4; Ac 5.36; 6.1; 7.38, 52; 10.26–7; 12.13; 14.17; 15.35; 20.24, 36; 21.18; 22.6), and three more go with the majority (Jn 16.25; Ac 2.13; 20.26). Five are unique. These are the three conflations at Jn 16.18; Ac 2.45; 13.28, the addition of *αυτον* at Ac 11.25, and the reading *αγνοουντες* at 13.27. Readings with less support are Ac 2.31 with a few minuscules, 33 with ℵ A B C* pc., and 13.45 with E. The remaining variants do not betray anything about the texts he knew. The variety may indicate an extensive knowledge of a number of textual traditions.

As to the effect of his corrections on the relationship of the Greek with the Latin column, only at Ac 19.29 does he adopt a reading found in the Latin. In seventeen other readings he introduces a discrepancy between them. In two more both D* and he have a different text from the Latin. Albeit he makes fewer corrections, his text is the most removed from the Latin of any corrector so far.

Although the relatively small number of corrections attributed to F makes assessment difficult, it seems that we find the milieu of Codex Bezae now to be essentially that of the standard Byzantine text.

CORRECTOR J[1]

The alterations to the text by Corrector J[1] are confined to one double page. At F160b/18 (Jn 15.2), he placed ↑ in the inner margin, and at the bottom of the leaf wrote

↓*ηδη ϋμεις καθαροι εστε δια τον λογον ον λελαληκα ϋμιν* ʻ
μινατε εν εμοι καγω εν ϋμιν καθως το κλημα ου δυναται καρπο̄
φερειν

Tischendorf does not record any variants for these words, omitted only in D*.

There are two corrections to the facing Latin page. At the bottom is added

iam vobis mundi estis propter verbum

Since the Latin *p.m.* omits the same amount as the Greek, the correction is incomplete. *Vobis* is in error for *vos* (caused by his correction in line 31?); *verbum* is read by Lvt (a q r[1]).

In line 31 (15.7) he added *vobis* after FIET, with Lvt (exc. d* e) Lvg.

CORRECTIONS BY HAND L

Both corrections to the text by this hand are in Luke.

8.41 (218b/31)
ΑΝΗΡ [ΤΗϹ ϹΥΝΑΓΩ]ΓΗϹ ΠΕϹΩΝ D*

ανηρ ω ονομα ιαϊρος και D^L d cet.
23.34 (278b/34–6)
add. *ο δε ις ελεγεν πατιρ / αφες αυτοις ου γαρ οι / δασιν τη ποιουσιν* D^L

While the International Greek New Testament Project's volume of Luke records a number of variants for 23.34, the majority of later manuscripts have the text used by D^L. The corrector added this verse, because it comprises a whole Ammonian Section, and his numbering would have been at fault without it. The need for a correction at 8.41 probably occurred to him because it was the beginning of a lection.

CORRECTOR K

Because of the heterogeneous material placed under this heading, there is no value in analysing it systematically. Only a couple of corrections need be mentioned. They are not all from one pen.

Matthew 15.11, 18, 20 (49b/22, 24; 50b/9, 14, 16)
κοινωνι . . . κοινωνει . . . κοινωνει . . . τα κοινωνουντα . . . κοινωνει $D^{*.K}$
κοινοι . . . κοινοι . . . κοινοι . . . τα κοινουντα . . . κοινοι D^D cet.

This roughly written restoration of D* (all by one hand) is possibly due to an antiquarian interest shown by a reader who then wants to make quite clear what this ancient codex read. The twelve places where the badly faded original letters have been rewritten (3b/33, 10b/31–3, 233/4, 250b/6, 258b/9, 260b/1, 312b/22, 419/30, 420b/9–13, 421/10–14, 462b/1, 464b/1) may indicate the same interest, as may the occasional substitution of a supralinear stroke for final *ν* with the letter itself. Note also

Matthew 21.5 (68b/15)
υποζυγιον $D^{*.K}$ Cyr Or
υποζυγιου D^A cet.

A few of the remaining corrections are possibly also fairly early. Most are from the Middle Ages or beyond, and contribute nothing to our understanding of the ancient use of this bilingual tradition.

Two other known Lyons manuscripts have illegible parts rewritten (see p. 166 below). It is therefore possible that at least some of K's activity may be associated with this period in the manuscript's history.

CORRECTIONS *SECUNDA MANU*

Although the great majority of corrections have now been described, there remain many which cannot be attributed to an individual hand. Most of them are erasures. There are also a number of corrections to the Latin whose source cannot be determined. Although they might be better described as *incerta manu*, I have thought it preferable to preserve Scrivener's usage.

These anonymous corrections have also to be examined, for our picture of the effect on Codex Bezae of its correctors to be a balanced one. So far, we have observed substitutions and insertions, but very few deletions. To analyse these corrections in the way that we have done hitherto would be unprofitable. Since we cannot determine the date of these corrections, we cannot use them in recovering the stages of the manuscript's history. We must therefore content ourselves with a more general appraisal of their character. To uncover the difficulties of interpreting this material, we begin with the more manageable group of Latin corrections.

Latin corrections *secunda manu*

It soon becomes apparent that there are very few significant changes to the text. The great majority are orthographical, or deletion of repeated letters, or removal of nonsense and wrong endings.

> Orthographic: consonants, seventeen times (*b* to *v* once, intrusive *s* five times); vowels, twenty-three times (*ae* to *e* eleven times); reduplication ten times; nonsense sixteen times; wrong endings fourteen times. There are three false corrections (F50/33, 135/27, and 269/2). There are also three places where the *p.m.* text has been rewritten (284/33, 461/1, 491/20), which like those attributed to K may be associated with the period of the supplementary leaves. Scrivener assigned other re-writings to K. Of the corrections of *ae* to *e*, four are made by marking the *a* with point above and obelus through (one in Acts); in the other seven (six in Acts) *a* is erased. Thus there is evidence for two or more hands even in this simple correction.

The remaining twelve significant alterations are unevenly distributed – there are five each in John and Acts 1.1–7.30, and one each in Luke and Mark. I use Scrivener's concise and clear Latin to describe how the corrections were made.

John 4.25 (117/3): *adnuntiavit* (scil. *-abit*) d*; *adnuntiat* d$^{s.m.}$ (*vi* punctis suprapositis abrogat); αναγγελλει D

6.28 (126/17): *operemur* d*; *operebimur* d$^{s.m.}$; ΕΡCѠΜΕΘΑ D*; εργασωμεθα D^{B}

The correction to d was itself erased later. The variant is complicated by a variation in the word order, though the hands of D agree.

6.51 (128/17): *descendit* d*; *descendi* d$^{s.m.}$; καταβας D

8.6 (135/3): INCLINATUS d*; *inclinatu* (sic) d$^{s.m.}$ (*s* puncto suprapposito abrogat); κατω κυψας D

8.40 (138/2): AUDIVIT d*; *audivi* d$^{s.m.}$ (*t* eras.); ΗΚΟΥCΕΝ D$^{*.H}$; ηκουσα D^{A}

Luke 3.32 (196b/column 2/15): SALOMON d*; *salmon* d$^{s.m.}$; σαλμων D

Mark 5.21 (300/25): AD EUM TURBA MULTA AD EUM d*; *turba multa ad eum* d$^{s.m.}$ (punctis suprapositis abrogat); ΟΧΛΟC ΠΟΛΥC ΠΡΟC ΑΥΤΟΝ D

There is considerable variation in the Old Latin manuscripts here, and d* represents a conflation of the two positions of the equivalent to *προς αυτον*. The corrector favours the reading of the majority of manuscripts.

Acts 1.11 (417/14): SIC ENIM VENIET d*; *sic veniet* $d^{s.m.}$ (punctis suprapositis et linea per *enim*); *ουτως ελευσεται* D

1.15 (418/1): CUM SURREXISSET d*; *surrexit* $d^{s.m.}$ (*cum* punctis suprapositis abrogat); *αναστας* D

1.21 (418/26): QUONIAM d*; *quo* $d^{s.m.}$ (punctis suprapositis et obelis *niam* abrogat); ΩC D

5.10 (432/14): ET CECIDITQUE CONFESTIM d*; *et cecidit confestim* $d^{s.m.}$ (punctis suprapositis *que* abrogat); ΚΑΙ ΕΠΕCΕΝ ΠΑΡΑΧΡΗΜΑ D

5.29 (434/20–1): *obtemperare* ... *honibus* (sic), *petrus* ... *eos* d*

D* also has the two clauses reversed. The correct order is indicated in both columns, but by different correctors.

Of these corrections, six (Jn 4.25; 6.28; Lk 3.32; Mk 5.21; Ac 1.11; 5.10) adopt the text of D*. Only three (Jn 8.40; Ac 1.21; 5.29) present a text different from D*. These three are all the majority (and Vulgate) Latin readings. Other interesting agreements are those at Jn 8.6 (with e) and Ac 1.15 (with Cyprian). In fact, these two corrections *could* be by the same hand, and the sanguine might wish to consider this double agreement with African witnesses to be significant.

The only clear conclusion that can be drawn from this evidence is that which completes our knowledge of the impact of the correctors on the relationship between the columns. The pattern of association with other manuscripts is bound to be entirely random, and the details of orthographical revision by an unknown number of hands is hopelessly generalized.

Let us therefore look even more briefly at the Greek corrections, summarizing their overall impact on the character of the volume.

Greek corrections *secunda manu*

There are 108 corrections which affect the relationship between the two columns. Of these, twenty adopt the text followed by the Latin column, and the rest introduce differences between the two texts. The details of the twenty are: Matthew four, John, Luke, and Mark two, Acts ten. Those of the other eighty-eight are: Matthew nine, John two, Luke five, Mark eleven, Acts sixty-one.

Many of the corrections to Acts consist in the removal of material distinctive to the longer text which is found in both columns. Clearly, these corrections have had a very obvious effect on the character of Codex Bezae as a bilingual.

Apart from these, there are again far more significant corrections to Acts than to the Gospels. Of these, we may note particularly that *και* connecting a participle and a finite verb is regularly removed. This idiom of D's, on which we have already remarked, and to which we will return in another chapter, is largely eliminated by the manuscript's correctors.

CHAPTER TEN

The supplementary leaves

S. Berger, *Histoire de la Vulgate pendant les premiers siècles du moyen âge*, Paris, 1893, pp. 61–4; A. Cabaniss, 'Florus of Lyons', *Classica et mediaevalia* 19 (1958), 212–32; M. Cappuyns, 'Florus de Lyon', *Dictionnaire d'histoire et de géographie ecclésiastiques*, ed. A. Bandrillart *et al.*, Paris, 1912ff, Vol. 17; C. Charlier, 'Les Manuscrits personnels de Florus de Lyon', *Mélanges E. Podechard*, Lyons, 1948, pp. 71–84; Charlier, 'Florus de Lyon', *Dictionnaire de spiritualité*, ed. M. Viller *et al.*, Paris, 1937ff, Vol. 5; J. Mizzi, 'The Vulgate Text of the Supplemental Pages of Codex Bezae Cantabrigiensis', *Sacris erudiri* 14 (1963), 149–63; H. Quentin, 'Le *Codex Bezae* à Lyons au IXe siècle? Les Citations du Nouveau Testament dans le Martyrologe d'Adon', *RB* 33 (1906), 1–25; Quentin, *Les Martyrologes historiques du moyen âge. Etude sur la formation du Martyrologe Romain*, Paris, 1908, chapter 7; S. Tafel, 'The Lyons Scriptorium', in *Palaeographia Latina*, ed. W. M. Lindsay, Part II (St Andrews University Publications 16), Oxford, 1923, pp. 66–73; *ibid.* Part IV (*ibid.* 20), Oxford, 1925, pp. 40–70. For Ado's Martyrology, see further Georges de Manteyer, 'Le Martyrologe lyonnais d'Adon (850) avec ses additions', Extrait du *Bulletin de la Société d'Etudes des Hautes-Alpes* 59 (1940), 5–203, Gap, 1940. For Charlier's work on Florus, see P.-I. Fransen, 'Le Travail scientifique de dom Célestin Charlier', *Interface* 87/24 (1987), Suppl., 5–8.

The extensive correction of the text comes to an end in the seventh century. One corrector may have touched the manuscript after its removal to Lyons.

By the ninth century, the manuscript had become incomplete, some gatherings being altogether lost. The long gap between Ff348 and 415 had already been formed. The school of Florus made no attempt to replace the whole of this lacuna. Only the final verses of Mark were supplied (this is certain because, although the end of 3 John appears on F415, *αρχεται πραξις αποστολων* is written on the opposite page, 348b*). Also added were a leaf in Matthew 3, and the middle of John 18 to the beginning of chapter 20 (see chapter 3 for details). It is actually in this late period that we find the bilingual character of the manuscript being taken seriously, for the first time since its youth.

Another manuscript that had missing portions supplied at Lyons is described by Tafel (Part IV, p. 49). It is Lyons Ms 443 (372), of Origen on the Heptateuch, made up out of a half-uncial and an uncial manuscript, with portions still missing supplied in Visigothic minuscule. Besides the programme of conservation referred to in chapter 3, we may note that the practice of rewriting illegible parts of manuscripts, which is quite common in D, is also paralleled in Tafel's research by Mss 2 (Lyons 604) and 18 (Paris Lat. 9550) in his list. It is, as we have seen, therefore likely that some at least of the rewritings ascribed by Scrivener to K and *s.m.* were in fact made at Lyons in the ninth century.

The restored Greek text is basically of good quality. A collation with the *textus receptus* (using *Η ΚΑΙΝΗ ΔΙΑΘΗΚΗ*, Oxford, 1973) yielded the following results.

The further evidence is drawn from Tischendorf, Legg (for Mark), Jülicher's *Itala*, and Wordsworth and White. The siglum δ denotes the Latin text of *Δ* (037); it is placed with Vulgate manuscripts because my source is Wordsworth and White.

MATTHEW 3.8–16

8: *καρπους αξιους*] *καρπον αξιον* c. ℵ B C pler. Lvt (exc. a) Lvg
της] OM
10: *και*] OM c. ℵ B C al. Lvt Lvg
16: *ανεβη ευθυς*] *ευθυς ανεβη* c. ℵ B W min. pc. Lvt (exc. d h) Lvg

JOHN 18.14–20.13

Chapter 18

14: *απολεσθαι*] *αποθανειν* c. ℵ B C min. pc. Lvt? Lvg?
20: *ο*] OM c. ℵ*·c B L 440
τη] OM c. ℵ A B C L pler.
24: *ο*] OM c. *Γ* pc.
27: *ο*] OM c. A B C L al.
28: *πρωια*] *πρωι* c. ℵ A B C L al.
*ινα*²] OM c. ℵ A B C* *Δ* 1 pc. Lvt (aur b c) Lvg (exc. E T^c W)
31: *ουν*²] *δε* c. A K U *Θ*^c P 1 pc. Lvt (r¹)
33: *εις το πραιτωριον παλιν*] *παλιν εις το πραιτ.* c. B C* L X Y *Δ* pc. Lvt Lvg
*ο*¹] OM
34: *απεκριθη αυτω*] *και απεκρινατο* c. Lvt (a aur c ff²) Lvg (exc. O T Y δ)
συ] OM c. ℵ* 59 Lvt (a aur c e f ff² r¹) Lvg (exc. δ)
σοι ειπον] *ειπον σοι* c. C* L
35: *οι*] OM
36: *ο*] OM c. ℵ A B C L plu.
*η βασιλεια η εμη*²] *η εμη βασιλεια* c. ℵ pc.
παραδοθω] *παραδω* c. 69
37: *ειμι εγω*] *ειμι* c. ℵ B L Y 1 13 pc. Lvt (a aur c f^m² ff² r¹) Lvg (D O*)
38: *ευρισκω εν αυτω*] *εν αυτω ευρισκω* c. Lvt (a)
39: *υμιν απολυσω*¹] *απολυσω υμιν* c. ℵ B K L *Δ Π* 1 al. Lvt (a aur e f q r¹) Lvg (exc. D G K M V Z^c)
*υμιν απολυσω*²] *απολυσω υμιν* c. ℵ A B K L *Π* 1 al. Lvt Lvg
40: *παντες λεγοντες*] *λεγοντες παντες*
τον] OM
ο] OM

Chapter 19

4: *ουν*] OM c. ℵ *Γ* 1 106 157 pc. Lvt (a aur c f q) Lvg
6: *σταυρωσον*^{2}] + *αυτον* c. Lvt (b f ff^2 j q) Lvg (E W δ)
αυτον υμεις] *υμεις αυτον* c. ℵ A X Y *Δ Π* al. Lvt (e q r^1)
7: *ημων*] OM c. ℵ B L *Δ* Lvt (exc. q) Lvg
του] OM c. ℵ A B pler.
11: *απεκριθη*] + *αυτω* c. ℵ B L 1 33 249 Lvt ([a] c j)
o^1] OM c. B E H K *Π* al.
ειχες] *εχεις* c. ℵ A L *Π* al.
ουδεμιαν κατ εμου] *κατ εμου ουδεμιαν* c. ℵ B K L X 1 33 124 157 Lvt (a aur b c e ⟨j⟩ r^1) Lvg (exc. δ)
σοι δεδομενον] *δεδ. σοι* c. ℵ B L Y
13: *τουτον τον λογον*] *τουτων των λογων* c. E H S Y *Γ Δ* 065 al. Lvt Lvg
του] OM c. ℵ A B L *Π* 065 al.
δε] OM c. ℵ
14: *ωρα δε*] *ωρα ην* c. ℵ A B L M U X *Δ Π* Lvt ([a] c j) Lvg
εκτη] *τριτη* c. ℵ^c L X^{txt} *Δ* 72 123*^{mg} 151 Lvg (δ)
16: *δε*] *ουν* c. A B al. Lvt (exc. f)
απηγαγον] *ηγαγον* c. E H K S Y *Γ Δ Λ Π**$^{.3}$ 065 al.
17: *τον σταυρον αυτου*] *εαυτου τον στ.* c. 238 299 Lvg
γολγοθα] *γολγοτα*
18: *αλλους δυο*] *δυο αλλους*
19: *δε*^{2}] + *το*
20: *ανεγνωσαν των ιουδαιων*] *των ιουδ. ανεγ.* c. Lvt ([r^1]) Lvg (J)
της πολεως ο τοπος] *ο τοπος της πολεως* c. ℵ A B L 065 pler. Lvt (q r^1)
21: *οι*] OM
αλλ] *αλλα*
23: *εποιησαν*] *ποιησαντες*
αρραφος] *αραφος* c. ℵ A E H K 065 pler.
24: *ουν*] *δε* c. Lvt (r^1)
εσται] *εστιν*
26: *ιδου*] *ειδε* (scil. *ιδε*) c. B M X *Λ* al.
28: *παντα ηδη*] *ηδην παντα* scil. *ηδη παντα* c. A B L U X Y *Π* al. Lvt (aur ff^2 v) Lvg
τετελεσται] *τετελειωται* c. 64
τελειωθη] *πληρωθη* c. ℵ 1 13 69 124 346 Lvt (b f q r^1)
30: *τετελεσται*] *τετελειωται*
31: *ην*^{1}] OM
εκεινου του σαββατου] *του. σαβ. εκεινου* c. L 69 73
34: *αλλ*] *αλλα*
35: *ινα*] + *και* c. ℵ A B H K L U X *Λ Π* al. Lvt (exc. e) Lvg (exc. D δ)
38: o^1] OM c. ℵ B E G K L M *Π* 1 33 al.
o^2] OM c. A B L 90
39: *ωσει*] *ως* c. ℵ B L *Γ Δ Λ Π* pc.

40: αυτο] + εν c. A Γ Δ Λ Π² al. Lvt (q r⟨1⟩) Lvg (S)
  τοις] OM
41: καινον] κενον c. 69 al.

Chapter 20

3: ο²] OM
8: και¹] OM
  και³] + ουκ
11: παρεκυψεν] ενπαρεκυψεν
12: εν ... καθεζομενους] OM

MARK 16.16–20

16: praem] + οτι c. 563 ℓ253
17: εκβαλουσι] εκβαλλουσι c. 579 697 (and Tischendorf adds the testimony of manuscripts B C G of the Acts of Pilate)
18: επι] επ
19: ανεληφθη] ανελημφθη c. A C W Δ Θ
  εκ δεξιων] εν δεξιων c. 485; εν δεξια C Δ pc.

Subscription ευαγγελιον κατα μαρκον / ετελεσθη' / αρχεται πραξις αποστολων'

This collation includes neither orthographic variants nor a few other peculiarities. These should not, however, be overlooked. They provide evidence that this copyist was a Latin of indifferent Greek scholarship:

F169b*/20] ραρρησια, where the first ρ = Latin *P*
  22 ϊουδαηοι = *iudaei*
170b*/27 ιουδαις = *iudaeis*
173b*/21 μινητ = *manet* (cp. *remaneret* Lvt (ff²))

While the intrusion of the wrong alphabet is easy in bilingual copying, its appearance here, along with the other errors, is more likely to indicate a Latin scribe, particularly since this scribe wrote only the Greek, and not both columns. The tendency to omit the article could also indicate that he was a Latin speaker (compare the frequency with which we have seen some of the early Greek correctors supplying articles where the first hand had omitted them). There are eighteen examples of this, eight with no Greek support. Some at least of the other ten may not have been in his exemplar.

His ignorance of Greek is shown also by F175b*/28 (Jn 20.11), where a medial point creeps into a word (εκλει·εν), and by numerous itacisms, of which the most blatant is confusion of long and short *e* and *o* sounds (e.g. 169b*1, 5 (Jn 18.14, 15) εν = ην; 170b*/4 (18.26), πετρως).

The regularity of agreement with ℵ or B is considerable. This should be expressed more precisely by comparison with the Vulgate. The type of Greek text used by the restorer contains elements in common with the base of the Latin materials. We note particularly

John 18.34: *και απεκρινατο* D^S d^S Lvt (a aur c ff^2) Lvg (exc. O T Y δ)
18.38: *εν αυτω ευρισκω* D^S Lvt (a)
19.6: *σταυρωσον σταυρωσον αυτον* D^S d^S Lvt (b f ff^2 j q) Lvg (E W δ)
19.20: *των ιουδαιων ανεγνωσαν* D^S Lvt ([r^1]) Lvg (J)
19.24: *δε* D^S Lvt (r^1)

The quality of the Greek text of the restorer gives us the confidence to believe that all these variants had a Greek base. There can be no question of the Greek text having been adjusted to conform to the Latin. There are in fact sixty-eight places where it has a reading that is different from the text of Wordsworth and White, although in many of these it does have other Latin support. But that it has not been latinized may be seen by collating it with the supplementary Latin column.

JOHN 18–20

Chapter 18

17: *η . . . πετρω*] *petro ancilla ostiaria*
18: *εστως*] OM
20: *παντοτε*] *omnes*
22: *των . . . παρεστηκως*] *assistens ministrorum*
23: *μαρτυρησον*] *perhibeo*
29: OM] *foras*
32: *θανατω ημελλεν*] *esset morte*
34: *ειπον σοι*] *tibi dixerunt*
37: *εγω* semel] *ego* bis
38: *αιτιαν εν αυτω ευρισκω*] *inuenio in eo causam*
40: *ουν*] OM
λεγοντες παντες] *omnes dicentes*

Chapter 19

2: *αυτου τη κέφαλη*] *capiti eius*
3: OM] *et veniebant ad eum*
4: *εξω ο πειλατος*] *pilatus foris*
λεγει] *dixit*
εξω] OM
6: *εκραυγασαν*] *clamabant*
ϋμεις αυτον] *eum uos*
7: *εαυτον ϋιον θυ*] *filium di se*

11: αυτω] OM
  εχεις] *haberes*
  ην δεδομενον σοι] *tibi esset datum*
12: εκραυγασαν] *clamabant*
  γαρ] OM
  βασιλεια εαυτον] *se regem*
13: OM] *autem*
14: ην] OM
  τριτη] *sexta*
16: αυτον αυτοις] *eis illum*
17: ουν] *autem*
  ηγαγον] *eduxerunt*
  ος λεγηται] OM
18: δυο αλλους] *alios duos*
20: των ιουδαιων ανεγνωσαν] *legerunt iudaeorum*
  εγγυς ην ο τοπος της πολεως] *prope ciuitatem erat locus*
  OM] *et*
23: τον ιν] *eum*
  ποιησαντες] *fecerunt*
24: δε] *ergo*
  εστιν] *sit*
25: ϊστηκεισαν] *stabant*
  του κλωπα] *cleope*
26: παρεστωτα] OM
  ειδε] *ecce*
28: πληρωθη] *consummaretur*
29: πλησσαντες σπογγον οξους και ϋσσωπω] *spongiam plenam acaeto hysopo*
  αυτου τω στοματι] *ori eius*
30: το οξος ο ις] *ihs* acetum
31: ινα μη μινητ . . . επι παρασκευι] *qm parasceue erat. ut non remanerent . . .*
  ημερα του σαββατου εκεινου] *dies ille sabbati*
  αρτωσιν] *tollerentur*
34: αυτον την πλευραν] *latus eius*
35: αυτου εστιν] *est eius*
36: αυτον] *ex eo*
40: εν] OM
  εστιν ϊουδαις] *iudeis est*

Chapter 20

1: η μαγδαληνη] *magdalenae*

MARK 16

16: οτι] OM
19: ο μεν ουν κς] *et dns quidem*

There has been no attempt to bring these two texts into conformity with each other. Thus D^{S} gives us a glimpse of a particular Greek text that was used in the West in the ninth century. The basic quality is impressive, and sheds light on the character of some Latin texts, particularly Lvt (q r^{1}). Along with Mizzi's demonstration that the restored Latin text is a good one, we have ample evidence of the high standards maintained in the Lyons *scriptorium*. The fact that the text has links with Latin manuscripts makes it unlikely that this is a text imported from the East. Either it was an ancient Lyons codex, or it was descended from one – or at least from a codex copied in the West.

The affinities of the Latin text of these leaves have been studied by J. Mizzi. His conclusion is that the Old Latin element in d^{suppl} is not considerable:

> The Vulgate portion of the Bezan Codex (d^{suppl}) presents a text which is more often in agreement with A[miatinus] and the best manuscripts as represented by W–W [Wordsworth and White] than with the Clementine printed edition. When it differs from A, W–W and [the] Clem[entine text] it is chiefly in matters of orthography and in these variants it has the support of some Mss of the Vulgate, particularly the Irish group, and of a few Old Latin codices. (Mizzi, p. 163)

Whilst his article achieves its aim of discrediting Scrivener's claim that d^{suppl} is closer to the Clementine edition than to 'Amiatinus and the best Mss' (p. xx), the value of the conclusions he draws from the orthographic variants is questionable.

One would like to be a little more precise in identifying the source of the Latin restoration. The only Gospel manuscript believed by Charlier to have been associated with Florus is Bibl. Munic. 431. This was, according to manuscript notes of Professor B. Bischoff (to whom I am grateful for permission to quote from them), written in the *scriptorium* of Saint-Amand in the third quarter of the ninth century. Since Florus died in 860, the probability of his having corrected in this manuscript is perhaps diminished. However, the text is close to that of D^{S}. Apart from orthographic variants (including twelve of interchange between *ae* and *e*), the differences are (placing the reading of 431 *before* the square bracket):

John 18.10: *auriculam eius*] *eius auriculam*
18.18: *calefaciebant*] *calefiebant*
19.4: *cognoscatis*] *cognatis*
19.11: *me tradidit*] *tradidit me*
Mark 16.15: *vero*] *autem*
16.18: *aegros*] *aegrotos*
16.19: *ihs*] OM
16.20: OM] *amen*

At three of the orthographical changes, the text of 431 has been corrected to that of d^{S}:

Matthew 3.2: *appropinquabit* 431*] *appropinquavit* 431^{corr} d^{S}

John 18.22: *adsistens* 431*] *assistens* 431^{corr} d^S
19.13: *lithostrotos* 431*] *lithostrotus* 431^{corr} d^S

Finally, the words originally omitted in d^S at Jn 18.25 form one whole line in Ms 431.

This evidence, though a very long way short of providing any kind of proof, indicates a strong possibility that Ms Lyons 431 is the source of the supplementary leaves.

Some idea of the standards held at Lyons, and of the abilities of its leading scholars, and especially of Florus who set and maintained them, may be gathered from the sadly truncated studies of S. Tafel. Tafel, a pupil of Traube, died in the Great War. He had been at work on a history of the Lyons *scriptorium*, and W. M. Lindsay drew together what he perceived to be Tafel's arguments and conclusions. Tafel stresses the continuity of ancient culture in Lyons, its schools of rhetoric in the fifth century, its importance in the transmission of Roman legal material, and above all he describes the ninth-century golden age of Lyonnaise literature. The scholarly gifts of Florus himself are glowingly described by Charlier in the *Dictionnaire de spiritualité*. Erudition wedded to critical ability issued in collections of both canon and civil law, in an edition of Jerome's *Psalterium iuxta Hebraicum* (of which only his own description survives), and in the transmission of patristic texts. Florus also engaged in theological debate, and was regarded by his contemporaries as a poet of note.

It is to these biblical and historical concerns at Lyons that we owe the supplementary leaves of the Codex Bezae. Ancient texts were precious in Florus' eyes, and there can be little doubt that he and others like him sought to supplement them with the most ancient materials he could find.

The scholars of Lyons treated Codex Bezae as more than a subject of antiquarian curiosity. Dom Henri Quentin, whose textual study preceded the palaeographical evidence linking the manuscript with Lyons, showed that the biblical citations in the Martyrology of Ado have traces of influence of a text like it.

The Martyrology was written when Ado was a monk in Lyons. This was between about 850 (before which he had spent a few years in Ravenna) and 859–60, when he became Archbishop of Vienne (Quentin, *Martyrologes*, pp. 672f and n. (p. 673)). As one might expect, it was not an independent work. It owed its inspiration to Florus' martyrology, itself a reworking of Bede's. It has as kin various other such works based on Florus. But Ado was clearly a scholar of some standing. Quentin lists as the sources of the Martyrology, eighty-nine hagiographical works, twenty-two patristic writings, and forty-two other references (*Martyrologes*, pp. 641f).

Quentin examined all the New Testament citations by Ado, comparing them with the Old Latin manuscripts b and c (for the Gospels), d and e (for the Pauline letters) and d e g^2 gig h p s t and the citations in Cod. Sangall. 133 (for Acts). The base of comparison in the Gospels was clearly too small, but that need not concern us here. The majority of quotations are from Acts (Gospels – eight, Paul – eight, Acts – forty-nine). Quentin found that they are closest in character to Codex Gigas. But he showed three places where Bezan influence is possible ('Citations', p. 19 – Ac. 11.27; 18.2; 19.1). More important, in his opinion, were places where Ado gives several possible Latin renderings. The first of these was Ac 6.9, where he has ... *cum eo disputantibus et conquirentibus atque altercantibus* ... Here *conquirentes* is read by g^2 gig p, *disputantes* by e t Lvg, and *altercantes* by d ('Citations', p. 21). The pattern of readings from gig, Lvg, and d is repeated at Ac 6.12 and 18.2–3 (*ibid.*). A second reading at Ac 6.9 contains readings found in gig and d.

The conclusion seems inescapable. Ado's basic text for Acts was close to that of Gigas. He also used the Vulgate, and added information which, so far as we know, he can have got only from Codex Bezae.

There were in fact, according to Quentin (*Martyrologes*, pp. 674f), three editions of Ado's work. Each is represented by a different group of manuscripts (for the manuscripts and text, see Quentin, pp. 466–77). Only the first was produced in Lyons. The second edition must date from after 25 August 865, when Ado was in Vienne. Quentin considers it impossible to decide whether the third edition was the work of Ado himself.

Some further investigation is required to ascertain whether the readings showing an agreement with D definitely come in the earliest, Lyons, edition. The brief note in Quentin's *apparatus* ('Citations', pp. 14f) states that most of the notice containing the citation including Ac 6.9 and 12 is missing in Mss F (Paris, BN Ms Lat. 12582) and Ge (=the collations of Vatican Mss. Regin. 511, 512, 514, given by Giorgi in his edition of the Martyrology published at Rome in 1745). These are all manuscripts representing the first edition. Since the presence of D in Lyons has been established by other means since Quentin's article, the question does not substantially affect our account of the history of the manuscript. But the problem deserves investigation.

CHAPTER ELEVEN

The development of the corrected text

At first sight, the total of fourteen hundred corrections to the Greek seems to indicate extensive changes to the text of Codex Bezae. But in fact over 320 of these are orthographic, whilst 380 are simply the removal of nonsense, and others are slight. In Part III we have devoted our main attention to only about 380 corrections. It is true that, for example, eighty-two definite articles are added to the text. But against the 11,837 articles apparently to be found in the Gospels and Acts of Nestle-Aland[26], this is a tiny number. And, given the remarkably distinctive character of the text, one wonders whether the correctors have made much impact in Acts, or any at all in the Gospels. We can test this by comparing the number of divergencies in text between the two columns in the fifth and the ninth centuries. The first hand shows, as we will discover in Part IV, a total of 860 differences between the two. The net increase as a result of corrections is by 142, to 1,002. This is not a startling change. The details (tables 34–6) show us that, apart from corrections by B, the move is slow.

It is clear that only G treats the two columns as a single tradition. Otherwise, there is a steady erosion of the peculiarities of the text, which is accompanied by a widening gap between the columns. The consequence of centuries of correction was the addition, not the diminution, of differences between the columns. The implications of this will be taken up in Part IV.

If we draw together the conclusions that we have reached about each corrector, we are able to describe the successive environments in which the codex found itself.

The earliest corrector, G, was a Latin speaker of some standing in the community for which the manuscript was produced. He had access to its exemplar, and made improvements to the style of the Latin version. He was the last handler of the D tradition to consider consistency between the columns desirable. The bilingual tradition virtually comes to an end with him.

The second hand, A, is a corrector on a small scale, a remover of nonsense and spelling errors. When he makes a larger correction, he seems to do so from memory rather than from a text open before him.

Table 34. *Introduction of differences between the columns*

Hand	Mt	Jn	Lk	Mk	Ac	Total
G	6	—	—	—	4	10
A	1	4	2	1	4	12
C	5	5	1	—	10	21
B	8	9	4	5	31	57
D	3	4	1	—	10	18
E	—	2	—	1	9	12
H	1	—	—	—	10	11
F	1	4	—	—	12	17
s.m.	9	2	5	11	61	88
Total	34	30	13	18	151	246

Table 35. *Removal of differences between the columns*

Hand	Mt	Jn	Lk	Mk	Ac	Total
G	7	—	—	—	13	20
A	2	—	1	1	6	10
C	1	2	2	—	9	14
B	2	1	1	—	11	15
D	2	—	—	—	9	11
E	—	1	—	1	4	6
H	1	2	—	—	4	7
F	—	—	—	—	1	1
s.m.	4	2	2	2	10	20
Total	19	8	6	4	67	104

Table 36. *Total number of differences (net for the correctors)*

Hand	Mt	Jn	Lk	Mk	Ac	Total
p.m.	76	87	150	226	317	856
Correctors	15	22	7	14	84	142
Total	91	109	157	240	401	998

Corrector C interested himself only in parts of the manuscript. His text is unusual: many of his readings seem to represent his own opinion of what should be read. His basic text is Byzantine, but with a small number of readings shared with Latin witnesses. He is not, therefore, far removed from the original Latin context of the manuscript. His activity seems to indicate a transitional and troubled stage in the history of D, looking both forwards and backwards.

The corrector who made most alterations, B, is a quite different figure. Working in the fifth century (and within at most a couple of generations of the original scribe), he used a text which is akin to that of the C correctors of the Codex Sinaiticus. This places him in a setting open to Caesarean influence. Besides this, we find that he knows readings that are out of the same stable as Codex Bezae. It is unlikely that the manuscript can have moved far from its birthplace by this stage. But either its original community has ceased to use Latin, or the codex has been moved to another place.

With D we have a related development. He was a scholar who knew a good New Testament text, closest among known witnesses to ℵ B.

The text of E is harder to describe, except that it is further on the Byzantine road. It is easier to see that H had a distinctive text, but he is in some ways like E, except that he shows slightly fewer readings which follow the ℵ B text.

In F we encounter at last the standard Byzantine text, and another distinctive period in the use of the manuscript.

Finally, in the period of the supplementary leaves, we find a quite different attitude to the codex. It is treated again as a bilingual, and interest is shown in the original character of the text. Some missing parts are replaced, and some words that are hard to read are rewritten. It even seems to have been regarded by Ado as an authority.

It should also be remembered that there are a number of corrections which cannot be dated, and above all that interest in the Latin column was never totally extinguished, even in the most Greek phases of this history. Undatable corrections, and ones that have been associated with known correctors, are the evidence for this. Only E and F have no corrections to the Latin column associated with them.

The main phases we have detected are

1. Bilingual; corrections against the exemplar (G)
2. Transitional – text not wildly different (A); vestiges of Latin influence (C)
3. Exposure to a quite different text (B – associated with $ℵ^c$ – and D – associated with ℵ B)
4. The growing (but far from total) influence of the Byzantine text (E and H)
5. Correction to the standard Byzantine text (F)
6. Renewed interest in the original form of text shown at Lyons in the ninth century

The evidence we have collected enables us to go beyond Fischer's classification according to linguistic milieu, and to observe the history of the manuscript according to the impact of other texts upon it. Most significant is the very small contact with any pure Byzantine text. Not least intriguing is the number of distinctive texts of which the correctors give us tantalizing glimpses.

Our study has been of the way in which Codex Bezae was altered against other textual standards. But in the text of Ado we saw an occasion where it influenced the text of someone who knew it. It must not be forgotten that the correctors whom we have been studying will, consciously or unconsciously, have taken readings of D away to their examination of other manuscripts. The fact that it was repeatedly corrected indicates that the tradition was a living one in the East for several centuries.

This can be expressed more pointedly. While it is clear that some of these correctors had a text quite different from that of D, the fact stands that they thought it worth correcting. Considering the extensive differences between it and the text known by, let us say, Hands B and F, this is a remarkable fact. Why was it not either ignored, or thrown away, or else more thoroughly corrected? The answer must be, that the correctors accorded the manuscript the respect of thinking it worth reading and emending. This respect will have led them to paying attention to its peculiarities and – consciously or unconsciously, as I have said – adopting some of its readings.

Now, it is clear that the subsequent influence of such readings may have been slight, and that in any case we can never isolate such a borrowing of a D reading. However, that it was a living tradition is clear. And there are occasional readings which could be of this type. They are rare. An instance in Acts could be 12.3, where *και ιδων* is read by D H L P al. pler., and *ιδων δε* by ℵ A B E al. Such a variant could have been taken into the majority text by a corrector of D later recollecting its reading. It must be emphasized that I am advancing this as a purely hypothetical case, simply in order to show that D continued to be used.

And possibly copied also. Some correctors, notably G but also C and H, are found only in some parts of the codex. One wonders, of the latter two in particular, whether they were not sampling the text, either out of interest or to decide whether it should be copied, or to prepare it for copying.

From the point of view of the relationship between East and West during this period, the smattering of corrections to the Latin is of some interest. Did Greek writers with a little Latin glance at the opposite column when the Greek text was particularly strange to them? Were they mildly intrigued at what must have been a great curiosity, a Latin text? Certainly, there is no absolute loss of interest.

The implications of this chapter for the history of the manuscript will be drawn out in Part V. We must finally ask in this chapter whether we have gathered any knowledge which will enable us to trace back the history of the tradition behind D.

In one clear way the result is negative. We have seen that, apart from G, the later tradition was not a bilingual one. In the main, D was handled as if it were merely a Greek manuscript. But we have seen that G certainly was in the bilingual tradition. It is clear from observing his activity that copying a bilingual will increase the divergency between its texts, while a corrector who is within the same tradition will reduce it. This point will be significant for our study of the divergencies, when we will be discussing whether or not the Latin column is independent of the Greek.

It is also clear that the Latin part of the tradition could be handled with some freedom, embellished and improved. This fact also will need to be borne in mind.

The corrections that are *not* made to the text are sometimes as interesting as those that are. For example, the spellings YMEIN and HMEIN are never touched. There are plenty of nonsense readings in D that have been allowed to stand, omissions by accident that have not been re-inserted, and so on. No doubt many of them will have survived in a copying of the text. There is here an important general point: we must beware of assuming that all nonsense readings are the work of the scribe of the manuscript in which we find them. Given the evidence for the care shown in certain matters by the scribe of D, I would suggest that some of these nonsenses are part of his inheritance.

It needs also to be noted how stubborn a text-type is. Even the considerable number of corrections made to Acts leave us with a text which is very recognizably that of Codex Bezae. The ability of a form to survive will also affect our examination of the divergencies between the columns.

There are therefore ways in which this part of our investigation will have helped us to understand the tradition behind D as well as the vicissitudes through which it passed.

PART IV

The bilingual tradition

CHAPTER TWELVE

The codex and the critics

> Mention was made of the *Earse* translation of the New Testament, which has lately been published, and of which the learned Mr. *Macqueen* of *Sky* spoke with commendation; but Mr. *Maclean* said, he did not use it, because he could make the text more intelligible to his auditors by an extemporary version. From this I inferred, that the language of the translation was not the language of the isle of *Col*.

This account (and I have no idea whether or not the inference was correct) comes from Dr Johnson's description of Col in his *Journey to the Western Islands*. It serves to introduce us to some of the dangers awaiting the student of a bilingual tradition. In the first place, the gap between intention and practice shows that a written document provides only partial evidence of what actually happened. In the second place, we have an instructive difference between written and extempore interpretation, which indicates that an account such as that describing the reading of Scripture in Jerusalem found in chapter 47 of the fourth-century *Peregrinatio Aetheriae* may not help us to understand a written text (see further chapter 15). Finally, the conclusion reached by Dr Johnson seems quite unjustifiable on this evidence. May not the venerable Mr Maclean have been objecting to the clarity of the translation rather than to the form of the Gaelic language which it represented? Or may he not have been prejudiced in favour of his own abilities against those of the translator?

How is the bilingual tradition of Codex Bezae to be interpreted? How and why did it arise? What effect did its creation have on the Greek and Latin texts it contains? Was it formed by making a translation of the Greek text before us, or was it created out of an existing Latin version? The proper way to attempt an answer to these problems is by establishing a correct method. To do that, we will find it helpful to review the explanations and the means that have been offered in the course of the past three centuries. The arguments of those who have claimed that the Bezan text approximates to the original hardly find room here. The reason is that their main concern has been to discredit other texts. For example, Clark's theory that the New Testament text is like a traveller losing a piece of luggage every time he changes trains, belongs to a more general discussion and not to the present investigation.

The following will not be an attempt exhaustively to list writings on Codex Bezae or opinions about it. There are already good bibliographies available. My aim is simply to describe the main outlines of research and interpretation. In doing this I shall deal in the main with writings devoted to the subject, rather than with general books on the New Testament text. For the history of the study of Codex Bezae, see F. J. A. Hort, *BBC* 3 (1926), 3–5. See also J. K. Elliott, *A Bibliography of Greek New Testament Manuscripts* (Society for New Testament Studies Monograph Series 62), Cambridge, 1989, pp. 37–42.

A history of the main theories of the relationship between the two texts of Acts is provided by B.-L., Vol. 1, pp. 3–10. The reader is referred thither in particular for the discussion of the two-edition theory. To the bibliography may be added the review of Blass (*Acta Apostolorum, Editio philologica apparatu critico*, Göttingen, 1895; *Acta Apostolorum secundum formam quae videtur Romanam*, Leipzig, 1896) by T. E. Page, *CR* 11 (1897), 317–20.

The story of the critical investigation of the manuscript begins with the *Novum Testamentum Graecum* of John Mill, published at Oxford in 1707 (Prolegomena, pp. CXXXI ff). It is generally stated that, in Mill's opinion, the Greek text had been Latinized. That is to say, it had been consistently altered to agree with the Latin column, thus losing any claim to significance as an ancient Greek witness. As a matter of fact, this is only part of his argument. He actually spends more time in discussing twenty-four readings where he thought D was correct, and it may be that he intended only to illustrate the more obvious errors of a bilingual copying. Since, however, the section devoted to the influence of the Latin on the Greek has received most attention, we shall examine it.

Theories of Latinization predate the critical study of Codex Bezae. Erasmus, in discussing the text of the Greek maiuscule manuscripts B and E (07), argued that they had been influenced by the Latin Vulgate.

H. J. de Jonge, 'Erasmus and the Comma Johanneum', *ETL* 36 (1980), 381–9.

To return to Mill: he held this view for two reasons. The first is, that the scribe was a Latin speaker. Here he follows an argument to be found in Simon which concerns the shape of the characters, and the purpose of such a codex. There is also the appearance of such words as *Ηρωδους, Ιωαννα, Ιωαννει, Σαμαριτανων, φλαγελλωσας, λεπρωσα*, and others. The second reason consisted in ten readings in which he believed assimilation to have occurred. These were to be the touchstone of the problem for most of the century. They are mostly examples of accidental rather than intentional Latinization. Five are of mistaken endings:

Mt 5.24: ΠΡΟCΦΕΡΕΙC D*; *προσφερε* cet.; OFFERES d
Mt 3.16: ΚΑΤΑΒΑΙΝΟΝΤΑ D; *καταβαινων* cet.; DESCENDENTEM d
Mt 11.28: ΠΕΦΟΡΤΙCΜΕΝΟΙ ΕCΤΑΙ D*; *πεφορτισμενοι* cet.; [ ]ESTIS d (lacuna)
Mt 18.22: ΕΠΤΑΚΙC D*; *επτα* cet.; SEPTIES d
Ac 5.9: CΥΝΕΦΩΝΗCΕΝ D; *συνεφωνηθη* cet.; CONVENIT d

There remain two particularly problematical readings.

Mt 11.22, 24: HN ΫΜΕΙΝ D; η υμιν cet.; QUAM VOBIS d
Mt 15.11, 18, 20; Ac 21.28: These variants are the ones where κοινωνεω is substituted for κοινοω.

Mitto alia, concluded Mill loftily. Yet the theory was allowed to stand on so narrow a basis until fairly recently. The influence of his argument may be gauged from the fact that in his eighth edition Tischendorf described two of these readings as Latinizations (Mt 11.28, and 15.11ff), and that Nestle-Aland[26] continues to maintain this tradition at Mt 11.28.

The views of Mill were further and most notably propagated by J. J. Wettstein (Vol. 1, pp. 28–38), who applied the theory to more manuscripts than D alone. Semler, writing in 1764, followed Wettstein (*Hermeneutische Vorbereitung*, Vol. 3, pp. 99–137). But in his *Spicilegium observationum*, written in 1766, he revoked his opinion – *istae accusationes omnes vacuae sunt et temerariae* – thereby challenging the accepted view.

Semler's later view was adopted in Griesbach's *Symbolae criticae* of 1787 and in the fourth edition of J. D. Michaelis' *Introduction (Einleitung in die göttlichen Schriften des neuen Bundes*, Göttingen, 1788). Our second halt is with the translation of the latter into English, with copious notes, by Bishop Marsh. (Herbert Marsh, *Introduction to the New Testament, Translated from the Fourth Edition of the German, Augmented with Notes*..., 4 vols., Cambridge, 1793–1801, Vol. 2, pp. 228–42; Marsh's notes are on pp. 679–705. I am indebted to these notes for some of the references in the previous paragraph.)

Michaelis' argument was this. Some of Mill's examples are very extraordinary – for instance καταβαινοντα at Mt 3.16. But the copyist may be freed from the charge of Latinization for two reasons. First, because there are differences between the two columns (e.g. Mk 11.12, ΕΞΕΛΘΟΝΤΑ against CUM EXISSENT). Second, because the Latin text has in some places been altered to follow the Greek (e.g. Ac 10.6, where d e follow D E in omitting the phrase *hic dicet tibi quid te oportet facere* which is found in the rest of the Latin tradition). Michaelis then draws attention to the agreements between D and several ancient versions, and particularly the Syriac, which he considers to be ten times as frequent as with any Greek manuscript. One could say rather that D has been assimilated to the Syriac. This is less probable than saying that its readings are genuine. He then examines a number of readings which are not correct, in which the Greek does not follow the Latin. These he describes as either *scholia*, or examples of *lectio facilior*, or tendentious alteration.

Michaelis certainly did not prove that there was no influence of the Latin on the Greek and it is unlikely that he intended to. But he achieved two important things. First, he showed that the Latin and the Greek are not identical. Second, he showed that the theory of Latinization was not able to solve the problem of the D text.

Marsh in his notes extended the discussion, stating a valuable canon for judging the possibility of Latinization in a particular reading: 'There is no reason whatsoever for ascribing any reading of a Greek Ms to the influence of the Latin, unless it can be proved that it could not have taken its rise in the Greek, and that it might easily have originated in the Latin' (p. 683, n. 90).

Kipling's transcription of the manuscript had appeared in 1793. An early scholar to make good use of it was David Schulz, the author of the first monograph on Codex Bezae (*De Codice D Cantabrigiensi disputavit D. David Schulz*, Bratislava, 1827). His thirty-three pages are filled with apt illustrations.

Thomas Kipling, *Codex Theodori Bezae Cantabrigiensis*, 2 vols., Cambridge, 1793. For two reviews, see Thomas Edwards, *Remarks on Dr. Kipling's Preface to Beza. Part The First*, Cambridge, 1793; Richard Porson, 'Codex Theodori Bezae Cantabrigiensis', *British Critic*, February, 1794, 139–47, 361–73. (The article by Porson is unattributed in the journal, but a manuscript note at the beginning of the Cambridge University Library copy (class mark Adv. c.79.72[10]) reads 'Every word of this Review is Porson's. *Kidd*, on the authority of *Nares*.')

After discussing the place where the manuscript was copied, and accepting Kipling's view that it was from Egypt, Schulz turns to the theory of Latinization, and produces an impressive list of readings to disprove it. In some of these the Latin style is shown to be dependent on that of the Greek; in others, Greek words have simply been transliterated; in others the Latin reading reproduces a corruption in the Greek (for instance, Ac 21.21 *gentes*, rendering ἐθνεσιν for ἐθεσιν); in others the translation is clearly false; and in yet another group an attempt has been made to reproduce the definite article.

He then goes on to argue that the Latin is not a translation of the Greek text now opposite it, but 'ex alio exemplo huic simillimo . . .; non ex hoc ipso, quantumvis interpretatio in locis plerisque omnibus ad Graecum exemplar appareat studiosissime, immo vero anxie accommodata, neque dubitandum sit, ex uno eodemque textum utrumque effluxisse fonte' (p. 13). This he demonstrates by means of examples of discrepancies between the columns.

Having dealt with these prior difficulties, Schulz turns to examine the origin of the Greek text. His conclusion (not a new one) is that it either depends (*pependisse*) on an Eastern version (perhaps Syriac), or that such a version was compared (*adhibitam fuisse*) with a Greek ancestor (*antigraphum*) of D (p. 16). Further on he seems to come down in favour of the latter alternative: 'alterius libri Graeci superioribus iam temporibus ad orientale archetypum accommodati antigraphum' (p. 21). To establish this he lists passages where D uses a synonym for the reading found in the rest of the tradition (such as Ac 2.2, παντα for ὁλον).

Whatever we may have today to say about this, there are four points about Schulz's book which continue to be important. First, he confined himself almost totally to the text of Acts, choosing not to weaken his theories by taking a few examples from each book. He did, however, assume that what was true for one book would be true for all. Second, he drew up a more convincing list of readings in support of his opinions than had been done hitherto. But, like so many other writers, he totally ignores readings which do not support his arguments. Thirdly, he distinguished between the separate problems of Codex Bezae: between that of the relationship of the columns to each other, and that of the singularity of the Greek text; and between this singularity and the question of the longer readings in Acts (these he did no more than list in the closing pages of his essay). Finally, he demonstrated that the text of D has a history, and that there are questions to be asked about a complex bilingual tradition, and not just about the manuscript itself.

Schulz was an able critic; in Scrivener's words, 'an excellent scholar'. He was so astute as to treat Kipling's transcription with caution: 'mihi aliquoties valde dubium visum esse, utrum recte necne codices verba legerit ac minores eius lacunas explevit' (p. 21). Although he was not able to produce a lastingly acceptable reconstruction of the history of the text, his work deserves to be remembered. It is a pity that more attention was not paid to his way of going to work – not least by Scrivener. He is quoted with approval by Gregory in the Prolegomena to Tischendorf's eighth edition (p. 372).

The question of the relationship between the columns does not seem to have been raised very much in the nineteenth century. Scrivener (p. xxxii) quotes Tischendorf as insisting, in the Prolegomena to his edition of Codex Sinaiticus, that the Greek is dependent on the Latin. But Hort called Mill's view 'a whimsical theory of the last century', in a passage which well sums up the state of research:

> As far as we can judge from extant evidence, it [the Western text] was the most widely spread text of Ante-Nicene times; and sooner or later every version directly or indirectly felt its influence. But any prepossessions in its favour that might be created by this imposing early ascendancy are for the most part soon dissipated by continuous study of its internal character. The eccentric Whiston's translation of the Gospels and Acts from the *Codex Bezae*, and of the Pauline Epistles from the *Codex Claromontanus*, and Bornemann's edition of the Acts, in which the Codex Bezae was taken as the standard authority, are probably the only attempts which have ever been made in modern times to set up an exclusively or even predominantly Western Greek text as the purest reproduction of what the apostles wrote. This all but universal rejection is doubtless partly owing to the persistent influence of a whimsical theory of the last century, which, ignoring all non-Latin Western documentary evidence except the handful of extant bilingual uncials, maintained that the Western Greek text owed its peculiarities to translation from the Latin; partly to an imperfect apprehension of the antiquity and extension of the Western text as revealed by patristic quotations and by versions. Yet, even with the aid of a true perception of the facts of Ante-Nicene textual history, it would have been strange if this text as a whole had found much favour. (Westcott and Hort, Vol. 2, p. 120)

In spite of these fine words, Mill's theory was revived at the end of the century on a grand scale, in J. Rendel Harris' study of Codex Bezae. Harris claimed to have found twenty-eight different kinds of Latinization, for which he adduced something over 230 examples. Most are from Matthew, and only sixteen come from John. This total which, he claims, shows that 'the Greek text has been thoroughly and persistently Latinized' (*Codex*, p. 107), is not high enough to demonstrate any such thing. In fact Harris drew attention to many very interesting readings although, as we shall see, an alternative explanation is often close at hand.

One of the strengths of Harris' study is that it explores a number of different aspects of the tradition. Chapter 3 ('Traces of an attempt at numerical verbal equality between the Greek and the Latin on the part of the scribes of the ancestry of Codex Bezae') raises questions relating to the development of the bilingual tradition. His discussion of the type of Latin found in the manuscript, although faulty in its conclusions, proved the stimulus for a whole new area of study.

In arguing that some readings of the manuscript reveal a Montanist influence, Harris also prepared the way for studies in the theological tendencies of certain readings.

In criticizing Harris, two points should be selected. The first is that he did not work out in sufficient detail the conditions under which bilingual manuscripts were copied and handed down. The second is that he discussed only those readings which were favourable to his own views. Time and again one finds an interesting passage, throwing new light on the text, which has been totally ignored.

For a thorough review of Harris, see A. S. Wilkins, 'The Western Text of the New Testament', *The Expositor*, Fourth Series, 10 (1894), 386–400, 409–28.

The arguments of Harris are today universally discounted. The possibility that the manuscript was written in Gaul has been long disallowed, and it is likely that the general consensus may emphasize the total dependence of the Latin on the Greek, rather than the reverse. But he did open up new lines of study for twentieth-century scholarship.

For the dependence of the Latin on the Greek, see e.g. Alands, *Text*, pp. 108, 185f; Fischer, 'Das NT', *ANTF* 5, p. 41 and n. = *Beiträge*, pp. 208f; Lagrange, *La Critique rationnelle*, Vol. 2, *Critique textuelle*, Paris, 1935, pp. 42, 430f; B. M. Metzger, *The Early Versions of the New Testament. Their Origin, Transmission, and Limitations*, Oxford, 1977, p. 318 and note.

Twentieth-century study has examined the manuscript and its text from a number of different angles.

The detailed linguistic examination of the codex has yielded few solid results. It is clear that phenomena in the Latin believed to be attributable to a particular area are simply typical of the late Latin of the period. Robert Stone's valuable work and concordance have made this quite clear (see chapter 2 above).

The exploration of the Greek style of the manuscript has been one aspect of a wider debate about the relative merits of allegedly Semiticizing and Atticizing readings.

Matthew Black, *An Aramaic Approach to the Gospels and Acts*, 3rd edition, Oxford, 1967; M.-E. Boismard, 'The Text of Acts: A Problem of Literary Criticism?', in Epp and Fee, pp. 147–57; T. C. Geer, Jr, 'The Presence and Significance of Lucanisms in the "Western" Text of Acts', *Journal for the*

Study of the New Testament 39 (1990), 59–76; among the writings of G.D. Kilpatrick, see e.g. 'Eclecticism and Atticism', *ETL* 53 (1977), 107–12; 'An Eclectic Study of the Text of Acts', in *Biblical and Patristic Studies in Memory of Robert Pierce Casey*, ed. J.N. Birdsall and R.W. Thomson, Freiburg, 1963, pp. 64–77; R. Sheldon Mackenzie, 'The Western Text of Acts: some Lucanisms in Selected Sermons', *JBL* 104 (1985), 637–50; A.J. Wensinck, 'The Semitisms of Codex Bezae and their Relation to the non-Western Text of the Gospel of St Luke', *BBC* 12 (1937), 11–48; M. Wilcox, *The Semitisms of Acts*, Oxford, 1965; M. Wilcox, 'Luke and the Bezan Text in Acts', in *Les Actes des Apôtres*, ed. J. Kremer, Leuven, 1979, pp. 447–55; J.D. Yoder, 'Semitisms in Codex Bezae', *JBL* 78 (1959), 317–21.

H.J. Vogels broke new ground, exploring the harmonizing readings of the Gospel text of D. He found 1,278 in all, showing this to have been a strong force in the development of the text. He explained these readings as coming from the Diatessaron. It is clear that far more rigid criteria than this are required to establish that a reading is Diatessaronic (see e.g. W.L. Petersen, 'Romanos and the Diatessaron: Readings and Method', *NTS* 29 (1983), 484–507, especially p. 490). In finding Syriac origins for this influence, Vogels was continuing a tradition that goes back at least as far as Wettstein, who believed D to have been the codex consulted by Thomas of Harkel in his revision of Acts. More recently, it had been championed by F.H. Chase, who claimed that D was descended from a hypothetical Graeco-Syro-Latin trilingual manuscript.

F.H. Chase, *The Old Syriac Element in the Text of Codex Bezae*, London, 1893; Chase, *The Syro-Latin Text of the Gospels*, London, 1895; Vogels, *Harmonistik*.

An important aspect of contemporary examination of Codex Bezae is the search for theological tendencies in its text.

E. Bammel, 'The Cambridge Pericope. The Addition to Luke 6.4 in Codex Bezae', *NTS* 32 (1986), 404–26; C.K. Barrett, 'Is There a Theological Tendency in Codex Bezae?', in *Text and Interpretation: Studies in the New Testament Presented to Matthew Black*, ed. E. Best and R. McL. Wilson, London, 1979, pp. 15–27; H.-W. Bartsch, 'Über den Umgang der frühen Christenheit mit dem Text der Evangelien. Das Beispiel des Codex Bezae Cantabrigiensis', *NTS* 29 (1983), 167–82; Matthew Black, 'The Holy Spirit in the Western Text of Acts', in Epp and Fee, pp. 159–70; J. Crehan, 'Peter According to the D-Text of Acts', *Theological Studies* 18 (1957); E.J. Epp, 'The "Ignorance Motif" in Acts and Antijudaic Tendencies in Codex Bezae', *HTR* 55 (1962), 51–62; Epp, *The Theological Tendency of Codex Bezae Cantabrigiensis in Acts* (SNTS Monograph Series 3), Cambridge, 1966; Epp, 'The Ascension in the Textual Tradition of Luke–Acts', in Epp and Fee, pp. 131–45; E. Ferguson, 'Qumran and Codex "D"', *Revue de Qumran* 8 (1972), 75–80; E.S. Fiorenza, *In Memory of Her. A Feminist Theological Reconstruction of Christian Origins*, London, 1983; R.P.C. Hanson, 'The Ideology of Codex Bezae in Acts' [a review article arising out of Epp's book], *NTS* 14 (1967–8), 282–6; Michael W. Holmes 'Early Editorial Activity and the Text of Codex Bezae in Matthew', unpublished Ph. D. dissertation, Princeton Theological Seminary, 1984; C.M. Martini, 'La figura di Pietro secondo le varianti del codice D negli Atti degli Apostoli', in *Settimana Biblica dei professori di Sacra Scrittura in Italia*, Vol. 19 ed. M. Laconi, Rome, 1966, pp. 279–89; P.H. Menoud, 'The Western Text and the Theology of Acts', *SNTS Bulletin* 2 (1951), 19–32; George E. Rice, 'The Alteration of Luke's Tradition by the Textual Variants in Codex Bezae', Ph. D. dissertation, Case Western Reserve University, 1974; since then, Rice has produced a series of articles in *Andrews University Seminary Studies*: 'Luke 3:22–38 in Codex Bezae: The Messianic King', *AUSS* 17 (1979), 203–8; 'The Anti-Judaic Bias of the Western Text in the Gospel of Luke', *AUSS* 18 (1980), 51–7; 'The Role of the Populace in the Passion Narrative of Luke in Codex Bezae', *AUSS* 19 (1981), 147–53; 'Is Bezae a Homogeneous Codex?', *AUSS* 21 (1984), 39–54. For the views of the Alands, see *Text*, pp. 69 and 107f.

Against the wider background of Hort's well known claim that 'there are no signs of deliberate falsification of the text for dogmatic purposes' (Westcott and

Hort, Vol. 2, p. 282) the argument concerns not the possibility of occasional emendation of the text to what an ancient presumed to be its true sense, but a theological redaction of some moment. The view has been trenchantly expressed by the Alands: 'The text found in Codex Bezae . . . represents (in its exemplar) the achievement of an outstanding early theologian of the third/fourth century' (p. 69). Although (as we have seen) Harris tried to establish links between the manuscript and Montanism, the theological redaction theory is usually associated with Epp's work. He has been closely followed by Rice. Holmes' contribution is of a somewhat different character.

The studies of Epp and Rice show a number of methodological faults which raise considerable doubts about the validity of their case. The first is the way in which they select variants to support it. Given the enormous number of places where Bezae's text is unique, the isolation of certain 'theological' tendencies in a number of them is likely to be arbitrary. As a matter of fact, any alteration to a theological text will by nature be a theological alteration, just as any change in the copying of a piece of music will be musical by nature, in that it will influence a performer's decision about what to play and how to play it. Even the format and style of printing may affect his attitude to it.

This shades off into the second problem, that of anachronistic interpretation. Both Epp and particularly Rice (in his thesis) use Conzelmann's redaction critical study (*The Theology of Saint Luke*, London, 1960 (1953, 1957)) as a guide to explaining the purpose of Luke, to which the reviser is supposed to have added an additional twist. But the only possible way to establish theological tendency is by comparison with the Fathers' understanding of the text: given *their* interpretations of Luke and Acts, the critic would then have to ask whether the Bezan reading can credibly be regarded as representative of one or more of them. A hypothetical example which brings these two problems together might be the well known reading of the seven steps at Ac 12.10. This, usually categorized as a reading relating to additional local geographical knowledge, could conceivably be claimed as a theological variant providing some mystical or allegorical sense to the passage. That is to say, it is at once arbitrary to select certain passages which, to the modern scholar taught to see Luke–Acts through Conzelmann's eyes, seem to present a theological bias, and anachronistic to interpret them from a twentieth-century perspective.

It is also a little strange that some of the alleged theological emphases of the reviser do not seem to be very far removed from what have, rightly or wrongly, been isolated as typically Lukan – for example, an 'interest' in the Holy Spirit. As far as that goes, it just indicates that what the text sets out to do is to give us Luke, only more of him. This point is implied by Martini, who demonstrates that not only Peter, but Paul also, has been given more prominence. That is, once one is expanding a story about the apostles, then it is a tautology to say that the apostles' role will be expanded.

A further problem with the approach is that it fails to provide a history of the text to support itself. The idea enunciated by Rice, that the copyist of D, working with a manuscript of the 'Western' text, was an editor not a copyist, is at variance with what we know about ancient scribes, and with what we have found so far in this study. The lack of textual history is exacerbated by the fact that those who find theological tendencies seem to ignore the Latin text altogether.

There is perhaps an analogy between this approach to the Bezan text and a certain kind of attempt to interpret Shakespeare theologically. For its analysis and a rebuttal, see R. M. Frye, *Shakespeare and Christian Doctrine*, Princeton and London, 1963.

Holmes' approach is a broader one. In studying the text of Matthew, he places the small number of variants he finds within a context of other kinds of editorial activity – harmonistic, expanding, and so forth.

The problem of describing some variants and not others as theological is heightened by the emphasis made on additions to the name of Jesus. This is generally regarded as a common feature of New Testament texts. We may, for instance, find *Χριστος* added to *'Ιησους* in many places. The discovery of subtle shades of Christological emphasis by Epp and Rice is likely to be spurious.

An alternative approach, which the present writer prefers, is to suggest that, undoubtedly, a reviser of the text will not have been a person without particular theological beliefs and a context in the church. In the process of revision, when many things were altered, some passages will have possessed for him a theological significance which he may have introduced into his revision. For instance, if he is taken to be working at a time when the relationship between Christianity and Judaism is far different from the situation envisaged in Acts, he will have taken some of this back into Acts: perhaps that the Gospel is addressed largely to Gentiles, so that the mission to Judaism is less important, will have been part of his assumptions. He will therefore have projected such a situation back into Acts, not as part of an anti-Judaic polemic, but because this was what he unconsciously assumed the situation to have been like.

That the transmission of texts *may* involve a degree of interpretation can scarcely be denied. But such problems have been taken as greatly significant only when they are encountered in translations – the Septuagint, for example. (See e.g. D. H. Gard, 'The Concept of Job's Character According to the Greek Translator of the Hebrew Text', *JBL* 72 (1953), 182–6.) There is in fact, as I will argue at a later point in this book, a very considerable theological character to the text of D. But I do not think that it consists in the kinds of things that others have written about, and I do not believe that the means which they have employed will help us.

A very clearly focussed case, integrated into a wider reconstruction, is provided by Fiorenza (p. 52). She draws attention to five places in Acts where the text of Codex Bezae reduces the role of women, or eliminates references to them from the text (Ac. 1.14; 17.4, 12, 34; 18.28). Here we have clear instances of the way in which all changes have a theological significance. We can also see how the text has been modified as a consequence of an issue within the early church.

Another valuable, and text-critically more extensive approach than Fiorenza's, has been followed by Michael Mees.

M. Mees, 'Lukas 1–9 in der Textgestalt des *Codex Bezae*. Literarische Formen in Dienste der Schrift', *VC* 5 (1968), 89–110; 'Sinn und Bedeutung literarischer Formen für die Textgestalt des Codex Bezae in Lukas 10–11', *ibid.* 7 (1970), 59–82; 'Jesusworte in Lukas 12 und ihre Komposition nach Codex Bezae Cantabrigiensis', *ibid.*, 285–303.

See also C.-B. Amphoux, 'La Parabole Matthéenne du Fils Prodigue: La Version du Codex Bezae (D05 du NT)'. *Langues Orientales Anciennes: Philologie et Linguistique* 1 (1988), 167–71.

Mees sets out to place the text of D within a literary context. The character of Q, the Gospel of Thomas, rhetorical technique, the influence of Semitic styles of writing, are some of the materials he uses to do this. By a careful examination of the whole shape of the narrative (this is particularly characteristic of the 1970 articles), he shows how D's variants belong together in the way the Gospel story is retold. An important advance in the future study of D will be to extend this work to other parts of its text.

Another approach is one that I have myself attempted elsewhere: a detailed analysis of the character of the Latin version.

D. C. Parker, 'Translation of *OYN*'

In this study, I came to two main conclusions with regard to Codex Bezae. First, that the Latin column is 'very consistent in all four Gospels . . . Acts was translated separately, according to a less rigorous system' (p. 275). In fact, d was more consistent in the Gospels than any other Old Latin text. But while in the Gospels *ergo* was used with great regularity, in Acts there are far more particles used – *autem*, *enim*, *ergo*, *itaque*, *-que*, *quidem vero*, *quidem ergo*, and *tunc quidem*. The conclusion was that Acts had been translated separately. This accords with all that we have already learned in this study of the manuscript. It would, of course, need the analysis of many more words before the matter could be regarded as proven from the vocabulary employed.

Whereas some texts showed traces of revision (for example, the Old Latin manuscript b uses *autem* and *igitur* as well as *ergo* regularly up to chapter 9 of John, but not beyond), there were no traces of revision in Codex Bezae. This, I suggested, showed that in spite of differences between the books of the kind we analysed in Part II, the Latin Gospels of D had a 'unity of origin' (p. 268).

In the same article, I tried to discover whether the readings under discussion shed any light on the relationship between the columns of Codex Bezae. It seemed that 'assimilation to the Latin was not the most important factor in the history of the Greek column' (p. 272). The main influence was of harmonization to Gospel parallels. Significant also was 'a stage of indifferent copying in the transmission of the text, that resulted in corruptions and false emendations' (p. 275). Rather than wholesale Latinization of the Greek, a far more subtle reciprocal process was at work, in which each column moulded the other. However, the chief influence was of the Greek on the Latin. Examples of the reverse were very rare.

The vocabulary deserves a book on its own, and cannot be included within the confines of this present study. Such an exploration would also need to be extended to include the grammar.

This survey has described the main ways in which the text of Codex Bezae has been analysed: Latinization of the Greek column; a Semitic style; harmonization of the Gospels; theological tendencies; the literary form.

In this work, we have attempted to explore different aspects of the manuscript and its text. The main part of this, the comparison of the columns, is our next theme. Hitherto, I have sought to uncover layers of tradition beneath the presentation of the text, to establish the circumstances under which it was transmitted, and to understand the characteristics and tendencies of a bilingual tradition. We have reconstructed the appearance of its exemplars, we have shown that the tradition was formed from several sources. Important questions remain with regard to the relationship between the two texts of Codex Bezae. Their comparison can provide us with a sort of binocular vision into the tradition.

To return to the questions with which the chapter began: Is the Latin a translation of the parallel text, or is it an existing version that was added to it to form a bilingual manuscript? Are there different answers to this question for different books of the manuscript? How far back can we trace differences between the columns? At what point did the Greek copying tradition cease to be a living one?

The examination of the differences between the columns will help us to begin to answer these questions.

CHAPTER THIRTEEN

A comparison of the columns

It has been known for many years that the two columns of Codex Bezae agree less closely with each other in some books than in others. This was first noted by J. A. Findlay.

'On Variations in the Text of d and D', *BBC* 9 (1931), 10–11.

He found 107 differences in reading between the columns in Matthew, 106 in John, 176 in Luke, 469 in Mark, and 607 in Acts: 1,465 in all. According to my examination, the numbers of differences are

Matthew	76
John	87
Luke	150
Mark	226
Acts	317
Total	856

Findlay argued that these figures reveal a revision that became increasingly less thorough. But, although this is true of the overall figures, a closer examination brings out a rather more complicated development. Table 37 shows the number of differences between the columns, chapter by chapter. It reveals that particular chapters contain high numbers of differences. The table is helpful because we have some idea of the passages involved, and there is some kind of division according to subject matter. But the chapters are of very unequal lengths, and not all are complete. Table 38 takes the codex by units of ten double-page openings where both columns are extant.

Were only a decreasing care of revision the cause of the figures revealed by the table, we might be entitled to expect a more constant increase in the number of discrepancies through each book. There is indeed a marked upturn at the very end of Luke and Mark (we do not have the last part of Acts). But the increase at the end of Luke may be due to the extensive textual problems of the last three chapters. It

Table 37. *Differences between the columns, by chapter*

Chapter	Matthew	John	Luke	Mark	Acts
1	(2)	lac.	6	10	4
2	(—)	lac.	5	10	19
3	(—)	(2)	4	17	7
4	2	7	4	9	18
5	2	6	7	16	20
6	(—)	17	4	19	6
7	lac.	6	8	11	27
8	lac.	13	5	15	(9)
9	(2)	2	6	16	lac.
10	3	1	6	19	(17)
11	1	7	8	11	15
12	6	3	6	15	4
13	4	3	8	10	21
14	1	—	7	26	14
15	1	1	8	21	17
16	5	6	4	(1)	19
17	3	8	6	/	20
18	5	(—)	8		18
19	3	lac.	7		30
20	3	(3)	5		(18)
21	2	2	5		(11)
22	3	/	8		(1)
23	3		10		/
24	11		9		
25	2		/		
26	(6)				
27	(6)				
28	—				

Numbers in brackets indicate that the chapter is incomplete in the codex.

may also be that we shall discover that the reasons for the differences vary between the books.

It is necessary, before we proceed, to define our terms. What constitutes a difference between the columns? First of all, anything must be eliminated that might simply be due to the way in which the Latin has been translated. For example, at Mt 5.15 d had UT LUCEAT for D's ΚΑΙ ΛΑΜΠΙ. This is simply a translator's choice. The translation of the historic present by the perfect (e.g. Mt 6.2 ΑΠΕΧΟΥϹΙΝ: PERCEPERUNT) is also to be ignored. So too are divergent word orders such as at Jn 15.10 – ΑΥΤΟΥ ΕΝ ΤΗ ΑΓΑΠΗ: IN CARITATE IPSIUS – and v. 15 – ΑΥΤΟΥ Ο ΚϹ: DMS EIUS. Besides these and similar grammatical differences which do not constitute a genuine variation between the columns, care

Table 38. *Differences between the columns, by pages*

Matthew		John		Luke		Mark		Acts	
3b–15	6	113b–123	15	182b–192	11	285b–295	41	415b–425	27
15b–34	6	123b–133	22	192b–202	9	295b–305	31	425b–435	42
34b–44	8	133b–143	16	202b–212	15	305b–315	38	435b–445	40
44b–54	5	143b–153	11	212b–222	12	315b–325	36	445b–464	37
54b–64	15	153b–163	5	222b–232	10	325b–335	31	464b–474	29
64b–74	6	163b–182 (9)	18	232b–242	13	335b–347 (12)	49	474b–484	40
74b–84	15			242b–252	23			484b–494	43
84b–94	7			252b–262	21			494b–508 (12)	58
94b–104 (8)	8			262b–272	14				
				272b–285 (13)	26				

must be taken in examining the vocabulary of the Latin column before a reading is pronounced to be a variation.

For bibliography on the subject of translation technique in the Latin versions, see chapter 14.

Where there is any possibility that a translator has translated what is in Greek D, even if it seems closer to a variant read by another Greek witness, we must discount the reading for present purposes.

Apparent differences, which are in fact due to the particular characteristics of late Latin, must also be ignored. This includes the present for the future (e.g. Mt 12.41 ANACTHCONTAI: RESURGUNT; 13.30 EPⲰ: DICO), as well as other tense changes; *in* with the ablative as equivalent to *in* with the accusative (e.g. Mt 12.9 EIC THN CYNAΓⲰΓHN: IN SYNAGOGA), and the reverse (Mt 12.24 APXONTI: PRINCIPEM), and so forth.

Differences which are due to casual scribal error I also discount, though here we have a difficulty of definition. It could be argued that most errors actually come under this head. But I really intend to eliminate what are clearly nonsense readings. An example is Mt 11.3 O EPΓAZOMENOC: QUI VENIS. D* is unique here, and is obviously in error for ὁ ἐρχομενος. Differences which may be due to itacism are also best ignored.

Mistranslation is sometimes a possibility. Such readings I have sometimes included, when I think that the difference deserves our attention.

Where it is uncertain whether a reading falls into one of these categories or is a genuine variant, the existence of other support for it should be weighed very carefully.

It is better to make the criteria for accepting a difference between the columns as rigid as possible. I have tended, therefore, having begun with more differences than Findlay, to end up with fewer.

Once the chaff has been winnowed away, what is left varies considerably in character. The most significant differences will be those where d can be shown to follow a text that is divergent from D's. Here other support will play an important part, particularly if it is Greek support. The evidence of other Latin witnesses is also significant. That of other versions must be treated with a great deal of care, and used only if the Greek behind both them *and* d can be established with a high degree of certainty. We will also need to be careful not to use the support of other witnesses too eagerly in readings where error may have arisen independently.

There are plenty of places where d has no other support at all. In each place it will have to be decided whether it can conceivably represent a lost Greek text, or whether the reading stems from the caprices or vagaries of successive Latin scribes.

The analysis in this chapter is undertaken with the working hypothesis that the Latin column of Codex Bezae is descended from a text translated from a Greek text similar to, but by no means identical with, the Greek column of D.

The question of revision, which Findlay raised, and which we must answer, poses a problem. We tried to establish (in chapter 8) that our manuscript Codex Bezae was copied from a Gospel book written in the order Matthew–Mark–John–Luke, and a separate exemplar containing Acts. The fact that Findlay's evidence suggests a revision of the books according to their present order, appears to be in direct opposition to the theory. The resolution of this problem, if one is possible, must await the conclusion of this chapter.

There is no alternative, if this study is to be of any value, but to work through all these readings, over eight hundred in number. The provision of a full *apparatus criticus*, with all witnesses and readings at each difference, will not be attempted. Variants will be given only where I think that there is a significant textual difference between the columns.

As in chapter 9, the reference to chapter and verse is followed by one to the folio and line number of the reading in the Latin column (or both columns where the variants are on different lines). Reading of D and d where I have not been able to find any other support are, as before, given in maiuscule letters.

THE GOSPEL OF MATTHEW

We begin with a reading which is in fact only a translation variant:

14.24 (48/20)
ην εις μεσον της θαλασσης / βασανιζομενος D
ERAT IN MEDIUM MARIS ET VEXABATUR d
erat in medio mari et iactabatur ff[1]

Both texts here essentially follow the synoptic parallel.

I also set aside the difference at Mt 23.34 (80/19):

αποστελω D 33 pc.; *αποστελλω* cet.; *mitto* d cet.

This could be a place where d has the present for the future. We turn instead to genuine differences.

1.23 (Isa. 7.14) (4/11): *καλεσεις* D 1391 ℓ184; *καλεσουσιν* cet.; *vocabit* d ff[1]
It might be tempting to link both readings with the variant at Isa. 7.14 (וקראת MT; וקרא IQIs[a]; *καλεσεις* LXX pler.; -*σει* א; -*σετε* Q L). However, the d reading is more likely to be influenced either by v. 25 (ET VOCAVIT NOMEN EIUS IHS) or by the fact that in Luke it is *Mary* and not Joseph who names the child, or simply by the previous word PARIET (here it would be making the same kind of error as Isa. 7.14 א). The third possibility is the most readily acceptable.
1.25 (4/18): AYTHC D*; OM d D[corr]
D* = Lk 2.7.
4.20 (10/31): *τα δικτυα* D; RETIAM d
d = v. 18 (1.27).

4.24 (11/13): ΑΥΤΟΥ Η ΑΚΟΗ D; *opinio eius* d
5.9 (12/6): *υιοι θεου* D; DEI FILIUS d
5.40 (15/5): ΚΑΙ Ο ΘΕΛΩΝ D; *και τω θελοντι* cet.; QUI VOLUERIT d
Here our concern is not with the casus pendens (for which see M.-H. 2,423–5; M.-T. 3,316; B.-D. §466(4)), but with the absence of a particle in the Latin.
9.18 (27/24–5)
ΑΡΧΩΝ / ΕΙCΕΛΘΩΝ ℵ^c C D E M W *Θ* al.
αρχων εις ελθων K S V *Δ Π* al.
αρχων προσελθων ℵ* 13 157 al.
αρχων εις προσελθων ℵ^b B
αρχων τις προσελθων C^3 G L U al. plu.
UNUS PRINCEPS / VENIENS d
princeps unus a aur b c f ff^1 l
quidam princeps k g^1 h
princeps veniens q
Here we can see the separate development of the two columns. The Latin follows the second or fourth of the Greek variants listed. The line division of the Greek column takes a different interpretation of the phrase. The sense-line division has taken no account of the Latin text.
9.22 (28/2): *εστη στραφεις* D; CONVERSUS STETIT d
10.2 (29/18): *των ιβ̅ αποστολων* D *Θ* pc.; *των δε ιβ̅ αποστ* cet.;
duodecim autem apostolorum d cet.
10.20 (31/6): ΤΟΥ ΠΑΤΡΟC D; *του πατρος υμων* cet.;
patris vestris d*; *patris vestri* d^{corr} cet.
10.32 (32/14): ΑΥΤΟ P^{19} D pc.; *εν αυτω* cet.; OM d 348 349 k^{corr}; *in ipso* k*; *illum/eum* cet.
11.12 (34/9): *απο των ημερων* D* sy^s Lvt (a) AMst; *απο δε των ημερων* D^A cet.;
a diebus autem d cet.
12.14 (37/3): *κατ αυτου* D; DE EO d
This seems to be a translation error: *κατα* has been understood as if it were with the accusative with the sense 'in respect to'.
12.21 (37/20): ΕΛΠΙΖΟΥCΙΝ D*; *ελπιουσιν* D$^{s.m.}$; *sperabunt* d
12.37 (39/7): *η* D Lvt (a c g^1) HIL PAU-N; *και* cet.; *et* d cet.
12.40 (39/15): ΩCΠΕΡΙ ΓΑΡ ΙΩΝΑC D; *sicut enim erat ionas* d
12.46 (40/11): *η μητηρ και οι αδελφοι αυτου* D; *mater illius et fratres eius* d
12.48 (40/16): *τω λεγοντι* D; DICENTIBUS d
The plural may be due to the influence of the par. passages in Luke and Matthew.
13.10 (41/14): *οι μαθηται* D; *discipuli eius* d
d is harmonized to Lk 8.9/Mk 4.10.
13.25 (43/10): *εσπειρεν* C D pler. Lvt (c k q); *επεσπειρεν* cet.; *superseminavit* d Lvt (cet.)
13.50 (45/31): *βαλλουσιν* ℵ* D* f^{13} pc.; *βαλουσιν* D^{corr} cet.; *mittent* d Lvt (cet.)
13.54 (46/10): *εν τη συναγωγη* D; IN SYNAGOGAS d
According to Aland's *Synopsis*, the Latin column has been affected by Mt 4.23. But see also Lk 4.15, immediately preceding the par. passage.

14.20 (48/13): εφαγον παντες D; MANDUCAVERUNT d
d follows par. Lk 9.17.
15.27 (52/3): απο της τραπεζης D; DE MENSIS d
This reading is probably due to the influence of *micis* in line 2.
16.18 (54/23–4): καγω δε σοι λεγω D; *et ego autem dico tibi* d
16.20 (55/1): O XPC IHC D Lvt (c); IHS XPS d ℵ^c C E F etc. W 118 209 Lvt (f l q); ο χριστος ℵ* B L al. Lvt (cet.) sy (c s)
16.22 (55/9): αυτω επετειμαν D 1 124 Or; *increpare eum* d cet.
ibid. (55/10): OY MH ECTH TOYTO COI D; ου μη εσται σοι τουτο cet.; NON ERUNT HAEC TIBI d
16.27 (55/31): την πραξιν ℵ^c B C D al.; τα εργα ℵ* F 1 al.; *opera* d Lvt (pler.); *opus* Lvt (aur l) Lvg; *factum* Lvt (e)
Πραξις is translated by d as *actio* (Lk 23.51) and *actus* (Ac 19.18); e has *actus* at Lk 23.51. It seems reasonably safe to assume that d here follows the reading of ℵ* F.
17.9 (56/32): ο ιης λεγων D; DICENS IHS d
17.10 (57/3): αυτον B C D al. Lvt (f ff² q); OM ℵ L W Z Θ 1 al. Lvt (d cet.)
17.15 (57/18–19): πολλακις ... ενιοτε D; ALIQUOTIENS ... SAEPIUS d
18.9 (59/24): EI KAI D; *et si* d
For the whole phrase in D (το αυτο ει και / *similiter et si*) see Harris, *Codex*, p. 96.
18.12 (60/6, 8): αφιησιν ... ζητει D pc.; αφησει ... ζητει B L 157 pc.; αφησει ... ζητησει Θ f¹³ 543; αφεις ... ζητει pler.; *relinquet ... quaeret* d
The future in both words is also followed by Lvt (e h) and some Vulgate manuscripts, which read *relinquet ... vadet quaerere.*
18.13 (60/10): επ αυτω μαλλον D; MAGIS IN ILLA d
18.14 (60/13): ημων D* pc. Lvg (Z*); υμων ℵ D^B W f¹; μου B F Θ al. f¹³ 157 al.; *vestro* d
18.33 (62/10): καγω σε ηλεηυα D; *et ego misertus sum tui* d
19.4 (62/27): ο δε D; *Iesus autem* d
19.8 (63/6)
και λεγει αυτοις D* 566 1187 1555 Lvg (B E H^c Θ K M O^gl V Z)
λεγει αυτοις D^corr cet. Lvt (cet.); *dicit eis* d e
Is d influenced by par. Mk 10.5?
19.24 (64/24): παλιν δε D Lvt (e f); παλιν F L V* Θ 1 565 al.; *iterum* Lvt (d a b ff¹ ff² l n q r¹); *et iterum* Lvt (aur c g¹ h) Lvg
20.15 (66/6): ECTIN D*; εξεστιν D^K; *licet* d
20.23 (67/24)
ουκ εστιν εμον τουτο δουναι C D W Δ Φ 085 33 al.
ουκ εστιν εμον δουναι ℵ B L cet.; τουτο ουκ εστιν εμον δουναι U 565 pc.
NON EST MEUM DARE d
non est hoc meum dare Lvt (q)
Tischendorf follows the C D text here, regarding the omission of τουτο as harmonization to Mk 10.40.
20.31 (68/26): εκραξαν ℵ B D L Z Π* pc.; εκραζον C N O W pler.; εκραυγαζον Θ f¹³; εκραυγασαν P⁴⁵; *clamabant* Lvt (d cet.) Lvg
21.2 (69/3)

μαθητας λεγων αυτοις ℵ B C D pler.
μαθητας αυτου λεγων αυτοις Θ f^{13} pc.
μαθητας αυτου λεγων 157
discipulos suos dicens Lvt (d b e ff^1 ff^2) HIL
discipulos suos dicens eis Lvt (c f g^1 l n q)
discipulis suis dicens eis Lvt (h [r^1])
discipulos dicens eis Lvt (a aur) Lvg
21.21 (71/5): *και τω ορει τουτω εαν* D S; *και τω ορει τουτω* W 565 pc.; *καν τω ορει τουτω* cet.; *et si monti huic* d cet.
22.1 (74/4): *αυτοις λεγων* D; DICENS EIS d
22.24 (76/2): *ο αδελφος αυτου* D pler.; *fratri suo* d
22.38 (77/1)
ΜΕΓΑΛΗ ΚΑΙ ΠΡΩΤΗ D
η μεγαλη και πρωτη ℵ B L (*η πρωτη*) Z f^1 f^{13} pc.
(*η*) *πρωτη και* (*η*) *μεγαλη* W Γ Δ Π mu. pler.
PRIMUM ET MAGNUM d
primum et maximum Lvt (f q); *magnum et primum* Lvt (e h r^1); *maximum et primum* Lvt (cet.)
23.3 (77/24): *ειπωσιν* D; *dixerunt vobis* d
23.6 (78/3)
ΤΗΝ ΠΡΩΚΛΕΙCΙΑΝ D = *την πρωτοκλισιαν* ℵ* B
primos discubitos Lvt (d a c f h r^1)
The plural is by harmonization to Lk 20.46b; Mk 12.39.
23.39 (81/4): *με ιδητε* D; VIDEBITIS ME d
24.3 (81/17): *ποτε ταυτα εσται* D; QUANDO ERUNT d
An accidental omission in d.
24.16 (82/19): *φευγετωσαν* D; FUGIAT d
The influence of the surrounding verbs has caused this reading in d. Note that, because *sunt* is absent, d makes sense.
24.26 (83/7): *ειπωσιν* D; DIXERIT d
This is a similar reading to 24.16.
ibid. (83/9): *τοις ταμειοις* D; CUBICULO d
24.29 (83/18): *των ουρανων* D; CAELI d
24.30 (83/20): ΟΥΡΑΝΟΙC D; *caelo* d
24.37 (84/15): *εσται και* D; *erit* d
Και is a harmonization to Lk 17.26.
24.38 (84/18): *και γαμουντες* $ℵ^c$ D L Lvt (a ff^2 h) sy (s); *nubentes* d cet.
ibid. (84/19): ΑΧΡΕΙ ΤΗC ΗΜΕΡΑC D*; *αχρει της ημερας ης* D^D; *αχρι ης ημερας* cet.; *usque in eum diem quo* d
24.41 (84/27): The second part of the verse (*δυο επι κλινης μιας . . . αφιεται*) is found only in D f^{13} (exc. 124) and some other minuscules, some Old Latin manuscripts, the Ethiopic, and $Or^{int\ 3.876}$ (*teste* Legg). It is derived from Lk 17.34 (not the D form).
μιας D etc Lvt (f)
OM d Lvt (cet.)
At Lk 17.4, *μιας* is omitted in B 1319 Lvt (c gat) Lvg (2 Mss) AU EP-L (*not* in D/d).

24.48 (85/10): ο κακος δουλος εκεινος D; *malus ille servus* d
25.6 (86/1): ΕΞΕΡΧΕΤΑΙ D*; εξερχεσθαι D^{p.m.} = εξερχεσθε pler.; ερχεται εξερχεσθε C³ W Θ al.; *exite* d
The correction by the scribe of D while the ink was still wet removes a difference between the columns. Which reading was in his exemplar?
25.20 (87/4): ταλαντα λαβων D; ACCEPERAT TALANTA d
This is transposition by d.
26.7 (90/13): ΑΝΑΚΕΙΜΕΝΟΥ ΑΥΤΟΥ D; DISCUMBENTIS d
Mk 14.3 reads κατακειμενου αυτου.
26.16 (91/5): παραδω αυτοις D Θ 892; παραδω cet.; *traderet* d
26.18 (91/9): ειπεν D; *dixit eis* d
The addition is from par. Mk. 14.13.
26.26 (92/1): το σω[μα μου] D; MEUM CORPUS d
This is transposition in d.
26.59 (95/13): αυτον θανατωσουσιν D; *mortificarent eum* d
26.61 (95/19): τον ναον του θεου D; *templum hoc dei* d
The Latin follows par. Mk 14.58: τον ναον τουτον; τον ναον D; *hunc templum* d.
27.22 (98/28): ποιησωμεν D 59 Lvt ([a] [b] c ff² h q) Or; *faciem* d cet
27.37 (100/8): αυτου D; OM d (lect. sing.)
27.41 (100/19): δε και D Γ Δ Π² pler Lvt (ff¹); και B K 1 33 al. pc.; *et* d Lvt (cet.); OM cet.
ibid. (100/21): λεγοντες D; *dicebant* d
27.48 (101/4): εξ αυτων D; EX HIS d
27.54 (101/25): ϋιος θεου D; *dei filius* d
At Mk 15.39, D 565 pc. Lvt (d ff² i k q) have θεου υιος instead of υιος θεου.

These variants may be ascribed to various causes.

1. Influence of the context
   On D: 24.30; 27.41²
   On d: 1.23; 4.20; 15.27; 24.16; 24.26 *bis*, 29
2. Translation error
   12.14
3. Harmonization to a Gospel parallel
   By D: 1.25; 24.37; 26.7
   By d: 12.46, 48; 13.10, 54; 14.20; 23.6; 26.18, 61; 27.54
4. Transposition
   By D alone: 4.24; 18.9
   By D with support: 16.22
   By d alone: 5.9; 9.22; 17.9, 15; 18.13; 22.1; 23.39; 25.20; 26.26
   By d with support: 16.18; 18.33; 24.48; 26.59
5. Textual differences
   5.40; 9.18; 10.2, 20, 32; 11.12; 12.37; 13.25, 50; 16.20, 22 *bis*, 27; 17.10; 18.12, 14; 19.8, 24; 20.23, 31; 21.2, 21; 22.24, 38; 23.3; 24.38¹, 41¹, 26.16; 27.22, 41¹

Several things deserve notice here. First, there is a tendency in the Latin to transpose pairs of words – most of those just listed are singular readings of d. We find this done only twice in the Greek. At 18.33; 24.48; 26.59; 27.54, d has other support for its transposition.

Secondly, there seem to be more synoptic harmonizations in the Latin than in the Greek. The context also seems to have influenced the Latin column more than the Greek. The readings at 24.29, 30 may belong here.

There are a few places where a fairly obvious error in one of the columns has led to the difference, whose place in this list is therefore more dubious: 12.21; 12.40; 20.15; 24.3, 38[2]; 25.6. At 27.48, the *his* of d is almost certainly in error for *eis*. At 27.37 also we have carelessness in the Latin.

We are left with about a third of the total number, where either there is other support for both readings, or it is reasonable to suppose that the Latin is founded on a different Greek reading. This group overlaps with that which we have classified as synoptic harmonization.

THE GOSPEL OF JOHN

In John, we have to disregard as differences several readings which still deserve notice:

16.2 (162b/23–4 = 163/23): *ο αποκτεινας υμας* D; QUI VOS OCCIDERIT VOS d

Here we see the word order actually being transposed in d. Such readings (we shall find others) suggest strongly that the scribe of this manuscript was responsible for at least a good many of these corruptions of the text.

17.23 (168/16)
τετελιωμενοι D cet.; PERFECTI CONSUMMATI d
consummati Lvt (b) Lvg; *perfecti* Lvt (cet.)
21.7 (180/27)
και ηλατο D*; *και ηλλατο* D[B]; *και εβαλεν εαυτον* cet.;
ET MISIT SE ET SALIBIT d
et misit se Lvt (cet.)

In these two readings, we see alternative renderings becoming established in the text. We may compare the activity of Corrector G.

We turn now to the differences.

3.34 (114/26): *διδωσιν ο $\overline{θς}$* D; *deus dat* d
3.35 (114/27): *ο πατηρ* D; $\overline{\text{DS}}$ d
4.3 (115/4): *την ϊουδαιαν γην* D; *terram iudaeam* d
4.25 (117/3): *αναγγελλει* ℵ* D; *adnuntiavit* d* cet.; *adnuntiat* d[s.m.]
4.33 (117/19): ΕΝ ΕΑΥΤΟΙϹ ΟΙ ΜΑΘΗΤΑΙ D; *discipuli ad invicem* d
4.48 (119/3): *εαν μη* D; SI d

4.50 (119/8): *αυτω* P^{66} ℵ B D; OM P^{75} K *Π* d
4.51 (119/11)
υιος σου P^{66c} D^K L^N *Γ Δ Λ Π*; *παις σου Θ Ψ* 063 f^1 pler.
παις αυτου P^{66*} P^{75} ℵ A B C W^s
filius tuus Lvt (⟦a⟧ b j); *filius ipsius* Lvt (r^1); *filius eius* d Lvt (cet.)
4.53 (119/18): *αυτου* D; OM d (lect. sing.)
5.4 (119/28): *τυφλων χωλων* D; CAECORUM ET CLAUDORUM d
5.13 (120/22): *οχλου οντος* D; *cum esset turba* d
5.19 (121/9): ΠΟΙΟΥΝΤΑ ΤΟΝ ΠΑΤΕΡΑ D; *patrem facientem* d
5.27 (122/3): *και* D *Γ Δ Λ Π* pler. Lvt (aur f q) Lvg (exc. *Δ* E); OM d cet.
5.32 (122/20): *η μαρτυρια μου* D* Lvt (e); *η μαρτυρια αυτου* D^A; *testimonium* d Lvt cet. (exc. b) Lvg c. ℵ B etc.
5.43 (123/15): *λαμβανετε με* D; *me accipitis* d
6.5 (124/5): *και* D sy (c); OM d cet.
6.7 (124/11): *αυτων* D *ΓΔ Λ* pler. Lvg (δ); OM d cet.
6.11 (124/20): *πεντε* D; OM d
ibid. (124/23): *ομοιως δε και* D M pc.; *ομοιως και* cet.; *similiter et* d
6.12 (124/25)
τα περισσευσαντα κλασματα D
FRAGMENTORUM QUAE SUPERARUNT d (order with Lvt (a))
6.18 (125/13)
δε D; *τε* cet.
quoque d Lvt (e); *vero/autem* Lvt (cet.) Lvg
6.19 (125/14): *ουν* D cet.; SED d
See Parker, 'Translation of *OYN*', p. 273.
ibid. (125/15): *ωσει* D; OM d
The rest of the Latin tradition translates the word.
6.20 (125/19): *ο δε λεγει αυτοις* D; *quibus ipse ait* d
6.30 (126/22)
σοι ποιεις D Lvt (aur b c e ff^2 q) Lvg (pler.)
facis tu d Gr. cet. Lvt (a r^1)
6.37 (127/10): *διδωσιν μοι* D; *mihi dat* d
6.41 (127/24): *δε* D; *ουν* cet. Lvt Lvg; ܕܝܢ sy (c s p); *ergo* d
6.50 (128/15): *ινα τις* D* cet. Lvt (e j m); *ινα εαν τις* D^C; *ut si quis* d Lvt (cet.) Lvg
6.51 (128/18): ΕΑΝ ΟΥΝ ΤΙϹ D; *si quis* d cet.
6.60 (129/18): OM D; *et* d
6.65 (129/32): *δεδομενον αυτω* D; *illi datum fuerit* d
6.70 (130/8): ΛΕΓΩΝ D; *και ειπεν αυτοις* ℵ; *et dixit* d Lvt (a)
7.4 (130/22): ΕΝ ΠΑΡΗϹΙΑ ΑΥΤΟ (*αυτος* D^H) ΕΙΝΑΙ D; *illut in palam esse* d
This is transposition in d.
7.5 (130/25): ΕΠΙϹΤΕΥϹΑΝ ΕΙϹ ΑΥΤΟΝ ΤΟΤΕ D; *crediderunt tunc in illum* d
Yoder (*Concordance*) takes *τοτε* as going with the beginning of v. 6 – *τοτε λεγει αυτοις* – although *λεγει αυτοις* is in the next line. Barrett (*The Gospel According to St John*, 2nd edn., London, 1978, p. 213) takes it to be harmonization to Ac 1.14 etc. We need to look also at the difference in the beginning of v. 6.

7.6 (130/26): *λεγει* D; *dicit ergo* d
If *τοτε* went at the beginning of v. 6, then the omission of *ουν* in D is explained. The phrase *επιστευσαν εις αυτον τοτε* is no kind of Greek at all. However, we also need to explain the origin of the Latin reading. If D represents a transposition in the phrase *επιστευσαν τοτε εις αυτον*, then the Latin is explained. The omission of *ουν* in v. 6 is a separate error on D's part.
7.8 (130/33): *εις την εορτην ταυτην* D; *in hunc diem festum* d
7.37 (133/15)
εν δε τη ημερα τη μεγαλη τη εσχατη D
in novissimo autem die magno d
This is transposition in D.
7.44 (134/1): *ηθελον εξ αυτων* D; *ex illis volebant* d
8.6 (135/3): *τω δακτυλω* D; *digito suo* d
8.8 (135/7): *τω δακτυλω* D; DIGITO SUO d
8.11 (135/16): OM D Λ al. Lvt (j ff[2] q); *et* d cet.
8.15 (135/30): OM D cet.; *δε* P[75] 238 253; *autem* d Lvt (f)
ibid. (*ibid.*): *κρεινω ουδενα* D; *neminem iudico* d
8.17 (135/33): *και* D; *sed et* d
8.23 (136/18): *εγω δε* D Lvt (f ⟨j⟩ q); *ego* d cet.
8.25 (136/26): *ουν* ℵ D 249; OM d cet.
8.29 (137/5): *αφηκεν με* D; *me reliquid* d
ibid. (137/6): *τα αρεστα αυτω* D; *quae illi placent* d
ibid. (137/7): *παντοτε* D; OMNIA d
8.49 (138/28): ΜΟΥ ΤΟΝ ΠΑΤΕΡΑ D; *patrem meum* d
8.52 (139/5): ΜΟΥ ΤΙϹ ΤΟΝ ΛΟΓΟΝ D; *si quis meum verbum* d
Transposition in D.
9.22 (141/27): *αυτον* $\overline{\chi\rho\nu}$ *ειναι* D; $\overline{\text{XPM}}$ EUM ESSE d
9.30 (142/14): OM D; ERGO d
10.33 (145/27): *καλου εργου* D; OPERE BONO d
11.23 (148/5): ϹΟΥ Ο ΑΔΕΛΦΟϹ D; *frater tuus* d
11.27 (148/12): OM D 157; *ei* d cet.
11.30 (148/20): ΟΥ D; *nondum* d
11.31 (148/26): *δοξαντες* D; PUTABANT ENIM d
A free rendering in d.
11.32 (148/29): *ωδε ης* D; *fuisses hic* d
11.42 (149/21): *ειπον* D; *dixit* d
Is this reading a mistranslation?
11.51 (150/14): *του ενιαυτου* P[66] D; *anni illius* d cet.
12.9 (151/23): ΔΕ D; *ουν* Gr. cet.; *ergo* d Lvt (aur f) Lvg pler.
igitur Lvt (r[1]); *autem* Lvt (⟦a⟧ e) Lvg (G)
See Parker, 'Translation of *OYN*', p. 265.
12.10 (151/27–8): *ϊνα και* D; *et ut* d
12.28 (153/17): ΚΑΙ ΕΓΕΝΕΤΟ D; FACTA EST d
13.8 (156/5): *νιψω σε* D; *te lavero* d
13.15 (156/22): *γαρ* D cet.; OM P[66]* 700 pc. d
13.27 (157/22): *ποιης* (*ποιησον* D[D]) *ταχειον* D; *citius fac* d

15.15 (162/14)
υμας λεγω D *Θ* 065 0250 f[1] f[13] pler.; *λεγω υμας* P[66] ℵ B L al. pc.
dico vos d Lvt (cet) Lvg; *vos dicam* Lvt (q)
16.2 (163/22): *ποιησουσιν ϋμας* D; *vos eicient* d
16.13 (164/20): *αλλα* D; OM d (lect. sing.)
16.16 (164/27): *ουκετι* P[66vid] ℵ B D L N W *Θ* al.; *ου* A 054 f[13] pler.; *non* d Lvt (cet.)
ibid. (*ibid.*): *θεωρειτε με* D; ME VIDEBITIS d
16.17 (164/31): *ουκετι* D W *Ψ* 33 pc.; *ου* cet.; *non* d Lvt (cet.)
16.19 (165/6): *θεωρειτε με* D; ME VIDEVITIS d
17.7 (167/4): *δεδωκας μοι* D; *mihi dedisti* d
17.10 (167/11): *τα εμε παντα* D; *omnia mea* d
17.12 (167/22)
ους δεδωκας μοι εφυλαξα D (C[3]) D *Θ* *Ψ* 054 f[1] f[13] pler.
ω δεδωκας μοι και εφυλαξα ℵ[2] B (C[A]) L W 33 pc.
και εφυλαξα P[66]* ℵ*
QUOS DEDISTI MIHI ET CUSTODiVI d
quos dedisti mihi custodivi Lvt (cet.) Lvg
17.14 (167/29): *εισιν* D; SUM d
17.20 (168/8): *πιστευοντων* D* pler. Lvt (b q); *πιστευσοντων* D[K] Cs Cac[2] Cb (mss);
credituri sunt d Lvt (cet.) Lvg
17.24 (168/20): *δεδωκας μοι* D; MIHI DEDIS d
ibid. (168/22): *δεδωκας μοι* D; *mihi dedisti* d
17.25 (168/23): *δικαιε* D cet.; *αγιε* 2; *sancte* d
Tischendorf also cites the Apostolic Constitutions 8.11 for the reading *ἅγιε*.
20.22 (178/32): OM D Lvt (cet.) Lvg (cet.); ET d Gr. cet. Lvt (f r[1]) Lvg (T δ)
20.25 (179/9): MOY[2] D cet.; OM d 1 pc. Lvt (a)
20.26 (179/17): *λεγει* D *Θ* 235 251; *dixit* d cet.
21.22 (182/10): MENEIN OYTѠC D; SIC MANERE d
21.23 (182/16): ΠΡΟC CE D; *quid ad te* d

As with Matthew, the several causes of these readings may be suggested.

1. Influence of the context
   6.19[1]; 8.17; 9.30; 12.28; 17.14
2. Translation error
   11.42
3. Harmonization to a Gospel parallel
   By D: 6.11[1]
4. Transposition
   By D alone: 4.33; 5.19; 7.4, 5, 37; 8.49; 11.23
   By D with support: 11.32
   By d alone: 8.52; 9.22; 10.33; 16.16[2], 19; 17.24[1]; 21.22
   By d with support: 3.34; 4.3; 5.13, 43; 6.12, 37, 65; 7.8, 44; 8.15[2], 29 *bis*; 12.10; 13.8, 27; 16.2; 17.7, 10, 24[2]

5. Textual differences
4.25, 50, 51; 5.27, 32; 6.5, 7, 11[2], 18, 30, 41, 50, 51, 70; 8.11, 15[1], 23, 25; 11.27, 51; 12.9; 13.15; 15.15; 16.16[1], 17; 17.12, 20, 25; 20.22, 25, 26

In addition, we suggest:

Errors in d, 4.48; 5.4?
Possibly there are errors in D at 11.30 and 21.23
Casual translation, 8.6, 8, 29[3]; 11.31
Omission in d, 4.53; 6.19[2]; 7.6; 16.13

The rejection of the conjunction at 6.20 anticipates quite a common occurrence in Mark.

As one would expect, the influence of the other Gospels is much weaker – there is only 6.11, where D follows all three Synoptists.

It is striking that there are far more instances of transposition of words – thirty-four examples in all, of which eight are in D (one with other support). However, of the d examples, nineteen are shared with other Latin manuscripts. The phenomenon is partly owing to the way in which the older Latin traditions handled the Johannine style. This list has already ignored the placing of the emphatic *ego* before the verb (e.g. 5.7 ερχομαι εγω/*ego venio*), and the very common order with the participle (e.g. του πεμψαντος με/*qui me misit*). The number of transpositions where d is alone are no more than in Matthew.

If the synoptic influence in Matthew is counted as part of the genuine textual variation, then there are fewer differences in John than in Matthew, with less than thirty readings where I take d certainly to support a different Greek text.

John 6.5–7.8, where there are a high proportion of differences (twenty-two in Ff123b–130), shows also a higher proportion of textual differences, since nine of these twenty-two may be counted as such.

THE GOSPEL OF LUKE

In Luke, we note separately the following readings.

4.39 (201/15)
παραχρημα ωστε D
CONTINUO UT ETIAM CONTINUO d
Again, we may see transposition at work.
6.16 (207/25–6): και A D pler; OM P^{75vid} ℵ B L W al.; *etiam et* d
This is a double rendering.
7.50 (215/25): σεσωκεν σε D cet.; *te salbam fecit* d (order with Lvt Lvg Marcion ap TE AM PS-AM AU PS-CY HI PAU-N LAU MAXn SED)
See also 8.48; 9.28, 30; 10.30; 11.27; 12.12; 18.33; 23.47.

At 18.11 the Latin translation interprets the Greek text wrongly. At 21.28 and 21.34 there is corruption.

Let us turn to the significant differences.

1.8–9 (183/24–5)
της εφημεριας . . . της ϊερατειας D; SACERDOTI . . . SACRIFICII d
vicis . . . sacerdotii Lvt (cet.)
Sacrificii may be a corruption of *sacri vicis*. The transposition in d must then be an error of memorizing.
1.9 (183/27): *του θυ* D; *dmi* d
The Latin may be a misrecognition of the nomen sacrum DEI as DNI or DMI.
1.13 (184/4): OM D Δ 1 579; *σοι* cet.; *tibi* d
1.26 (185/11): *εν δε τω εκτω μηνι* D; *in mense autem sexto* d
1.61 (187/29): *οτι* D cet.; OM 1 22 al ℓ184 d Lvt (a aur b c e ff² g¹ 1 q r¹) AM
Elsewhere in Luke, *ὅτι recitativum* is translated (and see W. E. Plater and H. J. White, *A Grammar of the Vulgate*, Oxford, 1926, pp. 119f).
1.66 (188/11): *το παιδιον τουτο εσται* D; *erit infans haec* d
2.8 (189/28): *αγραυλουντες* D; *cantantes* d
The International Greek New Testament apparatus suggests that d represents the word *αυλουντες*, or at least arises from a confusion between the two words. But it is to be noted that earlier in the verse, D has ΕΝ ΤΗ ΧΑΡΑ ΤΑΥΤΗ. The error in the Latin may arise from an association of ideas.
2.11 (190/3): *χρς κς* D; *xrs ihs* d
2.13 (190/8): *συν τω αγγελω πληθος* D; MULTITUDO CUM ANGELO d
2.17 (190/21): *του λαληθεντος* D; *quod factum est* d
2.35 (192/6): *δε αυτης* D; IPSIUS AUTEM d
3.2 (194/5): *θυ* D; *dmi* d
In spite of the Greek support for its reading, the reading of d is likely to arise out of the same cause as that at 1.9.
3.4 (194/14): *ϋμων* D Ath; *αυτου* cet.; *eius* d
3.9 (194/31): *καρπους καλους* D; *fructum bonum* d
Compare v. 8, where D/d have singular for plural. The plural here is from par. Mt 7.17.
3.17 (195/26): *αυτου* D cet.; OM d 827 Bas Clem Iren Or
4.6 (198/16): *της (την* D^D*) εξουσιαν ταυτην* D; HANC POTESTATEM d
ibid. (198/17): *τουτων* D 700; *αυτων* cet.; *eorum* d
4.35 (201/1): ΑΝΑΚΡΑΥΓΑСΑΝ ΤΕ D; *και κραξαν* 903[c]; *exclamans* d; OM cet.
Ανακραυγαζω is rare. Chrysostom, *Hom. XVII in Hebr.*: *μέγα ἐπ' ἐκείνῃ τῇ φρικτῇ ἡσυχίᾳ ἀνακραυγάζων* (ed. Ducaeus, *Tom. VI in N.T.*, Paris, 1636, p. 858).
4.36 (201/5): *ο λογος ουτος* D; *hic sermo* d
5.5 (202/17): *επι δε τω ρηματι σου* D; IN TUO AUTEM VERBO d
5.14 (203/13–14): ΕΙС ΜΑΡΤΥΡΙΟΝ ΗΝ D*; *εις μαρτυριον η* D^{corr};
sit in testimonium d
5.20 (204/9): *σου αι αμαρτιαι* D; *tibi peccata tua* d
D = par. Mt 9.2; Mk 2.5.
5.21 (204/13): *εις* D; *solus* d

D = par. Mk 2.7. Although in the Latin tradition *solus* is generally used for μονος, at Jn 17.3 Lvt (a) reads *unus*.

5.23 (204/17–18): σου αι αμαρτιαι D; *tibi peccata* d

Again D is taken from par. Matthew and Mark. The Latin may be harmonized to different texts of the same parallels.

5.26 (204/27): OM D; OMNES d

D and d have totally omitted the first half of the verse; d is here borrowing from the missing opening phrase (και ἐκστασις ἐλαβεν ἁπαντας).

5.27 (204/28–9): ΕΛΘΩΝ ... ΠΑΡΑ ... OM D; VENIT ... AD ... AUTEM d

This is an addition at the beginning of the verse that is unique to Codex Bezae. The first half is closely, the second freely taken from par. Mk 2.13. The Latin is rather inept.

6.4 (206/17): ειπεν D; *et dixit* d

This is in the story of the man working on the Sabbath. It produces in d the construction *videns ... et dixit*.

ibid. (206/20): EI D; OM d

This is in the same pericope.

6.29 (208/31): σου το ϊματιον D; *tunicam tuam* d

This is either transposition, or harmonization to Mt 5.40.

6.42 (210/8–9): και ϊδου η δοκος εν τω σω οφθαλμω ϋποκειται D Ss;
ET ECCE TRABIS IN TUO OCULO EST d

The form in D is essentially that of par. Mt 7.4. Υποκειμαι is a hapax legomenon for the New Testament. It may be due to a confusion with the following word, υποκριτα (written as ΥΠΟΚΡΕΙΤΑ in D).

7.1 (211/7): ταυτα τα ρηματα D; *omnia verba* d

The verse has been totally recast in Codex Bezae. The majority of Greek manuscripts read παντα τα ρηματα in their form of the verse.

ibid. (211/8): ηλθεν εις καφαρναουμ D; VENIT CAFARNAUM d

7.6 (211/22): μου ϋπο την στεγην D; *sub tectum meum* d

The D order = par. Mt 8.8.

7.12 (212/4–5): εγενετο δε ως ... εξεκομιζετο D; ως δε ... και ιδου εξεκ. cet;
factum est autem ... et ferebatur d

The grammar of d suggests that it has been partly but not wholly assimilated to the Greek column.

ibid. (212/8): CYΝΕΛΗΛΥΘΙ ΑΥΤΗ D; *cum ea erat* d

D is a recollection of Jn 11.33.

7.27 (213/24): OM D 1009 2766; σου cet.; *tuam* d cet.

7.41 (215/1): δανιστη τινι D; *cuidam faeneratori* d

7.47 (215/19): ΔΕ D; OM d

D = par. Mk 14.9.

8.29 (218/25): φυλασσομενος D; ET CUSTODIEBATUR d

8.38 (219/23): ειναι D; *ut esset* d

The d reading = par. Mk 5.18.

8.39 (219/27): εποιησεν αυτω D; *illi fecit* d

8.45 (220/11): συνεχουσιν σε D; *te comprimunt* d

8.49 (220/24): CΟΥ Η ΘΥΓΑΤΗΡ D; *filia tua* d

9.6 (221/25)
ΚΑΤΑ ΠΟΛΕΙϹ ΚΑΙ ΗΡΧΟΝΤΟ D; διηρχοντο κατα τας κωμας cet.
circa civitates transibant d
Some Old Latin manuscripts have *castella et civitates* or *civ. et cast.* This is probably under the influence of 8.1. The construction in D is εξερχομενοι . . . και ηρχοντο. d is a transposition of the majority Greek text; it therefore represents a different text from that of D.
9.9 (222/1–2): τις δε εστιν ουτος D; QUIS EST AUTEM HIC d
ibid. (222/3): αυτον ειδειν D; *videre eum* d
9.12 (222/15): τον οχλον D; *turbas* d
The plural = par. Mt 14.15.
9.22 (223/15): μεθ ημερας τρεις D; *post tres dies* d
Compare
Mt 16.21: μετα τρεις ημερας D (τη τριτ. ημ. cet.)
Mk 8.31: μετα τρεις ημ. D cet. (*tertia die* d).
This is transposition in d.
9.26 (223/27): εν τη δοξη αυτου D; *in regno suo* d
Is the d reading a recollection of Mt 16.28?
10.2 (227/14): OM ουν[2] D Lvt (e); ουν cet.; *ergo* d Lvt (cet.) Lvg
10.5 (227/20): ΕΙϹΗΛΘΗΤΕ ΠΡΩΤΟΝ ΟΙΚΙΑΝ D*; εισηλθητε οικιαν D[corr] (A?); *intraveritis domum* d
The omission of πρωτον is probably a harmonization to par. Mt 10.12, as the change in word order could also be.
10.23 (229/16): προς τους μαθητας D; *ad discipulos suos* d
10.31 (230/6)
κατα τυχα ϊερευς D; κατα συγκυριαν δε ιερευς pler.; κατα συγκυριαν ιερευς P[45]; *forte autem sacerdos* d; *fortuitio sacerdos* Lvt (a q r[1])
10.38 (230/26): τις D cet.; OM d (lect. sing.)
10.40 (230/33): ου μελι σοι D; *non tibi cura est* d
11.7 (231/31): τα παιδια μου D pler.; τα παιδια C* M 1 157 al.; *pueri* d
11.9 (232/3): ϋμειν λεγω D; *dico vobis* d
11.11 (232/8): τον πατερα ο υιος αιτησει D W pc.; τον πατερα αιτ. ο υιος pler.; *patrem suum filius petit* d
Petit, also found in Lvt (aur q r[1]) Lvg, may be due to *petit* in v. 10. *Suum* is unique to d.
11.28 (232/27): του $\overline{θυ}$ D; $\overline{\text{DMI}}$ d
The reading in d is a miscopying of $\overline{\text{DEI}}$.
11.31 (234/8): αυτους D; *eam* d
d = par. Mt 12.41.
11.41 (234/33): εσται ϋμειν D; *et erunt vobis* d
11.43 (235/6): την πρωτοκαθεδριαν D; *primas sessiones* d
The plural is harmonization to par. Mt 23.6 or to Lk 20.46. Note that at Mt 23.6 also we have variation between singular and plural in the witnesses.
11.49 (235/28): και εξ αυτων D; *ex eis* d
The omission = par. Mt 23.34.
12.18 (238/5): μου τας αποθηκας D cet.; OM μου d W ℓ1074 Lvt (a c ff[2] i l) AM AU

12.38 (239/27): D recasts almost all of this verse. Where it reads ΚΑΙ ΤΗ ΤΡΙΤΗ, d and e have *vel tertia*.
12.40 (239/31): δε D; OM P^{75} ℵ B L Θ 157 al. Lvt (cet.) Lvg; ουν cet.; *ergo* d
12.42 (240/4): καταστησει D; *constituit* d
The past tenses come from par. Mt 24.45.
12.45 (240/14)
ΜΕΘΥϹΚΟΜΕΝΟϹ D; και μεθυσκεσθαι cet.
et inebriari d Lvt (cet.) Lvg; *et inebrietur* Lvt (e)
d has not been assimilated to this minor D reading.
12.53 (241/3): διαμερισθησονται μητηρ D; *dividetur mater* d
The variant in the addition stems from the variation in the occurrence of the verb at the beginning of the verse
διαμερισθησονται P^{45} P^{75} ℵ B D L 157 al. Lvt (d pler.)
διαμερισθησεται cet.
13.4 (241/33): του σιλωαμ D ℓ1056 MarcEr; εν τω σιλωαμ cet.; *in siloam* d
13.6 (242/9): ΑΠ ΑΥΤΗϹ D; εν αυτη cet.; *in ea* d
13.14 (242/31): εργαζεσθαι D; CURARI d
This is caused by *curavit* (l. 32) and *curamini* (l. 32).
13.15 (243/1): ιησους D al.; κυριος al.; *dominus* d
ibid. (243/3): ΚΑΙ D; η cet.; *aut* d
13.18 (243/12): δε D; *ergo* d
The reading δε may be by attraction to v. 6.
13.23 (243/25): τις αυτω D; EI QUIDAM d
13.34 (244/30): προς αυτην D; *ad te* d
Te = par. Mt 23.37 D Lvt Ss
14.7 (245/19): δε και D; *autem* d
δε και is a reading produced by the context, v. 12.
14.9 (245/26): εση D; αρξη cet.; *incipiens* d Lvt (cet.); *eris* Lvt (e)
14.12 (246/12): τω κεκλητοκι D; *ad eum qui invitaverat eum* d
d is adopting the beginning of v. 7 – προς τους κεκλημενους.
14.17 (246/21)
παντα ετοιμα εστιν D 827 2766 Lvt (a e); ετοιμα εισι/ετοιμα εστι/ετοιμα εστι παντα cet.
parata sunt omnia d Lvt (aur f r^1) Lvg
The addition of παντα is harmonization to Mt 22.4. Do the two word orders represent two separate harmonizings?
14.21 (246/31): παντα ταυτα D; HAEC OMNIA d
14.23 (247/6): φραγμους D; IN SAEPES d
14.26 (247/15)
ετι δε και A D cet.; ετι τε και B L al.; ετι και P^{75}
adhuc etiam d Lvt (ff^2 l); *adhuc autem* Lvt (aur c f) Lvg
adhuc et Lvt (e r^1); *etiam et* Lvt (b q)
15.4 (248/17): ανθρωπος εξ ϋμων D; *ex vobis homo* d
ibid. (248/19): εξ αυτων εν D; *unum ex eis* d
εν εξ αυτων = par. Mt 18.12.
ibid. (248/21): ΑΠΕΛΘΩΝ ΤΟ ΑΠΟΛΩΛΟϹ ΖΗΤΕΙ D; *vadit et quaerit quod perierat* d

The d order follows par. Mt 18.12.

15.8 (248/33): και απολεσασα D; *et si perdiderit* d

The reading in D is based on v. 6. The Latin seems to combine both Greek readings.

15.15 (249/21): εκολληθη D; ADHESIT IBI d

Ibi may be taken from v. 10.

15.19 (249/33): COY ΫΙΟC D; *filius tuus* d

15.21 (250/7)

Ο ΔΕ ΥΙΟC ΕΙΠΕΝ ΑΥΤΩ D; ειπεν δε ο υιος αυτω P⁷⁵ B L 1 157 pc.

ειπε δε αυτω ο υιος cet.; *dixit autem filius eius* d

ibid. (250/9): COY ΫΙΟC D; *filius tuus* d

16.1 (251/10): δε και D pler.; δε S V 5 22 al.; *autem* d Lvt ([b] l r¹)

16.2 (251/14): φωνησας D pc.; + αυτον cet. Lvt; *uocans eum* d

16.11 (252/12): ὑμειν πιστευσει D; *credet uobis* d

16.29 (254/3): ειπεν δε αυτω D pc.; λεγει pc.; λεγει δε P⁷⁵ ℵ B L al.; λεγει αυτω al.; λεγει δε αυτω A W pler.; *dixit autem* d

17.2 (254/14): CYNΦΕΡΕΙ ΔΕ D; *expediebat* d

Συμφερει is from par. Mt 18.6. So is *expedit*. Is the imperfect of d a corruption of this?

17.8 (255/2)

ετοιμασον D pler.; ετοιμασον μοι ℵ pc.

para mihi d Lvt (b f q r¹); *para* Lvt (pler.) Lvg

17.23 (256/10)

ιδου ωδε ιδου εκει D al.; ιδου ωδε και ιδου εκει pc.

ιδου ωδε η ιδου εκει pler.; *ecce hic aut ecce illic* d

The reading ἤ is from par. Mt 24.23 (or Mk 13.21 variant).

17.28 (256/23)

και ως D pler.; καθως P⁷⁵ ℵ B L 157 al.

sicut d Lvt (aur f i r¹) Lvg

17.32 (257/2): μνημονευετε D; ET MEMENTOTE d

17.36 (37) (257/14): συναχθησονται D; συναχθησονται και U al.; *congregabuntur et* d

The D reading = par. Mt 24.28 (where there is a variant in 565 al. showing the reading of U etc. found here).

18.5 (257/26): παρεχειν μοι κοπον D; LAUOREM MIHI PRAESTAT d

18.13 (258/16): τους οφθαλμους D; *oculos suos* d

18.14 (258/22): ο δε D; *et qui* d

και ο possibly = par. Mt 23.12 (και οστις; *et quicumque* d ff²; *et qui* cet.) or Lk 14.11 (και ο; *et qui*).

18.18 (258/33): τις αυτον D; *eum quidam* d

18.19 (259/4)

εις ο θεος D cet.; εις θεος ℵ* B*

unus ds pater d; *unus/solus deus* Lvt (cet.)

18.27 (259/25): δυνατα παρα θω εστιν D; *apud dm possibilia sunt* d

18.32 (260/8): ενπτυσθησεται D; *espuent in eum* d

d = par. Mk 10.34.

18.41 (260/27): σοι θελεις D; *vis tibi* d

19.5 (261/10)
και εγενετο εν τω διερχεσθαι αυτον D
και εγενετο εν τω διερχεσθαι τον ιησουν 157
και ως ηλθεν επι τον τοπον cet.
et factum est cum illac transiret d
The whole phrase has been recast in D; *illac* in d corresponds to *επι τον τοπον*.
ibid. (261/11): *σπευσον* D Λ 16 al. Lvt (e q); *σπευσας* cet.; *festinans* d Lvt (cet.)
16 is a bilingual which we met in chapter 4. The Latin was never copied here.
19.9 (261/21): *ο ιης προς αυτον* D; *προς αυτον ο ιησους* cet.; *Iesus* d Lvt (e)
19.14 (262/4): *εμεισουν αυτον* D; ODERANT d
19.21 (262/22): *γαρ ει αυστηρος* D; *es enim austeris* d
19.31 (263/17): *ϋμας ερωτα* D; VOBIS DIXERIT d
d = par. Mk 11.3.
19.34 (263/18): *απεκριθησαν* D; SIC DIXERUNT d
Both columns seem separately to attempt to restore the sense after the loss of v. 33.
20.17 (266/6): *ουν εστιν* D; *est ergo* d
20.25 (266/33): ΕΙΠΕΝ ΔΕ D; *ο δε ειπεν* pler.; *ille autem dixit* d Lvt (e f)
20.28 (267/11): *την γυναικα* D; *uxorem eius* d
The addition is from either Mt 22.24 or Mk 12.19 (where there is a similar variant).
20.31 (267/16): ΩϹΑΥΤΩϹ D; *similiter et* d
20.35 (267/23): *εκεινου* D; *huius* d
21.7 (269/4): *επηρωτησαν δε αυτον οι μαθηται* D
επηρωτησαν δε αυτον pler.; INTERROGAVERUNT AUTEM DISCIPULI d
21.9 (269/13): *ταυτα* D; HOC d
21.11 (269/16): *τε* D cet.; OM d A pc. Lvt (g[1]) Lvg AM
21.22 (270/12): *αυται εισιν* D; *sunt istae* d
21.25 (270/22): *αστροις* D; *in sideribus* d
Lvt (e f) also have *in* before *luna*.
22.17 (272/32): OM *και*[2] D Lvt (e) Ss Sc Cb (mss); *και* cet.; *et* d
22.22 (273/7): *οτι μεν ο ϋιος* D; *filius quidem* d
The omission of *οτι* = par. Mt 26.24.
22.27 (273/20–2)
εγω γαρ εν μεσω ϋμων ηλθον ουχ ως ο ανακειμενος αλλ D
εγω δε ειμι εν μεσω υμων pler. (*εγω γαρ* Bas AMst)
ego autem sum in medio vestrum veni non sicut qui recumbit sed d
The text of d shows partial assimilation to that of D.
22.37 (274/17): *το* D; OM d
22.38 (274/18–19): *δυο μαχαιραι ωδε* D; *duo machaerae* d
22.60 (276/14): *λαλουντος αυτου* D; *eo loquente* d
ibid. (276/15): *εφωνησεν αλεκτωρ* D; *gallus cantauit* d
The Latin = par. Mt 26.74 or Mk 14.72.
22.61 (276/18–19): *τρεις απαρνηση με μη ειδεναι με* D; *ter abnegavis me* d
Here D follows v. 34.
23.9 (277/33): ΟΥΚ ΑΠΕΚΡΙΝΑΤΟ ΑΥΤΩ ΟΥΔΕΝ D; *nihil respondebat illi* d

23.11 (278/3–4): *εξουθενησας δε αυτον ο ηρωδης* D;
EXPROBANT AUTEM EUM ET HERODES d
d places *exprobant autem eum* with v. 10 (*et* is found in Lvt (a) in the sense of 'also').
23.14 (278/15)
ουδεν ευρον αιτιον εν αυτω D
ουδεν ευρον εν τω ανθρωπω τουτω αιτιον pler.
NIHIL MALI INVENI IN EO d
This is poor assimilation of d to D, using v. 22.
23.27 (279/13): ΤΟ ΠΛΗΘΟC ΑΥΤω D; *illum multitudo* d
23.36 (280/7)
οξος τε προσεφερον D; *οξος προφεροντες αυτω* P[75] ℵ A B C* L al.
και οξος προφεροντες αυτω pler.; *acetum offerebant ei* d Lvt (r[1])
acetum offerebant illi Lvt (e); *et acetum offerentes* Lvt (c)
Again, d has been partially assimilated to D.
23.37 (280/9–10): *εριτεθεντες αυτω και ακανθινον στεφανον* D;
inponentes illi et de spinis coronam d
The reading of D is from Mt 15.17. The plural in d is found in Mt 27.29 and Jn 19.2.
23.40 (280/17): *τον θν* D; *dnm* d
Again, compare 1.9.
ibid. (280/17–18)
εν τω αυτω κριματι ει και ημεις εσμεν D
εν τω αυτω κριματι ει pler.; *in ipso iudicio et nos sumus* d
23.43 (280/24)
αποκριθεις δε ο ιησους ειπεν αυτω τω επλησοντι (επιπλησοντι D[D]) D Et ORI
respondens autem iesus dixit qui obiurgabat eum d
Again, this is a poor piece of assimilation to D in d.
23.46 (280/32): *τουτο δε* P[75] ℵ B C* D W pc. Lvt (c r[1]); *και τουτο* K L P Θ al.;
και ταυτα cet.; *et hoc* d Lvt ([b] e l q); *et* Lvt (a)
24.5 (282/8–9)
τα προσωπα P[75] ℵ B D Θ 1 157 al.; *τον προσωπον* pler.
τα προσωπα αυτων C*; VULTOS SUOS d
24.18 (283/3): *εις* D pler.; *εις εξ αυτων* P Θ 13 157 al.; *unus ex eis* d
ibid. (283/5): *ιερουσαλημ* D P[75] ℵ A B pler.; *εν ιερουσαλημ* cet.; *in hierusalem* d Lvt (*ab hier.* c e)
24.31 (284/11): ΗΝΥΓΗCΑΝ D; *διηνοιχθησαν* cet.; *aperti sunt* d
This is part of an addition by D, shared with Lvt (c d e).
24.32 (284/14)
ην ημων κεκαλυμμενη D; *ημων καιομενη ην* pler.
nostrum erat coopertum d
This is poor assimilation in d.
24.39 (284/32): *το πνα* D; *οτι πνευμα* cet.; *quoniam sps* d
ibid. (284/33): *καθως εμε* D; SICUT ET ME d
24.45 (285/11–12): *διηνυξεν αυτων τον νουν* D; ADAPERTI SUNT EORUM SENSUS d
24.47 (285/17): ωC ΕΠΙ D; *εις* cet.; *super* d; *usque in* Lvt (c e); *in* Lvt (cet.)

These differences may be divided between the following causes.

1. Influence of the context
   On D: 13.18; 14.7; 15.8
   On d: 2.8; 13.14; 14.12; 15.15
2. Translation error
   8.29; 12.38
3. Harmonization to a Gospel parallel
   In D: 3.9; 5.20, 21, 23; 6.42: 7.6; 7.12^2; 7.47; 17.36
   In d: 8.38; 9.12, 26; 10.5; 11.31, 43, 49; 12.42; 13.34; 15.4^2, 4^3; 18.14, 32; 19.31; 20.28; 22.22, 60^2
   In both: 23.37
4. Transposition
   By D alone: 15.19, 21^2; 23.9, 27
   By D with support: none
   By d alone: (1.8f); 2.13, 35; 4.6; 5.5; 7.1^2; 9.9^1; 13.23; 14.21; 16.11; 18.5
   By d with support: 1.26, 66; 4.36; 5.14; 6.29; 7.41; 8.39, 45, 49; 9.9^2, 22; 10.40; 11.9; 15.4^1; 18.18, 27, 41; 19.21; 20.17; 21.22; 22.60^1
   A few of the transpositions in d may have the purpose of avoiding hiatus: 20.17; 22.60^1 (this is also a possible explanation of the difference at 23.27)
5. Textual differences
   1.13, 61; 3.4, 17; 4.6^2, 35; 7.1^1, 27; 9.6; 10.2, 31, 38; 11.7, 11; 12.18, 40; 13.4, 6, 15 *bis*; 14.9, 17, 26; 15.21^1; 16.1, 2, 29; 17.8, 23, 28; 18.19; 19.5^2, 9; 20.25; 21.11; 22.17; 23.46; 24.5, 18 *bis*, 39^1, 47
6. Corruption in the Latin
   1.9; 2.11, 17; 3.2; 10.23; 14.23; 18.13?; 20.35?; 21.9, 25; 23.11, 40^1; 24.39^2, 45

Of particular importance are a number of places where D has a unique, or at least a very characteristic reading, and d has something that is halfway between it and the more common reading. That is to say, it has been partially assimilated to the text of D. These are

7.12; 12.45; 19.5^1; 21.7?; 22.27; 23.14; 23.36, 40^2, 43; 24.31, 32

The implication of this is that, where it differs from D, d represents an older form of text, lacking the distinctive variations of the Greek column. The significance of these readings is something to which we will return.

There are a number of other differences that are caused by mistakes in copying – 11.28, 41; 17.2 (?), 32; 19.14; 20.31; 22.37, 38(?).

THE GOSPEL OF MARK

The task of ascertaining the differences in Mark is of a quite different order. The number of possible differences, beginning with nearer four hundred than three, has to be reduced considerably once it is realized that the parallel texts are presented to us by Codex Bezae in a careless and corrupt form. The many obvious errors which contribute to this state of affairs must be tackled separately. To include them would be to obscure our main purpose. Readings to be set aside include pieces of such extraordinary character as

ΚΑΙ ΗΓΑΓΟΝ ΤΟΝ ΠΩΛΟΝ ΠΡΟϹ ΤΟΝ ΙΗΝ
ΚΑΙ ΕΠΙΒΑΛΛΟΥϹΙΝ ΑΥΤΩ · ΤΑ ΪΜΑΤΙΑ ΑΥΤΟΥ

(11.7; F324b/20–1)

There are also signs that the Latin version does not set out to provide so precise a translation as it has in the previous Gospels. For example, the conjunction is occasionally omitted, I think intentionally:

10.4 (320/12): *οι δε ειπαν* D; *qui dixerunt* d
10.42 (324/1): *και προσκαλεσαμενος αυτους* D; *quos cum advocasset* d

The same has been done at 1.8; 4.39; 6.24; 8.5, 17, 32, 33; 9.33, 36; 10.11; 14.20; and possibly also at 9.42, 47; 14.9.

Parataxis is rejected at 1.35; 6.1; 14.61.

There are two translational variants in 1.31, and at 5.21 we can see transposition being introduced. Besides this, there are several other interesting readings which cannot be included as discrepancies. (From here on I shall indicate Old Latin manuscripts solely by their letter, without the prefix Lvt.)

6.53 (307/30): *διαπερασαντες* D cet.; *cum transfretasset* d r[1]
See also par. Mt 14.34 in ff[2]*, which has *cum transfretasset* for the same Greek.
6.55 (308/5): *ηκουσαν* D 472; *ηκουον* cet.; *audierant* d i; *audissent* a; *audiebat* ff[2]*; *audiebant* cet.
This reading in d could be a copying error, where an uncial *B* was misread as *R*. If not, then we have an interesting use of the pluperfect.

There are several readings where the Latin tradition has embellished the text.

9.25 (317/26): *μηκετι* D cet.; *cabe ne* b d
This is an embellishment of the text by b d.
10.19 (321/20): ΠΟΡΝΕΥϹΗϹ D; *occidas* d
D is in error for *φονευσης*. The reading is an example of misrecognition. Note that both D and d have the word in a different place from all other witnesses.

Leaving these, let us turn to the significant differences.

1.6 (286/15): *ην δε* D; *et erat* d
The reading in D etc. follows Mt 3.4.
1.7 (286/19): *ερχεται* D; *veniet* d
The d reading is from par. Lk 3.16 aur b c q r[1] (*venit* d cet.).
1.9 (286/23): *εν ταις ημεραις εκειναις* D; *in illis diebus* d
See M.-T. 4,24f.
1.11 (286/30): *σοι* D; QUEM d
d follows Mt 3.17.

1.13 (286/32): ημερας μ̅ D; xl· *diebus* d
D follows par. Mt and Lk.
1.14 (287/2): και D; *sed* d
1.27 (288/4): τις D; *quaenam est* d
D=par. Lk 4.36.
1.28 (288/8): αυτου D pler.; αυτη Θ; *iste* d c ff² r¹; *haec* e; *hic* [b] q; *eius* Lvt (cet.)
1.31 (288/17): αυτοις D; *ei* d
d=par. Mt 8.15.
1.38 (289/1): ΕΙϹ ΤΑϹ ΠΟΛΕΙϹ D; *civitates* d
2.1 (289/20): εισελθων παλιν D; *iterum intravit* d
2.5 (289/33)
σου αι αμαρτιαι ℵ B D L W Θ; σοι αι αμ. C* al.
σοι αι αμ. σου A C³ Γ Π 157; *tibi peccata tua* d a c f q; OM *tua* cet.
2.7 (290/5): OM D; *solus* d
2.9 (290/10): αρον C D L f¹ 33 157 al.; και αρον cet.; *et tolle* d cet.; OM f l q Lvg (Mss)
For this textual difference, see that at 2.11 below.
2.10 (290/13): εξουσιαν εχει D; HABET POTESTATEM d
2.11 (290/16): αρον D; *et tolle* d
d follows Lk 5.24.
2.16 (291/3–4): ΤΩΝ ΑΜΑΡΤΩΛΩΝ / ΚΑΙ ΤΩΝ ΤΕΛΩΝΩΝ D; *publicanis / et peccatoribus* d
2.21 (291/21): επι ϊματιον παλαιον D; *vestimento veteri* d
2.22 (291/25): οινον νεον D; NOUELLUM UINUM d
2.23 (291/31): OM αυτου D; *eius* d
2.26 (292/9): εξεστιν D; *licebat* d
The Old Latin reading is derived from par. Mt 12.4.
3.2 (292/14): εν D; OM d
This is a harmonization not listed by Vogels (*Harmonistik*). D follows Lk 6.6.
3.4 (292/19): εν D; OM d
The addition is from v. 2.
3.5 (292/24): συνλυπουμενος D pler.; OM W; INDIGNATIONIS d
The d reading is a reduplication of *ira* (c. e f l Lvg) and *indignatione* (Lvt cet. exc. a [b]), with the omission of συνλυπομενος (=*contristatus/doleus/tristis*). Does it therefore follow W?
3.6 (292/30): ΠΟΙΟΥΝΤΕϹ D; *faciebant* d
3.8 (293/3): OM D pc.; απο cet.; *ab* d cet.; OM c
3.9 (293/7): OM D; *in* d
Corruption in d.
ibid. (293/8): προσκαρτερη αυτω D; *sibi deserviret* d
3.11 (293/13): ΟΤΑΝ ΟΥΝ ΑΥΤΟΝ ΕΘΕΩΡΟΥΝ D; OM ουν cet.; εθεωρει A Γ al. f¹ 157 al.; CUM VIDERET ILLUM d
There are three differences in this phrase – the inclusion of ουν by D (because of the ending εθεωρουν?); the difference in number between the verbs; and the word order, which may be transposition in d.

3.12 (293/17): *αυτον φανερον ποιωσιν* D; *manifestarent illum* d
3.13 (293/18): *προσκαλειται* D; *vocavit ad se* d
d is following Lk 6.13 (b ff² l q r¹)
3.17 (293/28–9): *ονομα* ... *ϋιοι* D; *nomina* ... *filius* d
3.20 (294/4): ΑΡΤΟΥϹ D; *panem* d
D is a corruption associated with the loss of *αυτους (αυτον Θ)*.
3.23 (294/12): *εν παραβολαις* D; *in parabolam* d
What concerns us here is not the accusative for the ablative (see p. 197 above), but the use of the singular in d.
3.27 (294/21): OM A D W *Γ* al. 157; *δε Θ*; *και* C²; *αλλα* ℵ B C*vid L f¹ al.; *autem* d a ff²; OM Lvt cet.
3.29 (294/30): OM d W; *εἰς* cet.; *in* d pler.; OM a b q
3.32 (295/2): ΠΡΟϹ ΤΟΝ ΟΧΛΟ D; *circum eum turba* d
The error in D is through l. 1, *προς αυτον*.
3.33 (295/7): OM D; *mei* d
The inclusion of the word is probably from par. Mt 12.48.
4.1 (295/13): Ο ΛΑΟϹ D; *turba* d
Perhaps D is following Lk 6.17.
ibid. (295/16): *ην* A D W *Θ Π*; *ησαν* ℵ B C L al.; ERANT d
The other Old Latin manuscripts have the verb in the singular.
4.3 (295/19): OM D; *seminare* d
This is saut du même au même in D.
4.8 (295/33): *εδιδου* D; DAT d
4.19 (297/2): ΑΙ ΜΕΡΙΜΝΑΙ ΤΟΥ ΒΙΟΥ D; SOLLICITUDINEM VICTUS d
Victus may be taken to be the equivalent of *βιου* – compare *saeculi* aur f l Lvg. The accusative is the result of a misunderstanding of the sense – a copyist probably took *errores* as being accusative also.
4.21 (297/11): *ϊνα* D; *et* d
d = par. Mt 5.15.
4.24 (297/18): ΤΑ D; *quid* d
The D reading is probably due to ωΤΑ in l. 17.
4.37 (298/20): *ηδη* D; OM d
This seems to be a widespread error in the Latin tradition.
4.41 (299/1): OM D; *ei* d
5.2 (299/4): *αυτω* D; *illis* d
This may be the influence of the context on d – *illis* in l. 3.
5.3 (299/6): *ειχεν την κατοικησιν* D; *domicilium habebat* d
5.4 (299/10): *εδησαν* D 565 700; *δεδεσθαι* cet.; *ligatus erat* d
D has a divergent text in this passage; d has not been fully corrected to it.
ibid. (299/12): OM D; *amplius* d
5.11 (299/27): *εκει* D; OM d (lect. sing.); *illic/ibi* cet.
At par. Lk 8.32, *εκει* is omitted by W. But d is more probably a separate error than related to this.
ibid. (299/28): *βοσκομενη* D; *pascentium* d

The same variant is found at par. Mt 8.30 (Greek and Latin witnesses) and Lk 8.32 (Greek only).
5.12 (299/30): ΑΠΕΛΘΩΜΕΝ D; *introeamus* d
Vogels suggests that here D follows par. Mt 8.32.
5.14 (300/6): *το γεγονος* D; OM d
Probably omission by homoioteleuton in d.
5.22 (300/27): *των αρχισυναγωγων* D; *archisynagogus* d
The case in d etc. may be derived from par. Mt. 9.18.
ibid. (300/28): ΠΡΟCΕΠΕCΕΝ D; *procidens* d
The d reading is taken from par. Lk 8.41 (*cadens*). Are d and e derived from a Greek text with *πεσων* (from Lk) here?
5.26 (301/6): OM D; *habebat* d
This is caused by homoioarcton with the following *ακουσασα* in D.
5.28 (301/9): ΚΑΝ D pler.; *si* d aur c e; *vel si/si vel* cet.
D has its own text here; d has been partially assimilated to it.
5.37 (302/3): *παρακολουθησαι αυτω* D; SE SEQUI d
5.38 (302/6–7)
κλαιοντων και αλαλαζοντων D 565; *κλαιοντα και αλαλαζοντα* cet.
flentem et lamentantem d; *plorantium et* ⟦*lam*⟧*entanti*⟦*um*⟧ a
5.39 (302/8): *κλαιετε* D; TURBATIS d
5.43 (302/23–4): *μηδεις γνοι / τουτο* D; *nemini dicerent /* d
d is taken from par. Lk 8.56 *nemini dicere*.
6.4 (303/8): *εν ταις συνγενεσι* (*συνγενευσι* D^{A}) D; *in genere suo* d
6.6 (303/14): *κυκλω* D; ET CIRCUMIBAT d
Here d has been influenced by the context.
6.12 (303/31): *εκηρυξαν* ℵ D B C al.; *εκηρυσσον* A N W Θ al.; *praedicabant* d pler.
6.15 (304/9): *οτι* D cet.; *quasi* d al.; OM cet
Both texts are in error – they should read *οτι προφητης ως εις των προφητων*. It may be that d has been partially assimilated to D.
6.19 (304/20): *ηρωδιας* D; *herodes* d
ibid. (304/21): *ηθελεν* D; QUAEREBAT d
Quaero is generally used for *ζητεω*. Has d been influenced by e.g. Mk 14.11?
6.22 (304/33): *δε* D; *και* cet.; *-que* d; *et* b f; *vero* c; *autem* a ff^2
6.23 (305/5): ΕΙ ΤΙ ΑΝ D; *οτι (ο) εαν* cet.; *quod quidquid* d i q
6.26 (305/13)
ΠΕΡΙΛΥΠΟC ΓΕΝΟΜΕΝΟC D; *και περιλ. γεν.* cet.
et contristatus est d al.; *tristis factus est* a; *contristatus factus est* q
6.28 (305/19)
δε A D N Θ f^{13} 157 al.; *και* B C L W f^1 al.
et d a c ff^2 i; OM aur l Lvg; *-que* cet.
6.33 (306/6): *αυτου* D; *ibi* d
6.34 (306/7): *εξελθων* D; EXIENTES d
6.35 (306/11): *δε* D; *et* d
D etc. follow par. Mt 14.25/Lk 9.12.

ibid. (306/14): *ηδη* D; *et iam* d
d etc. are harmonized to line 11 (see above).
6.39 (306/24): OM D (lect. sing.); *illis* d
6.41 (306/31): *αυτου* P^{45} A D N W *Θ Π* f^1 f^{13} 157 al.; OM ℵ B L 33 al.; OM d (lect. sing.); *suis* cet.
6.45 (307/8–9): / *αυτος δε απολυει* D; *dum ipse* / *demitteret* d pler.
6.47 (307/11): *ην παλαι* D; *iam erat* d
6.51 (307/25): *ανεβη* D; *ascendens* d
Compare Mt 14.32 ASCENDENTIBUS. Is this reading synoptic harmonization in d?
7.2 (308/15): *αυτου* D; SUORU͡ d
This is influence of the context (preceding DISCIPULORUM) on d.
7.4 (308/23): *απ αγορας οταν ελθωσιν* D W; CUM VENERINT A FORO d
7.6 (309/3): *αγαπα* D W; *τιμα* cet.; *honorat* d; *diligat* a b c TE
Compare par. Mt 15.8, where D has *τιμα*, d al. *diligit*. Isa. 29.13 reads *τιμωσιν*.
ibid. (309/4): ΑΦΕCΤΗΚΕΝ D; *est* d
The reading *est* seems to be following par. Mt 15.8 D 1424 sy
7.8 (309/7)
βαπτισμους ξεστων και ποτηριων D *Θ* 12 28 330 (565) OM cet.
baptizantes orceos et calices d a ff^2 i ⟨r^1⟩
baptismos calicum et urceorum b c q
The addition is from v. 4. The rendering in d is a separate translation (at v. 4 it reads *baptismos calicum et orceorum*), suggesting that a reviser, bringing it into agreement with the Greek, did not recognize the doublet.
ibid. (309/10): *κρατειτε* D; *tenentes* d
Is this influence of the context on d?
7.12 (308b/21, 309/20)
ΟΥΚ ΕΝΑΦΙΕΤΑΙ D; *ουκετι αφιετε* pler.
iam non missum facitis d al.; *non sinetis* a; *et ultra* aur f l Lvg
7.20 (310/12–13): *το* . . . / *εκπορευομενον* D; *quae* . . . / *exeunt* d
The Old Latin tradition seems unanimously to be following par. Mt 15.18, where d has *qui . . . exeunt*.
7.21 (310/16): *πορνεια* D; *adulteria* d
The singular in D may simply be caused through the influence of the neuter plural endings in the context.
ibid. (*ibid.*): *φονος* D W (prim. *φονοι*) Ss Sp; *φονοι* cet.; *homicidia* d cet.
7.26 (310/28)
ΦΥΝΙCCA D (with ΟΙ written above the line over Υ)
συροφοινικισσα pler.
syrophoenissa d cet. (spelt variously)
phoenissa i
8.2 (311/33): ΕΠΙ ΤΟΥ ΟΧΛΟΥ ΤΟΥΤΟΥ D; SUPER ISTAM TURBAM d
8.3 (312/3): ΕΙC ΟΙΚΟΝ ΟΥ ΘΕΛΩ D; NOLO IN DOMO d
Transposition in d. *Εις οικον* is not, as is the rest of the addition, from par. Mt 15.32.
8.6 (312/10): *λαβων* D; *accepit* d
Harmonization of d to par. Mt 15.36

8.10 (312/20–2)
ANEBH ... KAI D; ενεβη ... και Θ 565 700; εμβας ... και W; εμβας ... OM cet.
ASCENDENS ... ET d; *ascendit* ... OM a; *ascendit* ... *et* f k q; *ascendens* ... OM cet.
The reading in d is a conflation of the D and majority readings (D = par. Mt 15.39).
8.11 (312/24): συνζητειν συν αυτω D; OM d (lect. sing.)
This is probably homoioteleuton in d, independent of the other authorities which omit the phrase.
8.13 (312/32): ENBAC D; *ascendit* d
8.17 (313/9)
πεπηρωμενη (ω above first η D) εστιν η καρδια ϋμων D 0143
ετι πεπ. εχετε την καρδιαν υμων A X Γ Π al.
εχ. την καρδιαν υμων ℵ B C L al.
sic obtusa sunt corda vestra d b c i
8.19 (313/16): πληρεις D pler.; OM $P^{45vid.}$ $f^{13pler.}$ al.; OM d al.; *plenos* f l Lvg
ibid. (*ibid.*): λεγουσιν αυτω D; *ad illi dixerunt* d
Compare l. 19 – d is adopting the words found there.
8.21 (313/20): πως ουπω D; *quomodo non* d
d = par. Mt 16.11 etc.
8.23 (313/28): βλεπεις B C D* Δ Θ 565; βλεπει cet.; *videret* d
8.25 (313/30): OM D cet.; EI d
8.30 (314/15): ϊνα D; OM d
d is harmonized (I think to Lk 9.21 rather than Mt 16.20).
8.31 (314/20): και αποκτανθηναι D; OM d
Homoioarcton in d.
8.36 (315/5): τον κοσμον ολον D; *universum orbem* d
9.3 (315/25)
λευκα λια (λιαν D^{B}) ως χιων D A al.; OM ως χιων P^{45vid} ℵ B C L W Θ
candida nimis d k; + *velut/tamquam nix* cet.
9.5 (315/29): τω ιηυ D; *ad ihm* d
d is harmonized to par. Lk 9.33.
ibid. (315/32): μωϋσει μιαν D; UNUM MOYSI d
Transposition in d. Compare par. Mt 17.4 *unum helias* q.
9.10 (316/13)
οταν D W f^{1} f^{13}; OM Θ; το cet.
QUOD d; OM k q; *cum* cet.
d seems to be a translation of το.
9.11 (316/16): OM D f^{1} pc.; οτι cet.; *quia* d aur c f l Lvg; OM cet.
9.12 (316/18): ελθων ... αποκαστανει ℵ* D; VENIT ... RESTITUERE d
Harmonization to par. Mt 17.11 in d.
9.18 (317/4): αυτο εκβαλωσιν D; EICERENT ILLUT d
Harmonization to par. Lk 9.40 in d.
9.19 (317/7): ανεξομαι ϋμων D; VOS PATIAR d
Transposition in d. Compare par. Mt 17.17 *vos patiar* ff^{1}; Lk 9.41 *vos sustineo* e.

9.30 (318/5–6): *επορευοντο / δια της γαλιλαιας* D; TRANSIEBANT / IN GALILAEA d
The preposition in d is from par. Mt 17.22. The verb is from the majority Greek reading.
9.34 (318/17): ΜΙΖΩΝ ΓΕΝΗΤΑΙ ΑΥΤΩΝ D; ESSE ILLORUM MAIOR d
9.38 (318/26): *απεκριθη . . . και* D; *respondens* d
d follows par. Lk 9.49.
9.39 (318/31): *γαρ εστιν* D; *est enim* d
ibid. (318/33): *ταχυ* D cet.; OM F* f[1pler.] 565; OM d pler.; *cito* aur f l q Lvg
9.42 (319/9): *ονικος* D; OM d (lect. sing.)
9.45 (319/20): *σοι εστιν* D; *est tibi* d
D is harmonized to Mt 18.8 (the parallel passage, but not the parallel phrase).
9.47 (319/28): *σοι εστιν* D; *est tibi* d
Harmonization to par. Mt 19.8 in D.
10.8 (320/24): *ουκετι* D; *non* d
This is likely to be simply a poor translation.
10.9 (320/25): OM D; *ergo* d
This reading could have been caused by the abbreviation *ο'* for *ουν* being confused with the preceding *ὁ*.
10.14 (321/6): *των γαρ τοιουτων εστιν* D; *talium est enim* d
Transposition in the Latin tradition.
10.15 (321/9): ΕΙC ΑΥΤΗΝ ΕΙCΕΛΕΥCΕΤΑΙ D; *intravit in illum* d
For the text of D, see Mk 10.23 and par.
10.25 (322/5): OM *εστιν* D; *est* d cet.; OM a
The Greek text of D is unique in this passage; d follows the normal text.
10.30 (322/26): OM D; *nunc* d
The omission seems to be a harmonization to par. Lk 18.30.
ibid. (322/29): *διωγμου* D; *persecutionibus* d
Is D a harmonization to Mt 13.21 par. Mk 4.17?
10.32 (323/2): *παραλαβων* D; *adsumpsit* d
Here there is harmonization in d k to par. Mt 20.17. But there d has *suscepit* (*adsumpsit* e cet.). At par. Lk 18.31 only d f have *adsumens* correctly (*adsumpsit* pler.).
ibid. (323/3): *τα μελλοντα αυτω* D; EI ESSENT d
10.35 (323/16): OM D 118 al.; *ινα* cet.; *ut* d pler.; OM b i k r[1]
ibid. (*ibid.*): *σε ερωτησωμεν* D; *petierimus te* d
10.38 (323/24): *πεινω* D; VIVITURUS SUM d (scil. *bibi-*)
d is harmonized to par. Mt 20.22.
10.40 (323/30): *μου* D; OM d (lect. sing.)
Hom. in d (I use this convenient abbreviation in the sense given it by Clark, *Primitive Text*, p. 1).
10.41 (323/32): OM D; *και* cet.; *et* d aur f k l Lvg; OM cet.
10.43 (324/7): *μεγας* D; *maior* d
At par. Lk 22.26, Codex Bezae has *μειζων*/*maior*. At the Matthaean parallel (20.26), D has *μεγας*, d *magnus* (*maior* cet.). Here it is therefore possibly separate harmonization to these passages in d cet.
10.44 (324/9): *ειναι πρωτος* D; *primus esse* d

At par. Mt 20.27 d has *esse primus* and D ειναι πρωτος: there they seem to be harmonizing to this passage. But here the harmonization appears to be in d, towards Mk 9.35 (OM D/d).
10.48 (324/22): ΕΚΡΑΞΕΝ D; *clamabat* d
Harmonization to par. Mt 20.31 (εκραξαν) in D.
11.2 (325/9): ΛΥCΑΝΤΕC ... ΚΑΙ D*; *solvite ... et* d
11.5 (325/16): τινες των D; *qui erant* d
The reading in b d i may be a partial harmonization to par. Lk 19.33.
11.6 (325/18)
ειρηκει D; ενετειλατο A Θ al.; ειπεν ℵ B C L W
praeceperat d a aur f l Lvg; *dixit* k; *dixerat* cet.
11.7 (325/22)
καθειζει D W f[1] al.; εκαθησαν ℵ* ℓ184 al.; εκαθισεν pler.
SEDEBAT d; *sedit* cet.
11.15 (326/13): ΕΙCΕΛΘΩΝ D; INTRAVERUNT d
D has been affected by par. Jn 2.14.
ibid. (326/14): ΕΝ ΤΩ ΪΕΡΩ D; *in templum* d
D is a harmonization to par. Jn 2.14.
11.19 (326/31)
εξεπορευετο ℵ C D Θ al.; εξεπορευοντο A B W *Π*
egrediebantur d aur c r[1]
11.25 (327/15): OM D; υμων cet.; *vestra* d cet.; OM Cy
11.30 (327/32): ΟΥΡΑΝΩΝ D; ουρανου cet.; *caelo* d cet.
11.31 (328/3): ΛΕΓΕΙ D; ερει cet.; *dicet* d; *dicit* b l
ibid. (*ibid.*)
ουν ℵ B C[2] D al.; OM A C* W al.
OM d cet.; *ergo* aur f l Lvg
12.1 (328/11): λεγειν D; *loqui* d
The reading in D is from par. Lk 20.9.
12.2 (328/18): του καρπου D; *fructibus* d
D is from par. Lk 20.10.
12.5 (328/27): πολλους D; *plures* d
Harmonization in d cet. to par. Mt 21.36.
12.6 (328/29): ουν D; ETIAM d
I suggested ('Translation of *ΟΥΝ*', p. 272) that *etiam* is a recollection of ετι ουν.
12.14 (329/20): ΑΥΤΟΝ ΟΙ ΦΑΡΙCΑΙΟΙ D; PHARISAEI EUM d
12.16 (329/32): ειπαν D; *dicunt* d
Harmonization to par. Mt 22.21 in d etc.
12.19 (330/7): OM D; *ut* d
Harmonization to par. Lk 20.28 by D.
12.26 (330/31): ως D; *quomodo* d; *sicut* q
D etc. has been harmonized to par. Lk 20.27.
12.30 (331/13): OM D; *est* d
The clause has been inserted from par. Mt 22.38, where εστιν stands in all witnesses. The omission here is hard to explain.

12.31 (331/14): ταυτῃ D; *illi* d

D here follows its own text of par. Mt 22.39; d follows, not its own text, but that of 1 33 69. The two columns have been separately harmonized to the Matthaean passage.

12.34 (331/27): μακραν ει D; *es longe* d

12.36 (332/1–2): ειπεν ... λεγει D; OM ... *dixit* d

There are two reasons for the difference here – the omission of the first verb in d, which was probably accidental, and the fact that D is harmonized to its own text of par. Lk 20.42.

ibid. (332/4): ὑποκατω D; *scamillum* d

The d text is harmonized to par. Lk 20.43.

12.38 (332/8)

δε D Θ 565; OM A W 157 al.; και ℵ B al.

et d c e k l q Lvg; *autem* aur c²; *at* cet.

The phrase in D is entirely different.

ibid. (322/11): ποιεισθαι D Θ 565; OM cet.; FACITIS d; OM cet.

The reading in d has been translated from a Greek text having the itacistic corruption ποιεισθε.

13.10 (333/31): OM D pler.; δε W Θ 565 al.; *autem* d al.; *enim* k; OM a aur l n q Lvg

13.11 (334/3)

AYTO D; εκεινο W f¹³ pc.; τουτο cet.

hoc d a i n r¹; *illut* k; *ipsum* c; *quid* ff²; *id* cet.

d seems to be following the majority Greek text.

13.17 (334/22): OM D; *autem* d

D has been harmonized to par. Lk 21.23.

13.22 (335/7): OM D; *etiam* d

Etiam is a harmonization to par. Mt 24.24.

13.25 (335/16): των ουρανων D; *caelestium* d

D has been harmonized to par. Mt 24.30.

13.26 (335/18): επι D; *cum* d

D has been harmonized to par. Mt 24.30. At par. Lk 21.27, q has *cum* for εν.

13.27 (335/23): ουρανου D; *caelorum* d

d cet. are harmonized to par. Mt 24.31 (though less exactly than r¹ which adopts the precise words, and not just the plural).

13.28 (335/27): το θερος εστιν D; *est aestas* d

13.30 (335/33): παντα ταυτα D; HAEC OMNIA d

d may have been harmonized to par. Mt 24.34.

13.33 (336/8): OM D W; εστιν cet.; *sit* d pler.; *veniet* e k; OM a c

14.1 (336/24): OM D; *dolo* d

D is probably harmonized to par. Lk 22.2.

14.2 (336/26): εσται θορυβος D; *tumultus fierat* d

d etc. have been harmonized to par. Mt 26.5.

14.3 (336/30): OM D (lect. sing.); *pistici praetiosi* d

D is harmonized to par. Mt 26.7.

14.8 (337/13): OM D; *unguento* d

d etc. (approximately) follow par. Lk 7.46.

14.9 (337/16): OM D pler.; οτι W min. pc.; *quod* d f i; *quia* a k; *quoniam* c; OM cet.
14.10 (337/20): EK D; *unus de* d
The Old Latin seems to be a conflation of the two Greek readings, but it is more likely to be taken from par. Mt 26.14. D could be from par. Lk 22.3.
14.12 (337/26): το πασχα εθυον D; *pascha immolabatur* d i q; *pasc. sacrificarent* k
The d reading is influenced by par. Lk 22.7, where there is a present infinitive passive.
14.15 (338/5–6)
ΑΝΑΓΑΙΟΝ ΟΙΚΟΝ ΕϹΤΡⲰΜΕΝΟΝ ΜΕΓΑΝ ΕΤΟΙΜΟΝ D
STRATUM PARATUM GRANDE d
stratum grande paratum ff[2]
There are many variants here, in both Greek and Latin. For the reading, see Harris, *Codex*, p. 80 and note. To this should be added the reading οικον in Θ at par. Lk 22.12. The two columns of D certainly present two different Greek texts, d and ff[2] following parallel Luke.
14.16 (338/8)
ΚΑΙ ΕΞΗΛΘΟΝ ΟΙ ΜΑΘΗΤΑΙ ΑΥΤΟΥ D; OM cet.
ET VENERUNT DISCIPULI EIUS d; OM cet.
d has attempted to make sense of the repetition in D, by altering the meaning of the second εξηλθον. In the next line, the same problem arises for d –
ηλθον D cet.; εισηλθον 49; OM ℵ*
VENIT d; *venerunt* cet.
14.29 (339/15): ΟΥΚ ΕΓⲰ ΟΥ D*; ουκ εγω D[s.m.]; *ego non* d
It seems that harmonization to par. Mt 26.33 has led to the readings in D.
14.31 (339/20): εαν D; *etsi* d
Par. Mt 26.35 has κἂν, and *etsi* ⟦⟨a⟩⟧ aur d, *etiamsi* cet. The text of d has been harmonized either to that, or to *etsi* at Mk 14.29. The latter is perhaps more likely.
14.36 (340/4): OM D; SI d
Harmonisation to par. Mt 26.39 in d only.
ibid. (340/6): αλλ D; OM d (lect. sing.)
This could be the influence of par. Mt 26.39 on d.
ibid. (340/6–7): ο ... ο D; *sicut ... sicut* d
Harmonization to par. Mt 26.39 in d c ff[2].
14.49 (341/10): εν τω ϊερω διδασκων D; *docens in templo* d
The reading in d could be harmonization to par. Mt 26.55 A W Γ al. It is more likely to be a transposition within the Latin tradition.
14.52 (341/16): γυμνος εφυγεν D; PROFUGIT NUDUS d
14.54 (341/21): ηκολουθησεν D; *sequebatur* d
The imperfect is harmonization to par. Mt 26.58 or Lk 22.54.
ibid. (341/24)
ΘΕΡΜΕΝΟΜΕΝΟϹ D; CALEFACIENTES SE d
Lvt (cet.) have the verb in the singular.
At Jn 18.18, r[1] reads *cal[e⟨fa⟩cie]ntes*. The reading in d may be a harmonization to such a reading.
14.56 (341/30–1): ΕΨΕΥΔΟΜΑΡΤΥΡΟΥΝ / ΕΛΕΓΟΝ D*; εψ. και ελεγον D[B]; *falsum testimonium* / *dicebant* d

Is D* a conflation of the Greek and Latin forms of the text? It is also possible that it is harmonized to the context – see v. 57.

14.57 (342/1): ΚΑΙ ΕΛΕΓΟΝ D; *dicebant* d

Here d has been harmonized to v. 56.

14.58 (342/4): OM D; *hunc* d

This is homoioteleuton in D.

14.62 (342/19): OM D; UENIENTEM d

14.64 (342/23): *την βλασφημιαν* D A Θ f¹³; *παντες την βλασφημιαν* W f¹ al.; *της βλασφημιας* ℵ B pler.; OMNES BLASPHEMIAS d; *blasphemiam* pler.

This is an error in d, where the plural *blasphemias* is due to a misconstruing of *omnes* as accusative rather than nominative. The basic text is that of W etc.

14.67 (343/1): OM D; *et* d

14.68 (343/4): OM D; *et* d

14.69 (343/8): *και* D; OM d

D may be harmonized to par. Mt 26.71 A C W f¹ f¹³ pler.

15.2 (343/26): *αυτω λεγει* D; *dixit illi* d

15.5 (343/32): *ουκετι ουδεν* D; *nihil amplius* d

15.7 (344/6): *πεποιηκεισαν φονον* D; *fecerat homicidium* d

15.11 (344/14): ΤѠ ΟΧΛѠ D*; *turbas* d

The plural is a harmonization to par. Mt 27.20 (*turbis* d).

15.20 (345/4): OM D (lect. sing.); *suis* d

15.24 (345/15–16)

σταυρωσαντες αυτον / *διαμεριζονται* D; *cruci adfixerunt eum* / *diviserunt* d

-entes ... -erunt aur l Lvg

D is harmonized to par. Mt 27.35.

15.26 (345/20–1): *επιγραφη ... επιγεγραμμενη* D; CAUSA ... INSCRIPTIO d

d is trying to harmonize with par. Lk 22.38 *inscriptio* a d.

15.27 (345/23): ΣΤΑΥΡΟΥΝΤΑΙ D; *crucifixerunt* d

D is harmonized to par. Mt 27.38 (apart from the fact that d does not translate the historic present).

15.29 (345/27): *ουα* D; OM d

d is probably influenced by par. Mt 27.40, even though D/d read *ουα*/*va* there.

ibid. (345/28): OM D; *illut* d

This is par. Mt 27.40 again. Here also D/d are alone in omitting the word there.

ibid. (*ibid.*): OM D; *in* d

At par. Mt 27.40 (again) D reads *εν*, d omits it. The harmonization could be in either.

15.30 (345/29): OM D; *et* d

d has been harmonized to par. Mt 27.40.

15.34 (346/7): *τη ενατη ωρα* D; *hora nona* d

ibid. (346/10)

ѠΝΙΔΙϹΑϹ ΜΕ D; *με εγκατελιπες* f¹ f¹³ 157; *εγκ. με* ℵ B L 565

me dereliquisti d

In order, d is following par. Mt 27.46, unless the copyist has transposed the two words. What is more important is that it has not adopted the unique reading of D.

15.36 (346/13): *πλησας* D; PLENA d

D is from par. Mt 27.48. So too is d – cp. *accepta spongia* – but independently.

ibid. (346/14): ΕΠΙΘΕΙϹ ΚΑΛΑΜѠ D; ET POTUM DABAT EI DICENS d
The corruption continues. Each column has omitted a different phrase. The Latin has been left making slightly less pronounced nonsense than the Greek.
15.41 (346/27–8): ΑΙ ΚΑΙ ... ΗΚΟΛΟΥΘΗϹΑΝ D; *αι και ... ηκολουθουν* N *Γ Θ* f[1] f[13] 565 al.; *αι ... ηκολουθουν* cet.; QUAE ... SEQUEBATUR d;
quae et ... sequebantur n;
quae ... sequebantur pler.
The aorist in D is from par. Mt 27.55. The text of d restricts the application of the clause to Salome.
15.43 (346/33): *ευσχημων* D cet.; *dives* d c ff[2] q
The d reading follows par. Mt 27.57.
ibid. (347/3): ΤΟ ΠΤѠΜΑ D; *το σωμα* cet.; *corpus* d
The Latin follows the majority Greek reading.
15.44 (347/6)
τεθνηκει D ℓ252; *τεθνηκεν* W *Θ* min. pc.; *απεθανεν* cet.
mortuus esset et d pler.; *defunctus esset* ff[2]
The reading *obisset* in l. 4 shows that here d follows the majority text.
15.46 (347/13): *εκ* D; *in* d
Harmonization to par. Mt 27.60 in d.
16.5 (347/28): *νεανισκον ειδον* D; *viderunt iubenem* d

As before, let us suggest the causes for these various differences.

1. Influence of the context
   On D: 2.16; 3.4, 6, 32
   On d: 5.2, 39; 6.6, 19; 7.2, 8², 21;, 14.57
2. Translation error
   4.37; 5.4²; 6.24²; 10.8, 32.

3a. Harmonization to a Gospel parallel
   In D: 1.6, 13, 27; 3.2; 4.1; 6.35; 8.2; 9.45, 47; 10.15, 30¹, 30², 48; 11.15¹, 15²; 12.1, 2, 19, 26, 36¹; 13.17, 25, 26; 14.1, 3, 29, 69; 15.24, 27
   In d: 1.7, 11, 14, 31; 2.11, 21, 26; 3.13, 33; 4.21; 5.22¹, 22², 43; 6.4; 7.6², 20; 8.6, 21, 30; 9.5¹, 12, 18, 30, 38; 10.32², 38, 43; 11.5; 12.5, 16, 36²; 13.22, 27, 30; 14.2, 8, 12, 36¹, 36², 36³, 54¹, 54²; 15.11, 26, 29¹, 29², 30, 34, 43, 46
   In both separately: 12.31; 14.10; 15.29³, 36¹

3b. Harmonization to elsewhere in Mark
   In D: 4.24
   In d: 6.19², 35²; 8.19²; 10.44; 14.31

4. Transposition
   By D alone: none
   By D with support: 15.7²; 16.5
   By d alone: 2.10, 22; 5.37; 7.4; 8.2, 3; 9.5²; 12.14
   By d with support: 1.9; 2.21; 3.9², 12; 5.3; 6.47; 8.36; 9.19, 39¹; 10.14, 32²; 12.34; 13.28; 14.49, 52; 15.5, 34²
   In either of the two: 9.34; 10.35²

5. Textual differences
   Where both columns are alone: 3.11; 8.10; 14.15; 15.41
   Where D is alone: 6.23, 26; 7.12, 26; 10.25; 11.30, 31; 13.11; 15.34[1], 43[2]
   Where d is alone: 3.5; 4.1[2]; 6.41; 8.25; 9.10; 11.7; 12.38[2]
   Where neither is alone: 1.28; 2.5, 9; 3.8, 27, 29; 5.11, 38; 6.12, 22, 28, 45; 7.6, 21[2]; 8.17, 19[1], 23; 9.3, 11, 39[2]; 10.35[1], 41; 11.6, 19, 25, 31[2]; 12.38[1]; 13.10, 33; 14.9, 64; 15.44

There are a higher number of places, as we said at the outset, where carelessness is the cause of the discrepancy. What Clark generically described as 'hom.' is found in D at 4.3, and in d at 5.14, 26; 8.11, 31; 10.40; 14.58. There are also errors in D at 2.7; 3.20; 4.41; 6.39; 10.9; 12.30; 14.56, 62, 67; 15.20; in d at 3.9, 17; 4.8, 19; 5.11; 6.34; 8.13; 9.42; 12.6, 36; and in both at 15.36[2].

At 2.1; 6.51; 11.2 we have the intrusion of the construction with a participle followed by *και* and a finite verb (see chapter 14).

The number of places where d has been partially assimilated to the text is lower than in Luke: we have 5.4[1], 28; 6.15; 7.8.

It will be noticed that the number of textual and harmonizing readings is particularly high in chapter 14, where there are three of the former and thirteen of the latter, and 15, where there are four and eight. This higher incidence is due to the nature of the material, where confusion between the Gospels is particularly prevalent, and not to a decreasing thoroughness of revision.

If we compare the degree of harmonization between the two columns, using Vogels' statistics (*Harmonistik*, p. 106) as a foundation, we find that 497 harmonizations are shared between them; there are 526 in D, and 546 in Mark – that is to say, D has twenty-nine not found in d, and d has forty-nine not found in D.

THE ACTS OF THE APOSTLES

In coming to Acts, we must draw up new criteria for identifying differences between the columns. This is because the Latin version has a quite different character from anything to be found in the Gospels.

A major problem in our undertaking is readings involving *δε* and *τε*, *autem* and *quoque*. The confusion between the two words in Greek is a regular feature of the textual tradition of Acts, and the problem is compounded by the inconsistency with which the words are rendered. Not only are several possible Latin words used, but there is also a tendency to omit the conjunction altogether. *Δε* is omitted in d where it is found in all Greek witnesses at 2.12; 3.6; 5.23; 13.34; 14.2; 16.12; 17.17; 18.17, 19; 19.5, 33; 20.2, 11; 21.14; where D reads *δε* and other witnesses *και* at 1.15; where D reads *τε* and other witnesses divide between *δε* and *και* at 8.8. It is translated by *et* at 13.43; 14.23; 15.7, 31, 36; 16.40; 20.8, 15. It is rendered by *-que* at

15.12; 16.16 (and 20.3?). *Τε* is often not translated, and *quoque* seems to have been used on occasion for δε as well as for *Τε*. *Και*, meaning 'even' or 'also', is omitted by d at 2.29. With this kind of confusion, it is very difficult to decide what Greek reading may lie behind d, where there is a variation. It may be presumed that sometimes the omission of δε (for example) follows a Greek variant, and sometimes reflects the decision of a translator. My rule has been to include such a variant where Tischendorf provides attestation by Greek witnesses, and to ignore it where he does not. This procedure is unlikely to meet with universal approbation, but it attempts to include some differences out of a group where a number may be presumed to indicate a genuine variation in text between the columns.

I have attempted to show ('Translation of *OYN*', p. 267) that such confusion extends to other conjunctions. Whereas the Gospels are fairly consistent in their rendering of *οὖν* by *ergo*, in Acts a far greater variety of words is used: *autem*, *enim*, *ergo*, *itaque*, *-que*, *quidem*, *vero*, *quidem ergo*, *tunc ergo*.

Another clearly marked habit in the Latin Acts of Codex Bezae is the use of the perfect indicative to translate a perfect participle, *without* the introduction of *et* or any other copula to connect the phrase with what follows. This may be found at 3.26; 15.4 *bis*; 16.19, 27 *bis*, 33, 35, 40(?); 18.5, 18; 19.14, 25; 20.13; 21.26. At 16.21, where d intends *praedicantes*, we have the opposite phenomenon. And as a further confusion, there are a few places where, as in Mark, the conjunction is dropped and *cum* used (e.g. 4.7 *cum stat*; see also 8.18; 13.16). At 2.14; 21.11, 15, the perfect and *et* translate a participle. Such differences are further confused by the construction consisting of a participle followed by *και* or *et* and a finite verb, which we have already mentioned.

The way in which prepositions are treated in the Latin column is also quite different. *Εἰς* with the accusative is generally ignored. *'Εν* may or may not be translated, or *in* may be found where the Greek has a simple dative (e.g. 16.40).

The appearance of *constructio ad sensum* in d (12.22) and the variation between the columns in 'hand' or 'hands', 'crowd' or 'crowds' cannot be treated as genuine differences.

I have not included places where there is real uncertainty as to the reading of either column, and have not taken into account the old collations of the bottom of F504b (Scrivener, pp. 446f) – these lines are treated as though they were lost, even though the collators do record readings that indicate a difference between the columns.

Once we have discounted the apparent differences that are actually simply part of how the Latin translation has been made, we find far fewer real differences to exist than had first been supposed. Findlay recorded 607. I began with a list of 753, but have reduced that number by more than half. Our hopes that this analysis may advance our understanding of the Bezan tradition are amply justified by what we learn about its text of Acts.

A number of interesting readings deserve separate mention. At 4.21 and 13.19 there is a double translation in the Latin, and at 12.23 d gives us a corruption of *sede* as an alternative translation of βηματος, so that its reading *a vermibus comestis* is the same as the D text. At 4.22 and 11.23 we may see transposition happening in D. The readings of d at 11.29, 13.47, 48 and 20.15 (*pridie*) are nonsense. At 11.11 the text of d could be a corruption of *eram*, which would give us the text ημην where D has ημεν. At 15.7 d intends to write *ut exquirant*, and at 15.31 it has a corruption of *exhortatione*.

It remains to be said that, as we found in studying the correctors, to collect the Latin evidence of Acts is not an easy task. Given what will prove to be the character of many of the differences, this is not too serious a problem. I have simply used Wordsworth and White. I have ignored all other versional evidence, even the Harklean, which so often supports the D text. Little patristic material is cited, though Lucifer's interesting evidence (drawn from Wordsworth and White) will be found.

1.3 (416/10)
ΤΕϹϹΑΡΑΚΟΝΤΑ ΗΜΕΡΩΝ D*; δι τεσσ. ημ. D[A]; δι ημ. τεσσ. cet.
POST DIES QUADRAGINTA d; *per dies quad.* pler.
1.5 (416/20)
ΚΑΙ Ο ΜΕΛΛΕΤΑΙ ΛΑΜΒΑΝΕΙΝ D*; OM D[s.m.]
et eum accipere habetis d
Transposition in d (see Ropes, ad loc.). This is in a longer reading.
1.7 (416/28): ϋμων εστιν D; *est vestrum* d
1.11 (417/14): d* alone reads *enim* (=γαρ??) after *sic*.
2.1 (419/12–14)
ΚΑΙ ΕΓΕΝΕΤΟ ΕΝ ΤΑΙϹ ΗΜΕΡΑΙϹ ΕΚΕΙΝΑΙϹ / ΤΟΥ ΣΥΝΠΛΗΡΟΥϹΘΑΙ ΤΗΝ ΗΜΕΡΑΝ / ΤΗϹ ΠΕΝΤΕΚΟϹΤΗϹ D
και εν τω συνπλ. την ημ. της πεντ. cet.
ET FACTUM EST IN DIEBUS ILLIS / ET CUM IMPLERENTUR DIES / PENTECOSTES d
It is clear here that d has simply had the longer D reading added in front of a translation of the majority reading.
ibid. (419/15)
ΟΝΤΩΝ ΑΥΤΩΝ ΠΑΝΤΩΝ D; ησαν παντες ομου cet.
erant simul omnes d; *erant omnes simul* Lvt (pler.)
2.2 (419/16): ΕΙΔΟΥ D = ιδου Cyr; OM cet.; OM d
2.6 (419/31–2)
ΚΑΙ ΗΚΟΥΟΝ ΕΙϹ ΕΚΑϹΤΟϹ / ΛΑΛΟΥΝΤΑϹ ΤΑΙϹ ΓΛΩϹϹΑΙϹ ΑΥΤΩΝ D
οτι ηκουον εις εκαστος τη ιδια διαλεκτω λαλουντων αυτων cet.
QUI (*quia* d[K]) AUDIEBANT UNUSQUISQUE / LOQUENTES EOS LINGUA SUA d
2.9 (420/8): OM και D (lect. sing.); *et* d
Is the error due to the preceding ελαμειται?
2.12 (420/21): τουτο ειναι D; *esse hoc* d
2.14 (420/24): ΤΟΤΕ ϹΤΑΘΕΙϹ D; σταθεις cet.; *cum stetisset autem* d

2.18 (421/10): απο του πνευματος μου D cet.; SPIRITUM MEUM d
This is carelessness in d.
2.24 (421/29): ουκ ην δυνατον D; POSSIBILE NON ESSET d
2.29 (422/18): της ημερας ταυτης D; *in hunc diem* d
2.30 (422/22–3)
ΚΑΤΑ CΑΡΚΟΝ ΑΝΑCΤΗCΑΙ ΤΟΝ ΧΡΙCΤΟΝ ΚΑΙ ΚΑΘΙCΑΙ D*; και καθ. D[s.m.];
το κατα σαρκα αναστησειν τον χριστον καθισαι P 049 462 al.; καθισαι pler.
secundum carne suscitare christum collocare d*; *collocare* d[s.m.]
2.32 (422/28): παντεις ημεις D; *nos omnes* d
2.39 (423/24): οσους D cet.; ους A C pc.; QUOS d; *quoscumque* cet.
2.42 (423/32): OM D cet.; εν A pc.; *in* d cet.
This may be a translation variant.
2.45 (424/8–9)
ΚΑΙ ΟΣΟΙ ΚΤΗΜΑΤΑ ΕΙΧΟΝ / Η D; και τα κτηματα και τας cet.
ET QUI POSSESSIONES HABEBANT / ET d
Here, it looks as if d has been partially altered from the majority to the D text.
2.46 (424/13–14)
ΚΑΙ ΚΑΤΟΙΚΟΥCΑΝ (κατοικους D[s.m.]) ΕΠΙ ΤΟ ΑΥΤΟ ΚΛΩΝΤΕC ΤΕ ΑΡΤΟ͞ / ΜΕΤΕΛΑΜΒΑΝΟΝ D
κλ. τε κατ' οικον αρτον μετ. cet.
ET PER DOMOS (+*in* d[G]) IDIPSUM CAPIEBANT PANES / ACCIPIENTES d
d has a text between those of D and the main Greek tradition.
3.5 (425/1): ΑΤΕΝΕΙCΑC D; επειχεν cet.; ADTENDEBAT d; *intendebat* pler.
3.10 (425/18): επι τη ωρεα πυλη D; IN PORTA ILLA PULCHRA d
3.13 425/33): ΗΜΕΙC D; υμεις μεν cet.; OM d (lect. sing.); *vos quidem* cet.
3.15 (426/10): ου D cet.; QUIBUS d; *cuius* cet.
3.16 (426/12–13): ΤΟΥΤΟΝ ... / ΟΤΙ (OM D[s.m.]) D; τουτον ου ... OM cet.;
hunc quem ... / OM d pler.
3.18 (426/20): Ο D; α cet.; *quae* d pler.
3.22 (427/1): ημων D pc.; υμων cet.; *vestris* d pler.
4.4 (427/29): ΚΑΙ ΑΡΙΘΜΟC ΤΕ ΕΓΕΝΗΘΗ D*; και αριθ. εγ. D[s.m.];
et factus est numerus d
ibid. (*ibid.*): χιλιαδες πεντε D cet.; *quinque milia* d cet.
4.10 (428/14): ιηυ χρυ D; *xri ihu* d
4.12 (428/23): ΟΥ ΓΑΡ ΕCΤΙΝ ΕΤΕΡΟΝ ΟΝΟΜΑ D; ουδε γαρ ον. εστιν ετ. pler.; NEQUAE ALIUD EST NOMEN d
This is a verse that has been completely recast in D.
4.14 (428/30): ΤΟΝ ΑΝΘΡΩΠΟΝ D*; τον τε ανθρωπον ℵ A B D[C] E al.; τον δε ανθ. P al. pler.; *hominem quoque* d pler.; *hom. etiam* gig p LUC; *videntes autem* h
ibid. (428/32): ΠΟΙΗCΑΙ Η D; OM cet.; OM d cet.; *facere aut* h
Apart from the impossible αυτων, these are the only two differences between D and B in this verse.
4.15 (428/33)
κελευσαντες (ΚΑΙΛ. D) D pc.; κελ. δε cet.
cum iussissent autem d al.; *iusserunt* h

4.16 (429/6): ΦΑΝΕΡΟΤΕΡΟΝ ΕCΤΙΝ D; *φανερον* cet.; *manifestum est* d pler.
4.17 (429/7): OM D lect. sing.; *αλλ'* cet.; *sed* d pler.
ibid. (429/8): ΟΥΤΟΙC D; *αυτοις* cet.; *eis* d pler.
4.18 (429/11–13)
CΥΝΚΑΤΑΤΙΘΕΜΕΝѠΝ ΔΕ ΑΥΤѠΝ ΤΗ ΓΝѠΜΗ / ΦѠΝΗCΑΝΤΕC ΑΥΤΟΥC ΠΑΡΗΓΓΕΙΛΑΝΤΟ / ΚΑΤΑ ΤΟ ΜΗ D
και καλεσαντες αυτους παρηγγειλαν καθολου μη pler.
CONSENTIENTIBUS AUTEM OMNIBUS NOTITIA / VOCANTES EOS PRAECEPERUNT ILLIS / NE OMNINO d
consent. autem hominibus vocantes ... Lvg (*Θ*)
consent. omnibus voc. ... Lvg (Bern. A.9)
Illis in d is merely translation of the *ellipsis obiecti*; *ne omnino* = *καθολου μη*. The D expansion is prefixed to this (*vocantes eos* could translate either text).
4.21 (429/22): *μη* D pc.; *μηδεν* cet.; *nihil* d e; *non* pler.
The phrase has been recast in D.
4.22 (429/26): OM D (lect. sing.); *τουτο* cet.; *hoc* d e; *istud* pler.; OM gig p IR LUC
4.24 (429/31)
ομοθυμαδον ηραν φωνην D pler.
UNANIMITER AUTEM VOCEM LEVAVERUNT d
unan. lev. vocem pler.
4.29 (430/17): *πασης παρρησιας* D; *fiducia omni* d
4.30 (430/18)
την χειρα σου D ℵ E P al.; *την χειρα* A B P al. pler.
manum d gig LUC; *man. tuam* cet.
4.33 (431/2): *παντας αυτους* D; EOS OMNES d
4.34 (431/4): *οσοι γαρ* D cet.; *quodquod* d Lvg (D); + *enim* pler.
5.1 (431/16): *ανηρ δε τις ονοματι ανανιας* D; QUIDAM AUTEM VIR NOMINE ANANIAS d
5.4 (431/27): OM D lect. sing.; *ση* cet.; *tua* d cet.
ibid. (431/29): ΠΟΙΗCΑΙ ΠΟΝΗΡΟΝ ΤΟΥΤΟ D*; *ποιησαι το πον. τουτο* D^B; *το πραγμα τουτο* cet.; *facere dolose rem istam* d; *hanc rem* pler.; *ut faceres ista* p
Again, it seems that the d reading is an alteration of the standard text towards equivalence to D.
5.8 (432/7–8)
ΕΠΕΡѠΤΗCѠ CΕ / ΕΙ ΑΡΑ ΤΟ ΧѠΡΙΟΝ ΤΟCΟΥΤΟΥ D
ειπε μοι ει τοσουτου το χωριον cet.
dic mihi / si tanti praedium d gig LUC
5.10 (432/18–19)
ΚΑΙ CΥΝCΤΕΙΛΑΝΤΕC ΕΞΗΝΕΓΚΑΝ / ΚΑΙ ΕΘΑΨΑΝ D
και εξενεγκαντες εθαψαν cet.
ET CUM EXTULISSENT / SEPELIERUNT d
5.15 (433/1–3): ΑΠΗΛΛΑCCΟΝΤΟ ΓΑΡ / ... / ѠC ΕΙΧΕΝ D;
και ρυσθωσιν ... ης ειχον E; *et liverabantur / ... / quem habebant* d e
This is in a longer reading.

5.19 (433/15): TOTE ΔΙΑ ΝΥΚΤΟϹ ΑΓΓΕΛΟϹ ΚΥ D; αγγ. δε κυριου δια (της) νυκτος cet.; PER NOCTE VERO ANGELUS DNI d
Again, d stands halfway between D and the majority reading.
5.20 (433/19): ταυτης D cet.; EIUS d
5.28 (434/14): ου ℵ^{c} D E P pler.; OM ℵ* A B; OM d pler.; *nonne* e p BED
ibid. (434/19): ΕΚΕΙΝΟΥ D*; τουτου D^{H} cet.; *huius* d pler.; *istius* Lvg
5.29 (434/20): δε (δει D^{A}) θεω D; DO OPORTET d
ibid. (434/21): Ο ΔΕ ΠΕΤΡΟϹ ΕΙΠΕΝ D; PETRUS VERO RESPONDIT d
5.32 (434/28): εσμεν μαρτυρες D; *testes sumus* d
5.34 (435/1)
εκ του συνεδριου D E; εν τω συνεδριω cet.
in concilio d pler.; *de conc.* e h p
5.35 (435/7): τοις ανθρωποις τουτοις D; ISTIS HOMINIBUS d
5.36 (435/11): εαυτον D cet.; IPSORUM d
Has the Latin text read the Greek as if it were εαυτων?
ibid. (435/12): ΚΑΙ D; OM cet.; OM d pler.
ibid. (435/14): ΑΥΤΟϹ ΔΙ ΑΥΤΟΥ D; OM cet.; OM d cet.
The passage has been rewritten by D.
5.37 (435/19): λαον πολυν C D Eus; λαον ικανον A^{2} H P al. pler.; ικ. λαον E pc.; λαον ℵ A* B pc.; OM P^{45}; *populum* d al. Lvg
5.38 (435/22): ΕΙϹΙΝ ΑΔΕΛΦΟΙ D*; αδελφοι $D^{s.m.}$; OM cet.; *fratres* d h
The difference occurs in a sentence whose beginning has been altered in D.
6.2 (436/17): ΠΡΟϹΚΑΛΕϹΑΜΕΝΟΙ D*; προσκ. δε D^{A} cet.; *convocantes itaque* d
This again is the beginning of a sentence.
ibid. (436/19): OM D cet.; ENIM d
It is possible that the word in d is actually the result of a confusion with INEM in the line above.
6.3 (436/22–3)
ΤΙ ΟΥΝ ΕϹΤΙΝ ΑΔΕΛΦΟΙ / ΕΠΙϹΚΕΨΑϹΘΑΙ D
επισκεψασθε δε αδελφοι ℵ B
επισκεψασθε ουν αδελφοι C E H P pler.
QUID ERGO EST FRATRES / PROSPICITE ITAQUE d
Again, d has adapted from one of the other two texts.
6.6 (437/4–5): ΟΥΤΟΙ ΕϹΤΑΘΗϹΑΝ ... / ΟΙΤΙΝΕϹ D; ους εστησαν ... και cet.; QUOS STATUERUNT ... / CUMQUE d
This is the beginning of a sentence.
6.15 (438/6): ΚΑΙ ΗΤΕΝΙΖΟΝ ΔΕ ΑΥΤΩ D*; και ατενισαντες εις αυτον D^{B} cet.; ET INTUITI IN EUM d
The phrase is the beginning of a sentence partially recast in D.
7.4 (438/20–1)
ΕΞΕΛΘΩΝ ... / ΚΑΙ ΚΑΤΩΚΗϹΕΝ D*; εξελθων ... κατωκησεν $D^{s.m.}$ cet.
exhibit (scil. *exivit*) ... / *et habitavit* d al.
7.5 (438/28–9): δουναι αυτω / εις κατασχεσιν αυτην D;
EI DARE EAM / IN POSSESIONEM d
7.7 (439/3): θεος D cet.; *dominus* d al.; *deus* al.

7.10 (439/15): ΧΑΡΙΝ ΑΥΤΩ D; *ei gratiam* d
ibid. (439/17): ηγουμενον D cet.; OM d lect. sing.
7.11 (439/19): ΕΦ ΟΛΗΣ ΤΗΣ ΑΙΓΥΠΤΟΥ D*; εφ ολης της γης αιγυπτου D[B]; εφ ολην την αιγ. ℵ A B C; εφ ολην την γην αιγ. E H P al. pler.; *super omnem terram aegypti* d e
7.16 (440/4)
του συχεμ D H al. plu.; εν σ. ℵ* B C al.; το εν σ. ℵ[c] A E pc.
ET SYCHEM d; *sychem* pler.
7.18 (440/8): ανεστη βασιλευς ετερος D; ALIUS EXURREXERIT REX d
7.20 (440/16)
ανετραφη μηνας τρις D
MENSIBUS TRIBUS EDUCATUS EST d
7.21 (440/20): ΑΝΕΘΡΑΨΑΤΟ D; και ανεθρεψ. cet.; ET VICI FILI EDUCAVIT d
7.24 (440/27)
ΕΚ ΤΟΥ ΓΕΝΟΥΣ D; εκ του γενους αυτου E; OM cet.
de genere suo d gig Par. lat. 11533; *de natione sua* e; OM cet.
7.28 (441/10): συ D cet.; OM pc.; OM d gig
7.30 (441/16): ΚΑΙ ΜΕΤΑ ΤΑΥΤΑ D; και cet.; ET POST HAEC ET d; *et post haec* d[s.m.]; *et* cet.
A translation of the D text has been tacked onto the front of d's rendering of the majority reading.
7.32 (441/22): εγω D cet.; εγω ειμι D; *ego sum* c d dem e gig p Lvg (mss) AU BED; *ego* al.
7.33 (441/28)
ΟΥ D*; εφ ω ℵ A B C D[B]; εν ω E H P al. pler.; *in quo* d cet.
7.34 (441/29): ΚΑΙ (OM D[s.m.]) ΙΔΩΝ ΓΑΡ (OM D[s.m.]) D; ιδων cet.;
INTUITUS ENIM d
The difference is at the beginning of a sentence.
7.35 (442/5): συν A B C D E al.; εν ℵ H P pler.; *in* d gig; *cum* pler.
7.36 (442/9): εν γη αιγυπτου D al.; εν γη αιγυπτω ℵ A E H P al.; εν τη αιγυπτω B C al.; IN AEGYPTO d; *in terra aegypti* pler.
7.39 (442/20): ΟΤΙ D; ω cet.; *cui* d pler.
7.45 (443/13): διαδεξαμενοι D cet.; OM d lect. sing.
ibid. (443/17): ΫΜΩΝ D; ημων cet.; *nostrorum* d
7.49 (443/25): ΜΟΥ ΕΣΤΙΝ D*; μοι εστιν D[H]; μοι cet.; EST MEUS d
7.50 (443/29): παντα ταυτα A C D E P al.; τα. παν. ℵ B H al.; *haec omnia* d pler.; *omn. h.* e
7.54 (444/9): ΚΑΙ ΕΒΡΥΧΟΝ ΤΕ D*; και εβρ. D[s.m.] cet.; *et stridebant* d pler.
7.56 (444/15): εκ δεξιων εστωτα του θυ D; *ad dexteram di stantem* d
7.60 (444/26–7)
ΘΕΙΣ ΤΑ ΓΟΝΑΤΑ / ΕΚΡΑΞΕΝ D*; θεις δε τα γον. εκ. D[A] cet.
CUMQ· POSUISSET GENUA / ET CLAMAVIT d
ibid. (444/28): ταυτην την αμαρτιαν D; *peccatum hoc* d
Transposition in one or the other (or both).

8.3 (445/7–8): την εκκλησιαν / κατα τους οικους D cet.; *ecclesias / per singulasquae domos* d; *ecclesias per domos* Lvg (B Θ); *ecclesias in domo* t
8.4 (445/12): διηλθον D cet.; ADNUNTIABANT d; *ibant/pertransiebant* pler.
8.6 (445/16–17)
ωC ΔE HKOYON ΠAN OI OXΛOI / ΠPOCEIXON D*
προσειχον δε οι οχλοι ℵ A B C D[C] al.; προσ. τε οι οχλοι E H P al. longe plu.
INTENDEBANT AUTEM OMNIS TURBAE / d
d has again been changed from the majority to the D text.
8.7 (445/21): πνευματα ακαθαρτα D cet.; SPIRITUM INMUNDUM d
8.9 (445/29): εαυτον D cet.; OM d; *se* cet.
Compare 5.36.
8.13 (446/9): KAI ΠPOCKAPTEPωN D*; προσκ. D[s.m.] cet; *et adherebat* d
ibid. (446/10): τε D pler.; δε pc.; τα B; OM d gig
10.14 (456/1): η D C E L P al.; και ℵ A B al.; *et* d pler.
10.15 (456/2): ΦωNHCAC ΔE D; και φωνη cet.; *et vox* d cet.
10.16 (456/5): ANEΛHMΦΘH ΠAΛIN D; παλιν αν. L P al. pler.; ευθυς αν. ℵ A B C E al.; ADSUMPTUM EST d
All the other Latin witnesses translate either παλιν or ευθυς.
10.21 (456/22): TI ΘEΛETAI H TIC H AITIA D; τις αιτια B; τις η αιτια cet.; *quid vultis quae causa* d; *quae causa* pler.
10.22 (456/24): TIC D; OM cet.; OM d cet.
10.23 (456/31)
TOTE EICAΓAΓωN O ΠETPOC EΞENICEN AYTOYC D
εισκαλεσαμενος ουν αυτους εξεν. cet.; τοτε προσκαλ. αυτους εξεν. E
TUNC ERGO INGRESSUS PETRUS HOSPITIO EXCEPIT EOS d
The sentence is recast in D.
10.25 (457/10–11)
EKΠHΔHCAC / KAI CYNANTHCAC D
Συναντησας is found in cet.; but this is a longer reading in Codex Bezae.
EXILIENS / ET OBVIUS FACTUS EST d
d is an alteration of an existing text to fit D, keeping the indicative found in other Latin witnesses (e.g. *obiavit ei* gig).
10.27 (457/15)
KAI EICEΛΘωN TE KAI EYPEN D*; και συνομιλων αυτω εισηλθεν και ευρισκει (ευρεισκι D[F]) D[F] cet.
et introibit et invenit d
et confabulans cum eo introivit et invenit p
et loquens cum illo intravit et invenit Lvg
We have here the omission of *loquens cum illo* or its equivalent in d, as the easiest means of making the two columns agree, where D has recast the text.
10.28 (457/18): ANΔPI D; OM cet.; OM d cet.
Is this error in D caused by 1.17?
10.29 (457/21): αναντιρ(ρ)ητως D cet.; SINE CUNCTATIONE d
Is this an error in d for *sine contradictione*?

10.33 (458/5): OM D*; σε D^C; *te* d
This is in a longer reading.
ibid. (458/7): NYN ΔΟΥ D*; *νυν ιδου* D^A; *νυν ουν* D^C cet.; *nunc ergo* d
ibid. (*ibid.*): *παντες ημεις* D; *nos omnes* d
10.35 (458/15): *αυτω εστιν* D pler.; *εστιν αυτω* pc.; *est ei* d al.; *est illi* pler.
10.36 (458/16): *γαρ* C*vid D pc.; OM cet.; OM d pler.
ibid. (458/17): *ευαγγελιζομενος* D cet.; EUANGELIZARE d
This may just be poor translation.
10.39 (458/28): *υμεις* A D; *ημεις* cet.; *nos* d cet.
11.1 (459/31–2)
ΑΚΟΥCΤΟΝ ΔΕ ΕΓΕΝΕΤΟ / ΤΟΙC ΑΠΟCΤΟΛΟΙC ΚΑΙ ΤΟΙC ΑΔΕΛΦΟΙC D
ηκουσαν δε οι αποστ. και οι αδ. cet.
AUDITO VERO / APOSTOLI ET FRATRES d
This seems to be another place where d has been partly altered to agree with D.
11.2 (460/9–10)
ΟΙ ΔΕ ΕΚ ΠΕΡΙΤΟΜΗC ΑΔΕΛΦΟΙ ΔΙΕΚΡΙΝΟΝΤΟ / ΠΡΟC ΑΥΤΟΝ D
διεκ. προς αυτον οι εκ περιτ. cet.
QUI ERANT DE CIRCUMCISIONE FRATRES IUDICANTES / AD EUM d
Iudicantes in d is assimilation to the context. Otherwise, it has adapted the word order of a translation of the majority text.
11.5 (460/16): OM D*; *εν* D^A cet.; *in* d cet.
11.7 (460/26): ΑΝΑCΤΑ D*; *αναστας* D^E cet.; *surgens* d
Compare 10.13 – has D* been harmonized to that passage?
11.8 (460/28): *η* D cet.; *et* d gig p Lvg (*Θ* T)
Compare 10.14 – d has probably been influenced by that passage.
11.9 (460/30)
ΕΓΕΝΕΤΟ D*; *εγ. δε* D^A; *απεκριθη δε* cet.
respondit vero d; *respondit autem* pler.
11.12 (461/5): OM D pc.; *δε* cet.; -QUE d; *autem* cet.
11.14 (461/13): *συ* D cet.; OM d (lect. sing.); *tu* cet.
11.19 (461/30): ΑΠΟ ΤΟΥ (OM D^s.m.) CΤΕΦΑΝΟΥ D; *επι στεφανου* A E al.; *επι στεφανω* ℵ B H L P al. pler.; *sub stephano* d pler.
11.21 (462/7): ΗΝ ΔΕ D; *και ην* cet.; *et erat* d pler.
11.26 (462/25–8): In this verse, which is presented in a quite different form in D, which has itself been revised by Corrector E, d has been roughly assimilated to the Greek column (for example, in the reading *et tunc primum*). But the following differences remain:
ΟΙΤΙΝΕC ΠΑΡΑΓΕΝΟΜΕΝΟΙ D
CONTIGIT VERO EIS d = *εγενετο δε αυτοις* cet.
ΟΧΛΟΝ ΪΚΑΝΟΝ D; ECCLESIAM d = *εν τη εκκλησια* cet.
ΕΧΡΗΜΑΤΙCΕΝ D; NUNCUPATI SUNT d = *χρηματισαι* cet.
ΟΙ ΜΑΘΗΤΑΙ ΧΡΙCΤΙΑΝΟΙ D; DISCIPULOS CHRISTIANOS d = *μαθ-ας χρ-ους* cet.
11.27 (462/33): CΥΝΕCΤΡΑΜΜΕΝΩΝ D; the whole phrase is omitted in all other Greek witnesses; REVERTENTIBUS d; *congregatis* p w R Par. lat. 342*
12.4 (463/24): OM D; *αυτον* cet.; *eum* d pler.

12.7 (464/5): ΕΠΕΛΑΜΨΕΝ ΤΩ ΟΙΚΗΜΑΤΙ D; ελαμψεν εν τω οικ. cet.; *refulgens in illo loco* d; *refulsit in illo loco* gig
This could be a paraphrase by d.
ibid. (464/8): ΑΙ ΑΛΥϹΕΙϹ ΕΚ ΤΩΝ ΧΕΙΡΩΝ ΑΥΤΟΥ D; αυτου αι αλ. εκ των χ. cet.; *eius catenae de manibus* d
The sentence is rewritten in D.
12.16 (465/15–16)
ΕΞΑΝΟΙΞΑΝΤΕϹ ΔΕ ΚΑΙ ΪΔΟΝΤΕϹ ΑΥΤΟΝ ΚΑΙ ΕΞΕϹΤΗϹΑΝ D*
ανοιξ. δε και ϊδ. αυτον εξεστ. D^{corr}
ανοιξ. δε ειδαν/-ον αυτον και εξεστ. cet.
et cum aperuisset viderunt eunt et obstupuerunt d
This also has been rewritten.
13.4 (467/4): ΚΑΤΑΒΑΝΤΕϹ ΔΕ ... OM D; κατηλθον ... τε/δε cet.; *descenderunt ... vero* d
13.5 (467/7): ΚΑΤΗΝΓΕΙΛΑΝ ΤΟΝ ΛΟΝ (scil. λογον) ΤΟΥ ΚΥ D; κατηγγελλον τον λογον του θεου pler.; *adnuntiabant verbum di* d p
13.6 (467/10): ΚΑΙ [ΠΕ]ΡΙΕΛΘΟΝΤΩΝ ΔΕ ΑΥΤΩΝ D*; διελθ. δε αυτων D^H; διελθοντες δε cet.; *cum progressi fuissent* d
13.7 (467/17): ϹΥΝΚΑΛΕϹΑΜΕΝΟϹ D; προσκαλ. cet.; CUM VOCASSET d
This is *probably* a genuine difference: συγκαλεω is rendered by *convoco* everywhere else in d.
13.12 (468/2): ΪΔΩΝ ΔΕ D; τοτε ιδων cet.; *tunc cum vidisset* d
13.18 (468/31): ΚΑΙ ΕΤΗ ·Μ· ΕΤΡΟΠΟΦΟΡΗϹΕΝ D; και ως τεσσερακονταετη χρονον ετροπ. cet.; *et annis ·xl· ac si nutrix aluit* d
13.23 (469/12)
Ο ΘϹ ΟΥΝ ΑΠΟ ΤΟΥ ϹΠΕΡΜΑΤΟϹ ΑΥΤΟΥ D
τουτου ο θεος απο του σπ. cet.
ds autem a semine huius d
Is d again an alteration of the majority reading?
13.25 (469/19): ιωανης (ιωαννης D^B) τον δρομον D; CURSUM IOHANNES d
ibid. (469/20): με ϋπονοειται D; SUSPICIMANI ME d
13.29 (470/4–6)
ΚΑΙ ΕΠΙΤΥΧΟΝΤΕϹ ... / ΚΑΙ ΚΑΘΕΛΟΝΤΕϹ ... / ΚΑΙ (OM $D^{s.m.}$) ΕΘΗΚΑΝ D
... καθελοντες ... εθηκαν cet.
ET INPETRAVERUNT ... / ET DEPOSUERUNT ... ET / POSUERUNT d
deponentes ... posuerunt cet.
13.30 (470/7)
ΟΝ Ο ΘϹ ΗΓΕΙΡΕΝ D; ο δε θεος ηγ. αυτον εκ νεκρων cet.
quem ds vero excitavit d; *deus vero suscitavit eum a mortuis* pler.
d can be seen to be an adaptation of the majority text.
13.35 (470/30): ΚΑΙ D; διο και C E H L P al.; διοτι και ℵ A B pc.; *ideoque et* d cet.
The phrase is recast in D.
13.42 (471/22): ρηματα ταυτα D; HAEC VERBA d
13.44 (471/30): ΘΥ D; DNI d

The sentence is omitted in all other witnesses.
ibid. (471/33): TE D; OM d
This is in another addition in D.
13.46 (472/8)
ΠΡωΤΟΝ ΗΝ D; *ην αναγκαιον πρωτον* pler.
oportebat primum d pler.
A corruption in D.
ibid. (*ibid.*): *θεου* D cet.; *domini* d CY; *dei* cet.
13.47 (472/13): OM D*; *ημιν* D^{D} cet.; *nobis* d cet.
13.48 (472/17): *θεου* B D E pc.; *του κυριου* ℵ A C L P pler.; *domini* d cet.
13.51 (472/30): ΚΑΤΗΝΤΗCΑΝ D; *ηλθον* cet.; *venerunt* d
14.1 (473/1): ΑΥΤΟΝ D; *αυτους* cet.; *eos* d
14.2 (473/7)
ΕΠΗΓΑΓΟΝ ΑΥΤΟΙC ΔΙωΓΜΟΝ D
επηγειραν και εκακωσαν τας ψυχας των εθνων pler.
incitaverunt persecutionem d
d has replaced *και . . . εθνων* with *persecutionem*.
14.4 (473/16): ΗΝ ΔΕ ΕCΧΙCΜΕΝΟΝ D; *εσχισθη δε* cet.; DIVISA AUTEM ERAT d; *divisa est autem* pler.
14.6 (473/23): CΥΝΪΔΟΝΤΕC ΚΑΙ D*; *συνιδοντες* D^{corr} cet.; *intellexerunt et* d cet.
ibid. (473/26): *την περιχωρον ολην* D E; *την περιχωρον* cet.; CIRCUM TOTAM REGIONEM d
14.7 (473/27): *ευαγγελιζομενοι ησαν* ℵ A B D al.; *ησαν ευαγγ.* C E H L P al. pler.; *erant euangelizantes* d, order c. al.
14.14 (474/22–3): ΔΙΑΡΡΗΞΑΝΤΕC. . . / ΚΑΙ D*; *διαρρηξαντες . . .* $D^{s.m.}$ cet.; *consciderunt. . . / et* d
14.18 (475/8): *του μη θυειν αυτοις* D; *ne sibi immolarent* d
14.19 (475/10): *επηλθον τινες ϊουδαιοι* D; *επηλθον/-αν δε. . . ιουδαιοι* ℵ A B H L P al.; *supervenerunt autem iudaei* d
14.22 (475/24): OM D cet.; ENIM d; OM cet.
This may have been caused by the following word, *animas*.
ibid. (475/25): *παρακαλουντες τε* $ℵ^{c}$ D; *και παρ.* L al.; *παρ.* cet.; *exhortantes* d e gig; *-tesque* pler.
14.23 (475/31): *κυριω* D cet.; DO d
14.24 (475/33): *διελθοντες* D cet.; REGRESSI d
15.2 (476/20): ΓΕΝΟΜΕΝΗC ΔΕ ΕΚΤΑCΕωC D; *γεν. δε στασεως* ℵ B C L; *γεν. ουν στασ.* cet.; *facta ergo seditione* d cet.
d has not followed D in the obvious corruption *εκτασεως*, and probably has the *Koinē* text form.
ibid. (476/22): CΥΝ ΑΥΤΟΙC D; *προς αυτους* cet.; *ad eos* d
ibid. (476/23): ΕΛΕΓΕΝ ΓΑΡ D; *dicebat autem* d gig; *docebat enim* w
This is in a longer reading.
ibid. (476/24): ΔΙΪΧΥΡΙΖΟΜΕΝΟC D; OM d gig w
This is in the same addition.
ibid. (476/28): *προς* D cet.; OM d Lvg (V); *ad* cet.

15.3 (476/32): δ21): ημειν D*; εν ημειν D[A] = εν ημιν E H L P etc.; εν υμιν ℵ A B C al.; *in nobis* d
15.17 (478/24): ΠΟΙΗϹΕΙ D*; ο ποιων ℵ[c] A C D[H] E H L P cet.; ποιων ℵ* B; *faciens* d cet.
15.20 (478/31): ΜΗ ΘΕΛΟΥϹΙΝ ΕΑΥΤΟΙϹ ΓΕΙΝΕϹΘΑΙ D; *volunt non fieri sibi* d
This is a sort of double transposition in d.
15.25 (479/22): υμων D pc.; ημων cet.; *nostris* d cet.
15.32 (480/11): ιουδας δε και D P al.; ιουδας τε και ℵ A B C E H L al.; *iudas quoque et* d gig; *iud. autem et* pler.
This seems to be a place where the columns differ, though it should be noted that at 10.24 d has *quoque* where there is evidence only of δε in Greek manuscripts.
15.38 (480/32–481/3)
ΤΟΝ ΑΠΟϹΤΗϹΑΝΤΑ ... / ... / ϹΥΝΕΛΘΟΝΤΑ ... / ... / ... ΕΙΝΑΙ D
τον αποσταντα ... συνελθοντα ... συνπαραλαμβανειν cet.
HIIS / QUI DISCESSERUNT ... / SIMUL VENERUNT ... / ... / ADSUMERENT d
Here d has totally misrepresented the sense of the passage. But it may be derived from the majority text – *adsumerent* is from συνπαραλαμβανειν rather than ειναι (see l. 6).
15.39 (481/6–7)
ΤΟΤΕ ΒΑΡΝΑΒΑϹ ΠΑΡΑΛΑΒΩΝ ΤΟΝ ΜΑΡΚΟΝ / ΕΠΛΕΥϹΕΝ D
τον δε βαρναβαν παραλαβοντα τον μαρκον επλευσαι H pc.
τον τε βαρναβαν παραλαβοντα (τον) μαρκον επλευσαι cet.
BARNABAS VERO ADSUMPTO MARCO / NAVIGAVERUNT d
D has made a separate sentence here; d has adapted another text (H pc.?) to it.
15.40 (481/8): ΕΠΙΔΕΞΑΜΕΝΟϹ D; επιλεξ. cet.; SUSCEPIT d
15.41 (481/12): παραδιδους τας εντολας D; *tradens autem mandatum* d; *(et) praecipiens praecepta* al.
This is in a longer reading.
16.1 (481/13): ΔΙΕΛΘΩΝ ΔΕ D; PERTRANSIENS d
This difference occurs in a longer reading.
ibid. (481/15): και ἴδου D cet.; ECCE d; *et ecce* cet.
ibid. (*ibid.*): ΕΚΕΙ ΗΝ D; *erat ibi* d
16.3 (481/23): εκεινοις D cet.; SUIS d; *illis* cet.
16.9 (482/10): ΕΝ ΟΡΑΜΑΤΙ D; οραμα cet.; *visum* d; *visio* pler.; *in somnis* e
16.13 (482/28): ΕΔΟΚΕΙ ΠΡΟϹΕΥΧΗ ΕΙΝΑΙ D; *oratio esset bidebatur* d
Transposition in d (besides corruption of *esse*).
16.14 (482/32): ΤΗϹ ΠΟΛΕΩϹ ΘΥΑΤΕΙΡΩΝ D; THYATIRUM CIVITATIS d
ibid. (482/33): ηκουσεν D* L al.; ηκουεν ℵ A B C D[s.m.] E H P al. pler.; *audiebat* d e gig Lvg (C T)
16.15 (483/5): ΤΩ ΘΩ D; τω κυριω cet.; *dno* d
16.16 (483/12): OM D (lect. sing.); αυτης cet.; *suis* d cet.
16.17 (483/14–15)
ΚΑΤΑΚΟΛΟΘΟΥϹΑ... / ΚΑΙ (OM D[s.m.]) ΕΚΡΑΖΟΝ D; κατακ. ... εκραζεν cet.
persecuta est ... / et clamabat d
subsecuta est ... et clamabat gig LUC
D (apart from the corrupt ending) has a participle followed by και with the indicative.

16.18 (483/22): ΕΥΘΕΩϹ ΕΞΗΛΘΕΝ D; *εξηλθεν αυτη η ωρα* cet.;
EADEM HORA EXIIT d; *ex. ead. hora* cet.
Here d has the wording of the majority text, but has adopted the order found in D.
16.19 (483/24)
ΑΠΕϹΤΕΡΗϹΘΑΙ ΤΗϹ ΕΡΓΑϹΙΑϹ ΑΥΤΩΝ D
εξηλθεν η ελπις της εργ. αυτων cet.
ISPES (*spes* $d^{s.m.}$) ET REDITUS EORUM d
exiit spes quaestus eorum pler.
ex. spes reditus eorum gig LUC
d is corrupt in omitting the verb, and adding *et* through taking the genitive *reditus* as if it were nominative.
16.21 (483/32–3): *τα εθνη* / *α* D* 1611*; *εθη α* D^{corr} cet.; GENTES / QUAM d
d has advanced the D corruption ('to the Gentiles things which it is not lawful . . .') to 'to the Gentiles, a thing which is not lawful'.
16.26 (484/19)
ηνεωχθησαν δε ℵ A B D E al.; *ηνεωχθησαν τε* C H L P cet.
APERTAQUAE (-que $d^{s.m.}$) SUNT d
16.30 (484/32–485/1)
ΠΡΟΗΓΑΓΕΝ / . . . / . . . ΑϹΦΑΛΙϹΑΜΕΝΟϹ / ΚΑΙ (OM $D^{s.m.}$) ΕΙΠΕΝ ΑΥΤΟΙϹ D
προαγαγων . . . εφη cet.
CUM PRODUXISSET . . . / . . . CUSTODIVIT / ET DIXIT ILLIS d
d seems to have inserted the D addition into the standard text.
16.34 (485/14): ϹΥΝ ΤΩ ΟΙΚΩ ΑΥΤΟΥ D; *πανοικει* cet.; CUM TOTA DOMU SUA d
ibid. (485/15)
ΕΠΙ ΤΟΝ ΘΝ D; *τω κυριω* min. pc.; *τω θεω* cet.
in domino d c* gig LUC; *domino* c^{corr}
16.36 (485/24): *τους λογους* B C D pc.; *τους λογ. τουτους* ℵ A E H L P al.;
HOS SERMONES d; *verba haec* cet.
17.1 (486/21): ΑΠΟΛΛΩΝΙΔΑ D; *απολλωνιαν* cet.; *apolloniam* d cet.
17.5 (487/5–6)
ΟΙ ΔΕ ΑΠΕΙΘΟΥΝΤΕϹ ΪΟΥΔΑΙΟΙ / ϹΥΝϹΤΡΕΨΑΝΤΕϹ D
ζηλωσαντες δε οι ιουδαιοι και προσλαβομενοι ℵ A B E al.
ζηλ. δε οι απειθουντες ιουδ. και προσλαβ. min. pler.
προσλαβ. δε οι ιουδ. οι απειθ. H L P al.
adsuptis vero iudaeis / *convertentes* d
ibid. (487/8): ΕΘΟΡΥΒΟΥϹΑΝ D; *εθορυβουν* cet.; TURBABANT d;
concitaverunt Lvg
ibid. (487/10): *εξαγαγειν* D; *προαγαγειν* pler.; *producere* d cet.
It is hard to be positive that this is a difference.
17.12 (487/33): ΤΙΝΕϹ D; *πολλοι* cet.; *multi* d
ibid. (488/1–3)
. . . ΗΠΙϹΤΗϹΑΝ / . . . ΕΥϹΧΗΜΟΝΩΝ / ΑΝΔΡΕϹ D
. . . CREDERE NOLUERUNT / . . . NON PLACENTIUM / ET VIRI d

This is in a longer reading. D has, as we already know, been revised here by Correctors B, E, and H.
17.14 (488/10): ΟΝ ΜΕΝ ΟΥΝ D; ευθεως δε τοτε cet.; *statimque* d (*-quae*) al.
17.15 (488/19): ΛΑΒΟΝΤΕC ΔΕ D; και λαβ. cet.; UT ACCEPISSENT d
The difference occurs at the join of a longer reading with the universal text; d has made it rather a strained one.
17.17 (488/28–9)
ΚΑΙ ΤΟΙC ΕΝ ΤΗ ΑΓΟΡΑ ΚΑΤΑ ΠΑCΑΝ ΗΜΕΡΑΝ / ΠΡΟC ΤΟΥC ΠΑΡΑΤΥΧΟΝΤΑC (παρατυγχανοντας D^{C}) D
OM τοις, et leg. παρατυγχανοντας cet.
ET HIIS QUI FORTE ADERANT / ET HIIS QUI IN FORO PER OMNEM DIEM d
Two lines have been transposed in d, and *et hiis* repeated (influence of the context) in the second.
17.19 (489/3)
μετα δε ημερας τινας επιλαβομενοι αυτω D 614
επιλαβ. τε αυτου cet.
post dies aliquos adpraehensumque eum d
apprehensumque eum AU
d has been altered by prefixing the D addition to its version of the majority text.
ibid. (489/4): ΑΥΤΟΝ D; OM cet.; OM d cet.
17.20 (489/9): εις τας ακοας ημων D cet.; ADVERSUS NOSTRAS D
17.21 (489/12): ΕΙC ΑΥΤΟΥC D; OM cet.; OM d cet.
17.25 (489/28): ΠΡΟCΔΕΟΜΕΝΟC D; ως προσδ. τινος ℵ* pc.; ως προσδ. cet.; *tamquam egeat* d
e gig also have *tamquam*.
17.27 (489/31): ΑΝΘΡΩΠΟΥ D; -ων cet.; *hominum* d cet.
ibid. (490/1)
ΚΑΤΑ ΟΡΟΘΕCΙΑΝ D*; και τας οροθεσιας D^{E} cet.
et determinationes d; *secundum determinationem* IR
ibid. (490/2): ΜΑΛΙCΤΑ D; OM cet.; OM d cet.
ibid. (490/4): η A D pc.; και cet.; OM d lect. sing.
17.31 (490/19)
ΚΡΕΙΝΑΙ D; εν η μελλει κρινειν cet.
iudicare d m AU; *iudicari* IR; *in qua iudicaturus est* pler.
ibid. (490/20): ΑΝΔΡΙ D; εν ανδρι. cet.; *in viro* d cet.
18.2 (491/8): ΑΥΤΩ D*; αυτοις D^{B} cet.; *ad eos* d pler.
This is corruption in D.
18.4 (491/14): ΚΑΙ (OM $D^{s.m.}$) ΕΠΙΘΕΝ ΔΕ D; επειθεν τε cet.; *et persuadebat* d; the verse is omitted in p and Lvg.
This is a reading where it could be argued that D, originally reading επειθεν δε for επειθεν τε, has had και added to force agreement with d.
18.5 (491/16): ΠΑΡΕΓΕΝΟΝΤΟ ΔΕ D; ως δε κατηλθον cet.; *ut vero advenerunt* d
ibid. (491/17): ΤΟΤΕ D*; ο τε D^{corr} cet.; OM d
The omission of ο τε by d is translational. The text of D is plainly corrupt.

18.10 (492/10)
ΤΟΥ ΚΑΚΩϹΑΙ ϹΕ D; *σοι του κακ. σε* cet.
te ut malefaciat tibi d; *tibi ut noceat te* cet.
18.11 (492/14): *αυτους* D 4; *εν αυτοις* cet.; *penes ipsos* d
18.14 (492/26): *τι* D cet.; OM d lect. sing.; *aliquid* pler.
18.15 (492/30): ΕΧΕΤΕ D; *εστιν* cet.; EST d; *est/sunt* cet.
ibid. (492/32): *εγω τουτων* D; *horum ego* d
18.19 (493/11): ΚΑΤΑΝΤΗϹΑϹ D; -*ησε* H L P al. pler.; -*ησαν* ℵ A B E al.; *devenerunt* d
ibid. (493/12): *κατελιπεν* D cet. (-*ιπ*-/-*ειπ*-); RELIQUERUNT d
18.21 (493/17): OM ℵ A B D al.; *αυτοις* cet.; *eos* d; *eis* e gig Lvg (R)
ibid. (493/18): ΠΑΝΤΩϹ D; OM d
This is in a longer reading.
18.23 (493/24): *ποιησας* D cet.; CUM FECISSENT d
Compare 20.3.
ibid. (493/27): *και* D pc.; OM cet.; OM d cet.
18.26 (or 27) (494/3): ΗΤΟϹ D*; *ουτος* D^{D} H pc.; *ος* P^{38}; *ουτος τε* cet.; *adque hic* d
ibid. (494/7): ΕΠΙΔΗΜΟΥΝΤΕϹ D; *επιδημησας* P^{38}; EXEUNTES d
This is in a longer reading.
ibid. (494/8–9): ΑΚΟΥϹΑΝΤΕϹ ΑΥΤΟΥ / ΠΑΡΕΚΑΛΟΥΝ D; AUDIERUNT EUM / HORTANTES d
19.1 (494/23): *διελθων δε* P^{38} D; *διελθοντα* cet.; *perambulantes* d
See also *perambulatis* gig – has d been modified from a similar reading? For the D text see 20.2.
19.3 (494/29): *ειπεν δε* P^{38} D pc.; *ειπεν τε* B H L P al. pc.; *ο δε ειπων* ℵ A E al.; *dixitque* d
19.9 (495/13): ΤΙΝΕϹ ΜΕΝ ΟΥΝ ΑΥΤΩΝ D; *ως δε τινες* cet.; *ut vero quidam eorum* d; *et cum quidam ex eis* gig
d has been altered simply by an addition.
19.10 (495/21): ΕΩϹ D*; *ωστε* D^{D} cet.; *ita ut* d pler.; *usque quo* e
ibid. (495/23): OM D* (lect. sing.); *τε* D^{D} cet.; -*que* d
19.12 (495/30)
τα τε πνευματα τα πονηρα εκπορευεσθαι D pler.
UT SPS MALIGNUS EXIRET d
19.14 (496/3): *εν οις* P^{38} D; IN QUO d
This and the next two differences are all in the same longer reading. This one may be only a translational variant.
ibid. (496/6): ΠΡΟϹ ΤΟΝ ΔΑΙΜΟΝΙΖΟΜΕΝΟ D; *προς δαιμονιζομενον* P^{38}; ADIMPLENTES d
ibid. (496/9): ΕΞΕΛΘΕΙΝ ΚΗΡΥϹϹΕΙ D; *κηρυσσει εξελθειν* P^{38}; PRAEDICAT EXIRE d
19.17 (496/20): ΦΟΒΟϹ ΕΠΕϹΕΝ D; *incidit timor* d
19.18 (496/22): *πολλοι δε* D pc.; *πολλοι τε* cet.; *multique* d pler.

19.19 (496/25): ÏKANOI D*; ικ. τε E; ικ. δε D^B cet.; *multi autem* d pler.
19.21 (496/33–497/2): διελθειν . . . / . . . / και D P^2; διελθειν . . . OM A E; διελθων . . . OM cet.; *transire* . . . / . . . / *et sic* d gig; *transire* . . . *et* e; *transire* . . . OM cet.
ibid. (497/4): και D cet.; OM d Lvg (S*); *et* cet.
19.22 (497/6): των διακονουντων αυτω D; *qui sibi ministrabant* d
ibid. (497/8): OM D cet.; *vero* d gig Lvg (Θ I M); OM cet.
ibid. (*ibid.*): ολιγον D 104; OM cet.; OM d cet.
19.23 (497/10): περι της οδου D cet.; DE HAC VIA DNI d; *de via domini* pler.
Hac=της.
19.24 (497/11): HN D; OM cet.; OM d cet.
19.25 (497/18): ημειν εστιν D; *est nobis* d
19.26 (497/20): ου μονον εως D; οτι ου μονον pler.; *quia non solum ipsius* d
ibid. (497/21): και D A L al.; OM ℵ B E H P al.; OM d cet.; *et* dem gig Lvg (F)
ibid. (497/24): ουτοι D; OM cet.; OM d cet.
ibid. (497/25): οι δια χειρων γενομενοι (γειν. D^B) D; QUI FIUNT MANIBUS d
19.27 (497/26): τουτο D cet.; OM d (lect. sing.); *haec* cet.
19.29 (498/3)
CYNEXYΘH OΛH H ΠOΛIC AICXYNHC D*
επλησθη ολη η πολις της συνχυσεως D^F
επλησθη η πολις της συγχυσεως ℵ* A B 181
επλησθη η πολις συγχυσεως $ℵ^c$ 13 al.
επλησθη η πολις ολη της συγχυσεως H L P 614 al.
επλησθη η πολισ ολη συγχ. E 69 175 309 pler.
REPLETA EST TOTA CIVITAS CONFUSIONEM d
erat autem totius civitatis magna confusio CAr
confusa est universa civitas gig
impleta est civitas confusione Lvg

This variant is important enough for us to dwell on it a little.

For the translation of συγχεω, and its Hellenistic form of συγχυννω, with *confundo*, see Ac 2.6 e Lvg AU; 9.22 Lvg; 19.32 d Lvg; 21.27 d. Συγχυσις is translated by *confusio* at 19.29 in d gig Lvg CAr.

Apart from the problems relating to the presence of the article and of ὁλη, and to the word order, our interest is focussed on the reading AICXYNHC in D. The rendering by *confusio* in d and Cassiodorus is the clue to its origin. *Confusio* has two meanings in late Latin: the traditional one, of mingling, or disorder; and another, of disgrace, or shame. According to Souter, it is a Christian usage, found from the second century onwards. This is an extension of the older meaning, 'a troubled state of mind, anxiety, consternation, embarrassment', to quote the *Oxford Latin Dictionary*, which cites Velleius: *quae senatus trepidatio, quae populi confusio*.

The best explanation of the D reading is that it is an expansion of συνεχυθη ολη η πολις (taken by Ropes, Clark, *Acts*, and B.-L. to be the original text of the longer recension) to include a misunderstanding of the Latin version.

ibid. (498/4): δε D pc.; τε cet.; *-que* d e; *et* pler.
19.32 (498/15): H ΓAP EKKΛHCIA HN D; *erat enim ecclesia* d

19.39 (499/10): ΕΝ ΤΩ ΝΟΜΩ ΕΚΚΛΗϹΙΑ D*; *εν τω νομω εκκλησιας* D[B];
εν τη εννομω εκκλησια D[D] cet.; IN LEGEM ECCLESIAE d
D is halfway to the d text.
19.40 (499/14): *της συστροφης* (primo *συντρ.*) *ταυτης* D; *de hoc concurso* d
20.3 (499/24): ΑΝΑΧΘΗΝΑΙ ΕΙϹ ϹΥΡΙΑΝ D; IN SYRIAM PERDUCI d
20.4 (499/27): ΜΕΛΛΟΝΤΟϹ ΟΥΝ ΕΞΕΙΕΝΑΙ ΑΥΤΟΥ D; *συνειπετο δε αυτω* cet.; *volente autem comitari eum* d; *comitatus est autem eum* Lvg
d is probably derived from a translation of the majority text – *comitor* is used in the Latin versions for *συνειπετο*.
20.5 (499/33): ΑΥΤΟΝ D; *ημας* cet.; *nos* d cet.; *eos* c
20.6 (500/5): ΕΝ Η ΚΑΙ D; *ου και* pc.; *οπου* ℵ A E; *ου* B H L P al. pler.; *in qua* d; *ubi et* IR; *ubi* cet.
20.7 (500/10): OM D (lect. sing.); *δε* pc.; *τε* pler.; *-que* d pler.
20.11 (500/24): *δε* D E pc.; *τε* cet.; *-que* d pler.
20.13 (500/33): *ως* D pc.; OM cet.; OM d
20.16 (501/10): ΜΗΠΟΤΕ D; *οπως μη* cet.; *ut non* d; *ut ne* e; *ne qua* cet.
20.18 (501/15): *ως δε* D cet.; AD UBI d; *qui cum* pler.
ibid. (501/19): Η ΚΑΙ D; ET d
In a longer reading.
20.21 (501/30)
την εις (τον) θεον μετανοιαν D cet.
QUAE IN DO PAENITENTIAM AGENT d
We have already noticed this as a likely piece of theological alteration.
ibid. (501/31): *δια*+genitive D; *εις*+accusative cet.; *in*+accusative d cet.
20.22 (501/33)
συναντησαντα μοι D al.; *-σοντα μοι/εμοι* cet.
mihi ventura sunt d; *mihi event. sunt* gig LUC; *vent. sunt mihi* cet.
20.23 (502/1): ΤΟ ΑΓΙΟΝ ΠΝΑ D; *το πν. το αγ.* cet.; *spm sanctum* d
20.24 (502/6): *μου* D* al.; OM D[s.m.] al.; OM d; *meam* Lvg (pler.)
20.25 (502/13): *ουκετι* D cet.; *ουκ* ℵ; NON d
20.26 (502/17)
ΑΧΡΙ ΟΥΝ ΤΗϹ ϹΗΜΕΡΟΝ ΗΜΕΡΑϹ D*
διο ϋμειν εν της σημ. ημερα οτι D[F]
διοτι μαρτυρομαι υμιν εν τη σημ. ημερα cet.
propter quod hodierno die d
propter quod contestor vobis hodierno die gig
quapropter contestor vobis hodierna die e
d is corrupt – apparently by having been partially assimilated to the text of D, in the omission of *μαρτυρομαι υμιν* but not in the change from *διοτι* to *αχρι ουν*.
20.28 (502/22): ΤΟ ΑΓΙΟΝ ΠΝΑ D; *το πν. το αγ.* cet.; *spiritus sanctus* d pler.
21.13 (505/13)
ΕΙΠΕΝ ΔΕ ΠΡΟϹ ΗΜΑϹ Ο ΠΑΥΛΟϹ D
τοτε απεκριθη ο π. και ειπεν ℵ A B C* E al.
απεκ. δε pler.; *απεκ. τε* al.; *απεκ. ο π.* pc.

RESPONDIT AUTEM AD NOS PAULUS d
ibid. (505/18): *ιηυ χρυ* D; XRI IHU d
21.14 (505/21): *του θεου* D pc.; *του κυριου* cet.; *domini* d cet.
21.15 (505/22): ΜΕΤΑ ΔΕ ΤΙΝΑC ΗΜΕΡΑC D; *μετα δε τας ημ. ταυτας* cet.; *post hos autem dies* d
21.19 (506/2): ΟΥC ΑCΠΑΜΕΝΟC D*; *και ασπασαμενος αυτους* D^B cet.; *cum salutasset eos* d
This difference comes at the beginning of a rewriting of a passage by D; d has been half altered to agree with it.
21.24 (506/25): ΑΛΛ ΟΤΙ ΠΟΡΕΥΟΜΑΙ ΑΥΤΟC D*; *αλλα στοιχεις και αυτος* D^D cet.; *sed ambulans ipse* d
Again, d has been partially changed.
21.25 (506/28): *απεστειλαμεν* B D pc.; *επεστ.* cet.; *scripsimus* d
21.27 (507/6): ΔΕ D; OM cet.; OM d cet.
21.39 (508/22–3)
ΕΝ ΤΑΡCΩ ΔΕ ΤΗC ΚΙΛΙΚΙΑC ΓΕΓΕΝΝΗΜΕΝΟC D
ταρσευς τησ κιλ. ουκ ασημου πολεως πολιτης cet.
TARSENSIS EX CILICIAE NON IGNOTAE CIVITATIS / CUIUS (scil. *civis*) d
Here, d has not been adapted to D.
ibid. (508/23)
ΔΑΙΟΜΕ ΔΕ CΟΥ CΥΝΧΩΡΗCΑΙ ΜΟΙ D
δεομαι δε σου επιτρεψον μοι cet.
rogo obsegro autem mihi d
The double translation in d has led to the loss of the equivalent to *συνχωρησαι/επιτρεψον*.
21.40 (508/25): ΚΑΙ ΕΠΙΤΡΕΨΑΝΤΟC ΔΕ D*; *επιτρεψ.* cet.; *et cum permisisset* d
22.1 (508/31): *προς ϋμας νυνει* D; *nunc aput vos* d

The mastering and evaluation of this number of differences is not an easy task. We begin with the kind that has been regularly present throughout the text – transposition.

In D alone: 1.5; 7.10^1; 16.1^3; 19.17, 32
In d alone: 2.24; 3.10; 4.33; 5.1, 29^1, 35; 7.5, 18, 20; 13.25 *bis*, 42; 16.14; 19.26^4; 20.3; 21.13^2; 22.1
In d and other manuscripts: 1.7; 2.12, 29, 32; 4.4^2, 10; 5.32; 7.56; 10.33^3; 14.18; 15.20; 16.13; 18.15^2; 19.22^1, 25, 40
Examples that could be in either column: 4.29; 7.49, 60^2; 19.14^3
The readings at 10.33^3 and 35 could be in order to avoid hiatus (the former with the preceding *ergo*).

Ignoring the last group, we see that there are six in which D is unique, seventeen in which d is unique, and fifteen where d has other Latin support. This agrees fairly well with what we have come to expect. It is interesting that only at 15.20 and 19.14^3 is the transposition (by d) in an addition to the text, though at 19.25 and

21.13^{2} the d text is an inversion of the reading found in D, and there is variation among the Greek witnesses.

It seems possible that a higher proportion of the Latin transpositions in Acts are translational (and see the Gospel of John).

Close examination shows how many of the differences, including nearly all the significant ones, occur in passages where D is the only witness to its text. These may be classed according to the character of their peculiarity. Eighteen of them are in additions to the text:

2.30; 4.14^{2}; 5.15; 10.33^{1}; 11.27; 13.44^{1}, 44^{2}; 15.2^{3}, 2^{4}, 41; 16.1; 17.12^{2}; 18.21^{2}, 26^{2}, 26^{3}; 19.14^{1}, 14^{2}, 14^{3} (the last of these has already been listed as a transposition)

Thirty-five are to be found in places where D contains a rewriting of the text:

2.1^{2}; 3.16; 4.12, 21; 5.8, 10, 36^{3}; 11.9, 26 (*quater*); 12.7^{1}, 16^{2}; 13.5, 29 (?), 35; 15.38; 16.18, 34^{1}, 34^{2}; 17.5^{1}, 5^{2}; 19.1, 10^{1},10^{2}, 26^{1}, 26^{2}, 26^{3}; 20.6, 16, 21^{2}; 21.19, 39^{1}, 39^{2}

Many more (and I list twenty-eight here) come at the beginning of a phrase or sentence, where the structure or wording is peculiar to the D tradition.

2.2, 14; 4.4^{1}; 5.29, 38; 6.2, 6, 15; 7.34, 60; 10.15, 33^{2}, 36^{1}; 13.4, 6, 12; 14.4, 19; 16.26; 17.14, 15; 18.5^{1}, 5^{2}, 19^{1}; 19.18, 19; 21.15, 40

The various problems with identifying the Latin equivalents to the particles means that there are probably more differences like this than those that we can list with certainty.

To all these should be added two other groups which we have noted as we encountered them: those where a version of the D text has simply been tacked onto the existing text of d: 2.1^{1}, 45; 4.18; 5.4; 7.30; 11.1; 17.19. And those where the text of d has been only partly altered to agree with D: 2.6, 46; 5.19, 29^{2}; 6.3; 8.6; 10.21, 23, 25, 27; 11.2, 26 *quater*; 13.18, 23, 30; 14.2; 15.39; 16.18, 30; 19.9; 20.4, 26; 21.13, 24. These readings number 110 – over a third of the total number in the book.

Beyond this, we find a large body of readings where d does not follow a smaller unique reading in D. There are about fifty-six of these.

2.9; 3.5, 18; 4.14^{1}, 17^{1}, 17^{2}, 22; 5.4, 28^{2}, 36^{2}; 7.11, 24, 33, 39, 45^{2}, 54; 10.22, 28; 11.5, 7, 19, 21; 12.4; 13.7, 46^{1}, 47, 51; 14.1, 6, 14; 15.2^{1}, 2^{2}, 17; 16.9, 15, 16, 17; 17.1, 12, 19^{2}, 21, 25, 27^{1}, 27^{2}, 27^{3}, 31^{2}; 18.2, 10, 15, 26; 19.24; 20.5, 7, 23, 28; 21.27

There are thirty-four where d presents a unique reading. In eight others it has a text with no Greek support:

1.11; 4.24; 5.20, 36^{1}; 6.2^{2}; 7.10^{2}, 16, 45^{1}; 8.4, 7, 9^{2}; 10.16; 11.12, 14; 14.6 (in a recasting not unique to D), 22^{1}, 23, 24; 15.3^{1}, 3^{2}, 40; 16.1^{2}, 3, 21; 17.20, 27^{4}; 18.14, 19^{2}, 23^{1}; 19.12, 23, 27; 20.21^{1}, 22

Text with no Greek support: 7.7; 8.13; 11.8; 13.46^{2}; 15.2^{5}; 19.21^{1}, 21^{2}, 22^{2}

In another thirty-five d follows a text supported by other Greek witnesses than D:

2.39², 42; 3.22; 4.15, 30; 5.28¹, 34, 37; 7.28, 32, 35, 36, 50; 10.14, 36², 39; 13.48; 14.7, 22²; 15.7, 25, 32; 16.14², 36; 18.21, 23²; 19.3, 22³, 29²; 20.11, 13, 24, 25; 21.14, 25

Although there are a few places where casual slips are responsible for the difference, we still have another 134 readings to add to the 110 already noticed. In many of this second set, it is striking how often d does not follow D in a change to the beginning of a sentence or phrase. It is persuasive to argue that a corrector would let just such differences stand in harmonizing two texts. He would often be seeking congruity of shape rather than precise conformity.

The evidence points clearly to the accommodation of an existing Latin text to Greek D. The places where the longer reading is placed alongside the shorter, with no attempt to make a grammatical connection between them, provide the clearest evidence. Also vital are the high number of places where d follows a different text, and the divergencies within longer readings. The conclusion is the surest, because based on the least equivocal evidence, of any that we have yet reached in this study.

The high number of unique D readings among the differences in Acts indicates that agreement was generally reached by altering the Latin. However, there is some evidence that the Greek was not untouched by this process. Its reading at 19.27 is a clear example. Ropes argued that places where D has a participle followed by και and the finite verb furnish others (p. lxxii), citing 14.6. This is indeed possible, though in fact many of these constructions occur, as we have seen, in only one column.

CONCLUSIONS

Before examining the differences, we raised a question regarding revision: the numerical evidence appeared to credit the supposition that the double text of the manuscript had been revised with the books in their present order. But it is now possible to show the obvious conclusion to be wrong.

The number of differences due to transposition is fairly constant throughout. Many of these are typical of the Latin versions. It also seems that a number are the creation of the scribe of this manuscript.

It is also clear that there is not a steadily rising curve of differences, which we would expect to be the case if a corrector is to be presumed to be slackening in assiduity as his work progressed. Instead, we have found passages where the number of differences suddenly increases. John 6 is one, although John as a whole has fewer *significant* differences than Matthew has.

The reason for the far higher number of differences in Mark and Acts lies in the textual history of these books. The main cause in Mark is the degree of synoptic harmonization that has occurred. Luke also has more harmonizations than has Matthew.

The differences in Acts arise out of the particularly strange character of the D text to which, we have suggested, d has been brought into somewhat approximate harmony from a rather different base. Proportionately, there are no more differences to a page in Acts than in Mark.

It must not be forgotten that the Greek text of D is least distinctive in Matthew and John. Matthew, we may note, was harmonized least of the Synoptists. The regular harmonizations of Mark, the unique readings of Mark and Luke, and the extraordinarily idiosyncratic text of Acts all contribute to the higher number of differences in the latter part of the codex. The fact that the more idiosyncratic the Greek text, the more the columns differ, shows that the Greek text is ahead of the Latin in developing its distinctive character.

Rather than a revision of the books in this order, we have five books each with a particular character with regard to the relationship between the columns. As a result, we may claim that the arguments which I have set forward with regard to the exemplars of the codex are untouched. Moreover, we gain from this examination some insight into the varying features of the Old Latin texts that constituted those exemplars. There is no single quality here.

I set out in the beginning with the hypothesis that d is a translation from a Greek text 'similar to, but by no means identical with, its present companion'. This now requires some modification. In the first place, we cannot make a single statement that will be true of all five texts. Indeed, we have to say that d contains translations from several Greek texts. But there is also a more theoretical matter to be resolved.

How close would the Latin columns have to be to the Greek, for us to decide that they were derived from it? Do the thirty or forty significant differences apiece of Matthew and John (that is, the readings listed for each book as item 5, 'Textual differences') constitute a sufficiently strong body for us to be able to deny that really the d text is the same as that of its Greek companion? Here the method of looking for differences can be seen to contain a danger. What about the places where the two columns agree against most or all other witnesses? For example, Vogels lists 220 places in Matthew where D harmonizes. We have only three where it does so without the support of d, and eight where d harmonizes and D does not. It must be conceded that the number of differences in Matthew and John is too insignificant to challenge the conclusion that the two columns of the manuscript present us with a single text of these two books.

In Luke, and even more in Mark, we find tendencies which reveal distinctive qualities possessed by the Latin column that are not shared with the Greek. Here we can clearly see a more forced correspondence.

Finally, the Latin text of Acts has manifestly been adapted to share the vagaries of the Greek. There is, behind the Latin, a text of Acts which, while by no means normal, lacked many of the additions and paraphrases so characteristic of D. The comparison of the columns has allowed us a glimpse of this older stage in the longer recension of Acts. The fairly low number of differences between the columns outside these additions suggests the older Latin version to have been derived from a shorter version of the present D text.

But this enables us to suggest a further conclusion. There existed a Greek text of Acts with this character. It existed, presumably, in the same milieu as D, since it was the source for D's Latin companion. This text, or one closely related to it, must have also been the one from which the present Greek text of D was worked.

We saw signs of a similar alteration to the Latin texts of Luke and, to a lesser degree, of Mark. There were fewer examples, but it seems possible that these Greek texts also had undergone some change and augmentation since the Latin translation based on it had been made.

The isolation of the earlier form of the Greek text of Acts is of the utmost importance. It is the foundation for the reconstruction of the textual history of the D text of Acts.

The history we have suggested for the Latin column of Acts also illustrates the way in which a distinctive text form like that of D increased its circulation. It took over an existing Old Latin version, and made it its own.

CHAPTER FOURTEEN

The character of the tradition

While the five books of Codex Bezae have been shown to be a gathering of texts each with its own characteristics, the fact remains that, in the comparatively normal Matthew and John as well as in Acts, they share a character that marks them off from other copies. These texts have been handed down in a particular way. Can anything more definite be said about this type of textual transmission? Can we ascertain its characteristics?

The problems of exploring the theme are considerable. We suggested (in chapter 12) that only Mees' approach does justice to the whole of the manuscript's text. But the provision of a textual commentary on Codex Bezae is a task for another day. The method that we shall follow owes its shape to the way in which my researches developed. The beginning is to take the readings used by J. R. Harris to support his theory of wholesale Latinization of the Greek. If his theory is wrong, then we should have a totally random sample of readings which will reveal to us what other influences are at work.

M. Black, *An Aramaic Approach to the Gospels and Acts*, 3rd edition, Oxford, 1967; C. F. Burney, *The Aramaic Origin of the Fourth Gospel*, Oxford, 1922; Burney, 'A Hebraic Construction in the Apocalypse', *JTS* 22, 371–6; R. H. Charles, *A Critical and Exegetical Commentary on the Revelation of St. John* (The International Critical Commentary), Edinburgh, 1920, Vol. 1; F. C. Conybeare and St. G. Stock, *Selections from the Septuagint according to the Text of Swete*, New York, 1980 (1905); A. B. Davidson, *Hebrew Syntax*, 3rd edition, Edinburgh, 1902; S. R. Driver, *A Treatise on the Use of the Tenses in Hebrew*, 2nd edition, Edinburgh, 1881; E. Haenchen, *The Acts of the Apostles*, Oxford, 1971; Harris, *Codex*; M.-J. Lagrange, *Evangile selon Saint Marc*, 4th edition, Paris, 1929; Parker, 'Dictation Theory'; W. B. Stevenson, *Grammar of Palestinian Jewish Aramaic*, 2nd edition, Oxford, 1962; James Willis, *Latin Textual Criticism* (Illinois Studies in Language and Literature 61), Illinois, 1972.

Harris claimed to have found twenty-eight different kinds of Latinization, and produced something over 230 examples. Most are from Matthew, and only sixteen come from John. This imbalance will be made up once we have studied his examples.

The theme of his first chapter was 'Traces of an attempt at numerical verbal equality between the Greek and the Latin on the part of the scribes of the ancestry of Codex Bezae'. Many of these examples are the addition of an auxiliary verb. In

Matthew we have 5.12; 11.28. At 10.10 the purpose is to avoid ellipse (with other manuscripts). At 17.2 we find that D has replaced hypotaxis with parataxis. At 15.32 a phrase (EICIN KAI) has been inserted to amplify the text.

The auxiliary verb is also inserted at 11.8; 12.10; 18.7; 19.26 and 24.32, all with the support of d and other manuscripts. These five readings are not mentioned by Harris. Nor are the three in John (1.6; 9.22; 17.10) and four in Luke (2.12; 11.34; 13.23; 24.27).

The only reading in John that Harris does mention is at 4.9. This seems to be a clumsy rewriting of the Greek. In Luke, the intrusion of ECTIN at 8.25 is found in many witnesses, and again its purpose is to avoid ellipse. The omission of *ἦν* at 15.24 is found in other witnesses. That of *παρακαλειν* at v. 28 is an obvious slip.

Some of Harris' examples from Mark are harmonizations (Mk 2.25; 6.3; 9.34 and 10.27). In at least three more we find again the rejection of ellipse (see M.-T. 3, p. 304):

5.40: add. ONTEC post *αυτου*
6.20: add. EINAI post *αγιον*
14.36: add. EICIN post *δυνατα*

The reading at Mk 5.9 (add. ECTIN post *μοι*) could be either of these two.

In two other readings D presents a periphrastic tense (noticed by N. Turner, M.-T. 3, p. 87; M.-T. 4, p. 20):
2.4: HN ... KATAKEIMENOC D
14.21: ECTIN ΓΕΓΡΑΜΜΕΝΟΝ D

The substitution of A EICIN for *των* at 4.31 is seeking a simpler style, and the reading ΑΠΟ ΠΟΤΕ at 8.2 (ΗΜΕΡΑΙ ΤΡΕΙC EICIN ΑΠΟ ΠΟΤΕ ωΔΕ EICIN for *ημεραις τριων προσμενουσιν μοι*) is described by B.-D. (§203) as 'quite vulgar'.

Harris provides six examples from Acts. At 4.34; 13.29; 17.6 the verb *εἶναι* has been inserted for the kinds of grammatical reasons that we have already encountered. At 5.38 and 21.21 the argument that the Greek has followed the Latin is quite strong, though one wonders whether it may not rather be adopting a very colloquial style.

In chapter 9 of his book, Harris divides examples of Latinization into twenty-six classes. To analyse them all would be tedious, adding little fresh information in proportion to the time spent. I have selected classes and readings that enable us to seek out the main tendencies of the tradition.

One of these is harmonization, either to a parallel passage in another Gospel, or to a similar phrase that is not strictly a parallel, or within a Gospel (the matter is thoroughly studied by Vogels, *Harmonistik*). A common example of the last is in John, where the addition of the demonstrative to the noun *κοσμος* is found at 17.11, 14, 15, 18 (*bis*), 25. This is under the influence of the passages 8.23; 9.39; 11.9; 12.25, 31 (*bis*); 13.1; 16.11; 18.36 (*bis*).

The influence of the context is very strong. I have discussed this elsewhere with regard to Acts, and concluded that it was the cause of many readings. In fact, it may be observed throughout the manuscript. It is likely that a high proportion of them is due to the scribe of D, and that this was one of his particularly strong idiosyncrasies as a copyist. There are three reasons for this, two of which I have suggested elsewhere:

> First, it is improbable that most of these accidental slips would last long in a tradition, certainly in such numbers: they would be either easily corrected, or falsely emended. We cannot expect a group of them to be perfectly preserved, as it were fossilised, through a succession of copyings.
>
> Second, a great many of these errors were corrected by the hand called G. He confined himself chiefly to correcting the errors – and generally the more obvious ones – of the scribe. (Parker, 'Dictation Theory', p. 106)

The third reason is that not a few of the scribe's corrections to his own work are of such readings.

Perhaps it should be added, apropos of the first reason, that some of these readings make some kind of sense (for example, the imitation of surrounding aorists, as at Lk 1.78 ΕΠΕϹΚΕΨΑΤΟ), and would be more likely to survive.

It would, of course, be misleading to burden the scribe of D with responsibility for such errors as if he alone were inclined to them. The influence of the context has been called 'Perseveration and anticipation' by James Willis. He describes it as 'one of the most prolific sources of error in manuscripts and in printing' (p. 92). The difference between this category, and what Willis classes as 'Preoccupation with other matter', including 'Literary reminiscence', is sometimes narrow. Into the latter class come the kinds of harmonizations which we have just listed. It indicates a consistency of factors in the formation of the Bezan text.

Further attention focusses on the literary style of the Greek column. All but one of Harris' examples of 'Confusion owing to the difference of genders in Greek and Latin' are *constructio ad sensum:*

Mt 3.16: ΚΑΤΑΒΑΙΝΟΝΤΑ. This was one of Mill's examples. (See p. 184 for bibliographical details.)
Mk 9.36: ΠΑΙΔΙΟΝ ... ΑΥΤΟΝ (cp. B.-D. §282).
Ac 5.32: ΠΝΑ ... ΟΝ (cp. B.-D. §296).

Four of his 'Instances where the corresponding verbs or prepositions govern different places in Latin and Greek' turn out to concern the accusative with verbs of touching:

Mt 9.25: ΕΚΡΑΤΗϹΕΝ ΤΗΝ ΧΕΙΡΑ leg. *της χειρος*
Lk 20.26: ΡΗΜΑ ΕΠΙΛΑΒΕϹΘΑΙ leg. *ῥηματος*
Mk 5.41: ΚΡΑΤΗϹΑϹ ΤΗΝ ΧΕΙΡΑ leg. *της χειρος*
8.23: ΛΑΒΟΜΕΝΟϹ ΤΗΝ ΧΕΙΡΑ leg. *της χειρος*.

For the rule, and the exceptions in D, see B.-D. §170.

At Mt 9.24, D reads ΚΑΤΕΓΕΛΩΝ ΑΥΤΟΝ. Corrector D changed this to the genitive. But note that the phrase *καταγελα ἀνθρωπον* comes at Sir. 7.11 (-*ου* ℵ).

A particularly interesting group of readings is described by Harris as 'Rendering of the participle (especially the aorist participle) followed by the verb as two verbs with a conjunction; and consideration of the effect of the same' (pp. 75–8). In fact, he here describes two different tendencies in D, at which we will look separately.

The first is straightforward parataxis. Using two finite verbs, rather than a participle or subordinate clause for one of them, is generally regarded as a Semitism, although it can also be seen as non-literary Greek (Moulton, *Proleg.* p. 12; M.-T. 4, p. 19). In fact, some of Harris' examples are more plausibly to be explained as harmonizations (Mt 13.4; 21.6f; 26.51; Jn 6.11; Lk 5.14). In discussing the style of Mark, Turner (M.-T. 4, p. 29f) raises the question as to whether any of the apparent Semitisms of D, in particular asyndeton and parataxis, could in fact be Latinisms, and therefore possibly authentic features of Marcan writing. The fact that they are not confined to Mark's Gospel makes this unlikely.

Black (p. 67f) refers to several passages where the Westcott and Hort text has the parataxis, and D hypotaxis (Mk 2.15; 5.28). We have already encountered one example in this chapter. There is another at Ac 8.26. And he also gives five readings where a variety of witnesses join D in parataxis (Mt 5.13; 17.7; Mk 12.21; Ac 13.12; 19.21).

The second, and stranger, group is of readings where D has a participle followed by *και* and a finite verb. This construction is not unknown in the New Testament (see M.-H. 2, p. 428f). But it appears far more regularly in D than anywhere else. A grammatical exposition will show just how many possible factors have to be considered in assessing the influences on the style of D.

First, the construction is frequent in classical Greek. It is discussed in Moulton and Howard (M.-H. 2, p. 428):

> Thucydides IV. 100: *ἄλλῳ τε τρόπῳ πειράσαντες καὶ μηχανὴν προσήγαγον*

Compare:

> Plato, *Theaet.* 144C: *ἀνδρὸς ... καὶ ἄλλως εὐδοκίμου καὶ ... κατέλιπον*

The examples given from Xenophon (*Cyrop.* II. 3.8 and eight other references) do not seem to me to be relevant.

Second, there is a similar Hebrew construction. 'When additional clauses are joined by *and* to a participial consn. the *finite* tense is usually employed, though not always' (Davidson, §100(e)). It is also an Aramaic construction (see Dan. 4.22; for the later extension of the participle's functions, see Stevenson, §21.9–15). Driver (*Tenses in Hebrew*, §117) discusses the usage in more detail. Burney took the further step of analysing Driver's examples and comparing them with the Septuagint. Out of twenty-five readings, the Septuagint translates literally six times (Gen. 49.17b;

Exod. 34.7; Num. 19.13; Isa. 14.17; 30.2; Amos 5.7). Elsewhere it translates idiomatically.

As well as sometimes adopting the Hebrew construction, the Septuagint also occasionally has a participle followed by *και* and a finite verb where the Hebrew has two finite verbs. Conybeare and Stock refer to two passages (§80), and suggest that the function of *και* is to emphasize the verb:

> Num. 21.11: *καὶ ἐξάραντες ἐξ Ὠβώθ, καὶ παρενέλαβον ἐν Χαλγαεί* (OM *και*² A F).
> 22.23: *καὶ ἰδοῦσα ἡ ὄνος . . . καὶ ἐξέκλινεν.*

I have also noticed 1 Sam. 9.11: *αὐτῶν ἀναβαινόντων . . . καὶ αὐτοὶ εὑρίσκουσιν.*

Thus, one construction appears in the Septuagint for two different reasons: to reproduce the Hebrew literally, and as a Greek idiom.

The Septuagint is one possible source for the construction in the New Testament. Another is the direct influence of Aramaic. Use of the participle for the indicative generally in D is described by Moulton as 'apparently arising from the literal translation of Aramaic' (*Proleg.*, p. 224). Whether the Semitism appears in the New Testament through the medium of the Septuagint, or directly from Aramaic, is not immediately relevant for us here.

Finally, the very same construction is also a feature of late Latin. As Stone writes, 'The present participle is found sometimes as the equivalent of the indicative. This usage was due to the widespread employment of the nominative absolute, and also the fact that in cases where forms of *esse* were used for the participle they tended to drop out, leaving the participle alone' (*Language*, p. 58). Stone refers us to two passages in E. Löfstedt's commentary on the *Peregrinatio Aetheriae* (pp. 158, 249) (though in neither passage of the *Peregrinatio* (5.11; 16.6) does the construction with which we are dealing occur).

It is fairly rare for this construction to be found in both columns at once. This rules out the possibility of the Greek having been Latinized, and the fact that a similar construction occurs in the Latin will play no further part in this discussion.

Setting Codex Bezae aside for the moment, let us fit what we have learned into the context of New Testament Greek.

Examples of the construction listed by Moulton and Howard or Moulton and Turner are as follows:

> Mt 13.22, 23 par. Lk 8.12, 14; Jn 1.32; 5.44 (not א); 2 Jn 2; Rev. 1.18; 2.2, 9, 20, 23; 3.9; 7.14; 14.2–3; 15.3.

Jn 1.32 can, however, be explained differently.

Burney finds the Hebrew construction to lie behind the New Testament examples (*Aramaic Origin*, p. 96f). So does Charles (pp. cxliv–cxlvi).

To return to Codex Bezae: the construction is not only more frequent; it is also much starker, often without the softening of intermediate clauses. The nearest comparison is with passages like Rev. 2.2.

The following list of the construction in Codex Bezae does not claim to be exhaustive.

Matthew 26.14: ΠΟΡΕΥΘΕΙϹ ΕΙϹ ΤΩΝ ·ΙΒ· ... ΚΑΙ ΕΙΠΕΝ
John 6.5: ΕΠΑΡΑϹ ΟΥΝ ΤΟΥϹ ΟΦΘΑΛΜΟΥϹ Ο ΙΗϹ ΚΑΙ ΘΕΑϹΑΜΕΝΟϹ ... ΚΑΙ ΛΕΓΕΙ
Luke 6.4: ΕΙϹΕΛΘΩΝ ... ΚΑΙ ... ΕΦΑΓΕΝ
9.6: ΕΞΕΡΧΟΜΕΝΟΙ ΔΕ ΚΑΤΑ ΠΟΛΕΙϹ ΚΑΙ ΗΡΧΟΝΤΟ
Mark 2.1: ΕΙϹΕΛΘΩΝ ... ΚΑΙ ΗΚΟΥϹΘΗ
5.27: ΑΚΟΥϹΑϹΑ ΠΕ ΤΟΥ ΙΗΥ ΕΛΘΟΥϹΑ ΟΠΙϹΘΕΝ ΚΑΙ ΗΨΑΤΟ
7.25: ΕΛΘΟΥϹΑ ΚΑΙ ΠΡΟϹΕΠΕϹΕΝ
11.2: ΛΥϹΑΝΤΕϹ ΑΥΤΟΝ ΚΑΙ ΑΓΑΓΕΤΕ
The influence of par. Mt 21.2 is strong here.
11.15: ΕΙϹΕΛΘΩΝ ΕΙϹ ΪΕΡΟϹΟΛΥΜΑ ΚΑΙ ΟΤΕ ΗΝ
14.1: ΠΩϹ ΑΥΤΟΝ ΚΡΑΤΗϹΑΝΤΕϹ ΚΑΙ ΑΠΟΚΤΕΙΝΩϹΙΝ
14.63: ΔΙΑΡΡΗΞΑϹ ΤΟΥϹ ΧΕΙΤΩΝΑϹ ΑΥΤΟΥ ΚΑΙ ΛΕΓΕΙ
15.46: ΠΡΟϹΚΥΛΙϹΑϹ ΛΙΘΟΝ ΕΠΙ ΤΗΝ ΘΥΡΑΝ ΤΟΥ ΜΝΗΜΙΟΥ ΚΑΙ ΑΠΗΛΘΕΝ
16.11: ΚΑΚΕΙΝΟΙ ΑΚΟΥϹΑΝΤΕϹ ΟΤΙ ΖΗ ΚΑΙ ΕΘΕΑΘΗ ΫΠ ΑΥΤΗϹ ΚΑΙ ΟΥΚ ΕΠΙϹΤΕΥϹΑΝ
16.15: ΠΟΡΕΥΘΕΝΤΕϹ ΕΙϹ ΤΟΝ ΚΟϹΜΟΝ ΚΑΙ ΚΗΡΥΞΑΤΕ
Acts 3.4: ΕΜΒΛΕΨΑϹ ΔΕ Ο ΠΕΤΡΟϹ ΕΙϹ ΑΥΤΟΝ ϹΥΝ ΪΩΑΝΝΗΝ ΚΑΙ ΕΙΠΕΝ
4.3: ΕΠΙΒΑΛΟΝΤΟϹ ΑΥΤΟΙϹ ΤΑϹ ΧΕΙΡΑϹ ΚΑΙ ΕΘΕΝΤΟ
5.21: ϹΥΝΚΑΛΕϹΑΜΕΝΟΙ ... ΚΑΙ ΑΠΕϹΤΕΙΛΑΝ
7.4: ΕΞΕΛΘΩΝ ΕΚ ΓΗϹ ΧΑΛΔΑΙΩΝ ΚΑΙ ΚΑΤΩΚΗϹΕΝ
8.2: ϹΥΝΚΟΜΙϹΑΝΤΕϹ ΤΟΝ ϹΤΕΦΑΝΟΝ ΑΝΔΡΕϹ ΕΥΛΑΒΕΙϹ ΚΑΙ ΕΠΟΙΗϹΑΝ
10.27: ΚΑΙ ΕΙϹΕΛΘΩΝ ΤΕ ΚΑΙ ΕΥΡΕΝ
12.16: ΕΞΑΝΟΙΞΑΝΤΕϹ ΔΕ ΚΑΙ ΪΔΟΝΤΕϹ ΑΥΤΟΝ ΚΑΙ ΕΞΕϹΤΗϹΑΝ
13.7: ϹΥΝΚΑΛΕϹΑΜΕΝΟϹ ΒΑΡΝΑΒΑΝ ΚΑΙ ϹΑΥΛΟ ΚΑΙ ΕΖΗΤΗϹΕΝ ΑΚΟΥϹΑΙ
14.6: ϹΥΝΙΔΟΝΤΕϹ ΚΑΙ ΚΑΤΕΦΥΓΟΝ
14.14: ΑΚΟΥϹΑϹ ΔΕ ΒΑΡΝΑΒΑϹ ΚΑΙ ΠΑΥΛΟϹ ΔΙΑΡΡΗΞΑΝΤΕϹ ΤΑ ΪΜΑΤΙΑ ΑΥΤΩΝ ΚΑΙ ΕΞΕΠΗΔΗϹΑΝ
17.1: ΔΙΟΔΕΥϹΑΝΤΕϹ ΔΕ ΤΗΝ ΑΜΦΙΠΟΛΙΝ ΚΑΙ ΚΑΤΗΛΘΟΝ
20.10: ΚΑΤΑΒΑϹ ΔΕ Ο ΠΑΥΛΟϹ ΕΠΕϹΕΝ ΕΠ ΑΥΤΩ ΚΑΙ ϹΥΝΠΕΡΙΛΑΒΩΝ ΚΑΙ ΕΙΠΕΝ

According to Lagrange, *και* has been inserted in these readings to produce an equivalent number of words in each column (p. lix). Black points out that, if this was the reviser's aim, he failed to achieve it (p. 68). Another approach has been to see D as a hybrid text. Thus Haenchen writes of the text at Ac 14.6 that 'This is not an Aramaism ... but a mixed reading, a hybrid of the B-text and the Latin (d and h)' (p. 421 n. 2). It is certainly possible that the reading at Mk 11.2 is a partial harmonization and therefore such a hybrid. However, the construction comes too regularly for this to explain all of its occurrences.

Serious consideration should be given to the possibility that this construction represents part of the style in which the texts contained in D have been recast. The stylistic peculiarities we have observed all point to an attempt to rewrite the material in a more vernacular style. Far from being Semitisms, many of the features of the language of Codex Bezae are homespun Greek. As against the Atticizing process, it seems that we have to reckon with the opposite: an attempt to explain obscurities – and what are perceived as such – by using a vernacular style. The many tiny expansions of the text, except for harmonizations, will be part of the same attempt.

See also T. Hirunuma, 'Matthew 16:2b–3', in Epp and Fee, pp. 35–45, esp. p. 43 and note. He suggests that the reading of D at Matthew 16.3 (AHP; cp. P Lond 991[10], *απο εδαφους μεχρι αερος*) 'might be a vernacular use with a general meaning'. His quotation is incorrect. B.L. Pap. 209 reads *απο εδαφου αχρι αερος*. Pap 991 has *απο θημελιου εως αερως*.

What elements mark out the Greek text of Codex Bezae? We have observed harmonization, not only between precise parallels, but also between similar phrases and within Gospels; the influence of the context; writing in an intentionally colloquial style.

The place of the Latin column *vis-à-vis* these characteristics is important. In fact it too contains them (hence Harris' belief that it was their cause). This suggests that it is derived from texts that already showed them.

These features are the common characteristics that make the Bezan text so immediately recognizable and distinctive. The participial construction which we have examined shows how particularly strong they are in Mark and in Acts. The fact that we were able to find in the Latin column of Acts the signs of a Greek text that showed such features without many of the longer readings, indicates that they are also long-established in the tradition.

Present opinion rightly discards the theory that wholesale Latinization of the Greek has occurred. However, the fact remains that in a number of places Latinization remains the best explanation of the text. The reading ΚΑΙ ϹΥΝΕΧΥΘΗ ΟΛΗ Η ΠΟΛΙϹ ΑΙϹΧΥΝΗϹ (Ac 19.29) is certainly one, and we have noticed a few others. It is worth asking under what circumstances such a reading could have arisen.

One possibility is that a copyist of a bilingual tradition sufficiently fluent in both tongues could unconsciously have put a Latin reading into Greek and written it down. It would have to be a Latin reading already known to him, since we have argued that the Greek page was written first. One could also imagine that in copying a bilingual text and finding one column either illegible or evidently corrupt, a scribe would consult the other in order to work out what he should write. It is also credible that a reader or copyist might consider the reading of the Latin column to be superior, and emend the Greek to accord with it.

Such factors might, over several copyings, exert enough influence for there to be a number of places where the Greek follows its Latin partner. It may be concluded that this is actually how it was with the Greek column of Codex Bezae. But it is only where other explanations fail that it should be adopted. It is salutary to recall Marsh's canon:

> There is no reason whatsoever for ascribing any reading of a Greek Ms to the influence of the Latin, unless it can be proved that it could not have taken its rise in the Greek, and that it might easily have originated in the Latin.
>
> (see chapter 12 above)

Another way, however, in which the text of the manuscript will have been affected by its bilingual nature, is in the lay-out. It is not hard to find places where the sense-lines do not accurately reproduce the sense of the text, with the consequence that the meaning has been altered, whole phrases being placed with wrong sentences, and sometimes altered as a result. And we have noted how the activity of Corrector B would have added to the number of such confusions.

One may also wonder whether the handling of the Greek text is not analogous to that of the Latin. That is to say, there was no authoritative Latin text for many centuries. Everybody, according to Augustine's famous complaint, who believed themselves to be competent produced their own version. In the G corrections, we can see this being done to d. With no fixed Latin text, transmitters of a bilingual tradition in a Latin environment may, consciously or unconsciously, have applied some of the freedom with which they handled the one column, to their reproduction of the other.

A further point remains to be made with regard to the considerably greater freedom of text shown in Mark and Acts. This is evident not only from comparison with other manuscripts, but from the greater disparity between the columns. The tradition is much more freely reproduced. The present order of the books may be not without significance in explaining this. The Gospels, we may suggest, are treated more carefully than Acts – or, at any rate, rather differently. Mark, however, regarded in the early church as a digest of Matthew, comes in for the most alteration, and is subsequently put at the end of the Gospel sequence. Acts is regarded as a text that can be handled much more freely, and we see that it is not only rewritten, but also considerably expanded. In the Gospels, material that is strictly additional, rather than harmonizing or added for the purpose of clarification, is rarer. A few *logia*, notably Jn 7.59–8.11; Lk 6.4; 22.44; 23.53, show that the transmitters of the text were not wholly averse to adding material. But at the end of Luke the tradition was so restrained as actually to *omit* material that opinion today would encourage it to have retained. The point here is that, even in this free textual tradition, there is a certain restraint. While the text of Acts is nothing less than an exhaustive rewriting, the Gospels are clearly recognizable as an attempt to reproduce Matthew, John, Luke, and Mark.

At the same time, the Gospel texts do not have the same kind of fixed form that is found elsewhere. The distinctions between the four Gospels (harmonizations) and between them and other traditions about Jesus (additions) are not clearly observed. And apart from these, there are the many other alterations we have seen. There are two possible reasons for this.

One is seen by comparison with a different kind of tradition. The Alexandrian text has often been described as representative of the best in ancient textual criticism, based on a careful preserving of classical writings, in the awareness that they may be permanently damaged by negligence or freedom in their transmission. By comparison with this, the Bezan text can be seen as bad scholarship, a failure to make every effort to secure the purity of the tradition.

Alternatively, an explanation could be given in theological terms (though the first is in fact a precondition); the texts do not have the kind of authority that requires their accurate preservation. They are simply part of a number of elements, perhaps including oral tradition, on which the church's teaching is based. In such a tradition, the material will be handled more freely; some will move from book to book; there will be less concern with handing on the precise wording from copy to copy.

Such appears to have been the situation out of which the Greek texts of D have come.

An implication of this is that to try to find a pure 'D text' is a useless undertaking. Its existence has only ever been assumed by analogy with the carefully preserved Alexandrian and the ecclesiastically approved Byzantine texts. The kind of text presented in D will, by its nature, never have existed in a controlled and definable form. Such a text contains many hybrids, but no species.

For example, we have found in Acts a Latin text and by inference a Greek original that was similar to D but shorter. To define either as the authentic D text is impossible. All that can be said is that the Greek text of D in Acts is the apotheosis of the free textual tradition.

It follows, and we are scarcely saying anything new here, that besides texts geographically recognizable, and texts of a particular period, we have texts of different genres. The relation of Codex Bezae to some of its supposed allies may be an affinity of this kind – rather than blood relations, they are kindred spirits.

In conclusion: the nature of D is determined by a number of characteristics. A tendency to recast the text in a more vernacular mould; harmonization in the Gospels, and the influence of the context (especially the close context) everywhere; the introduction of material from other sources; interaction between the columns; and, explaining how all this came about – a freedom to transmit the text loosely.

One may well feel ambivalent about this freedom. As textual critics, we can only deplore it (except as a source of absorbing activity). Humanly and theologically, there seems something admirable in this willingness to seek out the authentic spirit at the expense of the letter.

It is at this point that we encounter a notable theological tendency in the Codex Bezae: an attitude to the text that has affected every page. We shall return to it, as well as to further implications for our studies of the columns and the textual tradition, in the final chapter.

PART V

Text and codex

CHAPTER FIFTEEN

The origins of the Codex Bezae

Having studied the internal evidence that provides information about the origins of Codex Bezae, that is to say, the character of the hand, the particularities of the correctors, and the nature of the text, we are in a position to enquire as to its place of origin and early history, setting the internal evidence within the context of the history of the church and of contemporary culture.

A remarkably varied number of areas have been suggested as the homeland of D, ranging from Gaul to Alexandria and from Africa to Jerusalem. Since the palaeographical evidence in favour of an Eastern origin cannot be ignored, we can pass over the Western theories quite quickly, to examine more thoroughly the Eastern possibilities.

Aetheria, *Ethérie, Journal de voyage* (Sources Chrétiennes 21), ed. H. Pétré, 2nd edition, Paris, 1957; J. N. Birdsall, 'Geographical and Cultural Origin' (see p. 23 for full bibliographical details); F.E. Brightman, 'On the Italian Origin of Codex Bezae. The Marginal Notes of Lections', *JTS* 1 (1900), 446–54; F. H. Chase, *The Old Syriac Element in the Text of Codex Bezae*, London, 1893; Clark, *Acts*, pp. lv–lxix; Fischer, 'Das NT', *ANTF* 5, pp. 40–1 = *Beiträge*, pp. 208f; Harris, *Codex*, especially chapter 4; K. Lake, 'On the Italian Origin of Codex Bezae. Codex Bezae and Codex 1071', *JTS* 1 (1900), 441–5; Lowe, 'The Codex Bezae', *JTS* 14 (1913), 385–8; Lowe, 'Two Fragments'; Lowe, 'A Note'; G. Mercati, 'On the Non-Greek Origin of the Codex Bezae', *JTS* 15 (1914), 448–51, reprinted in *Opere minore* 3 (= Studi e testi 78), Vatican, 1937, pp. 332–5; Schulz, *Disputatio*, pp. 7–9; Scrivener, pp. xxix–xxxi; K. Sneyders de Vogel, 'Le Codex Bezae, est-il d'origine sicilienne?', *BBC* 3 (1926), 10–13; A. Souter, 'The Original Home of Codex Claromontanus (D^{PAUL})', *JTS* 6 (1905), 240–3; Stone, *Language*, pp. 12–16, 66–8.

Perhaps the most remarkable theory of all is that advanced by J. A. Bengel, who, in Schulz's words, dared to conclude that the manuscript had been copied in *Britain*, on the basis of a comparison with the Anglo-Saxon version (*Disputatio*, p. 7). It is only fair to point out that this claim is found in the posthumous (1763) edition of his *apparatus criticus* (Vol. 1, §28), edited by his son-in-law Philip David Burk.

The theory that the manuscript came from *Southern Gaul* goes back to J. M. A. Scholz (1794–1852; *Novum Testamentum*, Leipzig, 1830–6, Proleg. 1. xl; ciii, cited by Scrivener, p. xxxi). It was later supported by Scrivener, Harris, and Sneyders de

Vogel. The view is quite worthless, being based as it is on an early stage in the understanding of the development of Latin into the Romance languages. The supposed Gallicanisms of the text are simply those typical everywhere of the stage of development that the language had reached. The last essay in favour of Gaul to be written (Sneyders de Vogel) attempted to prove, on the basis of linguistic phenomena, that the manuscript was copied in the diocese of Lyons and Vienne. It provoked a reply by Lowe ('A Note') which showed once and for all that Gaul is ruled out on palaeographical grounds. Stone has since demonstrated that two phonological errors especially prevalent in texts from Gaul (confusion between *i* and *e*, and *o* and *u*) are not particularly frequent in Codex Bezae. Only the tendency for third-conjugation verbs to move into the second, shared with the *Peregrinatio Aetheriae*, is particularly Gallican (Stone, p. 66).

North Africa can also be discounted. There is no similarity between the script of d and the well developed African style of Codices Bobbiensis and Palatinus, the Leningrad Augustine, the Vatican Hilary, and other manuscripts known to be of African origin (see *CLA Supplement*, Introduction).

Sicily was advocated by Ropes. It is unfortunate that there is a lack of evidence to substantiate the case – there are no known Sicilian manuscripts for comparison. Ropes argued not from claims for proof but from probability. One of his stronger points was to suggest that the Muslim invasions of the East, which drove many Greeks into Western exile, is the cause of the lack of corrections to the Latin text, since the predominant language of the area was changed to Greek. But this would put an impossibly late date on the early Greek correctors, and still leave a large gap between Corrector G and the period of the invasions and expatriations.

Souter was in favour of a *Sardinian* origin. Having shown that the Codex Claromontanus was Sardinian, he found a historical reason for its production in the fact that in the year 533 this thoroughly Romanized island came into the possession of the Byzantine emperor. He then suggested that Codex Bezae and the Laudian Acts were also written there. Unfortunately, the earlier date now to be attributed to D rules out this theory.

The first to suggest *South Italy* were Lake and Brightman, in a joint article. Lake's part of the work was based on the fact that the text of 1071 (Laurae A. 104, a twelfth-century codex of the Gospels containing the Jerusalem colophon) 'essentially agrees with D' in the *Pericope Adulterae*. He lists eight agreements against all other manuscripts, one disagreement, and four readings unique to 1071. This established, he seeks a point of association. 1071 was written in the West, for it contains illuminations with Latin words in them, such as a picture of John containing the phrase *in principio erat verbum*. The manuscript can be traced back to Italy from the Laura: Lake suggests that it came to its present resting place from a ruined monastery nearby called Morfinon, which was founded in the twelfth century by monks from Amalfi, near Salerno. It seems reasonable to assume that they took the manuscript with them. Gregory had already observed that 'In Calabria nisi fallor exaratus . . . partim litteris Neritinis' (*Prolegomena*, p. 603). That the text of the *Pericope Adulterae* entered the manuscript's ancestry in Italy is shown by the fact that no other members of the Western group of manuscripts with this colophon (which include *Λ*, 157, 262, 565, and 829) have the same form of it. Lake therefore concludes that an ancestor of 1071 had this form of the passage added to it from the text of D, in Italy. It was necessary for Lake to show that Codex Bezae was in Italy in the twelfth century, and he does this by denying that it was ever in France at all, suggesting that Beza acquired it from some other source. We now know that it was in Lyons by the ninth century, so the argument cannot stand. Apart from this, everything we know about the oldest Italian manuscripts makes it impossible that D could be counted among their number. Only the arguments of external evidence, that Greek-speaking communities existed in the South of Italy, give the claim any force. However, a detailed examination makes these untenable, on the same grounds as those of Ropes have to be rejected.

Brightman's contribution set out to show that the type of lectionary system used by the later hands could not have been added in Gaul, but could have been in Italy, where the rite was Byzantine. He suggested an area comprising Calabria, Apuleia, and the Basilicata, which from the time of Leo the Isaurian (717–40) up to the Norman Conquest was within the jurisdiction of the Patriarchate of Constantinople. The problems with fitting this into the dates for the various hands of D are equally insuperable.

We need only very briefly note that Lowe advanced *Sicily* and *Dacia* as 'reasonable enough hypotheses', but 'mere guesses', without advancing any evidence ('A Note', *BBC* 4, p. 13 = *Pal. Papers* 1,227).

Compared to the suggestions of whole provinces of the empire by those who have advocated a Western origin for the manuscript, those who have placed it in the East have generally favoured particular cities. The reason for this is that one can be far more precise about conditions in the East with regard to the extent of Latin Christianity and learning. Since the physical evidence is so decisively in favour of a Greek place of writing, the possibilities must be more carefully weighed.

Egypt has been advocated by scholars ever since Thomas Kipling. J. S. Semler (1725–91) had suggested that the manuscript's *exemplar* was from Egypt (see Thomas Edwards, *Remarks on Dr. Kipling's Preface to Beza*, Cambridge, 1793, p. 32). Marsh argued that the writer used a manuscript of the 'Alexandrine edition' (see Edwards, *ibid.*, referring to Marsh's translation of Michaelis' *Introduction*, pp. 683 and 708). Schulz also argued for an Egyptian origin (*Disputatio*, p. 8f). Clark, who had at one time favoured Jerusalem, became a leading modern proponent of this theory (*Acts*, pp. lviii–lxiv). His evidence is as follows. First, the extensive number of other Egyptian bilingual manuscripts; second, that they are written in sense-lines; and third, the similarity between the texts of D, the

Michigan Papyrus P[38], the 'codex *Thomae*' (as he calls Thomas of Harkel's source), *Pap. Oxy.* 405, and the Sahidic version. Further pillars of his claim are Tischendorf's view that the Claromontanus comes from Egypt, the agreement of the order of the books with some Egyptian texts, and the use of the forms of the *nomina sacra* IHC and XPC. Let us examine these points.

First, it is true that there are many Egyptian bilingual manuscripts. In fact, more than half of the New Testament bilinguals of which one language is Greek come from Egypt. But in fact all these are Graeco-Coptic manuscripts. Thus there is evidence that bilinguals were well established in the Christian literature of Egypt, but no evidence that these included Graeco-*Latin* manuscripts. Apart from these New Testament texts, there are a number of bilingual texts including Cicero, Virgil, and Aesop, all Graeco-Latin (see chapter 4). It is fairly clear that these were school texts. A basic Latin education was available in Egypt, as elsewhere. But these texts provide no evidence of a Christian community needing a Graeco-Latin text. They are all the relics of a society needing to learn Latin from the beginning, and producing basic aids for the study of Latin writers.

The argument that sense-lines are a feature of Egyptian bilinguals overlooks the fact that they are a feature of most other bilinguals (see chapter 5).

The textual arguments cannot be used, because the survival of more texts in Egypt than elsewhere is likely to distort our understanding of the distribution of text-types. It is also questionable how close these witnesses, and particularly the Sahidic, actually are to Codex Bezae.

The other arguments have no weight to them at all. It is true that the Catholic Epistles come before Acts in the Bohairic and Sahidic versions. But it is not the case that these versions place the Catholic epistles directly after the Gospels – an equally accurate description of the order of the books in D (even assuming that the missing part of D actually contained the Catholic Epistles – a matter which we discussed in chapter 1). Nor do they place the Gospels in the order Matthew–John–Luke–Mark. The forms of the *nomina sacra* are simply an earlier type than ις and similar two-letter contractions (see chapter 6).

None of Clark's evidence has any cogency. He produces no evidence for any group in Egypt that could possibly need such a text as Codex Bezae. Indeed, the history of Egyptian Christianity is of Hellenistic Alexandria on the one hand, and of a rural Coptic church on the other. Unless research reveals the existence of a Latin community in Christian Egypt of a kind from which Codex Bezae could have come – and so far it has done nothing of the kind – then the evidence must be taken as showing it to be impossible that it could be Egyptian in origin.

The most recent advocate of *Antioch* seems to have been F.H. Chase. He believed that the codex's idiosyncrasies are to be traced back to a second-century Graeco-Syriac manuscript. Sanday argued for an Antiochian origin for the Latin column (*The Guardian*, 18 and 25 May 1892; cited by Chase, pp. 143ff). There is no point in offering formal rebutment of a theory which is presented with such slight support.

A much stronger case has been made for *Jerusalem*. This has been argued by Stone, on the grounds that its creation at such a centre may have been a reason for the manuscript's preservation (surely one of the accidental truths of history), and that Jerusalem was a Christian centre in 'a region imperfectly Hellenized' (p. 67f). The case has been most recently made by Birdsall. Here arguments are used which seek to explain the use of a bilingual in known church practice at a particular place.

The evidence is derived from the *Peregrinatio Aetheriae*. Aetheria, a cultivated lady of Galicia, visited Palestine at a time now fixed to between the Easters of 381 and 384 (for a full bibliography see J. Quasten, *Patrology*, Vol. 4, Westminster, Maryland, 1986). She describes the way in which the readings and the bishop's address were delivered at Jerusalem just before the year 400. They were first given in Greek, and then translated into the vernacular (Syriac and Latin) for the benefit of non-Greek hearers in the congregation. Further references to the use of several tongues in the liturgy may be found in Epiphanius (*Adv. Haer.* 3.2.21 (*PL* 42.825)), and Jerome (*Ep.* 108.29 (*CSEL* 55.348)). Other passages cited by Clark are not relevant.

A difficulty with Aetheria's account is that we cannot be sure that bilingual (or even Chase's hypothetical trilingual) *manuscripts* were used. The precise wording suggests rather an extempore translation, or even something of a paraphrase: 'quia sunt alii fratres et sorores graecolatini, qui latine exponunt eis' (47.4). According to its usual meaning, *expono* could be more easily taken in this sense. What is interesting for our purposes in this account is why the bishop, even if he knew other tongues, used Greek. It was not only because 'pars populi et graece et syriste nouit, pars etiam alia per se graece' (47.3), but rather because 'necesse est graece legi' (47.4). That is, whether or not anybody understood a word of it, Greek had to be used, because it was the proper liturgical language, and because the sacred text was Greek. Thus a fully Latin-speaking church, with or without a few educated people who knew Greek (and a lector who could at any rate read the characters), might still have a bilingual Gospel Book. Codex Bezae will then have been produced for a Latin-speaking community still close enough to the Greek origins of the church for Greek to be the language *necesse legi* because of its sacred character. But the language of the community will have been Latin. Such, to take an example far enough removed from Codex Bezae not to be confusing, might have been the case in the church at Rome in the period immediately before the abandonment of the Greek liturgy. The use of Latin in the West long beyond its use by the majority of people would be another parallel.

Two important objections to the theory that Codex Bezae was used for pilgrims to Jerusalem lie in the activity of the correctors. It may be assumed that there would have been some concern to ensure that the material read in the various tongues corresponded with each other. But, as we have observed, only G corrected both columns. Moreover, the subsequent corrections, all to the Greek, show the Latin to have fallen out of use. But there is no reason why Jerusalem should have ceased to use so valuable a book, when it continued as a place of pilgrimage as long as it was accessible to Western travellers.

A final piece of evidence adduced by Birdsall concerns the minuscule 1071, used by Lake in his arguments for an Italian origin. This codex contains the Jerusalem colophon. But further research would be necessary to show that the text of the *Pericope Adulterae* found in this manuscript came from its collation with manuscripts 'in the holy mountain'. The fact that its allies do not contain the same form of text in fact makes it unlikely that it did.

On the grounds, therefore, of the precise nuance of Aetheria's description, and of the evidence from the correctors of the way it was used, the view that Codex Bezae was written in Jerusalem has to be discounted. It may be added that there is no palaeographical evidence to support such a view. It is true that there is very little evidence of any kind about Latin manuscripts from Jerusalem. What there is, however, does not support a connection with Codex Bezae. The conventions of the *scriptorium* of Rufinus, on the Mount of Olives, have been painstakingly sought out by Dr C. P. Hammond.

'A Product of a Fifth-Century Scriptorium Preserving Conventions used by Rufinus of Aquileia', *JTS* N.S. 29 (1978), 366–91; 'Products of Fifth-Century Scriptoria Preserving Conventions used by Rufinus of Aquileia', *ibid.* 30 (1979), 430–62; 'Products of Fifth-Century Scriptoria Preserving Conventions used by Rufinus of Aquileia. Script', *ibid.* 35 (1984), 347–93.

In citation, punctuation, and *nomina sacra* (forms $\overline{dms}$ and $\overline{is}$), the conventions of Rufinus, as reflected in Ms Lyons 483, are quite different from those of Codex Bezae. The third article deals with script, and argues that the growth of half-uncial is derived from the copying of texts in monasteries founded by Rufinus' disciples Pinian and Melania, if not from the monastery of Rufinus himself. Although at first glance this last fact appears to strengthen the case against D having had any connection with the area, Dr Hammond also demonstrates that at this period half-uncial was used for the quick copying of *patristic* texts. Such a *scriptorium* as she describes might have chosen quite a different script for copying a *biblical* text.

Now that arguments have been advanced against every suggestion hitherto made, the writer is faced with the much harder task of attempting to substantiate a new proposal. Let us begin by recollecting the evidence that has to be used, and the criteria that must be met.

First, there is the palaeographical requirement: the manuscript was written in the East, by a Latin-trained scribe who was used to copying legal texts and who had a working knowledge of Greek.

Second, the chronology and character of the early correctors must fit in with the historical information that can be gathered from other sources.

Third, there is the requirement to find a place where Latin was spoken, so that Latin scriptures were needed, but where the reading of Greek was still possible.

The importance of this requirement has sometimes been overlooked in the past. For example, it should have been asked whether the reading of the Scriptures in Greek could be supposed in Augustine's Africa, before Africa was suggested as a possible place of writing.

Our conclusions (in chapter 5) about the sense-lines of D require a community old enough already to have worn out at least one copy (the exemplar).

On the other hand, a place must be sought where the existence of such a *Greek* text as that of D is also within the bounds of possibility. Places of significant textual activity, and those with which known texts are associated, must be discounted. Here the textual characteristics of the correctors of D have also to be taken into account.

It must be recognized that the number of Eastern locations where Codex Bezae could have been copied is severely limited by the fact that Latin was not commonly spoken.

Cassian, *De institutis coenobiorum*, *CSEL* 17; Jerome, *Epistulae*, *CSEL* 54–6; Libanius, *Opera*, ed. R. Foerster, Vol. 3, *Orationes XXVI-L*, Leipzig, 1906 (Bibliotheca Teubneriana).

G. Bardy, *La Question des langues dans l'eglise ancienne, Vol. 1* (the only one to appear), Paris, 1948; A. H. M. Jones, *The Later Roman Empire*, Oxford, 1964, Vol. 2, pp. 988f; H.I. Marrou, *Histoire de l'éducation dans l'antiquité*, Paris, 1948.

Jerome's letters bear testimony to this. In one, he writes from Syria (admittedly the desert) of a letter from some friends that 'illae hic tantum Latine sciunt. hic enim aut barbarus semisermo discendus est aut tacendum est' (*Ep.* 7.2 (*CSEL* 54.27)). This may be a comment on the quality of the local Latin. But in another he writes 'Grandem Latini sermonis in ista provincia notariorum patimur penuriam' (*Ep.* 134.2 (*CSEL* 56.263)). And elsewhere he complains that it is very hard to find Latin scribes in the East: 'in hac provincia Latini sermonis scriptorumque penuria est' (*Ep.* 75.4 (*CSEL* 55.33), written from Bethlehem in 399). And he says in the Prologue to Book X of his commentary on Isaiah that he has been hindered by, amongst other things, 'notariorum penuria' (*PL* 24.363 = *CC* 73.397): this at a time when many Westerners were fleeing from an Italy devastated by barbarians. In 398 the Spaniard Lucinius sent his own servants to Bethlehem to make copies of some of Jerome's works (*Ep.* 71.5 (*CSEL* 55.5)).

Cassian tells the story of an Italian monk in Egypt with a useless skill – the ability to write a Latin bookhand: nobody in those parts knew the language. This confirms Jerome's statement that Latin scribes were hard to find – they were never needed.

Jones' account describes the growing lack of Latinity in the East, from the fourth century onwards. 'Broadly speaking', he writes, 'it is true to say that Greeks learnt Latin only from interested motives . . . In the fourth century Latin was the official language of the empire even in the eastern parts, and a knowledge of the language was, if not essential, a useful asset to a man who aspired to rise in the administration, the army, or the law' (p. 988). He goes on to show that the use of Latin in administration was actually very limited – 'even in the fourth century Greek was almost exclusively used in the provincial offices and in that of the Augustal prefect' (*ibid.*) Latin was used only for internal communications at higher bureaucratic levels, and for translating important institutions. The Augustal prefect (the highest official in the Egyptian administration) used Latin for judicial proceedings down to about 440.

In the army, Latin seems to have been used down to the early sixth century, for purposes of 'formal administrative communications' (p. 989).

The consequence of the slow decline of Latin from its comparative importance in Diocletian's reign is that the opportunities for learning diminished with the demand. An intriguing instance of the slow breakdown of communication between East and West is provided by the Ann Arbor papyrus listed in chapter 4 (Michigan Pap. 457). The recto of this roll is a first- or second-century Latin legal text, and the verso contains Aesop's *Fables*, each fable preceded by a Latin version of the moral. Presumably an unwanted Latin document was used to produce a school text for teaching Latin speakers *Greek*. This document illustrates the decline both of general Latin knowledge and of Latin law.

It should be noted that the Latino-Greek manuscripts we studied in chapter 4 do not altogether support the other evidence. Their distribution by centuries is

II and III – two
IV – two
IV-V – three
V – six
V-VI – two
VI – one

Though the survival of so many more from the fifth than from other centuries could be chance, the evidence – unless Lowe's datings are to be seen as erring in caution – suggests that there was still a considerable number of Greek speakers wanting to read the *Aeneid* even at the end of the sixth century.

According to Libanius, the fourth-century pagan orator, teacher of John Chrysostom and Basil, and opponent of things Roman, Antiochene children had to go to Berytus or even Italy to learn Latin to a high standard (*Or.* 48.22). However, Jones suggests that 'a full Latin education in both grammar and rhetoric was always available at the imperial capital' (p. 990). There were ten chairs of Latin grammar and three of rhetoric established when the state university of Constantinople was founded in 425. But the occupants, particularly when they were Greeks (witness John Lydus), were not of a high calibre. However, some distinguished Westerners were also appointed to these chairs.

There is also manuscript evidence for the continuing Latin scholarship that was practised in the capital. Lowe, in an article to which we have already referred ('Greek Symptoms': see p. 9), suggests that the legal manuscripts that he isolated as being in b-r uncial and containing certain Greek features were produced in a *scriptorium* at Constantinople. These codices of the fifth and sixth centuries include the magnificent Pandect of the Justinian Code now in the Biblioteca Laurenziana. At the same time, the Greek influence on these copyists shows how isolated this particular tradition was from the rest of the Latin world. It may be added that the scripts of this group of texts have no connections with any of the hands found in the pages of D. This reduces the likelihood of the latter having been copied in Constantinople.

Elementary knowledge of Latin was easier to come by: the diglot school texts from Egypt were produced to serve precisely this purpose.

Gregory Thaumaturgos writes of the preliminary Latin studies that he undertook in his native Cappadocia, before setting out to train in law. It was in fact mainly in legal studies that Latin was, and continued to be, necessary (Socrates, *Eccl. Hist.* 4.27 (*PG* 67.535); Marrou, p. 349).

The centres for advanced study in the law were few.

H. F. Jolowicz and B. Nicholas, *Historical Introduction to the Study of Roman Law*, 3rd edition, Cambridge, 1972; Jones, *Later Roman Empire*.

According to Jolowicz, there was only Rome in the West, and in the East, as we learn from Justinian's *Constitutio Omnem* §7 (a text dealing with legal education), Alexandria, Caesarea in Palestine, Constantinople, and Berytus (Beirut). The last was the greatest of them.

Since Berytus has already been mentioned, in connection with the Latin script of Codex Bezae, let us examine its history and claims in detail.

It was the suggestion in Bischoff (*Palaeography*, pp. 74f) that the Latin hand may be associated with Berytus which prompted me to undertake the following study (see chapter 1, p. 28).

Agathias, *Historiae*, ed. B. G. Niebuhr (Corpus Scriptorum Historiae Byzantinae 3), Bonn, 1828; Athanasius, *Apologia (secunda) contra Arianos* (*PG* 25. 248–410); Eusebius, *De martyribus Palestinae*, ed. E. Schwartz, Leipzig, 1908 (*GCS* 9/2; L = long recension, S = short recension); Gregory Thaumaturgos, *Panegyr. ad Origenem* 5 (*PG* 10.1065f); Libanius, *Orationes* (see above) and *Epistula 1–839* (in *Opera*, ed. Foerster, Vol. 10, Leipzig, 1921); Philostorgius, *Historia Ecclesiastica*, ed. J. Bidez, 3rd edition, rev. F. Winkelmann, Berlin, 1981 (*GCS* s.n.); Sozomen, *Historia Ecclesiastica*, ed. J. Bidez and G. C. Hansen, Berlin, 1960 (*GCS* 50); Theodoret, *Historia Ecclesiastica*, ed. L. Parmentier, 2nd edition, rev. F. Scheidweiler, Berlin, 1954 (*GCS* 44).

F. P. Bremer, *Die Rechtslehrer und Rechtsschulen im römischen Kaiserreich*, Berlin, 1868; Paul Collinet, *Histoire de l'Ecole de Droit de Beyrouth* (Etudes historiques sur le Droit de Justinien 10), Paris, 1925; Collinet, 'Beyrouth, Centre d'affichage et de dépôt des Constitutions Impériales', *Syria* 5 (1924) 359–72; Adolf Harnack, *Die Mission und Ausbreitung des Christentums*, 2nd edition, Leipzig, 1906; J. N. D. Kelly, *Jerome*, London, 1975; K. Miller, *Itineraria Romana: römische Reisewege an der Hand der Tabula Peutingeriana*, Stuttgart, 1916.

For a reasonably full list of references to Berytus, see the article by I. Benzinger in *Paulys Real-Encyclopädie der klassischen Altertumswissenschaft*, ed. Georg Wissowa, Vol. 3, Stuttgart, 1899, cols. 321–3. See also K. Ziegler, H. Gärtner, and W. Sontheimer (eds.), *Der Kleine Pauly*, 5 vols., Stuttgart, 1964–75.

Such was its importance that Libanius could simply describe it as ἡ τῶν νόμων μήτηρ (*Ep.* 652 (566 in Wolf's numeration)), and that its fifty-century teachers were honoured as οἱ τῆς οἰκουμένης διδάσκαλοι. The school was founded in the late second century, although it did not receive an official *privilegium* or charter until the beginning of the fifth. It continued until the city was destroyed by an earthquake, tidal wave, and fire, on 16 July 551. The school was transferred to Sidon, but never recovered its pre-eminence (Agathias, 2.15). The city had not been rebuilt by the time it fell into Muslim hands in 635.

Berytus was described by Gregory Thaumaturgos as πόλις Ῥωμαϊκωτέρα πως καὶ τῶν νόμων τούτων . . . παιδευτήριον (*Pan. ad Orig.* 5). Nonnos, writing in Egypt in about 400, in a flight of fancy derived from the law school's fame, invents a legend of Beroë which includes Hermes holding Λατινιδα δελτον, a conceit revealing how closely he associates the city with Latin learning (*Dionys.* 41.155f). Jerome speaks of it as *Romana colonia*. The phrase is intended technically, as it is taken by Harnack (Vol. 2, p. 99) and by Bremer, who discusses a reference by Mommsen to the Commentary of Gaius *ad legem Iuliam et Papiam* ('Iuris Italici sunt Τρωας, Βηρυτος, Δυρραχιον') (p. 80).

According to Collinet, the law school was founded around the year 200, possibly as a result of Berytus already having been selected as a centre for the depositing and publishing of laws.

As a result, Berytus was one of the most important centres of the East:

> Au IVe siècle, il semble que se manifeste une tendance à la concentration du haut enseignement; du moins un certain nombre de centres d'étude apparaissent alors au premier plan: Alexandrie, Beyrouth (pour le droit romain), Antioche, Constantinople, la nouvelle capitale, et bien sûr, toujours Athènes. On aime à prononcer à leur sujet le mot d' 'université' et il n'est pas trop anachronique. (Marrou, p. 295)

According to Collinet, seeking to explain Berytus' unique fame amongst ancient universities, 'Beyrouth est une ville plus romaine que toute autre en Orient. Sa "romanité" s'accuse par ses monuments . . . Elle s'accuse surtout parce qu'on y enseigne le droit romain dans l'esprit de Rome' (*Histoire*, p. 305). Mommsen described the city as a Latin island lost in a sea of Hellenism.

Besides the law school, Berytus was important as a port for the Syrian hinterland, providing trade links with the rest of the Orient and, through Brindisi, with Italy (Collinet, *Histoire*, p. 25). The coast road runs through it from the north down to Sidon and Tyre. If you wished to travel overland from Constantinople to Alexandria, your route lay through Berytus. Another road ran inland to Heliopolis, linking with the north–south road down the Orontes valley from Damascus (see Miller, *Itineraria Romana*, pp. 806–7 and maps 257–60). In the Pseudo-Clementine Homilies, Peter spends several days in Berytus while on his way north from Sidon to Tripolis (7.9.1–8.1.1; *GCS* 42 (2nd edition), 120–2). The route south from Berytus to Sidon is the one given by the unknown pilgrim of the *Itinerarium Burgidalense*, who in 333 wrote an account of his journey overland from Bordeaux to Palestine (583, 8; *CC* 175.12). Jerome describes Paula's winter journey by ass from Seleucia through Berytus and Sidon to Sareptah and the holy sites (*Ep.* 108; *CSEL* 55.313; according to Kelly, *Jerome*, pp. 116f, it is likely that he accompanied her on the journey, at least from Antioch). The same route was followed by the pilgrims of the *Antonini Placentini itinerarium* (1–2; *CC* 175.129; see also the second recension, 1b–2a, *ibid.* 157–8), shortly before the city's destruction. This evidence indicates that, for Western pilgrims, Berytus was the gateway to the holy places (see also the article by H. Treidler in *Kleine Pauly*).

The language used at the law school was Latin, apparently from the beginning, and certainly at the time of Gregory Thaumaturgos. The foundation of Constantinople had only increased the importance of Roman law in the East, leading as it did to the promulgation of much new legislation, all in Latin and requiring the study and re-application of existing Roman law. Collinet produces sufficient evidence to show that Latin was still used in 381–2 (Libanius, *Or.* 2.44). But the earliest teachers to be accorded the title *της οἰκουμενης διδασκαλοι*, Cyril the elder and Patricius, were teaching and writing in Greek in 410–20 and 424 respectively (Collinet, *Histoire*, pp. 211f). The change from Latin to Greek as the teaching language of the school was therefore made between the early 380s and 410.

Not that the need for knowing Latin disappeared. Most of the primary material remained untranslated. However, the change from Latin to Greek as the teaching language of the school must indicate a significant shift in the requirements of the legal profession. It is noteworthy that Greek could be used for formal written judgements after 397, and for the wills of Roman citizens after 439. Does this indicate that at this time Latin became redundant for the ordinary legal practitioner, and was needed only by a scholarly few who studied the laws? This is supported by Jones (p. 990):

> In the fourth century then a rather rudimentary knowledge of Latin was required of notaries and of civil servants in certain branches . . . A competent grasp of the language was needed only by jurisconsults and by barristers who were not content to be mere orators . . . A full rhetorical knowledge was essential only for the clerks of the *sacra scrinia* who drafted imperial resolutions . . . In the fifth century . . . it ceased to be necessary for barristers, notaries, or civil servants, except in the military offices and the *sacra scrinia* . . . Latin became a learned language needed only by academic lawyers and legal draftsmen.

Besides being part of the general shift in Eastern culture, this change is paralleled by the demise with Ammianus Marcellinus of the Syrian Latin literary tradition (Collinet, p. 212).

All the evidence presents Berytus as the main Latin centre of the East, *until* the first decade of the fifth century. But it should not be overlooked that Greek also was used in the city. The surviving names of students and their provenances (Collinet, *Histoire*, chapter 3) lead one to suppose that the school was at least primarily for Easterners, not Westerners, and that they were bilingual speakers whose first tongue was Greek. An interesting insight into the standard of Greek spoken at the school is provided by a story in Sozomen (*HE* 1.11.8–9 (*GCS* 50.23)). A certain Tryphillius, Bishop of Ledrae in Cyprus, affected an Atticism that infuriated his teacher and fellow bishop Spyridon of Trimithus. Tryphillius rejected even Matthew and Luke's amelioration of Mark's *κραββατος*, preferring to describe the paralytic's bed as *σκιμπους*. Tryphillius had been a student of law at Berytus, and at the least it can be said that his stay there had not barbarized his style. This story is apparently from the 340s (Gams dates Spyridon's episcopate as 325–44, and Tryphillius' as beginning in 344: see p. 273 below for bibliographical details), so Tryphillius will presumably have been a student there in the 320s or thirties. His career had been a successful one, according to Sozomen. On his conversion to Christianity, he left Berytus for Cyprus, and a no less distinguished future. Jerome includes him in a list of leading Christian writers, along with names such as Pamphilus, Eusebius of Caesarea, Titus of Bostra, and the Cappadocians, as ones who 'in tantum philosophorum doctrinis atque sententiis suos referserunt libros, ut nescias, quid in illis primum admirari debeas, eruditionem saeculi an scientiam scripturarum' (*Ep.* 70.4; *CSEL* 54.706f). His style was evidently more congenial to the polished Jerome (assuming he had actually read him) than to the shepherd bishop of Cyprus.

The reasons for the change at Berytus from Latin to Greek do not concern us here. But the fact is of considerable interest. Nor need we be too worried by the fact that perhaps far more Greek than Latin was spoken in the city as a whole. It must be stressed that the law school was the best in the world, as well as the chief centre of Latin studies in the East, a study that was of the utmost importance to society. Nor, we must note, was the school the only important legal service provided. Berytus was also, in Collinet's words, 'le siège d'un dépôt auquel étaient transmises, pour l'affichage et la conservation, les constitutions intéressant certaines des provinces de l'Orient' (*Histoire*, pp. 20f; 'Beyrouth, centre d'affichage'; see also Marrou, p. 388).

So important and busy an institution as the law school and the legal archives will have generated its own Latin culture. Native Latin speakers will have been attracted Eastwards – language teachers and scribes and lawyers. That Westerners went to teach Latin at Constantinople is evidence for this. Certainly there will have been a demand for many scribes, experts in the conservation and copying of all kinds of legal texts. They will have maintained a living Latin tradition in this Greek world.

Such was the character of Roman life in Berytus. What of its Greek environment?

The history of the Greek church in Berytus cannot be reconstructed in detail. References to it in the ancient historians of the Greek church are scant and generally occur apropos of something else. Bishops of whom we know are few in number. But they provide us with a beginning.

Gams, *Series Episcoporum ecclesiae catholicae, quotquot innotuerunt a beato Petro Apostolo*, Regensburg, 1873, p. 434 (Gams' information, though not his dates, is derived from Michel Le Quien, *Oriens Christianus*, 3 vols., Paris, 1740, Vol. 2, cols. 815–20); W. Smith and H. Wace, *Dictionary of Ecclesiastical Biography*, 4 vols., London, 1877–87. For individual bishops, see:

Eusebius – G. Bardy, *Recherches sur St Lucien d'Antioche et son école*, Paris, 1936; A. Lichtenstein, *Eusebius von Nikomedia*, Halle, 1903; J. Quasten, *Patrology*, Vol. 3, Utrecht, 1960, pp. 190–3
Timotheus – Smith and Wace 4, 1029; J. D. Mansi, *Sacrorum conciliorum nova et amplissima collectio*, Vols. 3 and 4, Florence, 1759ff, reprint, Graz; Le Quien; H. Lietzmann, *Apollinaris von Laodicea und seine Schule*, Tübingen, 1904
Eustathius – Collinet, *Histoire*

Gams lists a number of bishops; in his catalogue, Berytus comes under the Patriarchate of Antioch, Province of Syria Prima. We transliterate the entry precisely:

Quartus, *discip. S. Pauli, apost.*
Eusebius, Arian. [cf. *Nicomedia*], *320*
Gregorius, Arian., 325
Macedonius, Arian., *344*
381 Timotheus, **449**
451 Eustathius, **458**
Aristus
Joannes, ex. saecul. 5
Marinus, *c.* 312–18 (he means 512–18)
c. 535 Thalassius
c. 869 Thomas, *tr. Tyrum s.* 879

For the legends about Quartus (Rom. 16.23), see *Acta Sanctorum* Novembris Tom. 1, Paris, 1887, pp. 585–6. According to Hippolytus, he was one of the Seventy-Two. The legend that he was appointed Bishop of Berytus is attributed by Le Quien 'ex spurio Dorotheo Tyri in Menologiis Graecorum' (817).

Eusebius, a disciple of Lucian of Antioch, was translated to Nicomedia shortly before 318 (Theodoret, *HE* 1.19; Athanasius, *Apol.* 6 (*PG* 25, 260); see also the *De Arii depositione* 1). He was again translated, this time to Constantinople, in 339, and died in about 342. He emerged as Arius' champion in about 320, which appears to have been the time at which he became bishop of Berytus. He is presented by Quasten as 'more an ecclesiastical politician than a theologian, experienced in worldly affairs and ambitious, ready for any intrigue' (*Patrology*, Vol. 3, p. 191). Certainly, as leader of the Arian party throughout the period after 320, he spearheaded the assaults on Athanasius and other leading opponents of Arianism (*Apol.* 6, *PG* 25, 257). His name figures with especial regularity in the *Apologia contra Arianos*, the *Historia Arianorum*, and *De Synodis*. It should be noted that his desire for preferment indicates something of the status of Berytus in the politics of the Eastern church – he was presumably only too glad to move. Athanasius' comment, though hardly unbiased, may have force: 'he relinquished his own, for which he had no affection, and took possession of another's, to which he had no right; he forgot his love for the first in his desire for another' (*Apol.* 6, *PG* 25, 257).

His successor was another Arian, listed by Arius in a letter to Eusebius of Nicomedia as one of those who had been excommunicated by the orthodox Alexander of Alexandria (see Theodoret, *HE* 1.5.2, 5 (*GCS* 44.26, 27)). He was one of Arius' stauncher allies – *τούτους μὲν οὖν συμφώνους ἔχειν ὁ Ἄρειος ἐσεμνύνετο* (*ibid.* 6 (*GCS* 44.27)). His name is found in the list of bishops at Nicaea. He was succeeded, according to Gams, by a third Arian, Macedonius.

There is then something of a gap, until we come to Timotheus. Whether Gams is correct in giving him an episcopate of sixty-eight years is perhaps debatable. We know that he attended the Council of Constantinople in 381 (Mansi, Vol. 3, col. 568), so at least the earlier date is fairly certain. His name is not in the list of bishops who attended the Council of Ephesus in 431 (Mansi, Vol. 4, cols. 1363–68). The dates provided in Smith and Wace are 381–99 (alleging the authority of Gams). Timothy was an Apollinarian, and fragments of his works survive (Lietzmann, pp. 277–86) – *To Homonius*, *Catechesis*, an Ecclesiastical History, and *Epistle to Prosdocius*. Along with Apollinarius, he was condemned in 377, although he seems to have subscribed to the canons of Constantinople. Theodoret preserves a Synodical Letter from Damasus of Rome, devoted to a condemnation of Timothy (5.10, *GCS* 44.295–7; in Latin in the *Historia ecclesiastica tripartita* 9.15, *CSEL* 71.516–18). We could gather more information about Timothy, but none of it relevant for present purposes.

The episcopate of Eustathius is marked by an attempt to increase the importance of the see of Berytus. He set out to free it from the metropolitan jurisdiction of Tyre, under which it had hitherto been. The attempt was sponsored by the emperor Theodosius, who wished to place six cities under the metropolitan jurisdiction of Berytus. The claim was recognized in 451 at the Council of Chalcedon and it was Le Quien's opinion that Eustathius' efforts in the Catholic cause at the Council of Ephesus prove it to have been merited. Eustathius was responsible for a magnificent and extensive building programme, including the Church of the Resurrection (the building is described by Zacharias Scholasticus in his *De opificio mundi*). We may suggest that, until the beginning of the fifth century, the city's importance as a Latin centre diminished its power in the East, so that only after the use of Latin had disappeared could such a bishop as the ambitious Eustathius provide it with influence and independence.

It may be noted in passing that Eustathius does not seem to have destroyed anything very ancient in his rebuilding programme. In describing the Arian occupation of Alexandria in 373, Theodoret pauses to vilify Magnus, one of Lucius' supporters. Magnus had been imperial treasurer and, according to Theodoret, had burned down the church of Berytus during Julian's reign, only to be forced to rebuild it again in Jovian's (Theodoret, *HE* 4.22.10 (*GCS* 44.252f)).

Other significant figures in the church are connected with Berytus only through the law school. The earliest of these is Gregory Thaumaturgos (Origen, *Ep. ad Greg., ad inc.*). The Caesarean martyr Pamphilus (see p. 147 above) was a native of the city, and grew up to study there, possibly in the law school (Collinet, *Histoire*, p. 28; Eusebius, *Mart. Pal.* 11 (*GCS* 9/2.934 L)). In the same work, Eusebius tells the stories of the brothers Apphianus and Aedesius. The first studied at Berytus *τῆς Ἑλλήνων παιδείας ἕνεκα κοσμικῆς* (4.3 S) and there, in the words of the long recension, *ποικίλων μαθημάτων συνείλεκτο παρασκευήν* (*ibid.* L). He later became a student of Pamphilus, and was martyred at Caesarea. Aedesius also studied at Berytus where *λόγων μετεῖχεν παντοίων καὶ παιδείας οὐ τῆς Ἑλλήνων μόνων, ἀλλὰ δὴ καὶ τῆς Ῥωμαίων ἧπτο, τῆς τε Παμφίλου διατριβῆς πλείονι χρόνῳ μετέσχησεν* (*ibid.* 5.2 L: the shorter recension says only that he was more highly educated than his brother, and that he began as a student of philosophy). Clearly, Roman law was only one of the academic options on offer in the city. In fact, Eusebius seems to have supposed the study of Roman law to be worth special mention, if that is the reference of the word *Ῥωμαίων*. Or does it mean that there was the opportunity to study other aspects of Latin culture besides law? If so, then the evidence for a wider Westernism in Berytus would be increased.

Evidence of Greek schools in Berytus is also provided by the career of Apollinarius the Elder, of Alexandria. Born in about 300, he taught Greek grammar at Berytus for some time, until 335 (so that his career may have overlapped with that of Triphyllius), when he moved to Laodicea. Described by Basil as 'never at a loss for an expression' (*Ep.* 263.4, *PG* 32.979), he produced (possibly with his more famous son) a tragedy called *Christus patiens* and a Psalter in Homeric hexameters, so as to get round Julian the Apostate's prohibition of Christians reading Greek literature. Apollinarius was regarded by some people as being too fond of pagan literature for his own good. This singing the songs of Sion by the springs of Parnassus accords with the rather precious Atticizing of Tryphillius, and gives us some idea of the Greek culture and church of the city.

The connections between this picture of Berytus and our reconstruction of the circumstances of the creation of Codex Bezae are strong.

First, we have the palaeographical arguments, which have already been set out. The argument is derived from Bischoff, and was described at the end of chapter 1. The scribe will have been a trained copyist of legal texts, who was also conversant with Greek but not expert in modern techniques of copying Greek texts.

Second, we may find in the history of the law school an explanation for the strange early history of the manuscript. Produced as a bilingual to meet the needs of Latin Christians in Berytus, and its Latin column corrected by G, its original use was suddenly lost when the school adopted Greek, and the Latin teachers and scribes were slowly dispersed. Henceforth, this Greek city showed interest only in the Greek column, with merely an occasional glance at that monument to its past Romanism, the Latin side. The destruction of the city in 551 may have led to the removal of the manuscript to another place, and to the distinctive attitude to it found in correctors H, F, J, and L. This place, according to what we have found from studying the hand of L, was also in Syria. Can it have been Sidon, to which the law school was transferred?

Thus there are palaeographical and historical arguments in favour of the manuscript's having been produced in Berytus. But objections may also be raised against the theory.

There does not seem to be any direct evidence that people whose *first* language was Latin came to Berytus. This could be because the sources are nearly all either Greek or oriental versions of lost Greek originals, with the exception of the *Expositio totius mundi* (Collinet, *Histoire*, p. 39f) and a brief reference to the city's destruction in the *Antonini Placentini itinerarium*. But the kind of Latin speakers who are likely to have come to Berytus will by no means all be people whose names are likely to have survived – scribes, clerks, and assistants.

It might also be suggested that the shift from Latin to Greek in the Berytus law school is only one example of the increasing loss of Latin that happened throughout the East during the fifth century. The precision with which the earliest hands of D can be related to the history of Berytus might be paralleled in many places, about which no information survives.

Another objection might be that it is quite clear that Christianity in Berytus was as Greek as anywhere else in the East. Indeed, Collinet suggests that this may have been a factor in the change from Latin to Greek at the school (*Histoire*, p. 217). It is probable that links between the (Greek) church and the law school were close. Collinet argues that in the fourth century the school's premises were adjacent to church buildings, and produces evidence that from the middle of the fifth they were in the precincts of Eustathius' Church of the Resurrection.

Could such a Greek text as that of D have been written in Berytus? It is true that, inasmuch as it was not an important ecclesiastical centre, a text of some antiquity and considerable peculiarity could have survived – to be corrected against more widely known models in the more expansive age of Eustathius. As far as we know, Berytus was not an important centre for the production of biblical texts, and it cannot be associated with any known text through patristic citations.

It is true that the kind of Greek style to be met with in people who had studied at

Berytus seems to have little in common with the popularizing revision of Codex Bezae. But there is more than one level of literary endeavour anywhere. In a big and culturally varied city like Berytus, there will have been room for plenty of people satisifed with Mark's κραββατος.

These possible objections are all fairly generalized and express the fact that we are dealing, not in certainties, rather in possible probabilities.

We began with the fact that by 400 Latin scribes and native Latin speakers were a rarity in the Eastern empire. The evidence reveals that Berytus was the only place where there was a concentration of Latin culture. A comparison of the history of Berytus with what we have reconstructed of the circumstances of Codex Bezae has shown that there is no incompatibility between the two.

The evidence for a strong Latin presence in Berytus can be demonstrated. The legal archives and school that had existed since the second half of the second century, and the role they played in teaching Latin to an advanced standard, all point to a need for direct contact with the West in education as in trade, and indicate a well established group of Latin-speaking inhabitants. Yet Berytus also meets the requirement of a place where Latin speakers are aware of Greek culture, and of the priority of the Greek scriptures.

Let us reconstruct the early history of Codex Bezae according to this theory. Copied in about or shortly before the year 400 and immediately corrected by G, the manuscript was produced in the final years of the strongly Latin tradition of the law school, for the benefit of Latin-speaking Christians drawn there by the needs and prestige of the school. The eclipse of Latin led to the Latin column falling into disuse, so that no further major corrections were made to it. The growing power of the Greek church of Berytus, where the manuscript remained, is reflected in the earliest Greek correctors. In the activity of Corrector B we see the growing influence of the church, and a corresponding susceptibility to outside influences, with the correction against a text of a Caesarean type, perhaps during the episcopate of Eustathius. With the destruction of the city in 551, the manuscript was taken elsewhere, beginning the travels that were in course of time to bring it to Lyons. In another home it found a new use. It was provided with a lectionary system and corrected against a standard form of text.

If the manuscript be from Berytus, then it may be suggested that the lay-out of the Gospels in its *Vorlagen* could reflect the centre's role in teaching Latin. The school books that presented the text for study in short lines with a translation beside them on the same page will have served as a model for a scribe used to doing this, and given a different task to complete.

The selection of Berytus has implications for our understanding of the yet earlier history of the text. If we suppose that this bilingual tradition was formed for the sake of Latin speakers at Berytus, then we are provided with a *terminus a quo* for its formation: the creation of the law school towards the end of the second century. If we allow a little time for the institution and the archive to gather momentum, we are left with a date from about 200 onwards. Given that Codex Bezae is copied from exemplars themselves bilingual, we may suggest that the tradition will have been formed in the early part of the third century.

CHAPTER SIXTEEN

The history of a text

H.-W. Bartsch, 'Über den Umgang der frühen Christenheit mit dem Text der Evangelien. Das Beispiel des Codex Bezae Cantabrigiensis', *NTS* 29 (1983), 167–82; C. M. Martini, *Il problema della recensionalità del codice B alla luce del papiro Bodmer XIV* (Analecta Biblica 26), Rome, 1966; C. H. Roberts, 'The Codex', *PBA* 40 (1954), 169–204; C. H. Roberts and T. C. Skeat, *The Birth of the Codex*, Oxford, 1983; E. P. Sanders, *Jesus and Judaism*, London, 1985.

In the course of this investigation, we have studied Codex Bezae in various ways. We have examined it codicologically and palaeographically; we have looked at the lay-out and orthography, at the correctors and at the differences between the two columns. We have made some attempt to discover the character of its text, and we have advanced a theory as to its place of writing. In this final chapter, we will bring the conclusions of these various explorations together and try to describe the history that emerges. Rather than repeat details which have already been given, we will content ourselves with the broad strokes of description. My object is not the recapitulation of facts, but to take the step, intuitive or deductive as you please, of describing the implications of the facts. Nor shall I provide justification for all that I say below – that will have to be found in the preceding pages.

We take up the story in the second century, at the period when four Gospels were given particular recognition in at least some churches. We are in the second half of the century. It is out of the combined authority of four Gospels, and comparison between them, that harmonization of the texts arises. The debate over Marcionism, with the issue of the *one* Gospel, may have been a significant factor. The Diatessaron of Tatian is the most significant result of such comparison; the text of Codex Bezae is another consequence. Besides the harmonizing, this text was characterized by a number of other features: the introduction of material about Jesus from elsewhere, and the tendency to rewrite the text in a more colloquial style. In general the text was fluid and susceptible of any number of changes. The text of Matthew was probably the most secure, while John (for obvious reasons) was the least harmonized. Acts was treated the most freely. At this period Latin versions were being produced which, apart from that of the Greek texts, had their own fluidity.

How old is the text we are describing? Do the features other than harmonization allow us to go even further back for its origins? This question does not have a simple answer. Since we have argued that this kind of text has no fixed form, we cannot claim a point at which it came into being. Any theory of a single editor or creative theologian being responsible for it is incorrect.

We can see that the development of free text forms shows a continuum with the growth of Gospel material in the oral period. There, the texts were in a constant process of being reshaped within the context of the church. The same is true of a free text. Moreover, if Papias preferred oral to written tradition, as he asserts, then we can easily see how the Gospel *books* of his period may have become depositories for loose pieces of tradition.

One may build a further point out of C. H. Roberts' argument that the production of Mark's Gospel was in a codex rather than a roll. If this was so, then the implication is that Mark was not published as a literary text in a final form, but intended for private circulation. Again, we can see how such a text might be regarded as fair game for emendment or development. This cannot be argued for Luke's work, published in two books on two rolls like any other literary work, although it may be that this status was subsequently eroded by association with writings like Mark.

The shaping of the oral tradition, the preservation of such material outside the written Gospels, and the lack of a definitive literary status for some of the Gospels, and therefore perhaps by custom for all of them, lead us into the world of the second-century free texts. This includes a variety of forms: versions of the Gospels later to be canonical; texts such as the Gospel of Thomas, which show how the processes at work in the creation of the four Gospels were still active long after the first century; Tatian's Diatessaron.

To the question, how old is this text?, we have to reply that since it is always changing, it is never precisely datable; but that the *kind* of text it represents is as old as the beginnings of the Gospel traditions. The statement concerns the *kind* of text, not the quality of its variants. (This argument is not an attempt to introduce through the back door a claim for the authenticity of the Bezan text.)

At a point early in the third century, the Roman law school at Berytus was burgeoning; more Latin speakers were arriving in the city, and beginning to establish their own society. Many of these knew little or no Greek, and the need for Latin scriptures became pressing. Up to this point we have no clear geographical location for the Greek and Latin texts that we have been describing. It may be, and this is the simplest possibility, that the independent Latin versions were the earliest stage of the non-Greek scriptures in Berytus, and that they were taken from the Greek texts already in use there. This would mean that the Latin texts would have been produced in the third rather than the second century. What is clearer is that at some point, after both groups of texts had developed beyond their state at the point when the versions were produced, a bilingual Gospel book was formed. This, written in short sense-lines modelled on educational texts (possibly used in the law school or in teaching programmes associated with it), contained the Gospels in the order Matthew–Mark–John–Luke. Its copying may be placed in the first part of the third century. From this, at a point between the middle of the third and the end of the fourth centuries, was made a second bilingual manuscript. This set out the Gospels in the order Matthew–Mark–John–Luke. It was the labour of two scribes, who divided their work somewhere around John 5. The manuscript had two columns to the page, one Greek and one Latin, and short sense-lines.

At some point in the same period, a bilingual codex of Acts was produced. This may have been at a later date than the first, and even than the second Gospel bilingual: the Greek text had so grown in length that the Latin needed quite substantially adjusting to it. Moreover, it seems to have had a single column to the page, and in lay-out to have been more like Codex Bezae itself. It used later forms of the *nomina sacra* for *dominus*. The character of the translation shows some differences from that (or those) of the Gospels.

Then, in about the year 400, a bilingual manuscript was written that contained the Gospels, possibly Revelation, the Johannine Epistles, and Acts. It adopted the one column to a page format, with the Greek on the left, and placed the Gospels in the order Matthew–John–Luke–Mark. A scribe from the *scriptorium* attached to the law school was engaged for the task, one who knew both scripts, although his primary skill was as a copyist of Latin legal texts.

Why was this new codex produced? Several things make it unlikely to have been for private use: the scale of the work, and the fact that no scholar who needed the books in Greek and Latin would want a bilingual copy – they could be studied separately. And any individual, if faced with the choice between copying the whole lot out and learning Greek, would surely prefer the latter. It is likely that the volume was for church use, so that the lections could be read in both the sacred Greek and a language understanded of the people. The absence of lectionary annotations does not make this unlikely: such notes are not found in other New Testament codices of the period. They were introduced at a later date.

Produced for Latin-speaking Christians in Berytus, the codex was examined at once by a person of some authority in the church, who made a considerable number of corrections and alterations in Matthew and the first chapters of Acts. These largely consisted in removing small errors in the Latin, as well as occasionally changing the rendering, and supplying several omissions. This person appears to have made use of the exemplars.

Latinity in Berytus, however, was not to flourish for much longer. With the demise of teaching in Latin in the first quarter of the fifth century, we have a loss of interest in the Latin column of the manuscript. A group of early correctors concerned themselves almost solely with the Greek side. The first of these, A, busied himself with correcting tiny errors; and where he makes bigger changes, his text is not dissimilar to that of the codex itself. Corrector C used a basically Byzantine form of text, yet some of his readings are shared with Latin witnesses. In fact, his seems to have been a mixed text. Hand B, the most assiduous corrector, used a text that came from Caesarea. It is known to us from the C correctors of Codex Sinaiticus. He also knew readings similar to those of Codex Bezae. The fourth hand, D, used a text like that of ℵ B.

Of these four hands, A can be dated to the first forty years after the manuscript was copied, B and C to the first fifty years, and D to around 450.

In the correctors of the period 450–500 (E, H, F, J^1) we find the increasing influence of the Byzantine text: growing in E, complete in F (admittedly H does not fit easily into the schema). This development reflects the episcopate of the powerful Eustathius.

There appears then to have been a gap of half a century, when no annotations were made to the manuscript. It seems not improbable that it had simply been abandoned, and regarded as providing an old-fashioned type of text. The destruction of Berytus by natural forces in July 551, the point at which the law school was transferred to Sidon, coincided with a renewed use of the manuscript. Extensive lectionary annotations and the Ammonian Sections were supplied by Hand L, who worked in Syria between 550 and 600. It may be that other more commonly used books had been destroyed in the catastrophe, and that Codex Bezae was brought out of a sheltered retirement to supply their lack. The full period of lectionary annotations, during which the *sortes* were scribbled in the margins of Mark, extends over the period between 550 and 650. It might be possible to bring the later date forward to 635, the year in which Berytus fell to the Arabs.

Although undoubtedly traumatic enough for those who experienced them – especially for the survivors in the ruins of so Greek a city as Berytus – these conquests were not marked by any systematic or more than sporadic persecutions of Christianity. The vision of a fleeing lector, scattering torn quires of the precious Codex Bezae, is unlikely to be realistic. But, whatever the precise circumstances, it seems reasonable to suppose that there cannot have been much left of Christianity in Berytus by the year 700, and that there can have been very little need indeed for such things as Graeco-Latin biblical manuscripts. What we know is that the Codex Bezae was left untouched after the middle of the sixth century; and that it may be presumed to have been complete up to that date. It is then lost to our sight for nearly two centuries. It reappears in Lyons, where between about 830 and 850 some of the missing leaves were replaced. The point at which the manuscript reached Lyons cannot be determined, but the lack of any activity in the Greek text after 650 may suggest that it found its way there much earlier than has been suggested hitherto. The role of Florus will then have been, not the importation to Lyons of an ancient and valuable codex, but the recognition of the importance of a volume lying on a Lyons bookshelf. His programme of restoration carried out on books actually copied in Lyons has already been described. Lyons played an important role in the conservation of ancient texts during the early medieval period. Not only did important patristic manuscripts find their way from further East in France and from Italy (not to mention so old a codex as D all the way from the Levant); Lyons was also, in the eighth century, a centre for the preservation of Latin law in the West. Was Codex Bezae brought to Lyons on its own, or was it part of what the scholars of Lyons rescued from the law libraries of Berytus? Later, in the 850s, Ado made some use of Codex Bezae in compiling his Martyrology.

And there the manuscript stayed until the sixteenth century. It appears to have travelled to the Council of Trent in 1546. In 1550 it was used for the first time as witness to the printed text, in Robert Stephanus' third edition. In 1562, the year in which Lyons was sacked by the temporarily Huguenot Des Adrets, the codex passed from the monastery of St Irenaeus into the possession of Theodore Beza. It therefore found its way to Calvin's Geneva. Beza did not visit Lyons himself (though he was in France and at the Battle of Dreux in 1563), but he maintained close friendships with its pastors, Viret, Chaillet, Vallet. There was a considerable influx of Lyonnaise refugees to Geneva after the second religious war, including many printers and booksellers. It seems more charitable to ascribe the codex's removal to Geneva to the love of books of one of these than, like Scrivener, to the spoliations of a looter.

I am grateful to Professor Alain Dufour of Geneva, editor of the *Correspondance de Bèze*, for communicating most of this information about Beza and Lyons, in a letter of 11 January 1982. He drew my attention also to a letter from the Lutheran Joachim Camerarius to Beza, of 26 August (1568?), in which he discusses the text of the New Testament (*Correspondance de Bèze*, ed. Hippolyte Aubert *et al.*, Geneva, 1960ff, Vol. 9, no. 630, especially n. 5). Unfortunately, Beza's part of the correspondence is lost. Professor Dufour tells me that they have not found anything new about Codex Bezae in the course of preparing the edition.

A thorough account of Codex Bezae in the sixteenth century (not lacking its own theological tendencies) is provided by Scrivener, pp. vii–x.

Then, in 1581, Beza presented the codex to the University of Cambridge, in whose successive University Libraries (when not in that of Richard Bentley) it has remained ever since.

A few leaves of the book may have had one other adventure, according to a story recently told me by Professor W. G. Lambert. He heard it from his teacher at Cambridge, C. P. T. Winkworth, who had heard it (one may guess in the 1920s) from an extremely elderly clergyman, who perhaps had heard it himself from a contemporary of the event. Professor Lambert has no doubt of the accuracy of Winkworth's recollections, and Winkworth found no reason to doubt those of the clergyman, so we may accept the story's credentials, and proceed to tell it. At some point at or just before the middle of the last century, it was noticed that the surviving leaves at the end of Codex Bezae were missing. Enquiry was made of the last person to have used the manuscript, a young Leipzig scholar called Tischendorf. In due course a packet arrived from Leipzig, containing the missing pages and an explanation that Tischendorf had run out of time in Cambridge, and so had taken them with him to finish his work. This story is an oral tradition of a century and a half in length, with reasonable attestation and certainly no lack of intrinsic probability. Unfortunately, there does not appear to be any written evidence in the library at Cambridge that would substantiate this living voice.

Such is our reconstruction of the history of Codex Bezae. What of its text?

One of the clearer things to have emerged is the speed at which it became obsolete: not only in the loss of its bilingual role, but also in the fact that within fifty years it was being compared disparagingly with other texts – Caesarean, Alexandrian, and finally Byzantine. It seems to have been old-fashioned even when it was copied in 400. Yet – and this bears out a point reiterated by the Alands in their introduction to the New Testament text – the codex survived in use through to the seventh century, and found a new lease of life at the other end of the Mediterranean in the ninth. It was long-lived, and its readings crop up in unexpected places.

But its impact may have been fairly slight, to judge by the witnesses that survive – although, of course, it may have been enormously popular in some areas and periods for which we now lack the evidence. But in the long run it was not to prove influential. And the reason is not far to seek. The Bezan text is not a *defined* text. Its main characteristic, we have suggested, is its lack of definition, its freedom in transmission. It will have been too subject to change and to outside influence to have had a strong influence on other texts. Thus, the apparent confederacy of what was once described as the 'Western text' is a similarity not in detail, but in character. We have not a text, but a genre. That is why the representatives of this free genre are distinct from all other types, but puzzlingly unlike each other.

Let us return to the suggestion that the *character* of text we have in Codex Bezae is very old, older than the writing of Gospels. Not all the implications of this suggestion can be followed up here. Clearly, there are theological ramifications of some interest with regard to the way the teaching of Jesus could be viewed and handed on by the early church. A pertinent discussion can be found in Sanders' book *Jesus and Judaism*. In his introduction, he discusses Gerhardsson's suggestion that the handing down of the traditions about Jesus was analogous to 'the dual transmission of the Hebrew Scriptures. There was a free transmission, one which altered Scripture appreciably, and which is represented in the haggada of the midrashim and the targums. There were also activities in which the precise text was maintained: worship, study, and the professional preservation and transmission of the written text' (p. 14). Sanders rejects this theory, since there never seems to be

> the concern for precise *wording* which Gerhardsson several times proposes as having characterized the preservation of the material about Jesus...
>
> I am persuaded by Gerhardsson that the Gospel material was not created and transmitted in the ways proposed by the form critics ... but we do not have a

> persuasive alternative, and the creativity itself is not to be denied. The most certain point is . . . the material was subject to all sorts of alterations, and we have it as it was transmitted by the church. (p. 15)

The issue, therefore, is not whether the early church was *able* to transmit texts *verbatim*, but whether it *chose* to.

In *The Birth of the Codex*, Roberts and Skeat advance an alternative hypothesis to the one suggested by Roberts in 'The Codex': that the new format originated at Antioch, on the analogy of the notebooks used by Jews for jotting down isolated decisions or rabbinic sayings (pp. 59f). It is tempting to suggest that the adoption of the codex by the early Christians indicates, not that they considered their writings to be less than literature, but that they believed the teaching of Jesus to be other than law. Certainly, they chose a format that eschewed comparison with either.

The text of Codex Bezae is our most eloquent witness to the fact that the early church could and did alter the transmitted sayings of Jesus. Moreover, it, or at least parts of it, did so right through to the fourth century (I speak of the canonical writings). There are reasons why such an attitude ought not to have so survived: the movement towards a standard ecclesiastical text is one; the need for a precise text to use in controversy is another (this was a major reason for the production of Origen's *Hexapla* as early as the middle of the third century).

Textually, there are also significant implications. The possibility that Mark at least was never officially published raises some interesting questions as to our precise task in reconstituting the text. The application of Alexandrian editorial techniques to such a book will have been a significant event in its history. Is the implication that this recensional work called a halt to the chaos at some point in about the year 200? If so, then the textual critic is in the same situation as that described by Sanders: 'we must conclude that the material was subject to change and may have changed, but that we do not know just how it changed' (p. 15). We are left needing either to apply this literary critical insight to textual criticism, or to affirm something like Gerhardsson's theory of two kinds of transmission. A text-critical argument that recognizes this is Martini's study of P^{75} and B. He concluded that the existence of the parallel traditions in the manuscripts bears witness to the different mental attitudes held in the early church towards the transmission of texts (p. 151). It does not appear that this present book has provided any evidence to justify making a pronouncement on the degree of trust which we may place in any one of these attitudes. To go further one would have to establish that the proto-Alexandrian recension had access to the Gospel texts at a sufficiently early stage in their transmission to give an accurate representation of them. But it makes one general point very clear: the care taken in copying. Codex Bezae is a free text, but is essentially not a careless one.

These wider questions lie beyond the scope of the present book. We must content ourselves here with the smaller canvas, on which we have attempted to delineate the history of a single manuscript and the text that it represents. A more thorough analysis, dealing with the way in which individual units were altered in the free text, would need to begin with Bartsch's study. He provides examples which illustrate precisely the parallel we have described between the earliest stage of the transmission and that of the free texts, whilst making it quite clear that D is 'für die Erstellung eines Urtextes zurecht wenig geachtet' (p. 167). It must be stressed again that the analogy between the free text and the early transmission of the material about Jesus is quite separate from the question about the authenticity of particular readings of that free text. The present argument does not require it to be established that even one of these readings has any claim to authenticity.

Such an analysis beginning with Bartsch as we have suggested should be extended throughout the codex in the way that Holmes has studied Matthew and Mees Luke (see pp. 191 and 192 above), using also some of the approaches found in the preceding chapters of this book. By this means, a good deal more could be uncovered of the early history of the text from which D is descended. If such results were to be examined in relation to the conclusions and further researches attainable through Martini's work, our knowledge of the text of the Gospels and Acts before the year 200 would be greatly enlarged, and many problems finally resolved.

We conclude by returning to the central theological point. We have in Codex Bezae a text that takes up a remarkable attitude, not only in its reproduction of the text, but in its recording of the sayings of Jesus and of the apostles. Theologians, not least moral theologians, need to be aware of its existence, if they are to do justice to the variety of thought alive in the early church. As a commentary on the character of this attitude, one can hardly do better than take the addition at Luke 6.4, where Jesus says, 'If you know what you are doing, then you are blessed; if not, then accursed and a transgressor of the Law.'

This text is even willing to change the content of the apostolic decree of Acts 15, interpreting its purpose for a different setting. It omits the reference to what is strangled, adding 'and that whatsoever they would not should be done to them ye do not to others' (Ac 15.20). Such a rewriting, of a piece with the addition at Lk 6.4, is one that takes the radical demands of the text very seriously.

The importance of this theology consists in its continuity with the earliest Christian transmission and its attitude to the sayings of Jesus.

APPENDIX I

Corrections to Scrivener's transcription of the codex

To give a list of errors to such a work as Scrivener's is to offer it the praise of being considered useful even when there is a facsimile edition available.

There are three sources to this list. The first was communicated privately by Yoder, being errors he noted whilst drawing up his concordance. The second is to be found in Stone's book on the Latin column (pp. 10f). The third comes out of my own use of the transcription, the facsimile, and the codex. Some of my alterations represent a different opinion rather than hard fact, and the reader may prefer to follow Scrivener.

Errors noted by Yoder or Stone have their name placed after the entry.

The readings of D are given in lower-case letters (**bold** in the case of the Latin). The first hand is denoted by p.m. (prima manus).

MATTHEW

3/15: for **ihm** read **ihm̄** (Stone).
3b/18: for *υ˙ιον* read *ϋιον* (cp. *Adn. ed.*).
4/4: for **vocavis** read **uocauis** (Stone).
4b/6: for *εκ* read *εξ* (and see appendix 2).
8b/12: for *γενο* *ται* read *γενω* *ται*.
9/25: for **temptavis** read **temptauis** (Stone).
12/28: for **videant** read **uideant** (Stone).
12b/12: for *υμειν* read *ϋμειν* (cp. *Adn. ed.*, which wrongly corrects to *υμειν*).
12b/26: delete *εως*.
13/4: for **omnia** read **omn**.
13/32: for **quadrantre** read **quadrantre** (and see appendix 2).
14b/11: delete the horizontal stroke over the double point.
16b/33: for *θησαυρουσ ουσ* read *θησαυρουσουσ* (cp. *Adn. ed.*).
26b/25: *εισ ελθων* is more likely to be a single word.
27/28: delete **e** in **ᵉum**.
28b/16: ultra-violet light confirms Scrivener's suggestion that the sponged-out letter is *ω*.

29/7: the letter after **au** in **autem** is **a**.
30b/13: the point after δια is a chance mark.
37/17: the point after **eius** is by Corrector G.
51/20: for **illym** read **illam**.
52b/4: for ⌒ read ζ̑ (Yoder).
54b/23: for *κερδη* read *κερδησ̑η* (Yoder).
57/14: for **eum** *prim.* read **cum** (Stone).
57/16: for **eum** read **cum** (and see appendix 2).
58/2: for **hic** read **hinc**.
59/1: for **convertamini** read **conuertamini** (Stone).
60/23: for **verbum** read **uerbum** (Stone).
75/4: for **hoc** read **ho**.
79/17: for **craviora** read **graviora** (Stone).
80/9: for **justorum** read **iustorum** (Stone).
80b/3: the blank left by Scrivener can be filled with the letter *υ* or *ϋ*.
85b/22: the question should be raised as to whether the breathing over *ω* is p.m. It certainly *looks* like his.
91b/16–18: should be indented further (as in the Latin).
95b/31: delete the double point in the outer margin (cp. *Adn. ed.*).
101b/29: from examination by ultra-violet light it is clear that p.m. wrote *των φυλακω* ⌒.
103/11: for **locu** read **locȗ** (Stone).

JOHN

116/3: for **davo** read **dauo**.
124/24: for **sui** read **suis** (Stone).
127b/33: note that p.m. wrote a medial point after *ημερα*.
128b/14: for *διδασκω* read *διδασκω̑*.
130b/11: delete the point after *ου*.
130b/32: the space between *ιησ̑* and *και* should be the same as usual.
131/33: delete the point after **miramini**.
136b/30: for *ημω* read *ημω* ⌒ (Yoder).
137b/6: p.m. wrote *εγεννηηημεν* (*ε* elot. sub *ν* 2a). Strange though the error seems, I still think (*pace* Tischendorf) that the middle *η* is not *θ*.
138/22: delete the point after **uos**.
138b/6: insert a point after *τηρησει*.
138b/23: delete the point after *ειμι*.
141/13: delete the point after **eos**.
144b/9: for *αλλ* read *αλλ'*.
147b/32: for *ϊδοιουσ* read *ϊδειουσ*.
149b/8: for *κ ιφασ* read *κφιφασ*.
149b/18: there is a point p.m. after *συναγωγη*.
150b/32: ultra-violet light shows the whole word *εορτην* of which Scrivener could make out only *εο*.

152b/21: add οτι at the end of the line.
154b/31: for λεντιω read δεντιω.
156b/23: for εγνω read εγνοι (and see *Adn. ed.*).
157b/20: the point after θησεισ is a double not a single one.
158b/5: the erasure at the end of the line begins with οι.
160b/6: for παρ read πηρ.
160b/19: what is erased includes ι[ ]σεισ.
166/6: for **inullum** read **nullum** (Stone).
167b/23: there is almost certainly a point p.m. after κοσμου.
168b/10: the presence of a point after ναζαρηνον is far from certain.

LUKE

186b/33: there may be a point after θελοι.
194/16: for **humiliab** read **humiliab̄**.
198b/26: add a point after αυτου.
205b/1 margin: for μα : read μ͡α : (cp. *Adn. ed.* ad loc.).
212b/2: for οφθικαια read οφθι και α.
212b/25: for τον read την (Yoder).
219b/3: σα above the line is not p.m., judging by the shape of α.
224/33: add a point after **est**.
224b/16: I am not certain that p.m. wrote a point after θυ.
226b/22: for ¨ιος read ϋιος (Yoder).
230b/4: it may be that there is no point after εξελεξατο.
230b/19: no point after σημερον.
235b/8: for λεγοντθς read λεγοντες.
246b/23–4: I do not think that the diaereses are p.m. They are larger than he generally writes them. That over ινα is more possibly p.m. than the other.
247b/8: for αυτο read αυτον. See appendix 2.
247b/31: for ουχ read ουκ (Yoder).
253/22: for **inustione** read **in ustione**.
270/25: for **slo** read **salo** (Stone).
278b/11: there is possibly a point after αγρου.
279b/15: a double point is written by p.m. after αυτον. That denoting the Ammonian Section is written separately.
279b/26: there was probably a point written by p.m., which has been incorporated into the double point for the new Ammonian Section.

MARK

287/3: for **galileam** read **galilaeam** (Stone).
287b/6: for π͡νευνα read πνε͡υνα (and see appendix 2).
293/18: add a point after **montem**.
293b/4: no point in this line.

293b/27: ι at the end of the line is, in my opinion, not p.m.
294/33 and 295/8: for **ejus** read **eius** (Stone).
301/7: no point in this line.
311b/20: the p.m. point may be a double one.
313b/13: ϵ above the line before ι is not p.m.
317/18: there is a point at the end of the line.
318b/30: for *γεεννα* read *γεενα* (Yoder).
319/28: what looks like a point is in fact part of a *τ* showing through from the verso.
319b/4: there is a p.m. point, used for indicating the new Ammonian Section.
321/5: for **prohi eos** read **prohi[bu]eratis eos**.
321b/5: the line should read *εισελευσονται* · *ταλειον καμηλος*.
324/4: there is a double, not a single point.
326b/3: there is a p.m. point as well as the Ammonian Section sign.
335/13: it is unlikely that there is a point.
335b/27: there probably is a point p.m. after *λαου*.
339b/7, 9, 20: there are p.m. points in all these places, re-used for the Ammonian Section double points.
342b/17: for *ιην* read *ιην*.
346b/33: for *η* read *μη* (Yoder).

3 JOHN

415/11: omit the **t** written above the line (see appendix 2).

ACTS

420, title: point necessary after **apostol**.
444b/20: p.m. reads *απο πολλοισ*.
465/26: for **inuenisse** read **inuenisset** (Stone).
474/17: for **ciuitate** read **civitate** (Stone).
474/27: for **dm** read **dm** (Stone).
478b/17: for *υμασ* read *ϋμασ*.
492, running title: for **actus a postol** read **actusa po stol** .

APPENDIX 2

Additions and corrections to Scrivener's Adnotationes editoris

Publication of the facsimile has not lessened the value of Scrivener's notes. However, the aid of ultra-violet light, and the benefit of his work, has enabled me to make a good many changes. I have not consistently attempted to emulate the admirable conciseness of his Latin notes, except in the use of p.m. for the first hand, and s.m. for any subsequent hand, when it cannot be determined which one was at work (for instance, in erasures). I have, however, used some of his phrases whenever they have proved useful.

There are many places where Scrivener suggested two possible hands as the source of a particular correction. Since my discussion of the correctors (chapter 9) always ascribes these to a particular hand, I indicate below which of the two I consider to have been responsible.

The readings of D are given in lower-case letters (**bold** in the case of the Latin); Scrivener's commentary is in *italic* type.

MATTHEW

3b/18: possibly the first oblique stroke of υ was written by p.m. under the first ϵ in ϵτϵκϵν.
4b/6: κ pro ξ eras. in ϵξ s.m.
10/8: the deletion is s.m. not G.
12b/5: this correction is certainly not F.
12b/30: the letters have not been erased. They are merely faded.
13/4: **ia** is added to **omn** in a modern hand.
13/32: G both placed a point over the second **r** in **quadrantre** and added a horizontal stroke for final **m**.
15/10: s.m. rather than G.
26b/13: αι prim. eras. s.m.
27/23: is it a point or **o** (sic!) above **s** in **utrisque**?
27/28: G not s.m.
28: for *l.28* read *l.29*.
28b/8: the correction to ϵσκυλμϵκοι is p.m. rather than A.

39b/7, 24: for *eras.* read *elot.*
41/30: the correction to **uadae** is obelo et puncto.
48/16: it should be added that the **ue** was supplied by G.
49/3: G not s.m.
51/20: the corrected letter is **a** not **y**.
52b/21: it looks as if an attempt has been made to replace the *ι* in *ιωνα* with *υ*. The alteration has subsequently been erased.
57/16: **e** for **c** in **cum** G.
58/2: the **n** above the line is p.m.
59b: ↑ is written and erased by G before and after the initial *λ* in *λελυμενα*.
εσται↓ is erased at the end of the addition by G in the bottom margin.
60/19: G not s.m.
erunt↓ is erased at the end of the addition by G in the bottom margin.
66b/19: I would follow Kipling against Scrivener in attributing this to A rather than p.m.
67b/7: the horizontal line thought by Scrivener to be written over *εικρου* in *μεικρου* is actually an underlining of *:τελος:* in the margin above.
67b/9: the marks by K in fact come at 71b/9.
68/21: G not s.m.
68b/8: Scrivener notes that Kipling ascribed the second *εχει* to s.m., which he thinks would be A, and the strokes over *εχει χρειαν* to p.m. According to Scrivener the *εχει* is p.m., the strokes are s.m. It seems to me impossible to attribute either to p.m. *εχει* is not Corrector A either. The *ε* is quite different, and with its upward-turning *hasta* is written by B.
69/26: G not s.m.
70/16, 19, 31, 33: G not s.m.
71b/9: see 67b/9.
71b/31: the way the correction is made is more like D than A.
75/4: the **c** is certainly by Corrector G.
76b/27: the correction is certainly not by G.
77/27: G not s.m.
77b/29: this correction is perhaps better attributed to C.
78/25: G not s.m.
78b/20: this is A rather than D.
79/33: *paretur* should be in roman type, not italics.
80/8: the correction of **urnatis** to **ornatis** is likely to be by G, but this cannot be demonstrated, since a tear in the leaf runs through the correction.
81b/16: the *β* of *βδελυγμα* contains a false stroke by p.m.
85/3: for *e* read *e prim.*
85b/8: there is no p.m. correction to *αρκεσει* – what Scrivener took to be an expunged *η* is a letter **p** on the recto.
86/14: the addition of **n** is not by G.
88b/17: the first *σ* in *επεσκεψασθαι* covers an *iota* – both are p.m.
90b/1: *και* punctis suprapositis abrogat s.m.
91b/6: there is nothing expunged under *ιν* in *αφεσιν*.
97b/2: the correction of *τοσα* to *ποσα* by a single vertical stroke is obviously hard to allocate to a particular hand. I prefer to see it as the work of F.

98b/28: for ϗ it might be safer to read *κ*.
100/29: this **a** is not by G.

JOHN

104b/15: the second *ο* in *ερχομενον* was begun as an *ϵ*.
104b/20: *ω* elot. sub *οι* in *αυτοισ* p.m.
114/3: for *elot. p.m.* read *eras. s.m.*
115b/22: the correction is not by H.
116/16: p.m. accidentally wrote the point after **mulier** twice, one slightly below the other.
121/1: I think it possible that the **o** added before **p** in **egoperor** is s.m.
123b/28: the letters expunged under *δωδεκατο* are *εκτωνπεν*.
124b/4: the final stroke of the second *ν* in *ανεχωρησεν* has been touched up by a later hand.
124b/27: the *αυ* in *αυτου*, erased by s.m., has been replaced by a late hand.
125b/20: the *ϵ* in *εστιν* was begun as a *τ*.
126/6: the correction of **hoc** to **huc** is not p.m. I cannot see any grounds for attributing it to A. Compare the **u** at 122/20, and 463/30. If it has to be attributed to a known corrector, then I would choose the one which wrote **fu** at 419/30, in the K group.
126/17: the corrector is not G.
129b/4: p.m. began to write *επιεν* before correcting himself to *ειπεν*.
130b/2: there are no grounds for disagreeing with Scrivener's hesitant decision.
134b/28: the erased letter is a *κ*.
135/27: **e** and **t** obelis notat G (not s.m.).
135b/30: the whole correction is by E: the tau of D is quite different.
136b/27: in my view this is p.m.
137b/3: the stroke is under *ϵ*, not under *ει*.
137b/4: s.m. adds a diaeresis over *υ* in *υμων*.
137b/6: s.m. placed a breathing over *ϵ* in *ενα*.
138b/26: *και παραγων* has been rewritten by L.
140/27: G not s.m.
143b/30: add *supraposito* after *puncto*.
144b/29: this is A.
145/12: the correction of **ego gnosco** to **cognosco** is, I suggest, p.m.
145b/9: there is no erasure, but a transfer of ink onto the page from elsewhere.
146b/33: *ϵ*, not *ο*, has been expunged.
147b/32: for *α pro ο* read *α pro ϵ*.
148/28: G not s.m.
148b/2: *ν* (sic) above *γ* in *λεγουσιν* s.m.
149b/8: s.m. has added a circumflex over *ω* in *ων*.
151/29: **o** in **iudaeorum** written over an **i** p.m.
152b/5: *σ* in *απολεσει* written over *ι* p.m.
152b/21: the erased letters *are οτι*.
156b/12: the *υ* had been marked with an obelus by p.m.
156b/23: one corrector wrote *ω* above *οι* in *εγνοι*; a second corrector erased the *ω* and altered *οι* to *ω*.

160b/1: the corrections attributed to J are by J'.
160b end of addition at bottom: for δυναται καρπο read δυνατα κκαρπο. The first κ has been altered to ι.
165b/10, 14: there is no point p.m. after πιστευετε or εστιν.
166b/20: ϵ in ϵν has been aspirated.
168b/3: there is no point p.m. after αυτου.
179/4: for *eras. s.m.* read *elot. p.m.*

LUKE

182b/11: to be precise, β has been erased.
183/11: not even with ultra-violet does any sign of an obelus appear: Kipling's statement should be ignored.
184: the marks 'manu recentissima' are as follows:

Points – l. 2 after **zacharia**; 7 after **gauderunt**; 8 after **dmi**; 9 after **bibet**; 12, 13, 17 at the end.
Apostrophes – l. 3 after **tua**; 17 at the end.
Apostrophe above a point – l. 5 after **iohanen**; 16 at the end.
Indeterminate strokes – l. 4 after **pariet** and **filium**.
In l. 14 the final letter in **heliae** has been partly rewritten.

The other points are all p.m.
184b/19: for *punctis* read *puncto*.
186b: for *v. 30* read *l. 30*.
188b/28: the correction is more likely to be D than B.
189b/9: the correction is not by H.
189b/16: this is more like B than D.
191b/27: apostrophe added by s.m. after ιερουσαλημ (possibly by C).
194/16: the stroke seems to me to be more probably p.m. Compare it with the line written above the nomina sacra.
196b/column 1/13, 23: neither correction is by H.
198b/6–7: not by H. Possibly the same hand as the μ that is added at F188b/20.
200b/18: αυτοισ p.m., changed to αυτουσ, probably also by p.m.
209b/9: the letter expunged was an ϵ; p.m. then began an ι, before finally writing ϵ after all.
210b/16: there is no erasure here.
211/15: **q** is correct.
212/28: **nos** and not **no** is expunged under **sit**.
218b/31: the erased words are τησ συναγωγησ πεσων. The correction cannot be by the same hand as the one which wrote τεθραμμενοσ εισηλθεν at 198b/6–7; it could possibly be attributed to L. For *αϊρος* read *ιαϊρος*.
219b/3: I do not think that the addition σα is p.m.
222b/11: the original letters seem to be more like τοδι, or even τοδν.
223/19: **sam** and not **sa** has been expunged.
225b and 226/5: the leaves have at some time become stuck together at the points where μη

and **prohibere** appear in their respective columns. This should be taken into account when using the facsimile.

228b/25: likely to be A.

234b/19: Scrivener is correct.

235b/8: the correction is, I think, from ε and not from θ.

240/12: the first **e** of **coeperit** was begun as a **p**.

240b/2: not by H, but a modern hand.

245b/2: ν has been washed out under σ in ποιησ.

247b/8: αυτον p.m. A point was placed over ν by s.m., and both point and letter subsequently erased.

248b/18: add *obelo* before *notat*.

250/31: for *s.m.* read *p.m.*

252/19: not **i**, but the beginning of **n**, is under the second **m**.

253b/20: the letters washed out are επτακεισετανοηση. The scribe then altered ισ to μ, before expunging the whole phrase. The last stroke of that μ has become the first vertical in the first η of the μετανοηση that stands.

254b/4: φ in φαγω was begun as a π, of which only the cross-stroke was executed.

256b/2: η has been washed out under θ in λωθ.

256b/10: this is B.

256b/15: examination by ultra-violet light confirms Scrivener's opinion. The letters ησο are, even then, scarcely visible.

261b/4: for ενεπεμψα- read ενεπεμψα⁀.

262b/34: the erasure under εαν ο may conceivably be ουτοι, though this is little more than a conjecture. But the top of the first stroke of υ may be made out between ε and α.

264/7: the letter under **sepaem** is not **t**. It is either **i** or the first stroke in **n**.

264/24: only **quid facerent** was written and then washed out. What Scrivener took for **ei** is μα from the verso.

266b/27: ε in εισαγγελοι has been aspirated by a secondary hand.

267b/26: Scrivener is correct in supposing that the correction of παντερ is not p.m. I would attribute it to A.

270b/11: it is hard to agree with Scrivener. The downward turn to the cross-stroke of γ is altogether habitual to the first hand.

270b/31: this is probably A.

274b/11: a double-point is written after ιην. It is the work neither of p.m. nor of L.

274b/23: I am confident that the letter **m** (Latin form) has been erased.

277/4: p.m. began to write **a** before beginning the **q** in **quid**.

279/33: it may be that the letter erased is **n**. The second upright is faintly visible. But the letter is really illegible.

279b/31: ε, and not ει, replaces η.

283b/13: the letter is not **n**, but **ei** or **en** (more probably the former).

283b/30: this is A, rather than B.

285/14: several short horizontal lines above **i** in **die** and **te** in **tertia** seem to have been made by p.m. in testing his pen.

MARK

287b/6: πνευνα has been altered by a later hand to πνευν.
287b/25: for ι read ι *prim.*
288b/12: μ washed out under δ in μηδενι.
292/6: it is doubtful whether p.m. did write **u** first.
298/27: nothing has been expunged under **i** in **sile**.
299/13: only the shape **C** has been expunged: either that **c**, or an incomplete **d** or **e**, was first written.
300/25: the deletion should be regarded as s.m.
301/25: nothing has been expunged; π shows through from the verso.
302b/8: I think that p.m. wrote τυισ, not ταισ.
304b/9: the point is certainly casu.
305b/9: a modern hand has added the elision sign and a smooth breathing in the phrase κατιδιαν.
305b/24: for δυο, read δυω *p.m.*
306/7: **tes**, and not **tm**, has been expunged.
306b/24: the hand cannot be identified.
307/33: there is no erasure. An accidental stroke comes after the second **o**.
308b/31: add. ι supra σ in εστιν s.m.
310b/1: the letter begun under ε is not α, but υ.
311b/22: ultra-violet light confirms Scrivener's opinion.
312b: various chance points appear on the folio. See ll. 15, 28.
313b/13: ε is added above the line before ϊ after συ, by a corrector.
314/20: for *secund.* read *prim.*
314/22: **b**, and not **r**, has been expunged.
314b/14: the whole correction is by B.
318b/13: the p.m. reading is σε. Corrector A altered this to εισ.
327b/1: for *puncto supra posito* read *punctis supra positis.*
327b/18: a scrolled line at the beginning, in a modern hand.
328/19: the points are undoubtedly accidental.
333b/2: what has been expunged is not ι, but the beginning of ω.
342b/16: the point is undoubtedly casual. It is s.m., and not p.m.
342b/17: ιην p.m. Corrected to ° ιησ by B.
346b/3: this correction is by B.

3 JOHN

415/11: **t** added above the line before **e** by s.m. (see appendix 1).

ACTS

416/21: for *obelis* read *obelo.*
416b/17: ε in εϊερουσαλημ puncto abrogat s.m.
417/1, 5, 14: s.m. not G.

417/29: **u** pro **b** in **perseberantes** G.
418/1: the points over certain letters of **cum surrexisset** are s.m. not G.
418/8, 11 (**m²** in **mercedem**), 26 (**niam** in **quoniam**): the corrections are s.m. not G.
420/25: s.m., not E.
420/32: s.m. not G.
421b/24: **nota** is added in the margin opposite this line, not l. 23.
422/5: add *et obelo* after *eras*.
422/15, 30; s.m. not G. In l. 21 the correction to **de** is by G, but that to **fructum** s.m.
423/27: s.m. not G.
424b/29: the correction is to the second occurrence in the line of *το*.
425/21: the presence of a point over the final **n** is not beyond dispute.
426b/20: s.m. not G.
428b and 429/20: neither correction is by E, or by any other principal corrector.
428b/3: the alteration is p.m. rather than A.
430/15,18: the parchment has been cut away. The superline is partly lost.
430/29: **n** in **possidebant** puncto abrogat s.m.
432b/4: the added *ξ* is by B, not E.
432b/13: not H.
433b/10: this is more possibly E than C.
433b/13: the corrector wrote *arχι*, not *αρχι* (that is, a Latin R, not Greek P).
434/20: **mi** added above **honibus** is late, and not E (cp. F483/16).
437b: for the first *l. 19*, read *18*.
438b/15 and 439/14: the points over the letters are casu.
438b/19: add. *γησ* supra. lin. post *τησ* B.
439b/19: this correction is by B. Cp., F444b/23, 27.
439b/20: the correction is above the letters *αυ*.
440b/17: sigma is inserted after *υ*, not after *σ*.
441b/14: the *σ* is more like p.m. – note the thickening before the initial stroke.
444b/20: p.m. read *απο πολλοισ*; H read *πολλοι*.
445b/23: this is fairly certainly A, not B.
464b/11: A rather than p.m.
471b/6 and 472b/12: both these are A.
472b/15: I have listed this correction under A.
476b/25: somewhat hesitantly, I attribute this to B.
477b/2: for *σ* read *σ secund.*
483/16: s.m., not E (cp. F434/20).
486b/32: for *ο secund.* read *ϵ secund.* From its style, the correction is by H rather than by B.
487b/24 and 26: these corrections are both D and not C.
487b/33: delete *minutum* from the description.
488b/29: this is more likely to be B than A.
488b/33: this is A.
492b/15: for *ο pro ω in αυτον*, read *ο pro ω in αυτων*.
492b/18: not H.
494b/3: ignore *sic*.
496b/30: the addition of *ν* by B is to *η*, not to *μελλει*.

497b/6: this correction is by D.
497b/18: correction by H, not D.
504b: R. P. Casey (*HTR* 16 (1923), 392–4) noted several errors in Scrivener's transcription from Dickinson's collation of the lines that had been lost in the interval. They are: v. 16 – for *nam μην non apparet, nec τινι κυριω*, read (*μην* enim non apparet) nec *τινι κυριω*; for *manus recentior ω* read fecit Man. Recentior *παρ ω ξενισθωμεν*; v. 17 – for *υπεδεξαντο* read *υποδειξαντο*.
504b/15: *ν* in *καρδιαν*: for *eras.* read *obelo abrogat.*
505/33: D, not F.
505b/2: for (*α eraso B*). read (*α eraso*) *B*.
505b/25: the correction is D, not B.
505b/28: D, not B.
508b/26: this is C, not B.

APPENDIX 3

Alterations to Scrivener's list of marginalia

67b/18–20: the following appears in the outer margin:

τω σαββα
τω [των προ]
φουτισματω

with a cross, its top looped like *rho*, on the left. It was later erased by L, who wrote the Ammonian Section *ΣΕ* over it. See Harris, *Annotators*, pp. 9, 35 (but he wrongly reads *φουτισματων*).

205b, last word of note: for *προσθεσεος* read *προθεσεος*.

ΙΥ

ΚΑΤ ΙΩΑΝ

ΤΑΕΡΓΑΤΟΥΠΕΜΨΑΝΤΟΣΜΕΕΩΣΗΜΕΡΑΕΣΤΙΝ
ΕΡΧΕΤΑΙΝΥΞΟΤΕΟΥΔΕΙΣΔΥΝΑΤΑΙΕΡΓΑΖΕΣΘΑΙ
ΟΤΑΝΩΕΝΤΩΚΟΣΜΩΦΩΣΕΙΜΙ
ΤΟΥΚΟΣΜΟΥ ΤΑΥΤΑΕΙΠΩΝΕΠΤΥΣΕΝΧΑΜΑΙ
ΚΑΙΕΠΟΙΗΣΕΝΠΗΛΟΝΕΚΤΟΥΠΤΥΜΑΤΟΣ
ΚΑΙΕΠΕΧΡΕΙΣΕΝΑΥΤΩΤΟΝΠΗΛΟΝ
ΕΠΙΤΟΥΣΟΦΘΑΛΜΟΥΣΑΥΤΟΥΚΑΙΕΙΠΕΝ
ΥΠΑΓΕΝΙΨΑΙΕΙΣΤΗΝΚΟΛΥΜΒΗΘΡΑΝ
ΤΟΥΣΙΛΩΑΜΟΕΡΜΗΝΕΥΕΤΑΙ
ΑΠΕΣΤΑΛΜΕΝΟΣ ΑΠΗΛΘΕΝΟΥΝ
ΚΑΙΕΝΙΨΑΤΟ ΚΑΙΗΛΘΕΝΒΛΕΠΩΝ
ΟΙΟΥΝΓΕΙΤΟΝΕΣΚΑΙΟΙΘΕΩΡΟΥΝΤΕΣΑΥΤΟΝ
ΤΟΠΡΟΤΕΡΟΝΟΤΙΠΡΟΣΕΤΗΣΗΝ
ΕΛΕΓΟΝΟΥΧΟΥΤΟΣΕΣΤΙΝΟΚΑΘΗΜΕΝΟΣ
ΚΑΙΠΡΟΣΑΙΤΩΝ ΑΛΛΟΙΕΛΕΓΟΝΟΤΙ
ΑΥΤΟΣΕΣΤΙΝΕΤΕΡΟΙΔΕΟΤΙΟΜΟΙΟΣ
ΑΥΤΩΕΣΤΙΝ ΕΚΕΙΝΟΣΕΛΕΓΕΝΟΤΙΕΓΩΕΙΜΙ
ΕΙΠΟΝΟΥΝΑΥΤΩΠΩΣΟΥΝ
ΗΝΕΩΧΘΗΣΑΝΣΟΥΟΙΟΦΘΑΛΜΟΙ
ΑΠΕΚΡΙΘΗΕΚΕΙΝΟΣΑΝΘΡΩΠΟΣΛΕΓΟΜΕΝΟΣ
ΙΗΣΠΗΛΟΝΕΠΟΙΗΣΕΝΚΑΙΕΠΕΧΡΙΣΕΝ
ΜΟΥΤΟΥΣΟΦΘΑΛΜΟΥΣΚΑΙΕΙΠΕΝΜΟΙ
ΥΠΑΓΕΕΙΣΤΟΝΣΙΛΩΑΜΚΑΙΝΙΨΑΙ
ΑΠΗΛΘΟΝΟΥΝΚΑΙΕΝΙΨΑΜΗΝΚΑΙΗΛΘΟΝ
ΒΛΕΠΩΝ ΕΙΠΑΝΟΥΝΑΥΤΩΠΟΥΕΣΤΙΝ
ΕΚΕΙΝΟΣΛΕΓΕΙΑΥΤΟΙΣΟΥΚΟΙΔΑ
ΚΑΙΑΓΟΥΣΙΝΑΥΤΟΝΠΡΟΣΤΟΥΣΦΑΡΙΣΑΙΟΥΣ
ΤΟΝΠΟΤΕΤΥΦΛΟΝ ΗΝΔΕΣΑΒΒΑΤΟΝ
ΟΤΕΤΟΝΠΗΛΟΝΕΠΟΙΗΣΕΝΟΙΗΣ
ΚΑΙΗΝΥΞΕΝΑΥΤΟΥΤΟΥΣΟΦΘΑΛΜΟΥΣ
ΠΑΛΙΝΟΥΝΕΠΗΡΩΤΩΝΑΥΤΟΝΚΑΙΟΙ
ΦΑΡΙΣΑΙΟΙΠΩΣΑΝΕΒΛΕΨΕΝ
ΟΔΕΕΙΠΕΝΑΥΤΟΙΣΠΗΛΟΝΕΠΕΘΗΚΕΝ

Plate 1 A double opening (F139b–40)

1cm 2cm

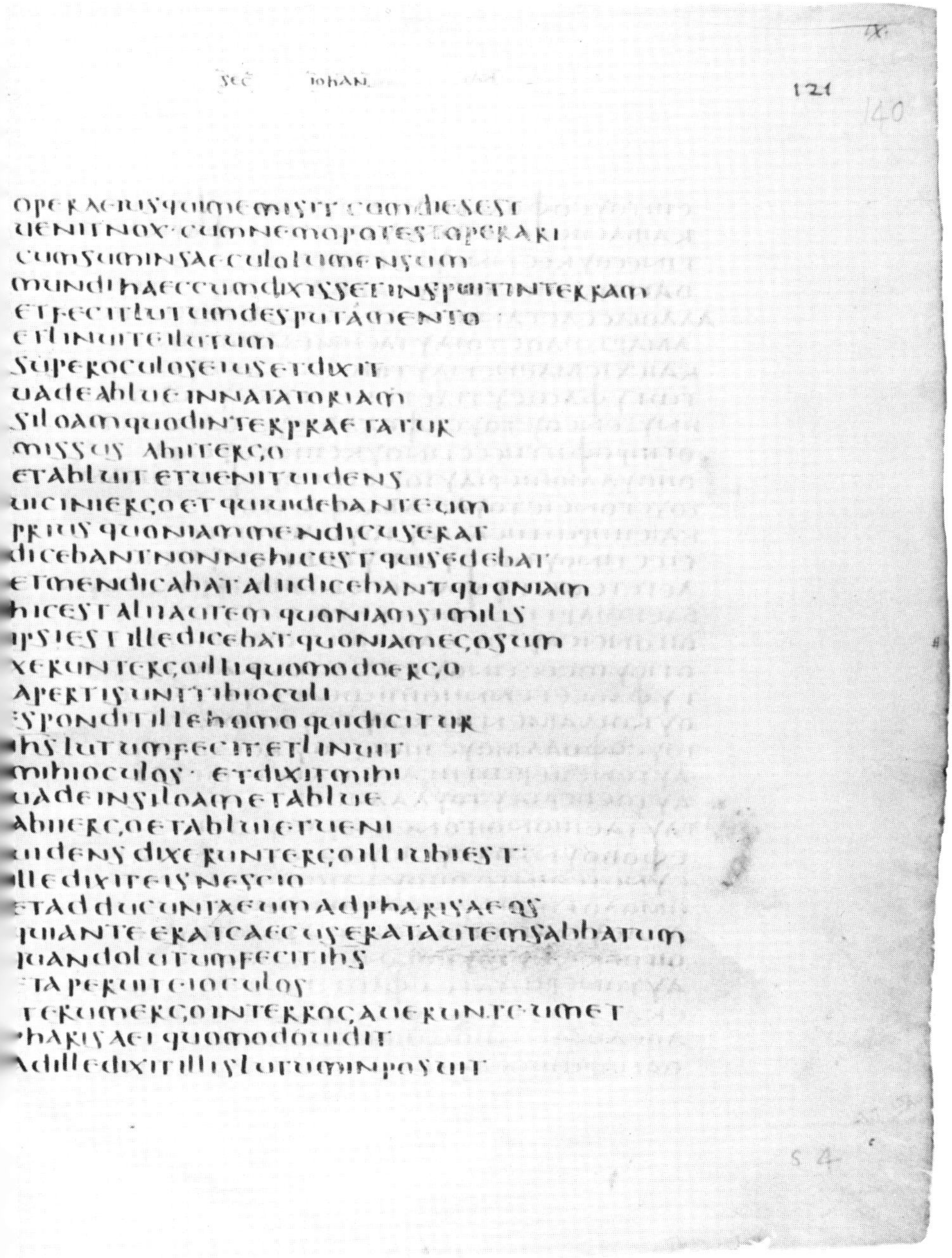

SEC IOHAN 121

140

operari eius qui me misit dum dies est
uenit nox cum nemo potest operari
cum sum in saeculo lumen sum
mundi haec cum dixisset exspuit in terram
et fecit lutum de sputamento
et liniuit ei lutum
super oculos eius et dixit
uade ablue in natatoria
siloam quod interpraetatur
missus abiit ergo
et abluit et uenit uidens
uicini ergo et qui uidebant eum
prius quoniam mendicus erat
dicebant nonne hic est qui sedebat
et mendicabat alii dicebant quoniam
hic est alii autem quoniam similis
ipsi est ille dicebat quoniam ego sum
xerunt ergo illi quomodo ergo
apertisunt tibi oculi
espondit ille homo qui dicitur
ihs lutum fecit et liniuit
mihi oculos et dixit mihi
uade in siloam et ablue
abii ergo et ablui et ueni
uidens dixerunt ergo illi ubi est
ille dixit eis nescio
et adducunt eum ad pharisaeos
qui ante erat caecus erat autem sabbatum
quando lutum fecit ihs
et aperuit ei oculos
terum ergo interrogauerunt eum et
pharisaei quomodo uidit
ad ille dixit illis lutum inposuit

54

1cm 2cm

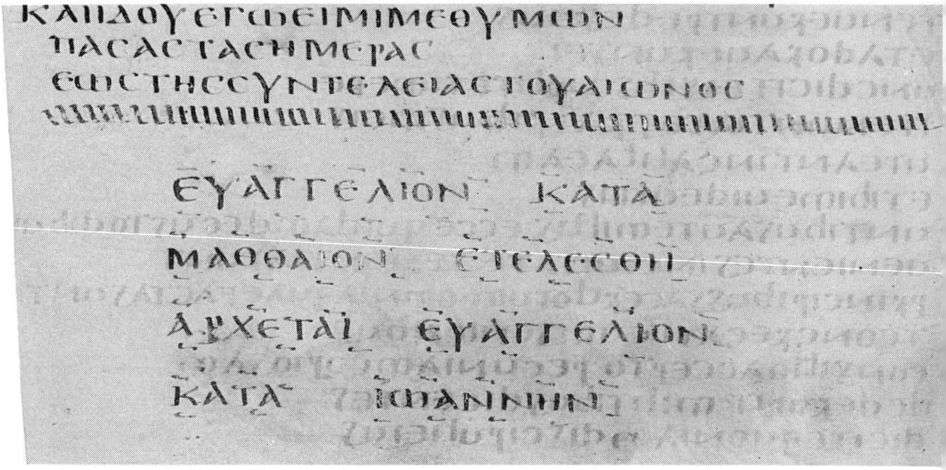

Plate 2a The Greek colophon to Matthew (F103b)

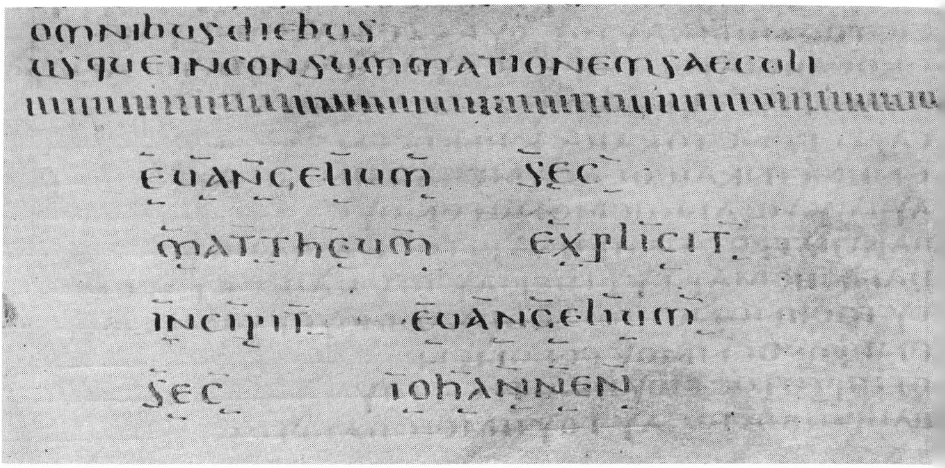

Plate 2b The Latin colophon to Matthew (F104)

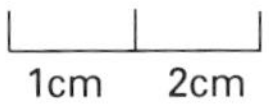

1cm 2cm

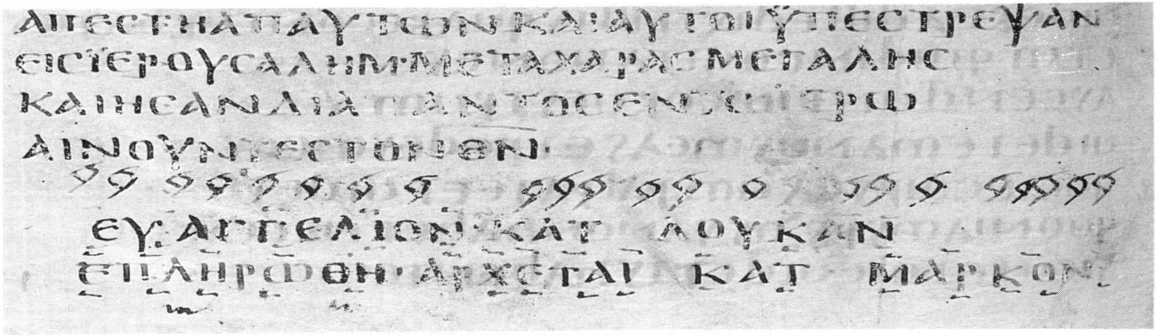

Plate 3a The Greek colophon to Luke (F284b)

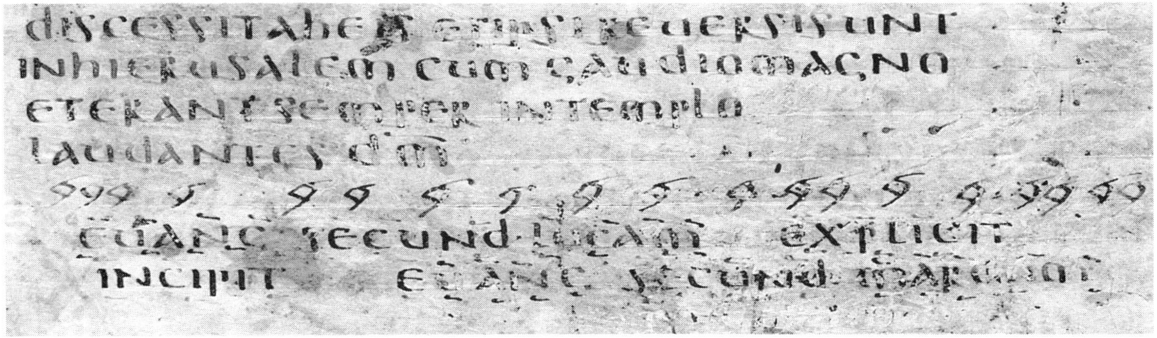

Plate 3b The Latin colophon to Luke (F285)

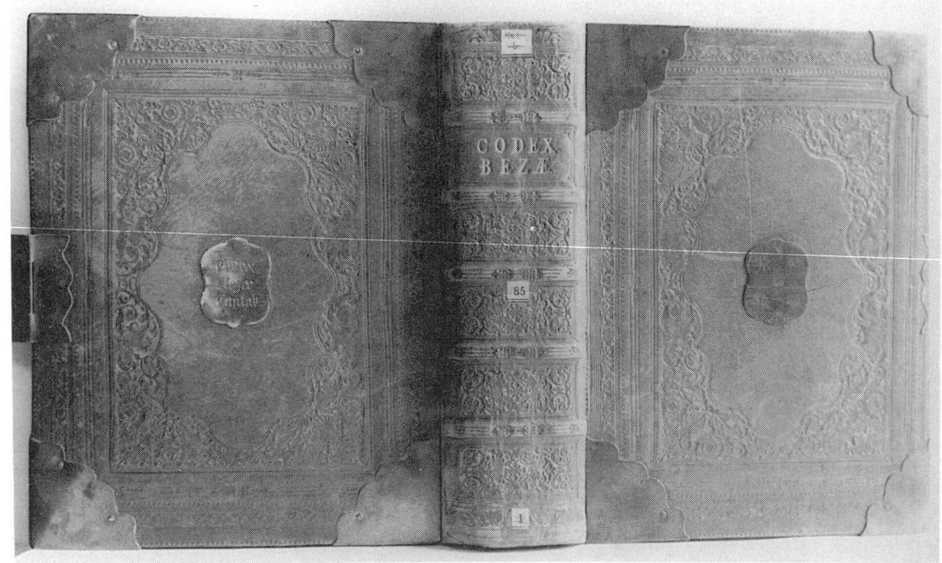

Plate 4 The previous binding

Plate 5 The unbound manuscript

Plate 6 Pressing and stretching the unbound sheets

Plate 7 The present binding

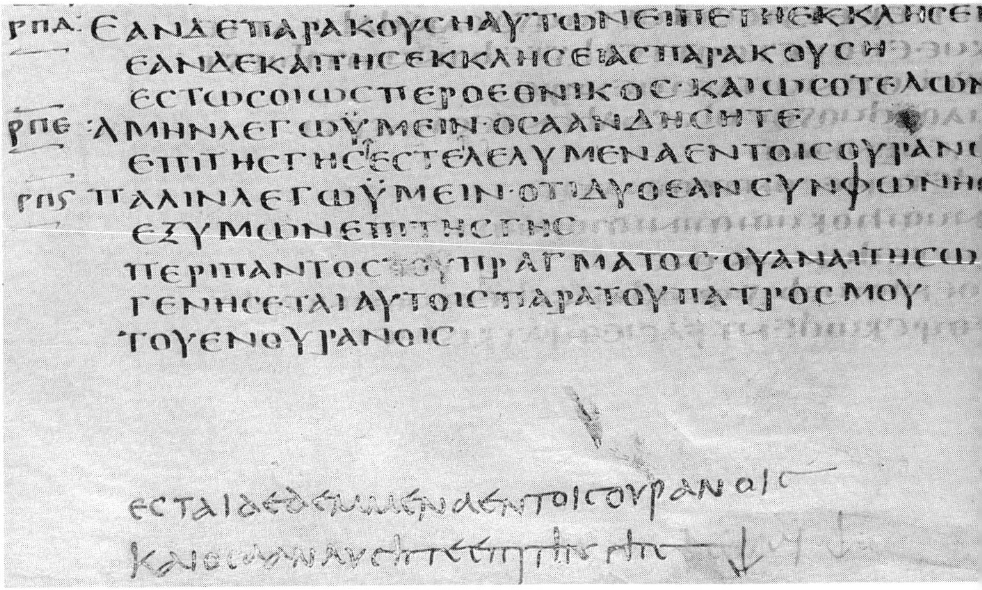

Plate 8a Corrector G (F59b, l. 28 to foot)

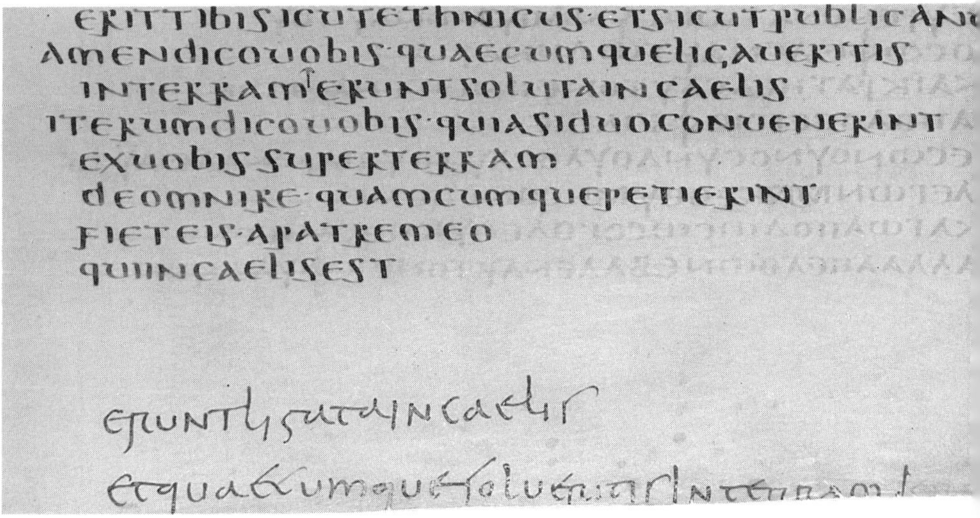

Plate 8b Corrector G (F60, l. 28 to foot)

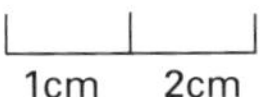

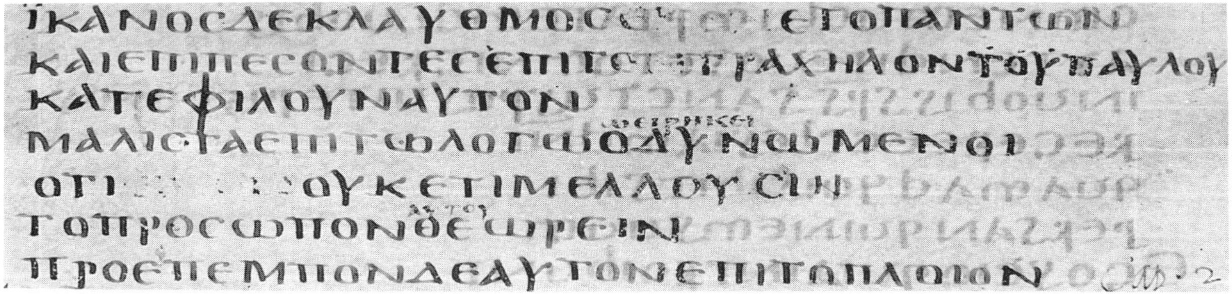

Plate 9 Corrector A (F502b/23)

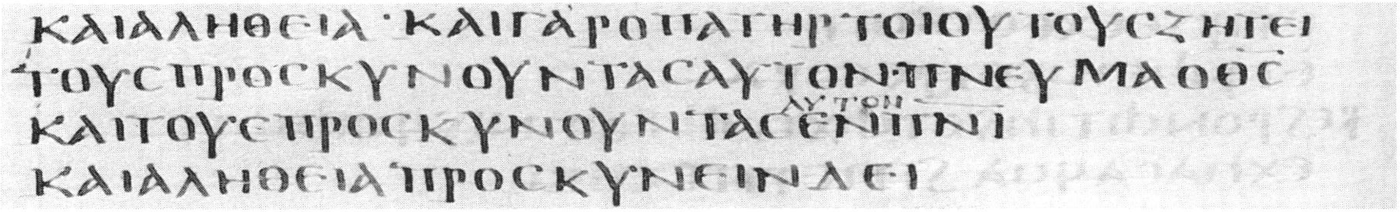

Plate 10 Corrector C (F115b/32)

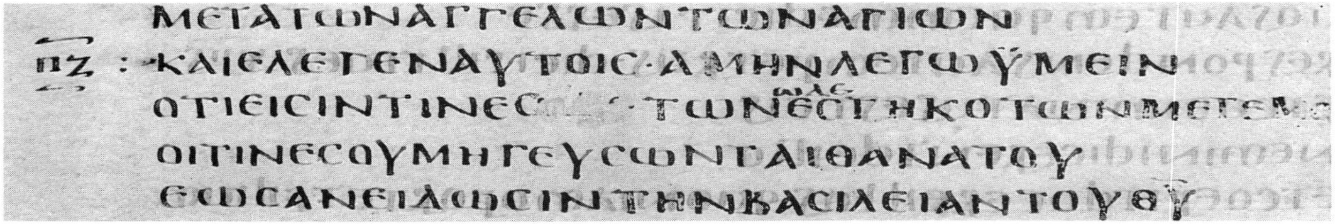

Plate 11 Corrector B (F314b/14)

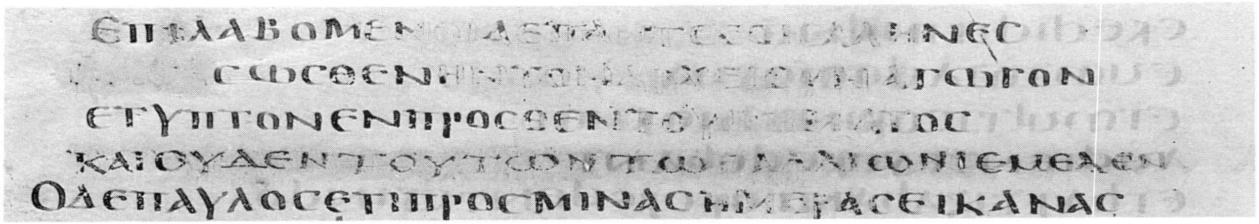

Plate 12 Corrector D (F492b/4)

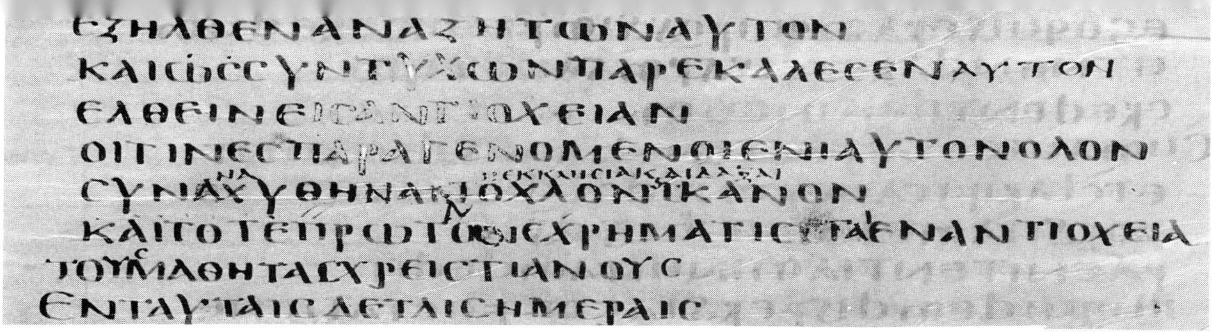

Plate 13 Corrector E (F461b/26–8)

Plate 14 Corrector H (F488b/28)

Plate 15 Corrector F (F163b foot)

Plate 16a Corrector J[1] (F160b, l. 30 and foot)

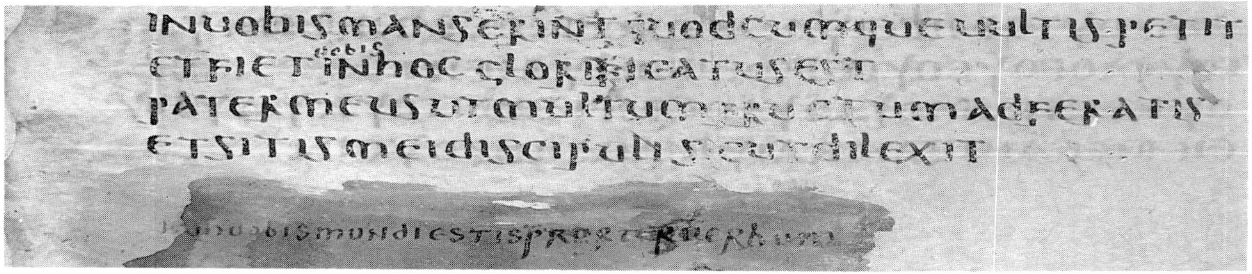

Plate 16b Corrector J[1] (F161, l. 30 and foot)

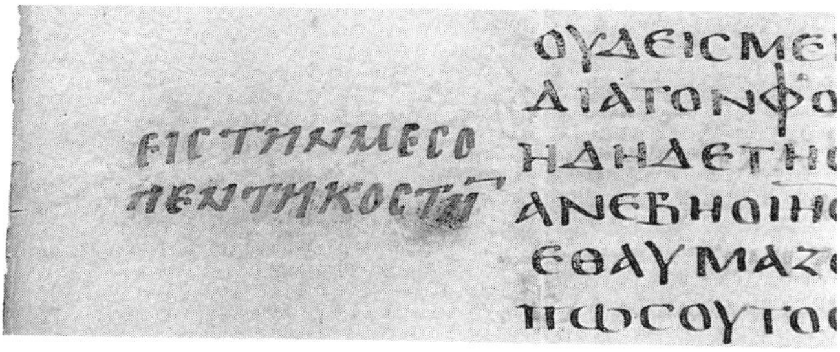

Plate 17 Annotator I (F130b/13–14, left margin)

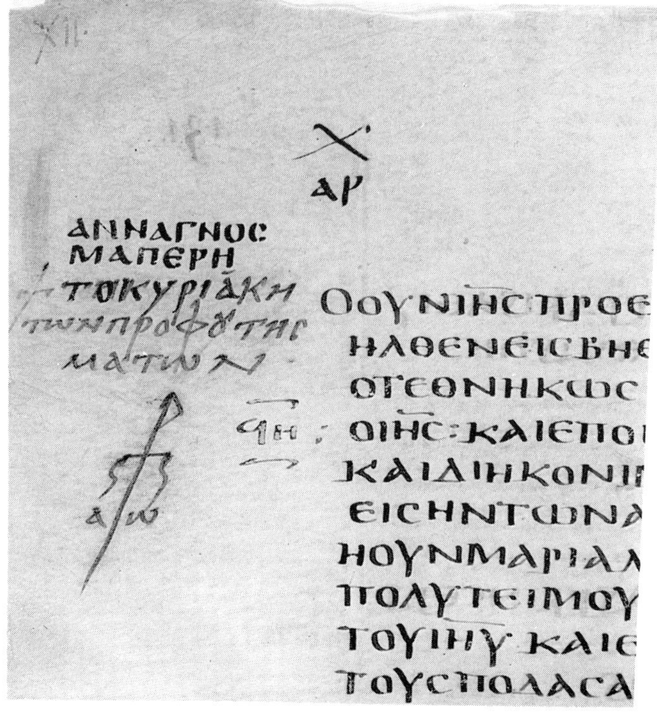

Plate 18 Annotators J and L (F150b top outside corner)

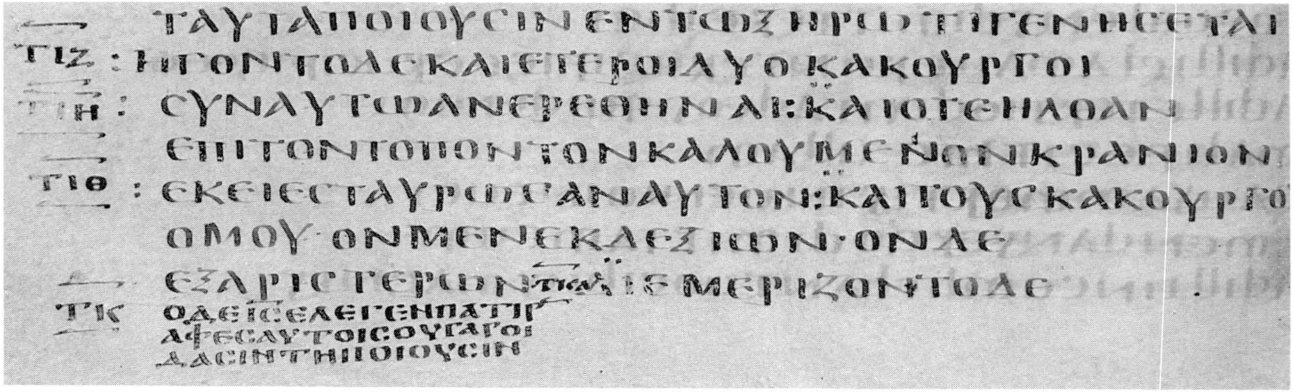

Plate 19 Hand L (F278b/27 to foot)

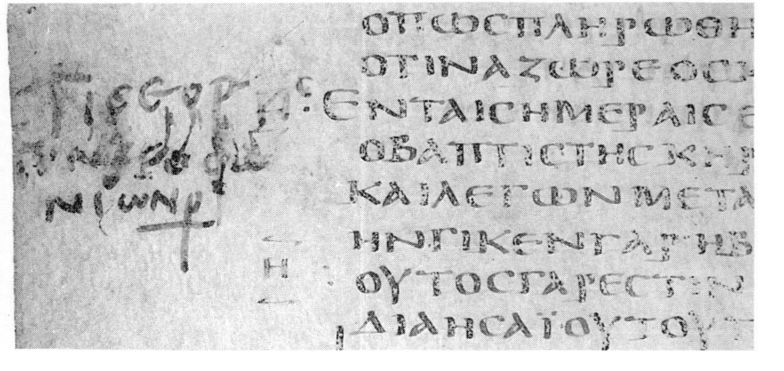

Plate 20 Annotator M (F6b/11–16)

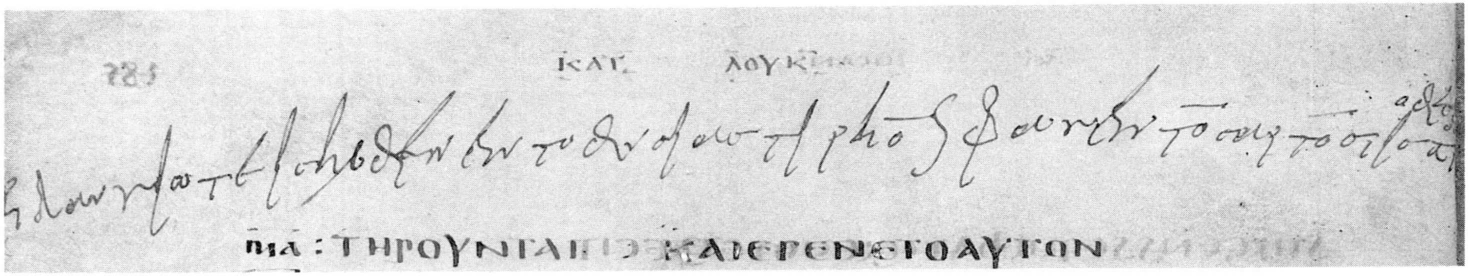

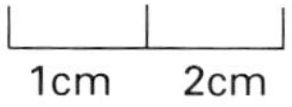

Plate 21 Annotator M[1] (F205b top margin)

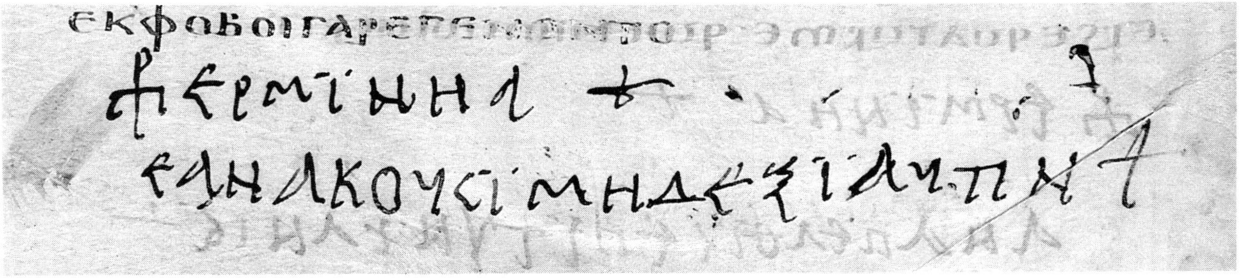

1cm 2cm

Plate 22 Annotator M[3] (F314b foot)

Plate 23 Annotator M[4] (F347b/10–15, left margin)

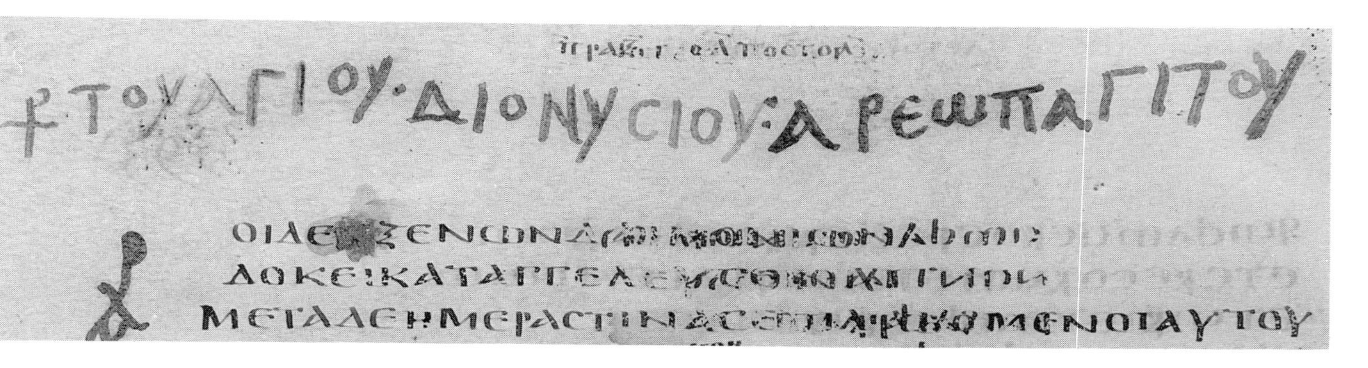

Plate 24 Annotator O (F488b top margin)

ταυταπαρακολουθησει'
εντωονοματιμου·δαιμονια
εκβαλλουσι' γλωσσειςλαλη
σωσινκαινεις· οφεισαρουσιν'
κανθανασειμον τιπιωσιν.
ουμηαυτουςβλαψη'
επαρρωστουςχειρας επιθησουσειν.
καικαλωςεξουσιν'
Ομενουνκ̅ς̅ μετατο
λαλησαιαυτοις·ανελημφθη
ειςτονουρανον·καιεκαθισεν
ενδεξιων του θ̅υ̅'
εκεινοιδε εξελθοντες.
εκηρυξανπανταχου'
τουκ̅υ̅συνεργουντος.
καιτονλογον βεβαιουντος.
διατωνεπακολουθουν τωνσημιων.
αμην'
ευαγγελιον καταμαρκον
ετελεσθη'
αρχεταιπραξις αποστολων'

haecsequentur'
Innominemeo·daemonia
eicient; linguisloquentur
nouis· serpentestollent,
etsimortiferu̅ quidbiberint.
noneisnocebit:
superegrotosmanusimponent.
etbenehabebunt'
etd̅n̅squidem·postqua̅
locutuse̅eis. assumptuse̅
incaelum·etsedit
adextrisd̅i̅'
Illiaut̅ profecti.
praedicaueruntubiq;·
d̅n̅o cooperante.
etsermonemc̅firmante
sequentib' signis:
amen'
euangelium sc̅d̅ marcu̅
explicit:
incipiuntactus ap̅lorum'

Plate 25a The supplementary leaves (F348b*)

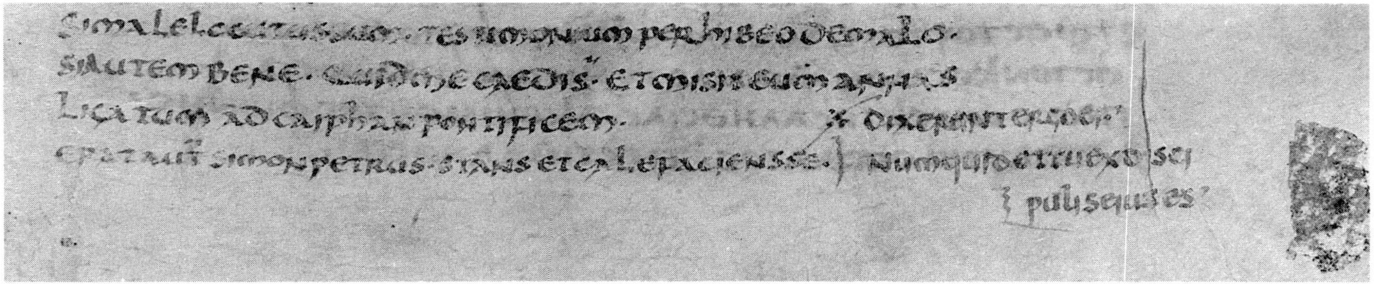

Plate 25b The supplementary leaves (F170*/31–3)

Notes on the plates

All the plates are the work of the Photographic Department of Cambridge University Library, and are reproduced by permission of the Syndics of Cambridge University Library.

The plates are derived from photographs taken of the manuscript itself.

1 A double opening virtually as it was left by the copyist (F139b–40).

2–3 The colophons

2a and 2b The Greek (F103b) and Latin (F104) colophons to Matthew. The scribe's rulings are very clear in Plate 2a.

3a and 3b The Greek (F284b) and Latin (F285) colophons to Luke.

4–7 At the rebinding of 1965

4 The previous binding.

5 The unbound manuscript.

6 Pressing and stretching the unbound sheets.

7 The present binding.

8–24 The correctors and annotators

8a and 8b Corrector G (F59b and F60, l. 28 to foot): use of *anchora* and addition to text (pp. 37, 91, and 126). *του* in the third line from the bottom of F59b has been erased by a secondary hand.

9 Corrector A (F502b/23): insertion of *ω ειρηκει* (p. 131). Two lines above, a corrector has placed points over *του* as an indication that this word should be omitted. In line 24, ΕΙΠΕΝ has been erased, and at the end of the line Corrector D has changed ΕΙ ϹΟΙ to *ουσιν* (p. 153). The *αυτου* in the following line is by Corrector E (p. 156).

10 Corrector C (F115b/32): insertion of *αυτον* (p. 135).

11 Corrector B (F314b/14): alteration of ΤΙΝΕ ϢΔΕ to *τινες* and insertion of *ωδε* after ΤϢΝ (pp. 40, 145).

12 Corrector D (F492b/4): insertion of *και ουδεν τουτων τ* before *ω γαλλιω, νι εμελ* before *εν* (p. 38, 152). In line 1, Corrector D changed ΑΠΟΛΑΒΟΜΕΝΟΙ to *επιλαβομενοι* (p. 152). The beginning of the second line is too thoroughly erased to be legible; *οταν* and *μετα* have both been conjectured (see Scrivener's *Adn. ed.*, p. 445 *ad loc.*).

13 Corrector E (F461b/26–8): alteration of text to *συναναχυθηναι τη εκκλησια ϗ διδαξαι οχλον ϊκανον χρηματισται πρωτως εν αντιοχεια τους μαθητας χρειστιανους* (pp. 38f, 156). The addition of *αυτον* three lines above is by Corrector F (p. 161). Earlier in the line, the points indicate that ωC should be deleted.

14 Corrector H (F488b/28): addition of *τι αυτος* (pp. 40, 159). The *υ* added at the beginning of the previous line is by Corrector E. OTI has been erased at the beginning of the following line; there is then an alteration (*διδους* for Ο ΔΟΥC) that is by Corrector B (p. 146).

15 Corrector F (F163b foot): replacement of *τι εστιν τουτο* with *ελεγον ουν τουτο τι εστιν ο λεγει το μικρο[ν] ουκ οιδαμεν τι λαλει ελε* (pp. 39, 160). The leaf has been stained with chemical.

16a and 16b Corrector J[1] (F160b and 161, l. 30 and foot): insertion of *uobis*, F161/30, and additions at foot of each page, marked in the Greek side by ↓ corresponding to ↑ above to show where the words should be inserted (line 18, not illustrated) (pp. 40f, 162). The Greek insertion runs *ηδη ϋμεις καθαροι εστε δια τον λογον ον λελαληκα ϋμιν μινατε εν εμοι καγω εν ϋμιν καθως το κλημα ου δυνατα κκαρπο̑ φερειν*. The first *κ* in *κκαρπο̑* has subsequently been partially scratched out to obtain the reading *δυναται*. The Latin insertion reads *iam uobis mundi estis propter uerbum*. In line 28, the first hand wrote a K which he then expunged. It is visible under the IN of INA. In line 31, *υμιν* is added by Corrector C (p. 135). In line 33, the alteration of MOY to *εμοι* is by Corrector B.

17 Annotator I (F130b/13–14, left margin): note *εις την μεσοπεντηκοστη̑* (p. 43).

18 Annotators J and L (F150b top outside corner): J wrote *†τη κυριακη των προφȣτησματων*; altered by L to *ανναγνοσμα περη το κυριακην* etc. (p. 40f).

19 Hand L (F278b/27 to foot): Ammonian sections and addition (p. 163).

20 Annotator M (F6b/11–16): note *τις εορτις τον θεοφανιων* ☩.

21 Annotator M[1] (F205b top margin): ☩ *δαυγι ωτε ισηλθεν ἐν το θυσιας τιρηο̑ και φαγιν το̑ς αρτο̑ς τις προθεσεος*.

22 Annotator M[3] (F314b foot): ☩ *ερμϊνηα + εαν ακουσϊ μη δεξϊ αυτιν +*. The fainter marks beneath are the hermenaia on the recto showing through.

23 Annotator M[4] (F347b/10–15, left margin): note ☩ *της αναλινψημου*.

24 Annotator O (F488b top margin): ☩ *του αγιου·διονυσιου·αρεωπαγιτου* (p. 43f). In the first line of text, N in ΟΙΔΕΝ has been erased. In the fourth line, *τον* has been added by Corrector B (for this proclivity, see p. 141). The modern Roman numeral in the top left-hand corner indicates the quire to which this leaf belongs.

25a and 25b The supplementary leaves

25a F348b*, final verses of Mark in Greek and Latin. The rulings can be seen between the columns.

25b F170*/31–3, correction to the Latin column (p. 47).

INDEX ONE

Of Greek New Testament manuscripts

Note 1: Manuscripts listed on pp. 17–19 are included in this index only if they are also mentioned elsewhere.
Note 2: The citation of manuscript support for readings is not included in this index.
Note 3: Manuscripts divided between more than one number in Aland's *Liste* (e.g. 029, 070) are generally indexed only under their first number.

INDEX TWO

Of Latin New Testament manuscripts

The citation of manuscript support for readings is not included in this index.

OLD LATIN

VULGATE

The following Mss may be found in Index 1, under the Gregory–Aland number indicated:

INDEX THREE

Of all other manuscripts

In this index, manuscripts are listed by location and shelf mark.

INDEX FOUR

Of biblical citations

Note 1: References which simply describe the extent of witnesses are not included.
Note 2: Passages referred to in the text only by their folio and line number in Codex Bezae are not listed separately here.

INDEX FIVE

Of folio references in Codex Bezae

Note 1: References are placed under facing pairs of pages, even though some references may in fact be only to one column.
Note 2: The folio numbers in the list on pp. 14–16 are not included here.

LUKE (*cont.*)

MARK

3 JOHN

ACTS

INDEX SIX

Of subjects

INDEX SEVEN

Of modern writers